CRIME AND PUNISHMENT IN EARLY MODERN GERMANY

Dedicated to Susan F. Levine

Crime and Punishment in Early Modern Germany

Courts and Adjudicatory Practices in Frankfurt am Main, 1562–1696

MARIA R. BOES
West Chester University, USA

Routledge
Taylor & Francis Group
LONDON AND NEW YORK

First published 2013 by Ashgate Publisher

2 Park Square, Milton Park, Abingdon, Oxfordshire OX14 4RN
711 Third Avenue, New York, NY 10017

Routledge is an imprint of the Taylor & Francis Group, an informa business

First issued in paperback 2018

British Library Cataloguing in Publication Data
Boes, Maria R.
Crime and punishment in early modern Germany : courts and adjudicatory practices in Frankfurt am Main, 1562–1696.
1. Criminal procedure--Germany--Frankfurt am Main--History--16th century. 2. Criminal procedure--Germany--Frankfurt am Main--History--17th century. 3. Crime--Germany--Frankfurt am Main--History--16th century. 4. Crime--Germany--Frankfurt am Main--History--17th century. 5. Corrections--Germany--Frankfurt am Main--History--16th century. 6. Corrections--Germany--Frankfurt am Main--History--17th century.
I. Title
345.4'3416405-dc23

The Library of Congress has cataloged the printed edition as follows:
Boes, Maria R.
Crime and punishment in early modern Germany : courts and adjudicatory practices in Frankfurt am Main, 1562–1696 / By Maria R. Boes.
pages cm
Includes index.
ISBN 978-1-4094-3147-3 (hardcover)
1. Criminal procedure--Germany--Frankfurt am Main--History--16th century. 2. Criminal procedure--Germany--Frankfurt am Main--History--17th century. 3. Crime--Germany--Frankfurt am Main--History--16th century. 4. Crime--Germany--Frankfurt am Main--History--17th century. 5. Corrections--Germany--Frankfurt am Main--History--16th century. 6. Corrections--Germany--Frankfurt am Main--History--17th century. I.Title.
KKC6717.7.B64 2013
364.943'416409032--dc23

2013000820

ISBN 978-1-4094-3147-3 (hbk)
ISBN 978-1-138-37975-6 (pbk)

Contents

List of Figures and Tables

Figures

Table

Preface and Acknowledgments

The city of Frankfurt am Main serves as the base for this in-depth analysis that meticulously traces the proliferation of increasingly disproportionate, selective adjudicatory practices during the early modern German period. The impetus to conduct such a study derived from quantitative fluctuations and qualitative sentencing reversals observed in one of Frankfurt's most important archival data collections: the Strafenbuch, Book of Punishments. It lists all criminal sentences, together with brief personal characteristics of the sentenced offenders, their respective crimes and the victims as well as the punishments meted out during the 1562 to 1696 period. Most noticeably, such seemingly aberrant sentencing patterns related to specific social groups. Women for example experienced a sentencing reversal for sex crimes toward the end of the sixteenth century in that they were now listed as the leading culprits, in contrast to men for the earlier period. Jewish crime sentences increased during the seventeenth century, while those who perpetrated crimes against them were meted out milder penalties. Similarly, soldiers were handed down increasingly milder punishments for violent crimes, while seemingly absurd, postmortem punishments were inflicted on the corpses of suicides. These various sentencing and penal trends called for explanations. While Frankfurt's Strafenbuch served as the quantitative/qualitative guiding force as well as dictating the time of this study, further research needed to be conducted and additional archival records consulted in order to discover the roots of these divergent sentences.

Probing general political, religious and socio-economic developments seemed warranted in the search for societal explanations. As Chapter 1 demonstrates, this approach yielded insightful information pointing to the emergence and solidification of certain socially, economically and religiously disadvantaged groups, especially toward the end of the sixteenth century, while registering the opposite for others. Documents such as those generated by the local guilds, the Zunfturkunden, disclosed details on their changing economic/cultural/gender and moral attitudes, resulting in negative societal ramifications, especially for women and for children born out-of-wedlock. Ample documentation evidenced that Jews were increasingly exposed to verbal and physical attacks culminating in an all-out attack on their quarters. By contrast, mercenaries had their description changed to soldiers, and experienced a concomitant positive group consolidation.

Chapter 2 not only traces the integration of these various denigrating and upgrading social values into Frankfurt's laws but also evidences that Frankfurt's legal and jurisdictional establishment intensified them in the process. Buttressing their relevant arguments with increased reliance on a foreign law, Roman Law, it was above all the agents of this foreign law code—those trained in Roman Law, Frankfurt's advocates—who initiated and executed these changes by exercising increasing legal and judicial influences. Their rapid proliferation as legal municipal and criminal penal advisors, and their symbiotic relationship to and increasing sway over Frankfurt's city councilors, those in charge of the judiciary, laid the foundation for ensuing selective crime sentencing. The extraordinary speed with which criminal trials were conducted aided this process.

Tracing Frankfurt's policing and crime/criminal detective and reporting methods constitute the focus of Chapter 3. The data consulted revealed that the authorities increasingly resorted to using visible avenues, such as by mandating multiple dress codes and other public-appearance related measures. Visible identification markers obviously facilitated criminal identifications and crime reporting. But they also encouraged, if not reinforced, the selective judicial process.

It was, however, the content of the individual criminal dossiers which disclosed the most momentous divergent crime-sentencing measures. The chapters on Gypsies, Jews, women, gays—to use the modern term—suicides and soldiers contain detailed, frequently harrowing and highly emotional trial renditions submitted by witnesses, the accused, barber/surgeons and midwives, and occasionally by the victims themselves. But it was the legal briefs by Frankfurt's advocates which proved to be the most stunning documents. Their written legal and penal deliberations convey a clear message: their own highly selective judicial judgments. By judicially denigrating certain social groups while upgrading others they created a judicial divide with ominous portent.

Acknowledgments

None of my scholarly endeavors could have come to fruition without the emotional support and years of patience with my "academic moods" by Susan F. Levine. This book is dedicated to her in gratitude.

My friend and former colleague Anne Dzamba also deserves a special thank you for her continued encouragement.

With sadness I also think of my former mentor Ruth Pike, who, unfortunately, left us much too soon but whose kind words of support and exemplary scholarly conduct I shall never forget.

In the professional realm I want to thank first and foremost everyone at Frankfurt's municipal archives, especially Dr. Roman Fischer, for their assistance in locating and submitting the relevant files and catering to my, what must have seemed at times, never-ending multiple requests with the greatest patience.

I am also grateful to many scholars whose valuable statements and contributions I still cherish, such as Hans Andersson, A.L. Beier, Tom Betteridge, Lloyd Bonfield, Bernard Cooperman, Pamela Cox, Ellen Dwyer, Clive Emsley, Janet McShane Galley, Rosemary Gartner, Andreas Gotzmann, Mary Gibson, Barbara Hanawalt, Merry Wiesner-Hanks, Peter King, Joanne M. Klein, Diethelm Klippel, Louis A. Knafla, René Lévy, William G. Naphy, Jutta Nowosadtko, Sheila Rabin, Xavier Rousseaux, Pieter Spierenburg, Robert M. Seltzer, Joy Wiltenburg, Heide Wunder and the late Barbara Weinberger.

Acknowledgments for Republication

Chapter 3 originally appeared in *Social Science History* 20/2 (Summer 1996): 259–79; Chapter 7 was published in *Criminal Justice History: An International Annual*, vol. 13 (Westport, CT and London, 1992), pp. 61–73; Chapter 10 appeared in Tom Betteridge, ed., *Sodomy in Early Modern Europe* (Manchester, 2002), pp. 27–45; Chapter 5 constitutes an expanded version of the earlier German publication "Zweifach im Visier: Jüdische Opfer von Straftaten und Rechtsprechung im Römisch-Deutschen Reich der Frühen Neuzeit," in Andreas Gotzmann and Stephan Wendehorst, eds, *Sonderdruck: Juden im Recht. Neue Zugänge zur Rechtsgeschichte der Juden im Alten Reich*, Zeitschrift für Historische Forschung, Beiheft 39 (Berlin, 2007).

Maria R. Boes
Professor Emerita
West Chester University

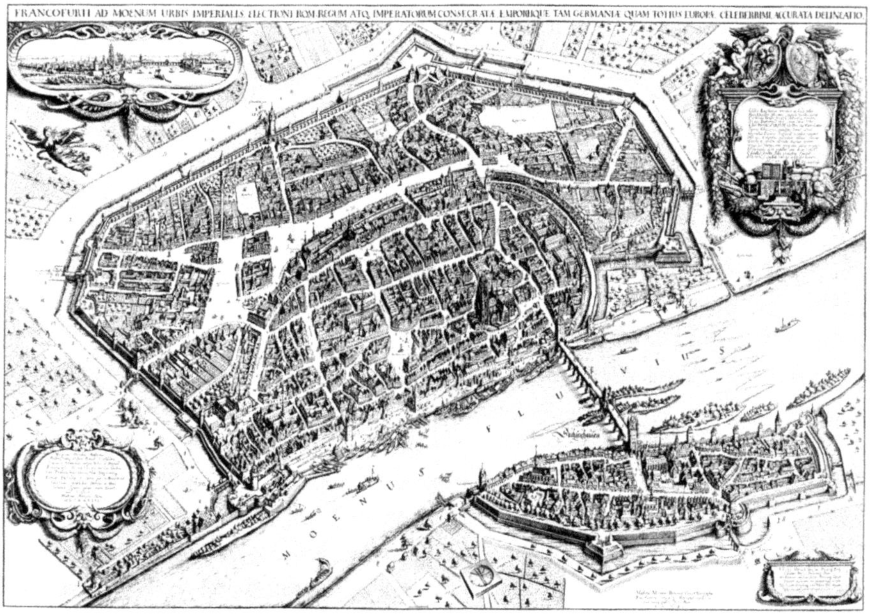

Frankfurt city map
Source: Map of Frankfurt, 1628. © Institut für Stadtgeschichte, Frankfurt am Main.

PART I
The City's Profile

Chapter 1
Socio-Economic and Religious Background

Governmental Structure

Frankfurt am Main is located on the navigable Main River, approximately halfway between the cities of Hamburg in the north and Munich in the south of what then constituted the Holy Roman Empire. This central geographical location at the crossroads of various trade routes played a key factor in Frankfurt's successful economic and political developments, as evidenced by two annual trade fairs of international reputation and its status as a free imperial city as well as the seat of imperial elections and coronations.

The mental dexterity of its inhabitants also played a decisive role in the acquisition of such far-reaching achievements. For years, perceptive locals pursued and successfully convinced various emperors either by purchase or astute political maneuvering to grant Frankfurt extensive self-rule rights as well as charters for its two annual fairs.[1] Furthermore, Frankfurt was successful in expanding its judicial authority. A 1387 imperial privilege entitled the city to adjudicate in both civil and criminal matters.[2] Frankfurt's municipal jurisdiction covered any offender, regardless of social status and regardless of where the crime had been committed. It also extended over former ecclesiastical prerogatives as the local court of the Catholic Church, the Sendegericht, had been dissolved in 1370.[3] Imperial and

---

[1] Michael Rothmann, *Die Frankfurter Messen im Mittelalter*, Frankfurter historische Abhandlungen, vol. 40 (Stuttgart: Steiner, 1998); Konrad Bund, "Frankfurt am Main im Spätmittelalter, 1311–1519," in *Frankfurt am Main: Die Geschichte der Stadt in neun Beiträgen*, Frankfurter Historische Kommission (Sigmaringen: Thorbecke, 1991), pp. 54–65; Friedrich Bothe, *Geschichte der Stadt Frankfurt am Main* (Frankfurt am Main, 1913) p. 23; Ludwig Heinrich Euler, "Rechtsgeschichte der Stadt Frankfurt am Main," in *Festschrift für den 10. Juristentag in Frankfurt am Main* (Frankfurt am Main, 1872), p. 6.

[2] Johann Anton Moritz, *Versuch einer Einleitung in die Stadtverfassung der Reichsstadt Frankfurt am Main* (2 vols, Frankfurt am Main: Andräische Buchhandlung, 1786), vol. 2, p. 29; Bothe, *Geschichte*, p. 226.

[3] Bothe, *Geschichte*, p. 253; Georg Ludwig Kriegk, *Frankfurter Bürgerzwiste und Zustände im Mittelalter* (Frankfurt am Main: J.D. Sauerländer's Verlag, 1862), p. 420; Johann, G.Ch. Thomas, *Der Oberhof zu Frankfurt am Main und das Fränkische Recht* (Frankfurt am Main: Jäger'sche Buch- und Papier-Landkarten-Handlung, 1841), p. 207; Euler, "Rechtsgeschichte," p. 27.

ecclesiastical authority was thus integrated into local government. Political prestige came when, with the inception of the "Golden Bull" of 1356, one of the most influential imperial documents for the Holy Roman Empire, Frankfurt am Main became the seat of imperial elections, a symbolic glamour heightened 200 years later when the city also became the site of imperial coronations.

With the acquisition of such far-reaching responsibilities, the administration of the city took more concrete forms, but not without serious challenges from within the city itself. While a city council stood at the apex of the local government consisting of three benches presided over by two mayors, the social composition or membership of the city council became a bone of contention. It became a matter of elite, local patricians versus a more general distribution of power and representation. The question of who or which group of the local citizenry should sit on each of these benches became of prime importance, especially considering the judicial powers invested in each branch: the first bench represented the local civil court, while all three benches were in charge of criminal matters, thus constituting the local criminal court.[4]

The offices of city councilors and mayors were elective ones; however, the electoral process to these offices became more and more restricted. Frankfurt's patricians were able to abrogate and keep the right to proper electoral procedures by co-opting their own members into the first two benches of the city council.[5] The guilds, despite a revolt, had to be content with the third.[6] In addition, since the pool for the mayoral positions was restricted to city councilors only, patricians easily won these positions as well. Throughout the entire sixteenth and seventeenth centuries no guild member ever reached the position of local mayor and no guild member ever entered the upper bench, the bench composing the civil court.[7]

The guilds were confronted with an additional problem in that city councilors did not receive any pay for their services.[8] This adverse monetary ruling did not seem to have had a major impact considering the continuity of guild members on the third bench.[9] First, the guild members sent to the city council were well

---

4 Johann Georg Rössing, *Versuch einer kurzen historischen Darstellung der allmählichen Entwicklung der heutigen Gerichtsverfassung der Stadt Frankfurt am Main* (Frankfurt am Main: J.E.B. Mohr, 1810), p. 39.

5 Kriegk, *Frankfurter Bürgerzwiste*, pp. 22–80, 354–95.

6 Bothe, *Geschichte*, p. 124.

7 Ibid., p. 116.

8 Ibid., p. 401.

9 Matthias Meyn, *Die Reichsstadt Frankfurt vor dem Bürgeraufstand von 1612 bis 1614: Struktur und Krise. Studien zur Frankfurter Geschichte*, Heft 15 (Frankfurt am Main: Verlag Waldemar Kramer, 1980), p. 178.

off themselves and second, the social status and prestige associated with being a city councilor made the work very attractive, in particular since not every guild had the right to send representatives to the city council.[10] Weavers, butchers, bakers, shoemakers and blacksmiths could send two representatives each and gardeners, fishermen, furriers and tanners only one each, leaving the majority of approximately 30 remaining guilds without such privileges.[11]

Frankfurt's city council thus did not represent a cross-section of the local population, but was—and would remain, at least during the time frame of this study—in the hands of the local patrician elite. The authority of the oligarchic patricians was not seriously endangered by the presence of artisans on the council.[12] On the contrary, they were able to solidify their power over the years, especially the two most prominent among them: the Alten-Limpurg and to a lesser degree the Frauenstein.

And up to a certain time period they did so by accommodating newcomers into their ranks, provided they had the necessary credentials such as money or a law degree. While the Frauenstein continued with a relative open policy, the Alten-Limpurg started to close ranks in 1584. Thereafter, no applicant was admitted whose parents, even grandparents, were descendants of artisans or small merchants.[13] Obviously, this process also led to endogamous intermarriages.[14]

As local patricians thus became an increasingly exclusive circle it is tempting to argue that they held unobstructed sway over Frankfurt's population. But this was not the case. The population at large shared implicitly and explicitly in the power structure, given the insular character and isolation of a walled city and the absence of any cohesive police or institutionalized military force. Frankfurt's patrician city councilors could not afford to impose their mandates over the

10 Ibid., p. 180.

11 Karl Bücher, *Die Bevölkerung von Frankfurt am Main im XIV und XV Jahrhunderts* (Tübingen: H. Laupp, 1886), p. 87.

12 Meyn, *Reichsstadt*, p. 180.

13 Wolfgang Klötzer, *"Keine liebere Stadt als Frankfurt" Kleine Schriften zur Frankfurter Kulturgeschichte II*, Studien zur Frankfurter Geschichte, 45, im Auftrag des Frankfurter Vereins für Geschichte und Landeskunde in Verbindung mit der Frankfurter Historischen Kommission herausgegeben von Dieter Rebentisch (Frankfurt am Main: Verlag Waldemar Kramer, 2000), pp. 219, 215; Meyn, *Reichsstadt*, p. 219.

14 Klötzer, *Keine liebere*, p. 251; Barbara Dölemeyer, *Frankfurter Juristen im 17. und 18. Jahrhundert*, in Ius Commune, Veröffentlichungen des Max-Planck-Instituts für Europäische Rechtsgeschichte, Sonderheft 60 (Frankfurt am Main: Klostermann 1993), p. XXIII; for an excellent discussion see Hermann Mitgau's article, "Geschlossene Heiratskreise Sozialer Inzucht," in Helmut Rössler, ed., *Deutsches Patriziat*, 1430–1740 (Limburg/Lahn: E.A. Starke, 1968), pp. 1–25.

population at will, as is clearly demonstrated by various socio-religious and economic developments.

Socio-Religious Developments

Cooperation among the city dwellers was necessary for survival and, toward that end, intramural audible and visible signals were introduced. It was in particular the pervasive sound of bells, which served as signals reaching everyone in town within a short amount of time. While originally the sound of bells emanated from church towers with a primarily religious message, Frankfurt acquired the right to use these bells for municipal purposes, starting by the mid-fourteenth century, such as the *Gemperlein* bell warning of possible impending dangers, soon to be supplanted by municipal bells mounted on the city hall and various city gates.[15] Two bells warned locals of impending danger, the guard bell and the fire bell. Other bells regulated monthly, weekly even daily local activities. The *Stadtglocke*, the municipal bell which was called "die Sturm," the tempest, rang to indicate when the city council would hold its meetings.[16] The *Marktglocke*, market bell signaled the opening and closing of the market; the *Zinsglocke*, the interest bell, warned delayed taxpayers to pay up; and the *Kehrglocke*, the cleaning bell, urged residents to clean the streets. The sound of bells even coordinated daily work and leisure times: such as the *Werkglocke*, the work bell, which indicated the beginning and end of the work period as well as the lunch break, and the *Schmiedeglocke*, smith bell, warned to limit noise-producing artisans, while the wine and beer bells signaled the closing of drinking hours in taverns.[17] Bells thus reminded locals of their duties and social obligations, such as to pay their taxes.[18] Their sounds filled the city with regulatory symbolic rhythms, an indispensible informative tool in a predominantly oral society.

But bells were not the only sounds regulating daily living. Intramural close living conditions also encouraged constant and speedy communication via street talk or window-to-window exchanges among the various inhabitants. Conversational

---

15 Isidor Kracauer, "Das Militärwesen der Reichsstadt Frankfurt a.M. im XVIII Jahrhundert," in Archiv für Frankfurts Geschichte und Kunst, 3 Folge, Bd. 12 (Frankfurt am Main, 1920), pp. 1–80, p. 3; Igor Jenzen, ed., *Urzeiten: Die Geschichte der Uhr und ihres Gebrauchs* (Frankfurt am Main: Jonas Verlag für Kunst und Literatur, 1989), p. 51.

16 Jenzen, *Urzeiten*, p. 51.

17 Ibid., p. 52.

18 Werner Moritz, *Die bürgerlichen Fürsorgeanstalten der Reichsstadt Frankfurt am Main im späten Mittelalter*. Studien zur Frankfurter Geschichte, vol. 14 (Frankfurt am Main: Verlag Waldemar Kramer, 1981), p. 103.

shouting was common practice and gossip flourished, serving as the weapon of choice for clandestine accusations and mutual supervision purposes.

Such verbal exploits even encouraged locals from circumventing laws, as clearly evidenced in the case of the poor and begging. Frankfurt had replaced the traditional poor relief handled through the agency of the Catholic Church, with its own municipal and secular administration. This ended not only the indiscriminate handing out of alms but also lowered the social status of the poor, whom the Catholics accorded a high esteem most vividly exemplified by mendicant orders.[19] In 1438 Frankfurt's city council initiated its first municipal poor relief endeavor, which already in 1476 resulted in sidelining the indiscriminate approach to poor relief by introducing gradations among the impoverished, splitting them into resident and non-resident with the objective of granting relief only to locals.[20]

Frankfurt was no exception in initiating such poor relief measures. Similar laws were promulgated in many other cities, such as in Nuremberg in 1478, Augsburg in 1522, Baden-Baden and Strasbourg in 1528 and also in Lyon and Paris. These laws eroded the religiously sanctioned status of the poverty-stricken, leading to a shift from indiscriminate charity to the policing of the poor.[21] And policed they were, for Frankfurt hired so-called Bettelvögte, beadles, who were to supervise the local poor, and oust the foreign beggars.[22] "Urban models" thus took the lead in begging reforms in both Germany and France, and since many of these laws were promulgated before the Protestant Reformation it is problematic to cite the Reformation as the decisive force of a changed poverty relief outlook as claimed by some scholars.[23] However, Protestant reformers,

---

19 Ibid.

20 Ibid.

21 Kriegk, *Frankfurter Bürgerzwiste*, pp. 142–5; for Strasbourg see Miriam Usher Chrisman, *Strasbourg and the Reformation* (New Haven, CT: Yale University Press, 1967), p. 44; for Lyon see Natalie Zemon Davis, "Poor Relief, Humanism and Heresy," in *Society and Culture in Early Modern France* (Stanford, CA: Stanford University Press, 1975), pp. 17–64; see also Robert Jütte, *Obrigkeitliche Armenfürsorge in Deutschen Reichsstädten der Frühen Neuzeit* (Cologne: Böhlau, 1984); for policing the poor, see Michael Mollat, *The Poor in the Middle Ages: An Essay in Social History*, trans. Arthur Goldhammer (New Haven, CT: Yale University Press, 1986), p. 250.

22 Moritz, *Fürsorgeanstalten*, p. 111.

23 Davis, "Poor Relief," pp. 39, 49, 50; such as suggested by Brian Pullan, "Catholics, Protestants, and the Poor in Early Modern Europe," *Journal of Interdisciplinary History*, 35/3 (Winter 2005): 441–56, especially pp. 447, 450. For a good thematic and historiographical summary, see Ole Peter Grell and Andrew Cunningham, eds, *Health Care and Poor Relief in Protestant Europe 1500–1700* (London: Routledge, 1997), as well as the reaction to this book by Thomas Max Safley, ed., *The Reformation of Charity: The Secular and the Religious in Early Modern Poor Relief*, Studies in Central European Histories, 30 (Boston, MA: Brill, 2003).

especially Martin Luther, intensified this pre-Reformation secular urban trend by further categorizing and dividing the poor into "deserving" and "undeserving."[24]

However, many of Frankfurt's people did not share this new derogative view of the poor, and this despite the fact that most of them had converted to Lutheranism. Side-stepping Martin Luther's admonition and circumventing Frankfurt's laws, they interfered with Frankfurt's beadles. When they heard the beadles approach to apprehend and escort beggars out of town, they hid them in their houses until the danger had passed. These clandestine defensive actions not only testify to the independent outlook and input of locals but also to the continuation of the Catholic mentality of the indiscriminate approach to poverty.[25]

Unfortunately, many locals were less inclined to step up for another underprivileged group, Jewish people. On the contrary, their frequent confrontations attest to at times strained and even violent outbursts reaching as far back as 1241, to the first Judenschlacht, Jewish battle, when local people seriously assaulted many Jews and forced them to leave town. Exactly when Jewish people returned is unclear but in 1281 they are again mentioned in the official records.[26] Another attack occurred four weeks after Emperor Charles IV had pawned his imperial jurisdiction over the Jews to the city of Frankfurt in 1349 who with this imperial sell-out, now became subject to the local city authorities. Many Jews were killed and the survivors left Frankfurt for the second time.[27] Twenty years later a few Jewish families resettled locally but their legal status was altered in that they only obtained legal burgher status for a specified length of time, mostly varying from one to five years, instead of for life as before. They were also barred from convening their own courts save for marriage and inheritance matters and minor civic affairs, which were handled by the Jewish Baumeister, a Jewish lay official.[28]

Starting in 1386, Jews were no longer registered in the local Bürgerbuch, the burgher book, and in 1403, they were required to pay a special annual city tax. This tax set the stage for the so-called Judenstättigkeiten, municipal charters,

---

[24] Ernst Schubert, *Fahrendes Volk im Mittelalter* (Bielefeld: Verlag für Regionalgeschichte, 1995), p. 365; Grell and Cunningham, *Health Care*, p. 3.

[25] *Corpus Legum Francofurtensium* (5 vols, Frankfurt am Main), vol. 4, p. 27. Similar resistance was shown by the population in Amsterdam: see *Pieter Spierenburg: The Spectacle of Suffering* (Cambridge: Cambridge University Press, 1984), pp. 128–9.

[26] Bücher, *Bevölkerung*, p. 532; Bothe, *Geschichte*, p. 63.

[27] Bücher, *Bevölkerung*, p. 534.

[28] Joseph Goldschmidt, "Die Rückkehr der Juden nach Frankfurt am Main in Jahre 1360," in Ludwig Geiger, ed., *Zeitschrift für die Geschichte der Juden in Deutschland* (Nendeln: Kraus Reprint, 1975); Bücher, *Bevölkerung*, p. 527; Moritz, *Versuch*, pp. 253–4.

specifying their rights and obligations, which on average lasted for three years—becoming more onerous with each renewal. But at least during the fourteenth and fifteenth centuries Jews were able to reside anywhere in Frankfurt. They had the right to acquire real estate and owned houses, vineyards and other landed property. At least topographically speaking they were intermixed with the local Christian population.

Relentless pressure from the Catholic Church coupled with antagonism from the guilds made their lives increasingly difficult. Already with the Fourth Lateran Council of 1215, the Catholic Church tried to introduce a special dress code for Jews and the formation of a Christian guild system precluded Jews from joining, and thus excluding them from practicing any kind of artisanal work.[29] During the Synod of Basel of 1434 the Catholic Church intensified its approach, decreeing that Christians were not to consult Jewish doctors, who, at least in Frankfurt, were held in high esteem both by the city council, who hired them as municipal doctors, and the local population.[30] Jews were to be prohibited from hiring Christian servants and, most devastatingly, they were to live in separate quarters.

While Frankfurt's city councilors ignored these exhortations, continuing with such practices as hiring Jews as municipal doctors and refusing to have local Jewish people relocated, they eventually succumbed to the combined pressure from many of Frankfurt's Christian population, and additional exhortations from the Emperor. In 1460 they decided to have the Jewish population move into special, segregated quarters: the Judengasse, the Jewish street.[31] When construction was finished two years later, Frankfurt's Jewish population—together with its synagogue located opposite the main local church and thus visually symbolizing the co-existence of Frankfurt's Jews and Christians—was removed to their new location, where its residents were not even allowed to own the land on which their houses were built but had to pay an annual fee.[32] The quarter was accessible only by three gates, which were locked at night, and on Sundays and holidays. Not surprisingly, Frankfurt's Jews called their painful removal and the bondage-like conditions "the New Egypt."[33]

---

29 Guido Kisch, *The Jews in Medieval Germany: A Study of Their Legal and Social Status*, 2nd ed. (New York: Ktav, 1970), p. 295; J. Friedrich Battenberg, "Des Kaisers Kammerknechte," *Historische Zeitschrift*, 3 (December 1987): 546–99, p. 561.

30 Heinz Ulrich Krauss, *Frankfurt am Main: Daten, Schlaglichter, Baugeschehen* (Frankfurt am Main: Societätsverlag, 1997), p. 443.

31 Isidor Kracauer, *Geschichte der Juden in Frankfurt am Main, 1550–1824* (2 vols, Frankfurt am Main: Kauffman, 1925), vol. 1, pp. 177–8, 199; Battenberg, "Kaisers Kammerknechte," p. 559; Bücher, *Bevölkerung*, p. 528.

32 Moritz, *Versuch*, vol. 1, p. 245.

33 Kriegk, *Frankfurter Bürgerzwiste*, p. 452.

Precise municipal ordinances regulated their comings and goings. Those who had to conduct business transactions "in town" were permitted to leave the Judengasse, but they had to be back at a certain hour. While in town they were not to assemble or stand/walk together in more than twos, and they were not to sit down but had to move constantly. Disregarding these rules meant paying a heavy fine.[34]

True, Frankfurt's Jewish inhabitants were not completely ousted beyond the city walls—a severe measure that occurred in many other cities and regions around the same time in Europe, such as Erfurt in 1458, Mainz in 1470, Bamberg in 1478, Magdeburg in 1493, Nuremberg and Ulm in 1499 and their infamous forced exodus from Spain in 1492.[35] England and France had already resorted to such rigorous steps in 1290 and 1306, respectively, without, however, gaining extensive historical or scholarly notoriety.

Professional and economic curtailments accentuated this litany of restrictions. Being pushed out of long-distance trading and having no access to the Christian guild system, they were left with few occupational and professional options, being largely relegated to lending money and running pawnshops. Frankfurt even excluded its Jewish population from receiving municipal poor relief, and this despite the fact that Jews were taxed more heavily than any other social or religious group in town.[36]

The Protestant Reformation did not change their plight, and this despite Martin Luther's astute assessment during a local visit: "They (Frankfurt's Jews) have no houses of their own, only furniture; and, indeed, they can only lend money upon houses or grounds at great hazard."[37] The reformer's seemingly sympathetic observations about Jews, however, were short-lived. Once he realized that Jews did not heed his proselytizing efforts, he abandoned his earlier stance and turned into an outspoken antagonist, as documented in his

---

[34] Dietrich Andernacht, *Regesten zur Geschichte der Juden in der Reichsstadt Frankfurt am Main von 1520–1616*, in Helga Andernacht, ed., Verbindung mit dem Institut für Stadtgeschichte Frankfurt und dem Arye Maimon-Institut für die Geschichte der Juden an der Universität Trier (2 vols, Hanover: Hahnsche Buchhandlung, 2007), vol. 1, p. 891, item 3521; p. 1096, item 4233.

[35] J. Friedrich Battenberg, *Das Europäische Zeitalter der Juden: Zur Entwicklung einer Minderheit in der nichtjüdischen Umwelt Europas* (2 vols, Darmstadt: Wissenschaftliche Buchgesellschaft, 1990), vol. 1, p. 163.

[36] Battenberg, "Kaisers Kammerknechte," pp. 560–61, 593; Kracauer, *Geschichte der Juden*, vol. 1, p. 452; Friedrich Bothe, *Beiträge zur Wirtschafts- und Sozialgeschichte der Reichsstadt Frankfurt am Main* (Leipzig: Duncker & Humblot, 1906), p. 89.

[37] *Table Talk of Martin Luther*, trans. and ed. William Hazlitt (London, 1857), p. 347.

private correspondence and public tracts.[38] In one of his letters to his wife, he even blamed his sexual inadequacy on the spell of 50 Jews whom he had passed in a village, exclaiming that "'(I) would have to devote myself to driving out the Jews," a theme he more virulently expressed in his various public writings.[39] In his tract "On the Shem Hamphoras," published in 1543, he advocated the burning of Jewish synagogues and private homes, instigations which in fact led to the outbreak of anti-Jewish violence in many Lutheran areas.[40] Reminiscent of the policies of the Catholic Church and Castile under Queen Isabella, Luther urged that Jews "be expelled from Christian lands," a mental stance he would never relinquish. Three days before his death in 1546, he asserted that "we will not suffer nor tolerate them (Jews) in our midst."[41]

The Reformation thus did not ease the plight of Jews. Lutherans proved to be as relentless as Catholics in their anti-Jewish stance. While in Frankfurt a Catholic city council had initiated the relocation of Frankfurt's Jews to the ghetto, its later exclusively Lutheran successor did nothing to ease the plight of its residents. Frankfurt's Lutheran city council, similar to its predecessor, also refused to include Jewish poor relief in its municipal system and this despite the fact that Jewish expertise in helping the sick was still widely acknowledged.

---

38 There are numerous monographs available on this topic; see especially Heiko A. Oberman, The Roots of Antisemitism in the Age of Renaissance and Reformation, trans. James I. Porter (Philadelphia: Fortress Press, 1984), pp. 9, 41; also Dean Phillip Bell and Stephen G. Burnett, eds, "Jews, Judaism, and the Reformation in Sixteenth Century Germany," Studies in Central European Histories Series (Leiden/Boston: Brill, 2006).

39 Cited in the excellent anthology edited by Susan C. Karant-Nunn and Merry E. Wiesner-Hanks, *Luther on Women: A Sourcebook* (Cambridge: Cambridge University Press, 2003), p. 193.

40 Robert M. Seltzer, *Jewish People, Jewish Thought: The Jewish Experience in History* (New York: Longmans, 1980); Bernd C. Sucher, *Luthers Stellung zu den Juden* (Nieuwkoop: DeGraaf, 1977), p. 85; Klaus Depperman, "Judenhass und Judenfreundschaft im frühen Protestantismus," in Bernd Martin and Ernst Schulin, eds, *Die Juden als Minderheit in der Geschichte* (Munich: Deutscher Taschenbuch, 1981), pp. 110–31; Jonathan I. Israel, *European Jewry in the Age of Mercantilism, 1550–1750* (Oxford: Clarendon, 1985), p. 10; Ronnie Po-Chia Hsia, "Printing, Censorship, and Antisemetism in Reformation Germany," in Philip N. Bebb and Sherrin Marshals, eds, *The Process of Change in Early Modern Europe: Essays in Honor of Miriam Usher Chrisma*n (Athens: Ohio University Press, 1988), pp. 135–48; Steven Rowan, "Luther, Bucer and Eck on the Jews," *Sixteenth Century Journal*, 16 (1985): 79–90.

41 Quoted by Hans Hillerbrand, "The 'Other' in the Age of the Reformation: Reflections on Social Control and Deviance in the Sixteenth Century," in Max Reinhart, ed., *Infinite Boundaries: Order, Disorder, and Reorder in Early Modern German Culture* (Kirksville, MO: Sixteenth Century Journal Publishers, 1998), pp. 245–69, pp. 252–3; Martin Luther's *Von den Juden und ihren Lügen/On the Jews and their Lies* of 1543.

It was in particular Jewish doctors who retained a high degree of esteem and respect. While unlike the former Catholic city councilors the Lutheran city councilors did not hire Jewish doctors as municipal doctors, they nevertheless issued frequent medical practicing licenses to Jewish doctors. And many of the locals continued to seek their medical advice, and some Jewish doctors even treated Frankfurt's poor free of charge.[42]

Visible denigrations also continued. While by the mid-fifteenth century the Catholic city council mandated that Jews wear special clothing and/or markers on their garments depicting them as Jews, the Protestants did not abandon this practice. And neither did they remove the defaming picture of Jews at the highly visible Brückenturm, a local bridge. Repeatedly, the Jewish community requested its removal because of its highly offensive depiction of the Judensau and a pictorial reference to an alleged Jewish ritual killing of a Christian child. While Frankfurt's city council conceded that it had led passers-by to take the depictions as incentives to charge Jews for such alleged crimes, they only had it covered temporarily for the 1612 imperial election.[43] Thereafter, it was restored to full view for centuries. At a time when most people were illiterate, and many took their lead from visible symbols, Frankfurt's move was not only imprudent but also provocative. However, as demonstrated, the blame for the various anti-Jewish actions does not rest solely with the city council. Large segments of the local population successfully pushed their own anti-Jewish agenda.

And it was also large segments of the local population who took the lead in other developments, such as the embrace of a different Christian denomination: Lutheranism. It was at the behest of Frankfurt's people that the city embraced Lutheranism for the first time in 1533. Pressure from the population at large and not the initiative of the city council led to the welcome reception of Lutheranism.[44] And once the basic religious change had taken root, religious

---

42 Andernacht, *Regesten*, vol. 1, p. 435, item 1844; p. 436, item 1848; p. 512, item 2103; p. 584, item 2360; p. 604, item 2435; p. 644, item 2590; p. 753, item 3004; 2, p. 827, item 3282; p. 891, item 3522; p. 897, item 3547. See also Robert Jütte, "Contact at the Bedside: Jewish Physicians and their Christian Patients," in Ronnie Po-chia Hsia and Hartmut Lehmann, eds., *In and Out of the Ghetto: Jewish–Gentile Relations in Late Medieval and Early Modern Germany* (Cambridge: Cambridge University Press, 1995), pp. 137–50.

43 Andernacht, *Regesten*, vol. 2, p. 1001, item 3926; p. 1014, item 3965; p. 1031, item 4021.

44 Sigrid Jahns, *Frankfurter Reformation und Schmalkaldischer Bund*, Studien zur Frankfurter Geschichte, vol. 9 (Frankfurt am Main: Verlag Waldemar Kramer, 1976), p. 411; this situation was not unique to Frankfurt. Other places in Germany experienced similar developments, as demonstrated by Marita A. Pantzer, *Sozialer Protest in süddeutschen Reichsstädten 1485 bis 1525* (Munich: Miscellanea Bavaria Monacensia Civ, 1982), pp. 259–60; A.G. Dickens, *Reformation and Society* (Norwich: Harcourt, 1966); Bernd

exclusivity followed on various levels, including the political and economic arena. Frankfurt's remaining small minority of Catholics was not allowed to join the local guilds, which automatically entailed exclusion from political say as well.[45] Lutherans ruled.

Economic and Demographic Developments and their Social Repercussions

Given Frankfurt's exclusionary religious attitudes in the city council and the guilds, it is surprising that by the mid-sixteenth century, Frankfurt welcomed predominantly Calvinist refugees to settle locally. By 1554, Flemish, Walloon and Dutch refugees arrived, setting up various industries and ushering in a local economic revival by overcoming the fifteenth- to mid-sixteenth century economic slump. Through their initiatives, Frankfurt began to change from a predominantly agricultural to a commercial and manufacturing center.[46] It was in particular the newcomers' expertise in the production of silk, coupled with their extensive trade connections, which contributed to Frankfurt's economic revival if not economic boom. They started a local flourishing silk industry, and stimulated Frankfurt's export trade, which in turn led to various money transactions and eventually to an extensive local banking system.

During the last decade of the sixteenth century the reputation of Frankfurt's fairs, including its local book fair, also reached new and international heights, even earning an accolade from the French King Francis I, who called it the most famous trading city of the entire world.[47] And so did the reputation of Frankfurt's diamond industry, which prompted Shakespeare to have one of his characters, Shylock, exclaim: "Why, there, there, there, there, a diamond gone, cost me two thousand ducats in Frankfort."[48]

Frankfurt's economic boom was also reflected in a demographic gain and a changed occupational structure. While at the beginning of the sixteenth century approximately 11,000 people resided locally, their numbers increased

Moeller, *Imperial Cities and the Reformation*, trans. Erik Midelfort and Mark Edwards (Philadelphia: Fortress Press, 1972); Miriam Usher Chrisman, *Strasbourg and the Reformation* (New Haven, CT: Yale University Press, 1967); Heinrich Richard Schmidt, *Reichsstädte, Reich und Reformation* (Stuttgart: Franz Steiner Verlag, 1980); Robert W. Scribner, *The German Reformation* (Atlantic Highlands, NJ; Humanities Press International, 1986).

45 Bothe, *Geschichte*, p. 381; Meyn, *Reichsstadt*, pp. 84, 172.

46 Alexander Dietz, *Frankfurter Handelsgeschichte* (2 vols, Frankfurt am Main: Druck und Verlag von Hermann Minjon, 1910) vol. 1, p. 305; Bothe, *Beiträge*, p. 76.

47 Bothe, *Beiträge*, pp. 38, 79, 156–7; Kracauer, *Geschichte der Juden*, vol. 1, p. 452.

48 *The Merchant of Venice*, Act III, Scene I: Venice. A Street.

to 18,000–20,000 during the last three decades of the century, of which the religious newcomers accounted for 4,000.[49] This immigration wave was paralleled by a large number of Jewish newcomers, whose numbers increased to somewhere between 2,000 and 3,000 by 1593.[50] True, compared to cities such as Cologne, Nuremberg and Augsburg—whose populations amounted to 30,000 to 40,000—Frankfurt was still a relatively small town, but its population was more heterogeneous compared to these towns.[51] And with the arrival of new industries came a different labor force. Both skilled and unskilled workers arrived in large numbers and sought and found work primarily in the textile industry, which increased employment in that sector from 156 workers in 1542 to 407 during the three-year span of 1586 to 1589.[52]

This local industry-specific demographic influx was paralleled by a general sixteenth-century demographic upswing and led to perceived or alleged structural problems, especially within the guilds.[53] The guilds, in particular guild masters, claimed overstaffing of their ranks; and in order to safeguard their own prestigious and financially rewarding positions they started to resort to exclusionary methods by both blocking the advancement of present guild members and increasingly preventing future applicants from joining their ranks. One of the means was to extend the travel periods for journeymen before they could apply to become masters; another was the increased insistence on a masterpiece.[54]

---

[49] Meyn, *Reichsstadt*, p. 204; Hans Mauersberg, *Wirtschafts- und Sozialgeschichte zentraleuropäischer Städte in neuerer Zeit* (Göttingen: Vandenhoeck & Ruprecht, 1960), p. 54.

[50] Kracauer, *Geschichte der Juden*, vol. 1, p. 31. See also Fritz Backhaus, "The Population Explosion in the Frankfurt *Judengasse* in the Sixteenth Century," in Fritz Backhaus et al., eds, *The Frankfurt* Judengasse*: Jewish Life in an Early Modern German City* (London/Portland, OR, Vallentine Mitchell, 2010), pp. 23–40.

[51] Dietz, *Handelsgeschichte*, vol. 2, p. 2; Martha Howell, *Women, Production, and Patriarchy in Late Medieval Cities* (Chicago: University of Chicago Press, 1986), pp. 156–7.

[52] Bothe, *Beiträge*, pp. 156–7; Meyn, *Reichsstadt*, p. 214.

[53] For the general sixteenth-century demographic increase see Hermann Kellenbenz, *Deutsche Wirtschaftsgeschichte* (2 vols, Munich: Beck, 1977), vol. 1, p. 216; Heinz Schilling, *Die Stadt in der frühen Neuzeit, Enzyklopedie deutscher Geschichte*, vol. 24 (Munich: Oldenbourg, 1993) pp. 2–17.

[54] Kurt Wesoly, "Lehrlinge und Handwerksgesellen am Mittelrhein: Ihre soziale Lage und ihre Organisation vom 14. bis 17. Jahrhundert," *Studien zur Frankfurter Geschichte*, 18 (1985): 268–9; Knut Schulz, *Handwerksgesellen und Lohnarbeiter: Untersuchungen zur oberrheinischen und oberdeutschen Stadtgeschichte des 14. bis 17. Jahrhunderts* (Sigmaringen: Thorbecke, 1985), p. 304; Frank Göttmann, *Die Frankfurter Bäckerzunft im späten Mittelalter: Aufbau und Aufgaben städtischer Handwerkergenossenschaften* (Frankfurt am Main: Kramer, 1975).

Barring future applicants proved to be an even more detrimental measure for years, if not centuries to come. Under the "cloak of utterly self-serving intentions" guild masters used the cover of alleged moral and ethical motives, and proceeded to bar people born out of wedlock, or "illegitimates" as they were called, from joining their ranks.[55] Only one other guild-initiated measure can be considered equally detrimental: the ousting and barring of women from their ranks.

Originally, women had access to the guilds. They were considered equal guild members, reaching also master's level.[56] Frankfurt's guilds demonstrate this pattern very clearly.[57] However, toward the latter part of the sixteenth century, guild masters reversed this admission and advancement policy by strictly enforcing the exclusion of women. Their exclusionary action was guided by the same selfish motivations that caused the barring of illegitimates. The barring of women and illegitimates thus unfolded simultaneously, culminating around the 1580s. And their intricately connected suffering was only to be compounded over the years.[58] While women in general had ranked among the poorest in society, the impact of the guild restrictions had an additional devastating effect on their lives. True, women stayed in lower occupational positions such as agricultural day laborers and domestic servants, but in both categories their income was at most half that of their male counterparts.[59]

Economic hardship and the lack of an alternate life-style as a guild member were further compounded by social and emotional hardship. Because of the

---

55 Rudolf Wissell, *Des alten Handwerks Recht und Gewohnheit*, 2nd ed. (2 vols, Berlin: Colloquium, 1971), vol. 1, p. 262; see also Edmund Salow, "Das Zunftwesen in Kassel bis zum Erlass der hessischen Zunftordnung von 1693," in Wilhelm Engelbach, ed., *Hessische Forschungen zur geschichtlichen Landes- und Volkskunde* (Hessisch Lichtenau: Vogt, 1978), p. 87, who calls it a "widerlichen Brotneid," disgusting bread-envy.

56 Edith Ennen, *Frauen im Mittelalter*, 3rd ed. (Munich: Beck, 1987); Karl Bücher, *Die Frauenfrage im Mittelalter* (Tübingen: Laupp, 1910); Wissell, *Alten Handwerks*, vol. 2, pp. 439–42; Merry E. Wiesner, *Working Women in Renaissance Germany* (New Brunswick, NJ: Rutgers University Press, 1986); Martha C. Howell, *Women, Production and Patriarchy in Late Medieval Cities* (Chicago: University of Chicago Press, 1986); Christina Vanja, "Mining Women in Early Modern European Society," in Thomas Max Safley and Leonard N. Rosenband, eds, *The Workplace Before the Factory: Artisans and Proletarians, 1500–1800* (Ithaca: Cornell University Press, 1993).

57 *Frankfurter Amts- und Zunfturkunden bis zum Jahre 1612*, ed. Karl Bücher and Benno Schmidt (2 vols, Frankfurt: Baer, 1914), vol. 1, p. 506 and vol. 2, p. 157.

58 Ibid., vol. 2, p. 261.

59 Karl Bräuer, ed., *Studien zur Geschichte der Lebenshaltung in Frankfurt am Main während des 17. und. 18. Jahrhunderts* (2 vols, Frankfurt am Main: Baer, 1915), p. 1:195; see also the excellent study by Sheilagh Ogilvie, *A Bitter Living: Women, Markets, and Social Capital in Early Modern Germany* (Oxford: Oxford University Press, 2003).

guilds' insistence on admitting only those born after an officially accepted and sanctioned marriage, previously accepted social patterns were turned upside down. Commonly practiced cohabitation without any legal marriage bonds and the mainly positive view of out-of-wedlock children were reversed as a consequence, setting in motion fear of pre-marital sex lest it lead to out-of-wedlock pregnancy. This negative change in mentality resulted in a general transvaluation of sexual mores entailing sexual shame and the rather preposterous idea of shame associated with giving birth to a child, albeit an illegitimate one.

By the end of the sixteenth century, this process culminated in the criminalization of various previously accepted sexual patterns such as fornication, that is, sex before marriage.[60] And women became the prime criminal targets of sexual criminal indictments and sentences, as demonstrated by Frankfurt's sexual sentencing practices in that during the 1595 to 1627 period a complete female–male sexual sentencing reversal occurred.[61]

Out-of-wedlock newborns were also dealt a terrible socio-economic blow due to no fault of their own. While in Frankfurt prior to the guild policies such children usually carried the name of the father (and it was also the father who took care of the sustenance and education of the child)—local patricians, following this non-discriminatory trend, even entitled them to inherit large estates such as the illegitimate brother of Claus Stahlburg the Rich—this attitude had been turned upside down by the end of the sixteenth century.[62] Illegitimate children, according to Frankfurt's revised, Roman Law infused law code of 1578, were now deprived of their father's socio-economic umbrella by being solely entrusted to their mothers' care and inheritance, that is to newly socially shunned unmarried women, many of whom barely made a living.[63] The guilds' stigmatizing of illegitimates, followed by Frankfurt's city council legal enactments, marked innocent youngsters for the rest of their lives.

And this was not a local phenomenon. Most guilds, including Frankfurt's, belonged to a guild network which, via the Bundesbriefe, letters of guild confederations, spread and enforced their rules and regulations all over

60 For a detailed analysis of this process see Maria R. Boes, "'Dishonourable' Youth, Guilds, and the Changed World View of Sex, Illegitimacy, and Women in Late-Sixteenth-Century Germany," *Continuity and Change*, 18/3 (2003): 345–72.

61 For detailed statistics see ibid. p. 359.

62 Georg Ludwig Kriegk, *Deutsches Bürgertum im Mittelalter: Nach urkundlichen Forschungen und mit besonderer Beziehung auf Frankfurt am Main* (2 vols, 1868; repr. Frankfurt am Main: Sauer & Auvermann, 1969), vol. 2, p. 278; Bothe, *Geschichte*, p. 262.

63 Helmut Coing, *Die Frankfurter Reformation von 1578 und das Gemeine Recht ihrer Zeit* (Weimar: Böhlau, 1935), p. 80 clearly stipulates that illegitimates were only to inherit from the mother.

Germany, and this for centuries. Not surprisingly, illegitimates thus remained on the fringes of society until well into the twentieth century.

While the guilds were responsible for these gender- and illegitimate-specific sufferings, an event unrelated to their policies affected Frankfurt's and other regions' people: the so-called price revolution of the sixteenth century.[64] It manifested itself primarily in an increase in food prices and the arrival of bad or debased coinage. Wage earners were particularly hard hit by the former, while the debasement of coins led to an ever-increasing monetary instability having a detrimental effect on Frankfurt's bi-annual fairs, which brought large amounts of money to Frankfurt but also many a bad coin.

Hardship resulting from these inflationary trends was soon coupled in the minds of many local people with the influx of foreigners, who were blamed for flooding the local industries and thereby reducing the natives' wages. The local guilds, resenting the competition from the religious refugees, echoed these allegations; and this despite the fact that many of the newcomers had acquired local citizenship.[65] Local Lutheran preachers intensified the chorus of these complaints by resenting the newcomers for religious reasons.

Frankfurt's city council, faced with this double-sided problem—an economic boom on the one hand stimulated by the religious newcomers and inflation coupled with local resentment directed against these newcomers on the other—succumbed to these concerted pressures from the population. It reversed its earlier flexible religious policy toward the Calvinists by curtailing their religious freedom in 1596. This momentous decision resulted in the exodus of many Calvinists, causing a serious blow to the local economy by triggering an economic slump.

Five years later, realizing the dramatic effect of their departure, Frankfurt's city council reversed its earlier decision, allowing Calvinists to set up a small church just outside Frankfurt's city walls. Many returned and with them came a second revival of the local economy. But despite previous experiences, the city council again restricted their religious services in 1608, bringing about the same, if not worse, devastating results, which contributed to sparking a serious local revolt four years later.

---

64 Wilhelm Abel, *Agrarkrisen und Agrarkonjunktur: Eine Geschichte der Land- und Ernährungswirtschaft Mitteleuropas seit dem hohen Mittelalter* (Hamburg/Berlin: Parey, 1978), pp. 104–51; Moritz John Elsas, *Umriss einer Geschichte der Preise und Löhne in Deutschland vom ausgehenden Mittelalter bis zum Beginn des 19. Jahrhunderts* (2 vols, Leiden: Sijthoff, 1936–49); Kellenbenz, *Wirtschaftsgeschichte*, vol. 1, pp. 291–3.

65 Dietz, *Handelsgeschichte*, vol. 2, p. 64; Bothe, *Beiträge*, p. 95.

The Tumultuous Seventeenth Century

The revolt of 1612–14—also referred to as the Fettmilch Uprising after its most conspicuous leader—was a very serious and a very complex event, unfolding as a threat and challenge to the city council, and a life-threatening experience for Frankfurt's Jewish population.[66] A mixture of mistrust and knowledge of corruption led many of Frankfurt's citizens to criticize their city council. They insisted on more transparency, a demand which soon escalated into a veritable list of grievances compiled into the so-called Gravamina, and presented to the city council by one of the revolt's ringleaders, L.V. Fettmilch, on August 25, 1612.

Foremost among the complaints was the social composition of the city council, especially the close inter-familial ties of its patrician councilors, which also extended to the city council's advocates, such as Christoph Keller, two of whose brothers were members of the council in addition to having familial ties to many patricians.[67] It was suggested that in future close relatives be prevented from sitting on the council so that an impartial administration be guaranteed. The second highest ranking complaint addressed the mishandling of the local jurisdiction and the need to have municipal decrees published.[68] While general corruption charges were levied, two legally trained advocates were singled out for serious improper behavior.[69]

The Gravamina also addressed various economic issues. However most of them targeted the local Jewish population. Usury was the key word used in the various allegations purporting that Jews were seriously bleeding the non-Jewish population. As a remedy, Frankfurt's guilds—similar to the requests voiced by many guilds throughout Germany—requested to have the Jewish population expelled from Frankfurt.[70]

Expelling the Jewish population turned into a relentless pursuit of the ringleaders of the uprising. In 1613, their demands escalated into concrete threats warning the city council that if the authorities failed to comply they would take action. These menaces reverberated in the Jewish community, causing fear and prompting some to save their belongings by trying to remove them from the

---

66 See Christopher R. Friedrichs' analysis of various historiographical interpretations of the Fettmilch uprising in "Politics or Pogrom? The Fettmilch Uprising in German and Jewish History," *Central European History*, 19/2 (1986): 186–228.

67 Friedrich Bothe, *Frankfurts Wirtschaftlich-Soziale Entwicklung vor dem Dreissigjährigen Kriege und dem Fettmilch Aufstand (1612–1616)* (2 vols, Frankfurt am Main: Baer, 1920), vol. 2, pp. 381–5.

68 Ibid., pp. 381, 388.

69 Meyn, *Reichsstadt*, p. 181.

70 Ibid., pp. 37, 48; Battenberg, *Europäische Zeitalter der Juden*, vol. 1, p. 593.

Judengasse, only to be ordered by the city council to have them returned. In 1614 the situation intensified. Jewish people were now increasingly being physically assaulted in Frankfurt's streets, which led to another outbreak of fear, if not panic. In May, many Jewish residents tried again—this time secretly—to remove their belongings, only to be intercepted by the rebels. The rebels, in turn, in a most curious note to the city council, suggested that the Jews should deposit their belongings with Frankfurt's burghers and guild-run places for safeguarding. They also declared that they would not do anything to harm them.[71]

Three months later the opposite occurred. Large segments of the population took matters into their own hands and attacked the Jewish population in the Judengasse on August 22, 1614.[72] Rumors about an imminent attack had reached the Jewish people one day prior to the actual assault and several families were able to take refuge in houses of friendly Christian locals. One city councilor protected more than 60 Jews, including 10 young mothers.[73] Those who had stayed behind tried to defend themselves but they were outnumbered. The attack by select local groups on Jewish life and property lasted for 13 hours. After the assault abated, Fettmilch and many other participants of the uprising forced the Jewish population to leave town.

As for the city councilors, they were unable to crush the uprising. In the end, imperial intervention was needed to suppress the uprising and restore calm. An imperial investigation was launched to determine the causes of the uprising and possible crimes committed during its course. This was the only time, at least from the 1562 to 1694 period, that an outside agency superseded local criminal jurisdictional authority. The imperial court pronounced the city council innocent of any major wrongdoing, while quietly removing two of its former members. Seven persons, mostly popular ringleaders, were sentenced to death; and an additional nine conspirators flogged and banished for life and 23 banished without flogging. All local guild members were found guilty of conspiracy and the guilds' power was considerably reduced. An additional 224 persons were pronounced guilty of conspiracy and had to pay considerable monetary fines.[74]

As to the crimes committed against Frankfurt's Jewish residents, the imperial authorities ordered that they were to be escorted back to town and that the fiscal damage done to them be reimbursed by the city of Frankfurt. While journeymen and their masters were held responsible for most of the damage, the

---

71 Andernacht, *Regesten*, vol. 2, p. 1037, item 4039; p. 1038, item 4044; p. 1041, item 4052; p. 1042, item 4055; p. 1066, item 4129; p. 1067, item 4131.

72 Ibid., p. 1072, item 4150.

73 Kracauer, *Geschichte der Juden*, vol. 1, p. 386.

74 Ibid., vol. 2, pp. 398–405.

majority of local citizens were also held accountable for having contributed to this conspiracy.[75] As a consequence, all citizens had to swear an oath to refrain from molesting Jews in and outside the Jewish Street. However, this oath did not preclude any further harassment. Physical threats persisted but they acquired a different face. The new avenue, concealed in nature, unfolded under the guise of criminal accusations and judicial manipulation. Jews were increasingly sentenced for no other reason than being suspicious, replacing previous "public anti-Jewish outbursts" with more "refined" judicial attacks.[76]

While the city council had gained an enhanced standing after the Fettmilch Uprising and acquired tighter control over the local guilds and artisans, the population could also register a partial success. The people had sent an unmistakable message to the patricians, who, in turn, could ill afford a future similar upheaval. A second intervention on the part of the Emperor might result in the loss of local autonomy, and thus the loss of the councilors' own power base.[77] And this turn of events was surely not lost on the city councilors or the population. No further local upheavals took place during the remainder of the seventeenth century. It thus seems as if a modus vivendi between the city council and the population had been established; but the various bellicose events starting with the Thirty Years War and ending with the French Wars added their share to this accommodation. A common threat from the outside fostered cohesiveness on the inside.

Initially, the outbreak of the Thirty Years War in 1618 affected Frankfurt only peripherally, mainly because of the city council's adroit handling of foreign affairs.[78] The drawn-out bellicose events, however, exerted an increasing strain on the local population. The pre-existing inflationary problem intensified during the

---

[75] Ibid., vol. 1, p. 391.

[76] See the detailed analysis on Jewish crime sentences in Frankfurt during the 1562 to 1696 period by Maria R. Boes, "Jews in the Criminal-Justice System of Early Modern Germany," *Journal of Interdisciplinary History*, 30/3 (Winter 1999): 407–35, especially pp. 425–7, 435. Unfortunately, Kasper-Holtkotte claims that no such studies existed: Cilli Kasper-Holtkotte, *Die Jüdische Gemeinde von Frankfurt/Main in der Frühen Neuzeit: Familien, Netzwerke und Konflikte eines Jüdischen Zentrums* (Berlin/Hamburg: De Gruyter, 2010), p. 15; also on p. 109 she asserts that 84 Jews committed criminal acts during the 1562 to 1696 period, basing her count on crime sentences, an erroneous deduction because crime sentences differ from actual crimes committed. Per Frankfurt's Strafenbuch, the actual number of Jewish people convicted for crimes was 94.

[77] Mauersberg, *Wirtschafts- und Sozialgeschichte*, p. 107; Christopher R. Friedrichs, "Urban Conflicts and the Imperial Constitution in Seventeenth-Century Germany," *Journal of Modern History*, 58 Supplement (December 1986): 98–123, pp. 100, 121.

[78] Karl Peter Jaeck, *Frankfurt und der Westfälische Frieden*, Archiv für Frankfurts Geschichte und Kunst, 4/1 (Frankfurt am Main, 1925), p. 218.

war, frequently resulting in a doubling if not tripling of the cost of general food products, causing serious food shortages—a problem which was augmented by the stationing of local soldiers. While local residents had originally defended the city, this policy proved to be ineffective, leading to the hiring of outside soldiers and to new taxes.[79]

While the actual numbers of locally stationed soldiers is rather sketchy, partly because of the lack of an in-depth study on the local military, a steady increase can, nevertheless, be observed especially during the war years. In 1618 for example, approximately 160 soldiers were recorded. Two years later this jumped to 750, reaching 1,200 in 1631.[80] When Frankfurt was directly drawn into the war with the arrival of the Swedish King Gustavus Adolphus in 1631, an additional 600 Swedish soldiers were stationed in a local garrison. Despite the fact that the Swedish King upheld Frankfurt's privileges and protected the city's trade—in return for a substantial amount of money—the stationing of Swedish troops caused considerable local hardship till 1635, when they had to retreat.[81]

Battles fought in Frankfurt's vicinity had an additional, and possibly an even more devastating effect on locals. Fields were demolished and harvests destroyed, and soon starvation began claiming its first victims. In addition, a seemingly endless stream of victims sought refuge in town. While the city council reacted by expelling many, especially peasants, large numbers were undeterred. They resorted to setting up huts for shelter outside the town walls. On top of this general disaster, Frankfurt experienced repeated outbreaks of the plague, which peaked in 1635 and resulted in catastrophic losses, claiming the lives of 6,943 registered inhabitants. But since only Lutherans were officially counted, the actual number was significantly higher.[82]

Despite these staggering casualties, Frankfurt fared better than many other towns in Germany during the war. It was the only town in south Germany whose trade, especially its bi-annual local fairs, continued throughout the war.[83] And by 1675 Frankfurt reached its prewar numbers of local residents.[84]

---

79 Bothe, *Geschichte*, pp. 440, 386.

80 Moritz, *Stadtverfassung*, vol. 1, pp. 419–20; Kracauer, "Militärwesen," p. 3.

81 Bothe, *Geschichte*, pp. 444–9.

82 Georg Ludwig Kriegk, "Frankfurt um die Mitte des dreissigjährigen Krieges," *Archiv für Frankfurt Geschichte und Kunst*, N.F 1 (1860): 260, 268, 251; Kracauer, *Geschichte der Juden*, vol. 2, p. 35.

83 Jaeck, *Westfälische Frieden*, p. 272; Hermann Meinert, *Frankfurts Geschichte* (Frankfurt am Main: Verlag Waldemar Kramer, 1958), p. 47; Bothe, *Geschichte*, p. 472.

84 Anton Schindling, "Wachstum und Wandel: Frankfurt 1555–1686," in *Frankfurt am Main: Die Geschichte der Stadt in neun Beiträgen*. Herausgegeben von der Frankfurter Historischen Kommission (Sigmaringen: Thorbecke, 1991), pp. 205–60, p. 209.

However, the war left an imprint on Frankfurt's military administration. Frankfurt's city council promulgated its own Kriegsartikel, articles of war, implementing how soldiers were to comport themselves and what punishments they could expect, for example, for stealing or sleeping while on duty.[85] The military also became more hierarchically stratified. In 1657, based on the prior division into 14 local city quarters, each of these 14 sections was united under a squad which consisted of two drummers, two musketeers, 20–25 corporals, one lieutenant and one captain.[86]

The outbreak of the French wars, especially the fight over the Palatinate, once again exposed Frankfurt to the immediate dangers of war. In 1673 Frankfurt was fortunate that an imperial army approached to save it from a French onslaught. But despite the fact that the city had hired additional soldiers, it could not prevent the French from setting two of its suburbs on fire in 1688. In addition to the French wars, the city also had to support the Emperor in his Turkish wars. While this generally bellicose situation entailed financial burdens, Frankfurt was spared any major war-related catastrophe.

The seventeenth century thus ended on a rather positive note. Frankfurt had weathered major bellicose upheavals that mainly raged outside its borders. But within Frankfurt the social composition had changed drastically, a process which had started by the end of the fifteenth century leading to an increasing split of the population along socio-economic and religious lines and resulting in an increase in disadvantaged groups by the end of the seventeenth.[87] The poor were first divided into local and foreign and subsequently into deserved and undeserved poor, creating four distinct categories. The concept of outsiders versus insiders—that is local versus foreigners—increased dramatically, highlighting the concept of boundaries even further.[88] Christian religious splits resulted in three local Christian religious groups—Catholics, Calvinists and Lutherans—while Jewish people were pushed into a ghetto. The guilds in turn created large margins between journeymen and masters while ousting illegitimates and women altogether, leading not only to increased gender divisions stressing marital status but also to the outcast status of illegitimates—the polarization of innocent

---

85 Bothe, *Geschichte*, p. 456.

86 Krauss, *Frankfurt am Main*, p. 83.

87 Sociological terms like "social stratification" and "Gemeinschaft versus Gesellschaft" with their multiple interpretations are deliberately omitted, and so are references to the linguistic designation of Randgruppen, Unterschichten or Aussenseiter used by some historians.

88 See Maria R. Boes, "Unwanted Travellers: The Tightening of City Borders in Early Modern Germany", in Thomas Betteridge, ed., *Borders and Travellers in Early Modern Europe* (Aldershot: Ashgate, 2007), pp. 87–111.

children. And the patricians, especially the Alten-Limpurg, increasingly closed ranks to prevent any "social pollution"; meanwhile the military resorted to creating its own internal structures, setting it increasingly apart from the rest of the people, especially during the seventeenth century.

These far-reaching urban divisions shattered an earlier, more egalitarian society where the concept of "Stadtluft macht frei," city air brings freedom, was held in high esteem but now no longer applied to everyone. That these divisions were to be reflected in the legal and judicial realm is almost a given. In fact, it fostered the emergence of an entirely new socio-professional group, advocates, who were increasingly consulted by Frankfurt's city councilors to assist them in their legal and general administrative tasks, soon gaining a stronghold over the legal system, as will be demonstrated in the following chapters.

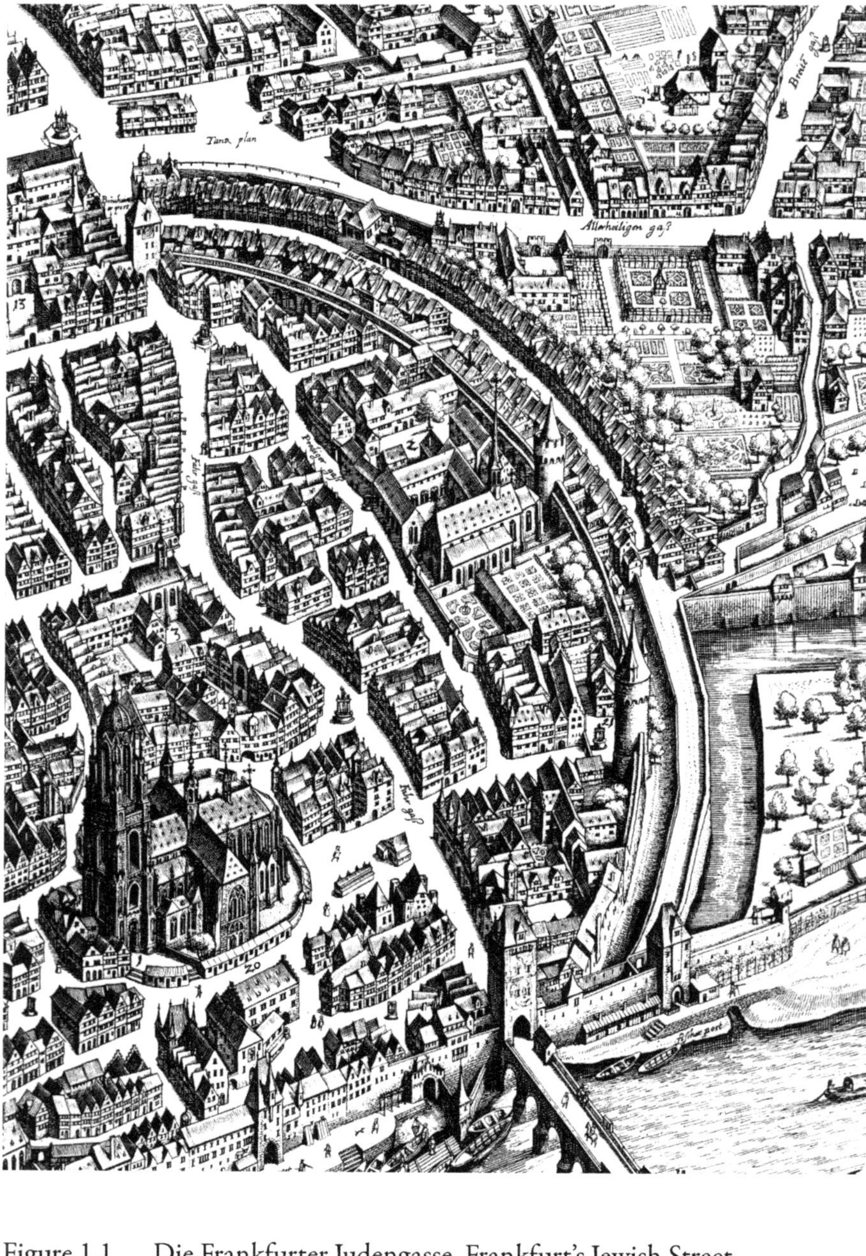

Figure 1.1 Die Frankfurter Judengasse, Frankfurt's Jewish Street
Source: © Institut für Stadtgeschichte, Frankfurt am Main.

Chapter 2
Legal/Judicial Setting

Historical Development

Arguably, one of the most contentious legal and adjudication issues of the late fifteenth and sixteenth centuries was the reception and integration of a foreign legal code, Roman Law, into the pre-existing Germanische Recht or Germanic Common Law. It ushered in a totally different legal approach and culture whose ramifications, both positive and negative, were felt by almost everyone in the Holy Roman Empire and beyond.

In order to assess the full extent of the legal implications, a brief overview of the Germanische Recht is warranted, especially with regard to criminal procedures. When a criminal act had been committed, it was the victimized person who had to avenge the deed. This seemingly personal revenge was, however, not conducted impetuously but through regulated procedural formalities. The victim or his family had to open the accusatorial procedure by making an oral complaint directly to the alleged perpetrator. In case the accused denied the charges, he had to prove his innocence. He could do this by taking recourse to so-called Eideshelfer, oath helpers—persons who knew him and who came to his defense by performing the Reinigungseid, a cleansing oath. This oath only backed the suspect's credibility. Oath helpers were character witnesses, not eyewitnesses; neither did they furnish the accused with an alibi. If this approach failed to convince the victim, ordeals, such as trial by fire, and judicial duels could be used. Both procedures took recourse to physical pain and implied divine interference in that God would side with the innocent. This Germanic Common Law approach to justice was a purely personal one in that the accusation and the defense were handled by the contesting individuals—that is without any governmental/state interference. It meant that the criminal offense was not considered an offense against the people or society as a whole.

The punishment, if the accused was found guilty, reflected this approach as well. The guilty person had to appease the victim or his family directly via a compositio, most commonly called the Wergeld, reflecting the value of the injured victim and partly the status of the offender.[1] It was only at this juncture

[1] Eberhard Schmidt, *Einführung in die Geschichte der deutschen Strafrechtspflege*, 3rd ed. (Göttingen: Vandenhoeck & Ruprecht, 1965), pp. 23, 36–7; Ludwig von Bar, *Geschichte des Deutschen Strafrechts* (Berlin: Weidmannsche Buchhandlung, 1882), p. 61.

that the community might step in to establish the appropriate value, but only if the parties could not agree. If the accused was unable to repay the loss, the victim or his family subjected the offender to their private revenge/punishment, an act which was, however, not carried out arbitrarily but was closely defined. Most importantly, for this revenge/punishment to be legal it had to be carried out in public in order to set it apart visibly from the criminal act.

Germanic Law thus had three central legal procedural and penal approaches. Of prime importance was the visibility and public nature of the entire trial from the accusation to the punishment, all of which unfolded under "freiem Himmel," open sky, or free sky in its literal translation.[2] All legal exchanges between the contending persons were conducted verbally and unfolded with minimal interference from the community. Criminal procedures were thus above all personal matters between the victim and the offender, and so was the penal structure. It was not a state monopoly.

Originally changes to Germanic practices occurred very slowly, targeting only specific practices such as the banning of ordeals by the Catholic Church during the Fourth Lateran Council of 1215, but they accelerated with the general reception of Roman Law toward the end of the fifteenth century. Already by the end of the fifteenth century, half of the members of the *Reichskammergericht*, the imperial court established in 1495, consisted of jurists trained in Roman Law.[3] And the first unified criminal code for the Holy Roman Empire, the *Constitutio Criminalis Carolina* of 1532, was the work of advocates trained in Roman Law. The reception reached its crescendo by the end of the sixteenth century, when this foreign law replaced Germanic practices—except for the public nature of executions.

However, while by the end of the sixteenth century the reception of Roman Law was complete, the discussion as to the cause and effect of this legal transition did not stop at the closing of that century, but has continued well into the twenty-first. Many books, treatises, and monographs were written about the reception of Roman Law. Its success was attributed to political, socio-economic, ecclesiastical/religious, and intellectual motives, as well as to power aspirations of a newly emerging professional group: jurists or advocates, a multi-causal phenomenon. Rulers, in their struggle for full sovereignty, sought to cement their aspiration by using this foreign law.[4] Similarly, German towns, in their

---

[2] Hans Fehr, *Deutsche Rechtsgeschichte*, 5th ed. (Berlin: Walter de Gruyter, 1952), p. 152.

[3] Wolfgang Kunkel, *Römische Rechtsgeschichte: Eine Einführung*, 4th ed. (Cologne/Graz: Böhlau, 1964), p. 163.

[4] Hans J. Wolff, *Roman Law: An Historical Introduction* (Norman: University of Oklahoma Press, 1964), p. 195.

striving for more political autonomy and increased independence, and for socio-economic reasons, followed suit.[5] The Catholic Church, by incorporating many Roman Law features and administrative procedures into its own legal body, reconfigured Canon Law, and thus was also seen as contributing to its reception and spread.[6] Humanism and its devotees, Humanists, emphasizing the study of classical antiquity, ipso facto also encouraged the study of Roman Law, which, in turn, led to the appearance of the agents of this legal change, a new professional group: advocates trained in Roman Law.[7] Later various Protestant reformers, scrambling to define their own legal system, fell back on Roman Law and further cemented its spread during the sixteenth century.[8]

While, obviously, this short synopsis points to a multitude of divergent scholarly views as to the contributing factors to the successful reception of Roman Law, its effect, especially on the people, has been given scant attention. Many legal scholars praise the new albeit foreign law for its "scientifically rational methods"—rather abstract descriptions devoid of any human connotation, as if legal systems operated in a social vacuum—ignoring if not negating the detrimental effect it had on large sections of the population.[9] Roman Law—with its inherent Roman values and ideas such as patria potestas and pater familias, the exalted status of men, the denigration of women and children, and its explicit encouragement of slavery and the abrogation of peasants' rights—did not lead to an open-arm reception.[10] In

---

[5] Hermann Conrad, *Deutsche Rechtsgeschichte* (Karlsruhe: C.F. Müller, 1966), p. 368.

[6] Georg Dahm, *Deutsches Recht* (Cologne and Stuttgart; W. Kohlhammer Verlag, 1951), p.127; see also Fehr, *Deutsche Rechtsgeschichte*, p. 340.

[7] Guido Kisch, *Studien zur humanistischen Jurisprudenz* (Berlin: Walter de Gruyter, 1972); see also Kaius Tuori, *Ancient Roman Lawyers and Modern Legal Ideals: Studies on the Impact of Contemporary Concerns in the Interpretation of Ancient Roman Legal History* (Frankfurt am Main: Vittorio Klostermann, 2007), who offers a somewhat different view.

[8] John Witte Jr, *Law and Protestantism: The Legal Teachings of the Lutheran Reformation* (Cambridge: Cambridge University Press, 2002).

[9] Proponents arguing for the "scientific rational methods" are Michael Stolleis, *Geschichte des* öffentlichen *Rechts in Deutschland* (4 vols, Munich: Beck, 1988), vol. 1, *Reichspublizistik und Policeywissenschaft*, pp. 66–7; Anja Johann, *Kontrolle mit Konsens: Sozialdisziplinierung in der Reichsstadt Frankfurt am Main im 16. Jahrhundert*, Studien zur Frankfurter Geschichte, Heft 46, Im Auftrag des Frankfurter Vereins für Geschichte und Landeskunde in Verbindung mit der Frankfurter Historischen Jommission, ed. Dieter Rebentisch (Frankfurt am Main: Verlag Waldemar Kramer, 2001), pp. 19, 51. The scientific label is cogently discussed by Tuori, *Ancient Roman Lawyers*, pp. 24–5, 54, 68 and especially on pp. 175, 182–3; see also Peter Bender, who presents a good historiographical survey in his *Die Rezeption des römischen Rechts im Urteil der deutschen Rechtswissenschaft: Rechtshistorische Reihe*, vol. 8 (Frankfurt am Main: Peter Lang, 1979), pp. 120–21, 128–9.

[10] For a detailed analyses of the complaints against Roman Law see Gerald Strauss, *Law, Resistance, and the State: The Opposition to Roman Law in Reformation Germany* (Princeton,

fact, the majority of the people did not embrace Roman Law as their law. While the full impact of Roman Law on European slavery cannot be assessed here, its detrimental effect on German peasants, women, and illegitimate children will, however, get due attention.

The German peasantry clearly suffered under the yoke of Roman Law because it empowered German rulers to evade, if not abrogate, various customary Germanic laws by utilizing and imposing the new *pater potestas* principle.[11] It deprived peasants, among others, of previously common-held properties such as grazing grounds, leading obviously to economic hardship. The peasants, aware of the legal appropriations of their common rights, resorted to public outcries escalating to the outbreak of the Peasants' War of 1524–25. Ranking high among their legal demands, clearly expressed in the Twelve Articles, was the restoration of previous customs and laws as well as the removal of the agents of this legal change, jurists/advocates who were seen as pushing the reception and dissemination of Roman Law.[12]

The Peasants' War and the peasants' disdain for Roman Law even prompted the Protestant reformer Martin Luther to speak up. But his involvement is perplexing. Barely three weeks after his initial "Friendly Admonition to Peace Concerning the Twelve Articles of the Peasants" of April 1525, which he addressed to the peasants, he wrote a virulent tract against them asking German rulers to use the utmost force "Against the Murderous and Plundering Hordes of the Peasants."[13] It was an astonishing and swift change of heart toward some of his most ardent supporters. It was, however, not his only shifting stance. He exhibited a similar attitude toward Roman Law and its agents, the advocates. In many of his writings, the reformer had clearly professed his deep dislike of anything foreign, especially the Roman curia, and his virulent statements against the agents of Roman Law, the jurists/advocates, are legendary.[14] He called the advocates "Schand-Juristen," dishonorable jurists, and bad Christians who only confused the people, and he suggested that they should have their "Zunge aus

NJ: Princeton University Press, 1986); see also Dahm, *Deutsche Rechtsgeschichte*, p. 122.

11 On the advantages for feudal lords see Wolff, *Roman Law*, p. 206.

12 Otto Stobbe, *Geschichte der Deutschen Rechtsquellen* (2 vols, Leipzig: Duncker & Humblot, 1864), vol. 1, pp. 51–2; Peter Blickle, *The Revolution of 1525: The German Peasants' War from a New Perspective*, trans. Thomas A. Brady, Jr and H.C. Midelfort (Baltimore: Johns Hopkins University Press, 1981), pp. 5, 20, 86. See also Johann, *Kontrolle*, p. 67, who cites article 46 of the peasants' demands, seemingly contradicting her former statement of a "rationalization."

13 Hans J. Hillerbrand, *The World of the Reformation* (New York: Charles Scribner's Sons, 1973), pp. 84–5.

14 See in particular Strauss, *Law, Resistance*, pp. 5, 23; Witte, *Law and Protestantism*, p. 119.

dem Hals reissen," tongues torn out of their throats, even admonishing his son that if he ever considered becoming a jurist he would "an ein Galgen hengen," hang him on the gallows.[15]

Reminiscent of his turnabout attitude toward the rebellious peasants, Martin Luther later reversed his stance by describing Roman Law as "heathen wisdom," this the very law that deprived many peasants of their livelihood.[16] This legal reversal is confounding. It becomes even more perplexing if one considers that Martin Luther now even encouraged youngsters to study this foreign law and become jurists, the agents of change whom he had so vehemently assailed. Practical religious reasons are being suggested by one of the leading legal Reformation scholars for this reversal, who claims that Martin Luther "needed the jurists to support his reformation."[17]

In contrast to Martin Luther's original reservations against the "heathen law," Philip Melanchthon, his fellow Protestant reformer, never voiced any such objections.[18] On the contrary, he enthusiastically supported it early on in his career and never wavered.[19] He even "taught university courses in Roman law."[20] His embrace of this foreign law was intricately linked to his admiration for the contemporary intellectual movement, Humanism, which stressed and imitated the various cultural aspects of antiquity, including the study of the Latin language.

For Melanchthon the Latin language was of prime significance in the study and understanding of Roman Law, as he claimed—somewhat arrogantly—that the "uneducated, [those] not conversant with the intricacies of the Roman language," were "as capable of dealing with important disciplines [such as Roman Law] as a donkey to play the harp."[21] He also stressed the importance

---

15 As cited by Notker Hammerstein, "Universitäten—Territorialstaaten—Universitäten," in Roman Schnur, ed. *Die Rolle der Juristen bei der Entstehung des modernen Staates* (Berlin: Duncker & Humblot, 1985), pp. 687–736, p. 695 footnote 21.

16 Witte, *Law and Protestantism*, p.115 cites the term "heathen wisdom"; Strauss, *Law, Resistance*, p. 5 also stresses Luther's later embrace of the study of foreign law, but fails to explain why he did so.

17 Witte, *Law and Protestantism*, p. 120.

18 Hammerstein, "Universitäten," p. 696; Isabelle Deflers, "Konfession und Jurisprudenz bei Melanchthon," in Christopj Strohms and Heinrich de Wall, eds, Konfessionalität und Jurisprudenz in der frühen Neuzeit (Berlin: Duncker & Humblot, 2009), pp. 33–46.

19 Guido Kisch, *Melanchthons Rechts- und Soziallehre* (Berlin: Walter de Gruyter, 1967), pp. 74–5, 90, 119.

20 Harold J. Berman, *Law and Revolution, II: The Impact of the Protestant Reformations on the Western Legal Tradition* (Cambridge, MA: The Belknap Press of Harvard University Press, 2003), p. 78.

21 Cited by Kisch, *Melanchthons Rechts-*, p. 87.

of its written format. To him, the written set-up served as a protection against despotism, and the "recklessness of the masses … for the protection of the peace."[22] His esteem for Roman values, including Roman Law, over Germanic practices is best presented by his argument that "Without a doubt, our culture gained considerably by accepting Roman literature and Roman Law [especially when] compared to the barbaric condition of previous centuries," and he claimed that "thanks to the Roman Law our people discontinued with brutal practices."[23] Not surprisingly, he also pressed to raise the status of those familiar with Roman Law, such as judges and advocates.[24]

Similar to Luther, the heathen origins of the "Weisheit der römischen Gesetze," wisdom of Roman laws, did not represent a stumbling block for Melanchthon. He argued that Roman Law was not based on human but on God's wisdom, that it was God who had infused the heathen Romans with this legal wisdom.[25] The religious gap between Roman heathens and Protestant Christians was thus bridged and crossed.

Considering the reformers' influence on many German rulers and city councils in many towns, their embrace of Roman Law could only strengthen the reception and application of this foreign law and its agents, the advocates/jurists, against the will and complaints of many.[26] While the Catholic Church had originally advocated many features of Roman Law and incorporated them into Canon Law, Protestants continued with this practice. Roman Law became now also religiously sanctioned in Protestant areas.[27] Melanchthon's embrace of Roman Law did not, however, prevent him from also making ample use of divine or biblical law, emphasizing its retributive aspect by arguing that "if they [rational creatures created by God to be like Him] strive against Him the order of justice [requires that] He destroys them."[28] For him "criminal punishments served as a form of divine retribution."[29]

Other reformers such as Jean Calvin in Geneva and his advocate friend Germain Colladon, both of whom were trained in Roman Law, had similar

---

22 Ibid., pp. 96, 86.

23 Ibid., pp. 86, 120.

24 Ibid., p. 88.

25 Hammerstein, "Universitäten," p. 696 citing Melanchthon's expression; Kisch, *Melanchthons Rechts-*, p. 117.

26 Hammerstein, "Universitäten," p. 697; for a good rendition of contemporary complaints by the people see Strauss, *Law, Resistance*, pp. 3–5. Even luminaries such as Ulrich von Hutten and Sebastian Frank were against it; see Stobbe, *Geschichte*, vol. 2, pp. 45, 47.

27 Witte, *Law and Protestantism*, pp. 150, 158.

28 Ibid., p. 134.

29 Ibid., pp. 132–5, Berman, *Law and Revolution*, pp. 79–81, 83; Kisch, *Melanchthons Rechts-*, pp. 80, 116–17; see also Deflers, pp. 33–46.

legal outlooks.[30] While Colladon, it was suggested, regarded Roman Law as "les regles d'or," golden rule, he also "invoque frequemment le droit devin," frequently invoked divine law.[31] The combination of Roman Law and divine/biblical law resulted in an at times perplexing legal amalgam and led to equally perplexing sentencing, such as in Geneva, where the Christian "heretic" Servetus was sentenced to death based on this legal mixture of heathen and divine laws.[32] Unfortunately, Servetus was not the only one to be subjected to this legal blend with a very harsh outcome. Some later Lutheran, legally trained jurists and writers, in particular Johannes Eisermann who argued "that a learned legal profession was essential to a Christian Commonweatlh", and Johann Oldendorp, for whom "the highest source and state of law was divine law," above all the "laws of the Bible," followed this lead with far-reaching impact on other Lutheran jurists.[33] This paradoxical combination of the "heathen" Roman Law coupled with Christian divine law as revealed in the Bible led to very harsh, albeit selective, sentences even in Frankfurt, as disclosed in the following chapters.

In addition to changes to substantive laws, Roman Law also affected and transformed criminal court procedures. It replaced the private, personal, oral, and public proceedings of Germanic Law—practiced without official or governmental interference—with written, secretive, impersonal, ex officio or governmental and authoritarian agents and procedures, to become known as inquisitorial court procedures.

The written procedures led to better record-keeping on criminals and facilitated the flow and exchange of data among the various courts, whose policing ability was thus enhanced. However, it also had an intimidating effect, especially on the illiterate—and most contemporaries, especially women, could neither read nor write—who found themselves having their words written down without any proof that what they said was properly recorded. What had once been a public, oral, and transparent approach turned into an opaque one: a terrifying experience which left the people's oral cultural safety net in shambles. How fearful many of them were is best exemplified, somewhat ironically, by one of the greatest writers, Shakespeare, who, in describing Jack Cade's rebellion,

---

30 For Jean Calvin see Robert M. Kingdon, *Adultery and Divorce in Calvin's Geneva* (Cambridge, MA: Harvard University Press, 1995), pp. 117–18, 121, 157; and for Germain Colladon see Erich-Hans Kaden, *Le jurisconsulte Germain Colladon, ami de Jean Calvin and de Théodore Bèze* (Geneva: Libraire de l'Universite George & Cie, 1974), especially pp. 48–9, 80–81, 96, 120.

31 As argued by Kaden, *Germain Colladon*, pp. 81–2.

32 For Geneva, Kingdon, *Adultery*, pp. 117, 121, 157.

33 Witte, *Law and Protestantism*, pp. 150, 158.

portrayed lawyers as the rebels' first selected targets because they used the written word as a tool of suppression.[34]

It was not only the lawyers' written words, which were frightening to many, but it was also their use of Latin and even Greek terms in their various legal opinions. In fact, the emerging legal terminology became so complex that already by the mid-sixteenth century it had led to the conceptualization and publication of legal lexicons—some reaching numerous reprints—which were to help none other than the advocates themselves.[35] That even legally trained advocates needed such legal linguistic assistance for clarification only emphasizes the loss and bewilderment those unfamiliar with the new procedures, that is, most of the people, must have felt.

While some legal scholars today voice their sentiments against the new procedures—rightfully claiming that it resulted in a separation between the Volksrecht, the people's laws, and the Juristenrecht, a lawyer's law code favoring the legal profession—others argue for its benefits, stressing, among others, the progressive and unifying character of the new procedures.[36] True, Roman Law was the driving force leading to the first unified criminal code, the *Constitutio Criminalis Carolina* promulgated in 1532 by the Catholic Holy Roman Emperor, Charles V, but this unified Roman Law-modeled code merits neither the unifying accolade nor its all-encompassing, allegedly progressive interpretation. First, local sentiments acted against such a unified enforcement from above, as clearly documented by the promulgation of an additional clause, the Salvatorische Klausel, or Saving Clause, which guaranteed the continuation of local rights, thus fostering the persistence of particularistic tendencies.

Second, to its credit, the *Constitutio Criminalis Carolina*—mainly structuring procedural law, especially the system of proof—officially displaced the former highly subjective usage of oath helpers and character witnesses and replaced them with actual witnesses, especially eyewitnesses. It also did away with the previous painful ordeals and judicial feuds. However, it did so by replacing them with another equally, if not more, painful procedure: judicial torture.[37]

---

34 In his play *Henry VI, Part 2*, of 1594.

35 Kisch, *Studien*, pp. 36–8.

36 Both Dahm, *Deutsches Recht*, pp. 121–2, 144 and Fehr, *Rechtsgeschichte*, p. 197 point to this split; Conrad, *Rechtsgeschichte*, p. 341 stresses its progressive format.

37 Fehr, *Rechtsgeschichte*, points to the influence of Roman Law entailing the use of torture, p. 152, stressing that as late as the thirteenth century the Sachsenspiegel, a regional Germanic law code, did not include its use; see also John Langbein, *Torture and the Law of Proof: Europe and England in the Ancien Régime* (Chicago: University of Chicago Press, 1977) and Edward Peters, *Torture* (New York: Basil Blackwell, 1982).

Torture aimed, of course, at eliciting a confession without which, in the absence of at least two eyewitnesses, a suspect could not be sentenced. Circumstantial evidence did not lead to a conviction. Torture was also used to extract the identity of alleged fellow villains. It could be inflicted in two ways: psychologically by displaying the torture instruments, which was (not ironically) called "mit Güte," with kindness; or physically by applying them, called "mit Wehe," with pain. Confessions made during the application of torture were only valid if they were ratified by the suspect a day or two after such an application. If the suspect refused to reconfirm his or her confession at a later date, torture could be reapplied. Thus while the evidence given by eyewitnesses marked a definite legal progress over the subjective deployment of oath helpers and character witnesses, the use of torture does not merit the accolade of a "totally indispensible" judicial procedure.[38]

Moreover, if a suspect withstood judicial torture without pleading guilty, he or she was to be discharged, which frequently, however, did not correspond to a full exoneration, especially if the authorities continued to harbor doubts about the innocence of the suspect. In that case they could and frequently did mete out a so-called Verdachtstrafe, punishment for being suspicious. Although such Verdachtstrafen were milder, mainly consisting of banishments, they constituted punishments nevertheless. Neither releasing the accused for withstanding torture—a procedure reminiscent of the former concept of ordeals—nor meting out punishments simply based on suspicion represents highly improved judicial approaches.

In addition, both eyewitness and torture procedures encompassed the new secretive legal approach. In contrast to previous publicly conducted trials, the questioning of witnesses unfolded in private, that is, in separate chambers behind closed doors in the presence of very few officials, who wrote down the various statements to be presented to the legal authorities at a later date.[39] And the application of judicial torture unfolded in a similar secretive fashion.

Also, and most revealing, while the Catholic Church started to use torture in its ecclesiastical courts by the early thirteenth century and continued to do so for years to come—the documents of the Inquisition speak for themselves—none of the initial Protestant reformers, such as Martin Luther or Melanchthon or subsequent Protestant reformers and preachers, including Jean Calvin and

---

[38] As claimed by Alfons Vogt, "Die Anfänge des Inquisitionsprozesses in Frankfurt am Main," *Zeitschrift der Savigny-Stiftung für Rechtsgeschichte*, vol. 68 (Weimar: Böhlau, 1951), pp. 234–308, p. 248.

[39] For a good rendition of secrecy in Roman Law, see Marie Theres Fögen, *Römische Rechtsgeschichten.* Über *Ursprung und Evolution eines sozialen Systems* (Göttingen: Vandenhoeck & Ruprecht, 2002), pp. 141, 162–3.

his friend, the advocate Germain Colladon in Geneva, advocated its abolition in Protestant areas.[40] Despite recent attempts at reassessing Luther's and other Protestant reformers' legal legacy, such efforts do not erase the fact that torture continued to be used for centuries in both Protestant and Catholic areas.[41] Protestant reformers did not reform criminal adjudication practices.

Frankfurt's Administration of Justice

During the time frame of this study, 1562 to 1696, Frankfurt's city council possessed full jurisdictional criminal autonomy, covering everyone in town regardless of social status or religious affiliation—including its local Jewish population and military personnel.[42] This also extended over foreigners regardless of where they had committed the crime. The sentences meted out were final, as during the Diet of Augsburg of 1530 appeals to a higher criminal court were abandoned. Once sentenced, an offender had no further legal recourse.

The city council, as previously stated, was composed of three benches presided over by two mayors. The first and second benches were staffed by local patricians, of which the family of the Alten-Limpurg held the biggest share, followed by the Frauensteiner with a considerably smaller numerical representation.[43] The third bench consisted of members of select guilds, whose

---

40 In a very detailed study Mathias Schmoeckel confirms that Luther did not oppose torture: *Humanität und Staatsraison. Die Abschaffung der Folter in Europe and die Entwicklung des gemeinen Strafprozess- und Beweisrecht seit dem hohen Mittelalter* (Cologne: Böhlau, 2000), p. 110. For Calvin see Kingdon, *Adultery*, and for Colladon see Kaden, *Germain Colladon*, especially pp. 83–91, 97.

41 Witte, *Law and Protestantism*, does not even list the term torture in the index let alone deal with it in the text; and neither does Berman, *Law and Revolution*, who devotes pages 133 to 137 to the use of torture but fails to have a single reference to Luther's acceptance of torture.

42 For the Jewish population, see the privilege issued by Emperor Charles IV on June 2, 1372: Andernacht, *Regesten*, vol. 2, p. 910, item 3591. See also Andreas Gotzmann, "Im Spannungsfeld externer und interner Machtfaktoren. Jüdische Gerichtsbarkeit im frühneuzeitlichen Frankfurt am Main," in Anja Amend et al., *Die Reichsstadt Frankfurt als Rechts- und Gerichtslandschaft im Römischen Deutschen Reich* (Munich: Oldenbourg, 2008), pp. 185–215, especially p. 195 where he cites a reaffirmation of these rights by Frankfurt's city council of 1622.

43 Gerald Lyman Soliday, A Community in Conflict. Frankfurt Society in the Seventeenth and Eighteenth Centuries (Hanover, NH: University Press of New England, 1974), p. 99.

exact social composition is still somewhat elusive.[44] By the time of this study all of Frankfurt's city councilors were Lutheran men; no Catholics, Calvinists, Jews, or women were admitted. This socio-religious exclusionary composition remained in effect throughout the time span covered in this book. However, despite this religious exclusivity, Frankfurt's Lutheran city councilors continued with their Catholic predecessors' admiration of Humanism and Roman Law. In fact, they adopted Roman Law as their legal guiding force and they fostered and hired advocates trained in Roman Law.

Substantive Laws

In substantive law, Frankfurt initiated and promulgated its own laws despite the introduction of the *Constitutio Criminalis Carolina* in 1532. Most interestingly, in 1509, Frankfurt's then Catholic city council issued its first Reformation—as the new compilation of local laws was called—including various features of Roman Law.[45] The later Lutheran city council not only followed this practice, but also amplified it by completing the integration of Roman Law into Frankfurt's revised Reformation of 1578. These two codes were complemented by numerous revised or new decrees and edicts pertaining to criminal behavior, many of which are contained in the voluminous Rathsbücher (Minutes of the City Council). While the sheer volume of these laws and edicts prevents one from drawing many inferences, one major characteristic, however, emerged from a brief analysis: ambiguity.

In particular, it was the coexistence of fines and physical punishments, which lacked transparency and objectivity. Not in all instances did the laws clearly stipulate when fines or corporal punishments were to be applied. For instance, article XVI of the 1578 Reformation stated that if someone prevented municipal functionaries from executing their duties, the offender was to be punished with fines or corporal punishments, depending on the circumstances.[46] But the circumstances were not explained. An edict of 1613 concerning adulteration of saffron was equally ambiguous. While specifying stiff monetary fines or corporal punishments, it did not, however, clarify when one was to be applied

---

[44] Johann, Kontrolle, points to some interesting name continuities possibly representing family-sequential representations similar to those of local patricians, p. 25 note. 63.

[45] Helmut Coing, Die Frankfurter Reformation von 1578 und das Gemeine Recht ihrer Zeit, eine Studie zum Privatrecht der Rezeptionszeit (Weimar: Böhlau, 1935), p. 3.

[46] Ibid., p. 280.

over the other.[47] The payment of the Schmägulden, or money of shame for sexual misconduct, which was to be remitted in public in one of Frankfurt's major squares announced by the beating of drums—thus entailing and enhancing considerable public exposure—could be averted based upon, among others, the wealth and status of the offender.[48]

Ambiguity also appeared in some laws aimed at religious and moral behavior. While issues such as blasphemous cursing were religion-specific, other behaviors were cloaked in the mantle of religion to scare locals by invoking the wrath of God, which in turn would befall the entire community. The 1608 edict prohibiting the lodging of prostitutes serves as an example, as does the 1629 edict.[49] They prohibit cursing, adultery, prostitution, and fornication, stating that the rules were to be followed in order to prevent God's anger, which could manifest itself in the plague and other communal punishments. In 1673 a municipal decree links cursing, blasphemous speech, adultery, fornication, excessive eating and drinking, and immoderate clothing not only to God's wrath but also to the imminent dangers of war.[50] The wrath of God was thus seasonally adjusted depending on the circumstances, from the emergence of diseases to the threat of war. Most curiously, however, not a single entry was found that tied fiscal matters or usury to the wrath of God.

This kind of quasi-moral/religious legislation did not always exist in Frankfurt. Although the city had incorporated the ecclesiastical court in 1370, it by no means immediately infused or criminalized many of its religious responsibilities. Frankfurt passed its first secular legislation on adultery only in 1441, followed by the introduction of monetary fines in 1452. But even after the promulgation of the 1452 law, it was not closely followed by the authorities.[51] It was only toward the end of the sixteenth century that there was an increase in not only measures to curb adultery but also in the scope of sexual legislation encompassing fornication and prostitution. Frankfurt, which had operated its own municipal brothels for centuries, outlawed prostitution in 1574, and thus

47 *Corpus Legum Francofurtensium* (*CLF*) in Frankfurt's Municipal Archives (5 vols, 1748), vol. 1, p. 85.

48 Ibid., p. 554; Philip Orth, Anmerkungen über die sogenannte erneurte Reformation der Stadt Frankfurt am Main (3 vols, Frankfurt am Main, 1751), vol. 1, p. 885.

49 *Concepta Edictorum Francofurtensium* (6 vols), vol. 4, pp. 208–9; vol. 5, no. 10.

50 *CLF*, vol. 4, p. 27.

51 Georg Ludwig Kriegk, *Deutsches Bürgertum im Mittelalter: Nach urkundlichen Forschungen und mit besonderer Beziehung auf Frankfurt am Main* (2 vols, 1868; repr. Frankfurt am Main: Saue & Auvermann, 1969), vol. 2, pp. 287, 189.

turned into a prosecutor of its own former practice.[52] But it was fornication in particular, that is, sex prior to marriage, which became a prime target.

As outlined in the previous chapter, a detailed analysis shows that the criminalization of previously acceptable sexual patterns was closely connected to guild policies barring women and illegitimates access to their ranks, which they had previously enjoyed.[53] Barring illegitimates for quasi-moral reasons from joining the guilds reversed previously accepted patterns, such as commonly practiced cohabitation as well as the mainly positive view of out-of-wedlock children, at the same time dragging down widely accepted sexual mores. The effect was a shift of sexual mores leading to the criminalization of many previously accepted sexual patterns, and illegitimates as well as women became the prime victims.[54]

Not surprisingly, Frankfurt's 1578 revised law code, the Reformation, reflects these changes. It not only coerced single people to marry, stipulating monetary fines for fornication if they got married, or punishment by imprisonment, flogging and banishment if they refused; it now also excluded illegitimate children from inheriting their father's property.[55] Women lost more rights as well. At the death of their husbands, they had no legal say over the administration of their children's estate but were immediately put under the power of a male guardian, in contrast to widowers who had full legal powers.[56]

This new patriarchal legal approach is not surprising considering that the 1578 Reformation substituted previous traditional legal practices with Roman Law.[57] It was the work of one of Frankfurt's advocates, Dr. Johannes Fichard,

---

52 Ibid., p. 336.

53 For a detailed discussion of this process see Maria R. Boes "'Dishonourable' Youth, Guilds, and the Changed World View of Sex, Illegitimacy, and Women in Late-Sixteenth-Century Germany," *Continuity and Change*, 18/3 (2003): 345–72.

54 See ibid., especially data on p. 359.

55 Coing, *1578 Reformation*, p. 80; *Sammlung der Verordnungen der Reichsstadt Frankfurt*, ed. Johann Conradin Beyerbach (6 vols, Frankfurt am Main: Hermann, 1798), vol. 1, p. 554.

56 Ulrich Trumpold, *Heinrich Kellner 1536–1589: Studien zu Recht, Verwaltung und Politik in Frankfurt am Main* (Frankfurt am Main: Verlag Waldemar Kramer, 1975), pp. 62–3.

57 Coing, *1578 Reformation*, p. 103; Anton Schindling, *Wachstum und Wandel: Frankfurt 1555–1685*, Archiv für Frankfurter Geschichte und Kunst, 41 (Sigmaringen: Thorbecke, 1991), pp. 205–60, p. 249; Stobbe, *Geschichte*, pp. 42, 317, 324–5. For an excellent study of the Romans' legal position on women, especially the patria potestas and pater familias, see Evelyn Höbenreich and Giunio Rizzelli, eds, *Scylla: Fragmente einer juristischen Geschichte der Frauen im antiken Rom* (Vienna: Böhlau, 2003), especially pp. 41, 56, 223.

trained in Roman Law, whose career will be discussed below. That the infusion of Roman Law incorporated concomitant Roman cultural ideas and values, such as the exalted role of men—patria potestas and pater familias—is quite obvious.[58] While the guilds became a male domain, the city council also flexed its patria potestas muscles.[59] Hence the claim that the 1578 Reformation was a rational legal code, one mirroring the "ethical values of Frankfurt's society toward the end of the sixteenth century," is at best presumptuous.[60]

The exalted standing of the father/husband was already included in the Roman Law infused 1532 *Constitutio Criminalis Carolina*. Article 118 stipulates that when a wife or virgin was abducted, only the husband or father had the right to launch legal proceedings. If they failed to do so, the state/government would not step in. A woman abducted against her will had thus no other recourse than to rely on close male relatives. Roman Law thus did affect women.[61] This anti-women trend in legislation did not fizzle out by the end of the sixteenth century. On the contrary, in 1604, 1611, and again in 1614 Frankfurt's city council promulgated edicts prohibiting burghers' widows and burghers' daughters, that is, women with burgher rights, to marry foreigners unless the future husband had either received or applied for citizenship. Failure to comply with these

---

[58] See Tuori, *Ancient Roman Lawyers*, who stresses the impact of Roman cultural ideas, p. 186; also Guido Kisch, "Die Humanistische Jurisprudenz," in Leo S. Olschki, ed., *La Storia del Diritto nel Quadro delle Scienze Storiche* (Florence: Olschki, 1966), pp. 469–90, especially p. 490. Coing's stance in *1578 Reformation* is puzzling if not inherently contradicting: while he claims on p. 11 that "Fichard only included a few Roman sentences with regard to patria potestas and it seems as if he did not subscribe to this idea," he, nevertheless, asserts on pp. 103, 107 that Roman Law fully replaced local law.

[59] This puts into question assertions that religious factors had the decisive impact, as advanced by Steven Ozment, *When Fathers Ruled: Family Life in Reformation Europe* (Cambridge, MA: Harvard University Press, 1983), pp. 29–30.

[60] As claimed by Johann, *Kontrolle*, p. 59.

[61] Unfortunately, this topic is hardly ever discussed despite many excellent studies on women for that period. Susan C. Karant-Nunn and Merry E. Wiesner-Hanks, ed. and trans., *Luther on Women: A Sourcebook* (Cambridge: Cambridge University Press, 2003), refer to the Roman concept of pater familias only briefly, p. 9; Martha C. Howell, *The Marriage Exchange: Property, Social Place, and Gender in Cities of the Low Countries, 1300–1500* (Chicago: University of Chicago Press, 1998) has a few but rather inconclusive references to Roman Law, pp. 212–14, 217; meanwhile Ulinka Rublack, *The Crimes of Women in Early Modern Germany* (Oxford: Clarendon Press, 1999), cites "The law was an important instrument," p. 2, and "The law took up such notions," p. 14 without, however, giving any specifics pertaining to these laws. Merry E. Wiesner, *Women and Gender in Early Modern Europe*, 3rd ed. (Cambridge: Cambridge University Press, 2008), while citing the impact of various classical sources, has no explicit referral to Roman Law despite a chapter entitled "Ideas and Laws Regarding Women."

municipal decrees would result in the loss of citizenship and banishment for the rule-breaking women.[62]

And the city councilors used every means at their disposal to make these laws known to everyone, in contrast to their previous negligence in publicizing other municipal decrees, as so clearly stated in the burghers' 1612 Gravamina, item 11. They had these marriage-restricting laws for women announced orally in Frankfurt's streets and publicly written up. But, most importantly, they also took recourse to local preachers, who had to broadcast these marriage restrictions from the pulpit in the various churches.[63] Quite obviously, disseminating marriage restrictions in churches added weight to their enforcement by implying God's sanction, a pattern reminiscent of previous Catholic practices.

Frankfurt's advocates played a decisive role in this development as well. They had not only produced Frankfurt's revised law codes, infusing and later replacing them with Roman Law, but also issued criminal legal opinions, which affected the individual penal structure, as will become evident in the following chapters. A closer look at Frankfurt's advocate is therefore warranted.

The Role of Frankfurt's Advocates

As already pointed out, the emergence and proliferation of advocates in the Holy Roman Empire and in Frankfurt is intricately linked to the emergence and proliferation of Roman Law: it was a symbiotic development. The spread of Roman Law depended on advocates; and advocates, in turn, depended on Roman Law for their very existence.[64] In addition, the contemporary elite's preoccupation if not obsession with Humanism, and hence the widely considered superiority of many aspects of Roman antiquity, cemented the proliferation of Roman Law and, ipso facto, enhanced the position of its standard bearers.

Since Roman Law emanated from Italy and was originally exclusively taught at Italian universities, German students had to travel and live in Italy to absorb it. And, to state the obvious, money was needed for such lengthy legal university studies. Sons of wealthy people—mainly from the nobility and urban centers—could, of course, afford this sojourn, which resulted in a close interdependence

62 *Concepta Edictorum*, vol. 4, p. 283; *CLF*, vol. 1, p. 93.

63 *Concepta Edictorum*, vol. 4, p. 283; *CLF*, vol. 1, pp. 80, 93; vol. 4, p. 27.

64 Adolf Stölzel, Die Entwicklung des gelehrten Richterthums in deutschen Territorien. Eine rechtsgeschichtliche Untersuchung mit vorzugsweiser Berücksichtigung der Verhältnisse im Gebiet des ehemaligen Kurfürstenthums Hessen (Stuttgart: Verlag der J.G. Cotta'schen Buchhandlung, 1872); Helmut Coing, *Die Rezeption des römischen Rechts in Frankfurt am Main* (Frankfurt am Main: Vittorio Klostermann, 1939), p. 151.

between wealth and the emerging legal profession.[65] While eventually Roman Law was taught at German universities, and the number of universities endowed with legal chairs increased considerably, entailing a concomitant increase in law students, the original interdependence between wealth and advocates continued and intensified.[66]

Frankfurt serves as the perfect example of this development. The initiative to foster the reception of Roman Law, and hence the corresponding legal studies in Italy, emanated from local patricians who held the majority in the city council. They were not only staunch supporters of the Humanist movement but were also cognizant of the political power vested in Roman Law. Both Humanism and Roman Law promised to enhance their prestige and position of power. Humanism, with its various Latin derivatives, thus became the powerful guiding force of supremacy by stirring above all the intellectual aspirations of men of the upper echelon of society while remaining a movement alien to most people in Europe: those frequently referred to—in a condescending if not pejorative way—as the "common" people.[67]

That Frankfurt's patricians clearly expressed admiration for Humanism is demonstrated by two vivid examples: the selection of first names for family members and the formation of a local Humanistenkreis, Humanist circle. The Holzhausen family, belonging to the Alten-Limpurg patricians, chose for one of their son's name Justinian, after the Roman Emperor. Justinian Holzhausen, in turn, only opted for Greek and Roman names for his sons, such as Trajan, Achilles, Johann Hector, Hieronymus Augustus, and Julius, the latter referring to Julius Caesar—all examples testifying to the absence of genealogical modesty.[68] The initiation of the formation of a local Humanist circle emanated

---

65 Erich Maschke, *Städte und Menschen* (Wiesbaden: Franz Steiner Verlag, 1980), p. 80; Stölzel, *Entwicklung*, demonstrated that the majority of students came from the nobility and from cities, p. 130.

66 For the increase in German universities teaching Roman Law and the increase in law students, see Hammerstein, "Universitäten," pp. 690 and 718. For the prerequisite of financial support see Strauss, *Law and Resistance*, p. 170; Johann, *Kontrolle*, p. 62; see also Walter Rüegg, ed., *Geschichte der Universität in Europa. II: Von der Reformation zur Französichen Revolution (1500–1800)* (Munich: Beck, 1996).

67 The emergence of this pejorative and arrogant description which, unfortunately, is still being used by many, is traced by Peter Burke, *Popular Culture in Early Modern Europe*, (Aldershot: Ashgate, 2002), p. 270.

68 Wolfgang Klötzer, "Keine liebere Stadt als Frankfurt," in *Kleine Schriften zur Frankfurter Kulturgeschichte II: Studien zur Frankfurter Geschichte*, 45, Auftrag des Frankfurter Vereins für Geschichte und Landeskunde in Verbindung mit der Frankfurter Historischen Kommission herausgegeben von Dieter Rebentisch (Frankfurt am Main: Verlag Waldemar Kramer, 2000), pp. 166, 219, 250.

from local patricians, who also made up its exclusive membership. Prominent among them were again members of the Holzhausen family as well as members of the Bromm family. In fact, both families maintained Humanist relationships beyond the Frankfurt circle, such as with Melanchthon, who was a frequent visitor. Justinian Holzhausen even studied under Melanchthon in Wittenberg. He garnered praise for his performance, as documented in a letter Melanchthon sent to his father.[69]

Obviously, the association with Humanism and known Humanists served to strengthen the patricians' self-esteem.[70] It should, therefore, not come as a surprise that they also sponsored and financed the study of Roman Law to promising students and promoted, if not pushed, for its deployment by subsequently hiring Roman Law trained advocates as municipal legal and penal advisors.[71] Frankfurt's patricians thus made two investments: adopting self-serving, Humanist practices at home and encouraging students to study Roman Law abroad. And they were successful in their aspirations.

Already by 1460 secular, Roman Law trained advocates replaced the former mainly Catholic-trained jurists.[72] The legal implications of that transition manifested themselves early in the sixteenth century when two municipal advocates trained in Roman Law started to include Roman Law in municipal legislation in the newly formulated local code, the Reformation of 1509. It was one of the first codes in Germany to include the foreign law.[73] Several decades later, Frankfurt's advocate Dr. Johann Fichard—who after he had finished his

69 Ibid., pp. 166, 228, 250.

70 Ibid., p. 251.

71 Frankfurt's city council offered money to Fichard for his studies of Roman Law in Italy, Stobbe, *Geschichte*, p. 57; see in particular Stobbe, Geschichte, p. 37; Konrad Bund, "Frankfurt am Main im Spätmittelalter," *Archiv für Frankfurter Geschichte und Kunst*, 41 (1953), pp. 53–149, p. 112; see also the seminal data assessment by Barbara Dölemeyer, *Frankfurter Juristen im 17. und 18. Jahrhundert*, in Ius Commune, Veröffentlichungen des Max-Planck-Instituts für Europäische Rechtsgeschichte, Sonderheft 60 (Frankfurt am Main: Vittorio Klostermann, 1993), pp. LII, LVIII, LXI.

72 Coing, *Rezeption*, p. 175. See also Stölzel, *Entwicklung*, p. 286; Johann, G.Ch. Thomas, *Der Oberhof zu Frankfurt am Main und das Fränkische Recht* (Frankfurt am Main: Jäger'sche Buch- und Papier-Landkarten-Handlung, 1841), p. 222; Stobbe, *Geschichte*, p. 643, B.J. Römer-Büchner, "Wohlleben und Prachtliebe der Gesellschaft Limburg zu Frankfurt am Main," *Zeitschrift für deutsche Kulturgeschichte* (1856), p. 137. Similar trends were observed by Dieter Stievermann for Württemberg, "Die gelehrten Juristen der Herrschaft Württemberg im 15. Jahrhundert. Mit besonderer Berücksichtigugn der Kleriker-Juristen in der ersten Jahrhunderthälfte und ihre Bedeutung für das landesherrliche Kirchenregiment," in Schnur, *Die Rolle der Juristen*, pp. 229–72, 304.

73 Trumpold, *Heinrich Kellner*, p. 59.

legal studies in Germany spent additional years in Italy to familiarize himself even more intensely with Roman Law—issued the revised municipal 1578 Reformation, which rounded off this transition by replacing Germanic practices and legal codes with Roman Law.

But Roman Law and Humanism were not the only binding force among the patricians, the city council, and its advocates. Informal connections played an equally decisive role: familial and social ties cemented their relationships.[74] Johann Fichard not only belonged to Frankfurt's Humanist circle but was also married to a patrician woman, thus gaining access to the Alten-Limpurg, the most famous and powerful of the local patricians. When Fichard, burdened by too much work, asked the city council for a fellow advocate, he submitted his own candidate, Dr. Heinrich Kellner, who also belonged to Frankfurt's patrician the Alten-Limpurg with relatives in the city council.[75] He was hired. When, in turn, Fichard's son, Raymund Pius, wanted to fill a new vacancy, Kellner returned the favor, and suggested him to the city council. He was hired.

This was only the beginning of the Kellner family interconnections. After Heinrich Kellner's death in 1585 Frankfurt's city council hired his nephew Christopher, who was also married to a woman belonging to the Alten-Limpurg. During the seventeenth century the Kellners of the Alten-Limpurg produced several generations of advocates and thus ranked highest not only in name-recognition among Frankfurt's municipal advocates but also in their patrician familial connections to the city council.[76] But the Kellners were not the only ones. Several other patrician-connected advocates exercised important legal functions, such as the advocate Maximilian Faust von Aschaffenburg, who continued his father's patrician predilection by twice marrying women from the same Alten-Limpurg, and Anton Glock, a Frauenstein patrician whose career lasted for over 40 years.

Several advocates did, however, come from non-patrician families; some even came from outside of Frankfurt. Via their legal studies, they climbed the social ladder and married into patrician families. Georg Schuster, whose father was a teacher in Memmingen, twice married women of the von Aschaffenburg family and thus entered the Alten-Limpurg. Johann Jacob Schütz, the son of a

---

[74] Peter Moraw, "Über Patrone und Klienten im Heiligen Römischen Reich," in Antoni Maczak, ed., *Klientelsysteme im Europe der frühen Neuzeit*. Unter Mitarbeit von Elisabeth Müler-Luckner, Schriften des Historischen Kollegs. Kolloquien 9 (Munich: Oldenbourg, 1988), pp. 1–18.

[75] Trumpold, *Heinrich Kellner*, pp. 45–6.

[76] Dölemeyer, *Frankfurter Juristen*, pp. LVIII, 98–9.

preacher from Tübingen, married a woman of the Frauenstein patricians and thus entered their ranks.[77]

By 1584, the Alten-Limpurg had made it more difficult to join their ranks, in contrast to the Frauenstein, who continued to practice a relatively open policy.[78] But even the Alten-Limpurg did not categorically exclude all advocates of non-patrician origin or those from outside of Frankfurt.[79] Some of "foreign" origin actually rose to fame and fortune in Frankfurt: such as Lucas Kupferschmidt, who eventually acquired local citizenship; Zacharias Stenglin, who, apart from writing legal penal opinions, also became one of Frankfurt's most eminent political representatives at various imperial meetings; and the Rasors, who became one of the most distinguished local jurist families.

Whether local or from outside of Frankfurt, all of them had two common denominators. First, similar to Frankfurt's city councilors, all belonged to the Lutheran faith and, not surprisingly, most of them had studied at Protestant universities such as Strasbourg, Giessen and Marburg.[80] Some in fact were sons of Protestant preachers.[81] Second, there existed significant professional as well as frequent social-familial close-knit alliances between them, local patricians, and patrician city councilors.

Social, legal and financial privileges followed.[82] Advocates developed into a special new professional group. Their exalted status, their frequent patrician familial interrelations with corresponding influence over the city council, and, of course, their outward appearances in the form of special garments did not go unnoticed. During one of the biggest local upheavals, the 1612–14 Fettmilch Uprising, various complaints by Frankfurt's people addressed these issues. They criticized the arrogant behavior of many patricians toward the people of Frankfurt, and in particular those relating to the administration of justice and criminal trial procedures.[83] As specific examples they cited the advocate

---

77 See also Rainer Koch, *Grundlagen bürgerlicher Herrschaft: Verfassungs- und sozialgeschichtliche Studien zur bürgerlichen Gesellschaft in Frankfurt am Main (1612–1866)* (Wiesbaden: F. Steiner, 1983).

78 Klötzer, "Keine liebere Stadt als Frankfurt," pp. 219, 215.

79 Ibid., p. XC.

80 Dölemeyer, Frankfurter Juristen, p. LXXIV.

81 Ibid.

82 Johan, *Kontrolle*, p. 64; for Germany in general, Stobbe, Geschichte, p. 54; for Nuremberg, Eberhard Isenmann, "Reichsrecht und Reichsverfassung (15.–17.Jh.)," in Schnur, *Die Rolle der Juristen*, pp. 545–628, p. 561; Hammerstein, "Universitäten," p. 710; for steady increase of financial rewards see Strauss, Law, Resistance, pp. 178–81.

83 Matthias Meyn, *Die Reichsstadt Frankfurt vor dem Bürgeraufstand von 1612 bis 1614*. Struktur und Krise: Studien zur Frankfurter Geschichte, vol. 15 (Frankfurt am Main: Kramer, 1980), pp. 63–4, 71, 75–6.

Kellner, whose two brothers were members of the city council, and the advocate Caspar Schacher, who was sharply criticized for his "boundless bribery." They complained about the opaque nature of new legislation and insisted that in the future all new laws and edicts be made publicly available.[84] While an imperial mandate, which sealed the end of the Fettmilch Uprising, stipulated that no more than 14 Alten-Limpurg were to join the city council and close relatives were not to be admitted, patricians continued to hold sway over the city council; and they increasingly sought the advice of advocates for criminal legal and penal deliberations, as a quantitative analysis clearly demonstrates.

The advocates' caseloads dramatically and steadily increased from 9.95 percent during the last three decades of the sixteenth century to close to 56 percent during the last decades of the seventeenth.[85] And these numbers are on the conservative side as this quantitative evaluation is based on sentences only. The actual figures might be considerably higher if cases that did not result in conviction are included. Also, starting at the beginning of the seventeenth century, the number of advocates evaluating any given criminal case increased from two to three. This quantitative jump is not unique to Frankfurt but corresponds to the general enrollment of law students at various German universities, and clearly points to an escalation of legally trained jurists not only in Frankfurt but also in Germany as a whole.[86]

Suspects, however, did not profit from this increase. They had little recourse to the legal finesse of advocates, who now increasingly presented their legal opinions spiced with Latin and Greek comments—a quasi-legal ruse possibly aimed to impress city councilors with their "learnedness"—rendering their services even more indispensable at the cost of transparency as so clearly evidenced by a case from 1570 when even the councilors had to have a Latin legal opinion "verteutscht" translated into German.[87] The advocates' legal sophistry did not extend to the suspects. On the contrary, during most of the time frame

---

[84] Ibid., p. 63.

[85] The data is based on entries in the Ratsprotokolle (RP) which exist for the years 1562–1625, 1627 and 1628–88. While the Ratsprotokolle are missing for the years 1628 and 1689 to 1696, the pattern is sustainable based on the 1,284 verifiable samples out of a total of 1,338 sentences.

[86] Stölzel, Entwicklung, lists 931 students at German law universities between 1526 to 1556, jumping to 1,595 during the 1556 to 1590 period, pp. 47–9. See also Hammerstein, "Universitäten," p. 718, who argues for an intense increase in jurists at universities, unlike Stolleis, Öffentliches *Recht*, p. 299, who claims that there was no "Juristenmonopol," a claim he based on the writings of various legal scholars' theoretical tracts rather than actual dispensation of legal practice in the form of handwritten legal opinions of the various advocates, or on any quantitative sources.

[87] BB June 13, 1570, p. 14.

of this study there was no legal advice available or given to assist, defend or plead the case of an accused. It was only toward the mid-seventeenth century that suspects increasingly sought such advice from outside jurists to help them formulate their written defenses. While such individual defense arguments also increasingly contained Latin/Greek legal renditions challenging the advocates' sophistication and their legal supremacy, it was only in 1727 that suspects were guaranteed legally trained defenders in Frankfurt. Thus, most of the accused were bereft of any legal aid in an increasingly bewildering legal field.[88]

And more bewildering it became. Frankfurt's growth and transition from a small, mainly agrarian town to a commercial center also resulted in more complex economic and political issues, and so did the emergence of more diverse socio-religious groups. All these developments seemed to have compelled the city councilors to consult advocates not only as criminal legal/penal experts but also as general special municipal advisors. The advocates' legal briefs increasingly reflected these additional political functions by suggesting penal recommendations, which advanced the city council's socio-political interests.

Yet, despite their prominence, neither the city council nor its advocates could operate without at least some input of the local population, many of whom served either as court experts or, most importantly, as crime reporting agents in the absence of an independent police force.

Frankfurt's General Court Procedures

One, perhaps, the most insidious initial cause for a criminal accusation and arrest was the legally accepted validity of general suspicion based on rumors or hearsay. Sheer rumor could and did lead to criminal arrests and none other than local inhabitants were deeply involved in this process. They were the ones starting the rumor mill, which was especially efficacious in a community of the size of Frankfurt where many people knew each other. This accusatorial method made for a shield-the-accuser process by precluding personal involvement since it was extremely difficult to find the source of the rumor or hearsay. Turning sheer suspicion into a viable reason for starting criminal proceedings is, of course, reminiscent of the equally vague and infamous Verdachtstrafe, punishment for being suspicious. While the latter was exercised by the city council and its advocates, the former fell into the domain of the people.

---

[88] Karl-Ernst Meinhardt, *Das peinliche Strafrecht der Freien Reichsstadt Frankfurt am Main im Spiegel der Strafpraxis des 16. und 17. Jahrhunderts* (Frankfurt am Main: Privately printed, 1958), p. 30.

The people also reported directly on criminal suspects, and many of them served as witnesses. In addition, they served as court experts who had to verify whether a crime had actually occurred, such as in infanticide allegations where it had to be proven that the baby had been killed rather than been stillborn. Accidental deaths had to be verified as such and delineated from possible suicides, which were considered a crime.

In most of these instances, court experts such as midwives and barber-surgeons were consulted. Obviously, the advice of midwives was sought to authenticate pregnancies and the possible deliberate death of a newborn such as by strangulation, while barber-surgeons had to establish whether an assault victim had died as a result of an assault or because of other and/or prior conditions. In cases where several people had participated in a deadly assault, they had to establish what weapons were used and subsequently who among the assailants had administered the final and deadly blow.

Teachers and preachers served as experts in libel cases where teachers had to verify the writing of the written allegations. Preachers by contrast had to talk to the accused to elicit a confession and at times to inform the suspect of the gravity of the wrong-doing and, of course, in proselytizing cases. In one instance, all of Frankfurt's preachers were repeatedly consulted because the accused showed signs of an impending conversion to Judaism.[89] Given under oath, the experts' statements were in most instances written down by a municipal clerk and subsequently submitted to the city council and/or the municipal advocates for legal comments.

The obvious next step was to find and arrest the suspect. Here Frankfurt's relatively small size proved to be advantageous because witnesses were readily available. The nature of the crime dictated the use of eyewitnesses. In many manslaughter cases, which primarily unfolded in public, eyewitnesses were readily available and could thus immediately be questioned. For more clandestine crimes such as burglaries and robberies the statements of circumstantial witnesses were sought; and, although their testimonies did not directly entail a verdict, their statements frequently led to a suspect.

Similar to court experts, witnesses were interrogated, frequently under oath, in a separate room, their testimonies written down and subsequently presented to the city council and/or submitted to the advocates for their assessment. Witnesses never appeared directly in front of the council; they were never cross-examined, but in some instances they had to confront the suspect. In cases of overlapping or contradictory testimonies a suspect might, and the stress is on "might," be released, or, most commonly, subjected to judicial torture.

89 RP 1617—nine meetings from June 4 to August 23.

Judicial torture first appeared in Frankfurt by 1375, but originally it did not apply to local citizens. It was only during the fifteenth century that burghers were more frequently subjected to this procedure; dates which in Frankfurt's case point to its Roman Law origins.[90] Torture was not to be applied automatically to every suspect. The decision rested with the city council as to who was to be tortured, by what means, and how often. However, its decision was in most cases based on the recommendation of the advocates. It was also the advocates who put together the questions torture suspects had to answer while undergoing pain. While Frankfurt's records demonstrate that every suspected criminal regardless of gender, age (both young and old), profession, religion, or place of origin could be subjected to torture—only in cases of sickness do the records specify exceptions in addition to pregnant women, who seemed to have been treated sparingly—the advocates' torture decisions exhibit flagrant partialities, as will be disclosed later.

An additional measure to assess a suspect's guilt, especially when he/she came from out of town, was to conduct a personal background check. To this end, Frankfurt frequently contacted the authorities of the place of origin of a suspect and/or other places where he or she had sojourned for any length of time in order to collect more personal and criminal implications. Such exchanges were taken very seriously because they could and did lead to harsher punishments, especially in cases of recidivism.

Religion also played an important role in the sentencing deliberations and the penal structure. Frankfurt's Lutheran advocates, following Melanchthon's lead, did cite specific religious passages, especially from the Old Testament, the lex divina, when formulating their penal approaches, with such references as "per göttlichem und gemeinem Recht" or "geistlichen und gemeinen Recht."[91] There was thus no separation between the religious and secular administration of justice during the sixteenth and seventeenth centuries.[92] However, the advocates' religious/legal references exhibit a flagrant selective approach, affecting women more negatively than men. Also, Jewish suspects, in contrast to Christians, were subjected to intense proselytizing efforts and, in case they did not convert, subjected to much harsher punishments than their Christian counterparts, such as being hung by their feet—sentences frequently accompanied by the wording

---

[90] Coing, *Rezeption*, p. 55; Vogt, "Die Anfänge des Inquisitionsprozesses," p. 301; Kriegk, *Deutsches Bürgertum*, vol. 1, p. 215.

[91] Strafenbuch (ST) 1582, 1590.

[92] In contrast to arguments advanced by Eberhard Schmidt, *Einführung in die Geschichte der deutschen Strafrechtspflege*, 2nd ed. (Göttingen: Vandenhoeck & Ruprecht, 1951), who cites a critical approach to the use of the Bible in jurisdiction, p. 139.

"died like a stubborn Jew."[93] Thus religious prejudicial factors frequently entered the legal process.

Frankfurt's Lutheran advocates' penal suggestions were by no means milder than their Catholic predecessors'. In an incest case from 1486, when a father had sexual intercourse with his own daughter he was branded on the cheek and flogged, and in 1512 a culprit who had had sexual relations with two sisters was flogged.[94] By contrast, Frankfurt's Lutheran advocates, referring to "geistlichem und weltlichem Recht," suggested the death penalty in 1582 when a father had sexual relations with his stepson's wife.[95] He was executed by sword for incest unrelated to his direct bloodline, unlike the 1486 case.

However, there existed two, admittedly slim, recourses to outside assistance, first in the form of so-called Aktenversendung, and second by personal pleas of family and friends. The Aktenversendung, a measure introduced in 1600 on the imperial level, consisted of sending a suspect's criminal dossier to a law faculty at a university for further legal advice.[96] This quasi-appeal was used in very complex cases or when not all advocates working on a given case were in agreement, or if an accused was very adamant about a revision. However, this procedure had a serious drawback, for the incurring cost had to be borne by the proposing party.[97] Not surprisingly, this avenue was rarely used. Only 10 such cases were recorded in Frankfurt's archives.[98] It also had inherent biases because it was Frankfurt's authorities that put together the criminal dossier in the first place, and any bias it contained would thus be passed on. Also, not surprisingly, Frankfurt's city council mainly selected Protestant law faculties; and their sentences were not necessarily milder, as has been claimed.[99] As late as 1694, the law faculty of the University of Jena suggested the death penalty in an incest case involving a father and his daughter, based on theological and secular law.[100]

---

93 Maria R. Boes, "Jews in the Criminal-Justice System of Early Modern Germany," *Journal of Interdisciplinary History*, 30/3 (Winter 1999): 407–35, p. 432.

94 Ferdinand Rau, *Beiträge zum Kriminalrecht der Freien Reichsstadt Frankfurt am Main im Mittelalter bis 1532* (Potsdam: Krämersche Buchdruckerei, 1916), pp. 154, 188.

95 ST February 16, 1582.

96 Gerhard Pätzold, "Die Marburger Juristenfakultät als Spruchkollegium," *Beiträge zur Hessischen Geschichte*, 5 (1966): pp. 20, 26.

97 Ibid., p. 29.

98 One in 1607; two in 1625; one each in 1659, 1681, 1684, 1687; two in 1688; and one in 1694.

99 Such as by Richard van Dülmen, *Theater des Schreckens: Gerichtspraxis und Strafrituale in der frühen Neuzeit* (Munich: Beck, 1985), p. 116.

100 ST July 10, 1694.

A suspect's best chance at being either freed or receiving a milder punishment depended on the intervention of relatives, close associates, and persons of higher social standing. They could plead with the city council on behalf of the suspect. But, again, this very personal out-of-court system had its built-in drawbacks in that not everyone had recourse to such a support system; and also not every plea was given the same weight by the city council.

However, various additional extenuating circumstances could have a mitigating effect on the punishment: self-defense in manslaughter cases; the return of stolen goods to their owner; long incarceration prior to being sentenced; disease, and even drunkenness in isolated instances. The penalty could also be mitigated in such cases where the offense had occurred years ago and the reconstruction of the crime itself had become too vague. However, there was no statute of limitations. In contrast to this extended, open-ended time frame to prosecute, the actual sentencing frequently took place with breathtaking speed.

Duration of Trials

The extreme speed with which suspects were sentenced and subsequently punished has hardly received any attention.[101] If twenty-first century trials and penal procedures provoke by their lack of speed seemingly endless legal depositions, lawyers' rhetoric and convoluted appeals, early modern criminal trials evoke the opposite sentiment: they shock modern observers by their startling swiftness.

Frankfurt's city councilors made the ultimate decision on corporal or capital punishments with incredible speed. In 205 instances, or 17.4 percent of all cases, they meted out the sentence based on one hearing; 357 cases, or 30.4 percent, were based on two court hearings; and 266, or 22.6 percent, were based on three.[102] This represents a staggering 61 percent of the 1,174 verifiable data for suspects sentenced. And this pattern remained almost constant throughout the period assessed in this chapter. True, most pertinent legal information had been collected prior to these city council meetings, but it was only read to the councilors during these mainly one-, two-, or three-time deliberations. The city

101 A notable exception is Robert Riemer, "Hamburg und Frankfurt vor dem Reichskammergericht: Ein Vergleich unter besonderer Berücksichtigung der Handels- und Handwerksprozesse," in A. Amend et al., *Die Reichsstadt Frankfurt als Rechts- und Gerichtslandschaft im Römisch-Deutschen Reich* (Munich: Oldenbourg, 2008), pp. 260–79, p. 270 who, analyzing the duration of civil trade and guild trials before the imperial court, comes to a similar conclusion.

102 Data is derived from the Ratsprotokolle; see footnote 85.

councilors thus allotted in the vast majority of the sentences only one to two hearings, during which they were briefed about the legal circumstances and during which they arrived at life-threatening punishments.

An analysis of the detention periods pending sentencing revealed a similar trend in that 168, or 14.3 percent, of the culprits were in fact sentenced after only one day of detention; another 79 (8 percent) after only two days; and a total of 410, or 34.9 percent, were detained for only one week prior to sentencing. The haste—or rashness—with which some suspects were sentenced was indeed quite phenomenal. Meting out the punishments after sentencing unfolded at an even faster pace. The majority, that is a total of 1,000 convicts, were punished only one or two days after sentencing, an additional 87 after three, and 76 after four days. Again, the pattern over time is consistent throughout the entire time span investigated in this book. A suspect could thus be arrested, sentenced and punished within one-to-two days as is most flagrantly demonstrated by the 29 offenders who were executed during that time frame: an extraordinarily frightful judicial speed.

Obviously, factors such as the timely availability of witnesses, the application of judicial torture frequently leading to quick real or pain-induced false confessions, and the lack of appeals to a higher court all fostered such an approach. While sending letters to universities for their input, submitting inquiries to other towns, listening to private pleas and conversion efforts could contribute to a slowing of a trial, these legal variables had little effect on contemporary trials and executions mainly because of their sporadic and selective application. The horrendous prison conditions a suspect had to endure while the trial unfolded might be considered as an encouragement for a fast trial or, conversely, as a hidden additional punishment. The faster a trial proceeded the less suffering it entailed for the suspect; but surely it was not worth the expense of his or her life to receive speedy sentencing.

How many innocent people were sacrificed for the sake of speed has to remain an open, or academic, question. It can, however, be ascertained that the German proverb "jemanden einen kurzen Prozess machen," to give someone a short trial, with its implicit meaning of a short-shrift trial has a real judicial base.

PART II
Criminal Detection Methods

Chapter 3

Public Appearance and Criminal Judicial Practices in Early Modern Germany

One of the most fascinating aspects of criminal adjudication is the method of identifying the criminal. Who committed the crime? While crime-detecting agents of the twenty-first century use an array of sophisticated methods, such as fingerprinting, psychology and DNA sampling, no such methods were available to their sixteenth- and seventeenth-century counterparts. In fact, during the early modern period there were hardly any police forces to speak of. How, then, did contemporaries detect and report their culprits? These intriguing questions are being addressed using Frankfurt am Main from 1562 to 1696 as a case study.[1]

A free imperial city, Frankfurt possessed extensive political and judicial autonomy, manifested by its criminal legislative and sentencing powers. The city's criminal jurisdiction extended to all local residents, regardless of their civic status or religious affiliation, and also to outsiders, whether or not they had committed their crimes locally, unless extradition requests were submitted for them to be tried in their hometown.

Despite Frankfurt's extensive legislative and jurisdictional power it did not have a uniformed, institutionalized police force, a problem other towns faced as well. True, a few municipal functionaries, such as the beadles who supervised beggars, exercised policing functions, but there was no independent agency to report crime and assemble the evidence to render indictments. Thus, a communal system had to be established in order to keep its citizens safe. Several historical factors led to the evolvement of contemporary policing methods. First among them was a shift in criminal adjudicatory practices, namely, the introduction of inquisitorial court procedures. By the fifteenth century Frankfurt, like many other European cities and regions, had replaced Germanic criminal practices with inquisitorial methods. With this transition the former Germanic use of oath helpers had been abandoned in favor of witnesses, especially eyewitnesses. Oath helpers had served as character witnesses only who knew and, in fact, were summoned by suspects to defend them by performing

1 Frankfurt's Strafenbuch, Book of Punishments (hereafter ST), served as the basic source. It is supplemented by the Bürgermeisterbücher (BB), minutes of the mayors' meetings; the Ratsprotokolle (RP), minutes of the city council meetings; and legal sources such as the *Corpus Legum Francofurtensium* (*CLF*, 5 vols, 1748), all located in Frankfurt's Municipal Archives.

the "Reinigungseid," cleansing oath. They attested only to the credibility of the accused: unlike eyewitnesses, they had not seen the criminal act; nor did they furnish the accused with an alibi. Eyewitnesses, quite obviously, recognized the offender and had observed the crime unfold. While oath helpers had stressed the inner or psychological makeup of a suspect, eyewitnesses focused on outward appearances. Criminal court procedures now favored visibly verifiable facts.

This conceptual change had far-reaching consequences for policing and sentencing. With the introduction of eyewitnesses, the number of potential judicial participants increased considerably, from a select few, such as the former oath helpers, to the entire population. In addition, the judicial power of eyewitnesses was considerable, because the testimonies of two were sufficient to convict a suspect. Witnesses were interrogated in private, secluded chambers, under oath and their statements were written down by clerks to be presented to the authorities at a later date. They were never cross-examined in front of an assembled court although, occasionally, the witnesses were confronted with the suspects. Once a suspect had been identified, the witnesses did not play any further role because, unlike the former Germanic process when the victim personally accused the suspect, the accusation was now launched ex officio, that is, by officials of the government.

Since everybody could now become a potential witness an avenue had to be established to persuade people to come forward to identify the suspects. Toward that end, Frankfurt, similar to other towns, initiated various policies to involve if not entice as many people as possible as crime-reporting agents. One way was to promulgate municipal decrees, such as in 1580 when Frankfurt's city council urged the people to intercede in brawls, even offering to pay those who arrested or devised plans to catch transgressors.[2] Another consisted of publicly beating drums, thereby summoning the people to assist in manhunts.[3] In Frankfurt everyone became a potential police agent. Indeed, out of 261 verifiable cases, 27 percent of the sentenced criminals had been captured in the act by locals.[4]

Direct and explicit crime reporting was supplemented by suspicion, an elusive form of criminal indictment that included rumor and hearsay. The latter were legally accepted methods of reporting crime and were grounds for arrest. In Frankfurt 47 percent of the suspects in the 261 verifiable cases were brought

2 *CLF*, vol. 1, p. 26.

3 Karl-Ernst Meinhardt, *Das peinliche Strafrecht der freien Reichsstadt Frankfurt am Main im Spiegel der Strafpraxis des 16. und 17. Jahrhunderts* (Frankfurt am Main: Privately printed, 1958), p. 94.

4 Based on entries in ST and BB.

to trial on the basis of "itz under die sag," general gossip, or "allgemeinem Stadgeschrei nach," according to general rumor around town.[5]

Incrimination based on rumor or hearsay covered a wide range of crimes, including prostitution. Frequently the records embellish a woman's citation with the words "wegen ihres Hurenlebens sehr beriichtigt," quite infamous because of her whorish lifestyle.[6] Witch trials also show the suggestive power of rumor and hearsay, the grounds on which many of the 15 persons accused of witchcraft in Frankfurt between 1570 and 1694 were arrested.[7] Rumors, moreover, were difficult to erase from the collective memory. In a 1605 case, some of the implicating "facts" reached back 13 years earlier, when the suspect had been the center of incriminating innuendo.[8] But it was not only a local phenomenon. On the contrary, it was clearly demonstrated for France where "Rumors ... took hold everywhere," and "having taken hold, were tenacious."[9]

While rumors could and did lead to arrests, appearing suspicious was sufficient grounds for sentencing. The Verdachtstrafe, sentence by suspicion, was meted out when the city council—despite a lack of evidence and despite a futile application of torture—harbored doubts about the innocence of the accused. The punishment was less severe, but the suspect was nevertheless made to suffer and was never fully exonerated.

In relatively small, contemporary, urban settings such as Frankfurt, where daily verbal communications were of paramount importance in a basically illiterate society, rumors could and did germinate. Local inhabitants initiated and conveyed them because it was safe to do so because the suspects had no way of knowing the identity of, and therefore no way of avenging themselves on, the persons who incriminated them. Gossip thus had great potential as a tool of mutual surveillance.

---

5 BB May 20, 1563, July 8, 1610, December 31, 1650; ST August 21, 1660.

6 ST July 27, 1678.

7 Walter Eschenröder, *Hexenwahn und Hexenprozess in Frankfurt am Main* (Gelnhausen: F.W. Kalbfleisch, 1932), pp. 47, 58. For similar findings see also Erik Midelfort, *Witch Hunting in Southwestern Germany* (Stanford, CA: Stanford University Press, 1972), p. 160; Gerhard Schormann, *Hexenprozesse in Deutschland* (Göttingen: Vandenhoeck & Ruprecht, 1981), p.110

8 ST January 3, 1605.

9 Arlette Farge and Jacques Revel, *The Vanishing Children of Paris: Rumor and Politics before the French Revolution*, trans. Claudia Mievielle (Cambridge, MA: Harvard University Press, 1991), p. 97.

Visual Identification

However, the crucial question remains: how did Frankfurt's population know whom to accuse, explicitly or implicitly? How did local inhabitants identify offenders, given the lack of passports, identification cards, and photographs? Contemporaries resorted to oral and visual forms of identification: for example, by adding to a first name one's birthplace or the designation of a physical feature, frequently a handicap, often in the form of a nickname.[10] In fact, the use of sobriquets was ubiquitous.

Another and more elaborate system of identification ascribed clearly discernible symbols to each person walking Frankfurt's streets. Specific dress, badges or color schemes described every aspect of a person's life—rank, wealth, religion, occupation, marital status, age, even bereavement. From birth to death, a person's whole life was mirrored and even regulated by outward appearances.

The concept of using visual aids for identification was introduced by Frankfurt's city council in the mid-fourteenth century.[11] At first it was a vague dress code, but by the end of the fifteenth century it had become more elaborate.[12] It was primarily during the sixteenth and seventeenth centuries, however, that *Kleiderordnungen*, dress regulations, multiplied, stratified, and were institutionalized.

The emergence and proliferation of dress codes paralleled Frankfurt's economic and demographic growth as well as its social diversification. During the late sixteenth century Frankfurt grew in population from approximately 11,000 to 18,000–20,000, and changed from a mainly agricultural town into a commercial and financial center. It even became the site of imperial coronations. Finally, its religious diversity increased dramatically. Most of Frankfurt's population converted to Lutheranism, leaving a small Catholic minority in addition to Jewish people, who had been forced to move to separate quarters, the Judengasse, Jewish Street; the city also saw the arrival of Calvinist refugees, mainly from the Netherlands. With the transition to a more populous and diverse social environment, governing the city became more complex, necessitating new administrative and policing strategies. The dress codes met

---

10 ST May 11, 1619; Karl Bücher, *Die Frauenfrage im Mittelalter* (Tübingen: Laupp, 1910), p. 474.

11 Karl Bücher and Benno Schmidt, eds, *Frankfurter Amts- und Zunfturkunden bis zum Jahre 1612* (Frankfurt am Main: Joseph Baer, 1914), p. 501.

12 Karl Bräuer, *Studien zur Geschichte der Lebenshaltung in Frankfurt am Main während des 17. und 18. Jahrhunderts*. Veröffentlichungen der historischen Kommission der Stadt Frankfurt am Main (Frankfurt am Main: Joseph Baer, 1915), p. 223.

these needs. A primarily illiterate society resorted to visual signs and symbols to convey messages.[13]

From 1572 to 1672, 11 identifiable dress codes were promulgated in Frankfurt.[14] With each citation of the codes, they became more stratified. While the 1572 dress code was rather vague with regard to birth and professional status, the 1593 code made it clear that everyone should dress according to their social standing, honor and wealth. For example, only nobles, doctors and patricians were permitted to wear jackets or coats made of velvet, damask, satin or other silk products. Even the yardage to be used for these garments was prescribed in that only well-known burghers and traders, merchants and city councilmen were permitted to use 2 yards of velvet for their clothing, while prominent retailers and notaries were entitled to use one.[15]

By 1621 five *Stände*, ranks, were cited: city councilors; distinguished and well-known burghers and tradesmen; notaries, advocates, artists, and distinguished retailers; general retailers and artisans; and those not qualifying as artisans or retailers, such as day laborers.[16] The members of each rank had to wear specific clothing, made out of specific material. In 1672 historical background or lineage became as important to one's social standing as honor, wealth, and profession. Municipal administrators or city councilors who wanted to join the first rank, held by patricians, had to furnish proof of their ancestors having held high municipal office. In most cases proof of service had to cover a 100-year period.

According to the various dress codes, city councilors were at the top of the social ladder. They "merited" such high status by virtue of their role as representatives of both the city government and Frankfurt's autonomous judiciary. And since the city council consisted of two-thirds patricians, they stood out as the most eminent social group. Their illustrious status was visibly conveyed to everyone by the clothing they wore, as cogently noted by a contemporary who wrote in his diary that the difference between a patrician and a burgher was most noticeable in their dress.[17] Visual symbols even conveyed the internal structure

---

13 On the importance of symbols, see Clifford Geertz, *Local Knowledge: Further Essays in Interpretive Anthropology* (New York: Basic Books, 1983); and David Freedberg, *The Power of Images: Studies in the History and Theory of Response* (Chicago: University of Chicago Press, 1989).

14 *CLF*, 1748, vol. 1.

15 *CLF*, vol. 1, p. 52.

16 *CLF*, vol. 3, p. 36.

17 *CLF*, vol. 4, p. 25; B.J. Römer-Büchner, "Wohlleben und Prachtliebe der Gesellschaft Limburg zu Frankfurt am Main," *Zeitschrift für deutsche Kulturgeschichte* (1856): 58–83, p. 76.

of the patrician families, many of which adopted distinctive color schemes. The Frauensteiner, for example, dressed predominantly in white and yellow.[18] Patricians also attached little bells to their clothing for easy identification by sound, which was captured in the proverbial saying: "Wo die Herren seien, do klingeln die Schellen," Where the gentlemen are, the bells ring.[19]

However, visual demarcations were not drawn only in secular society. The Catholic Church had long used habits and color combinations to distinguish orders. Franciscans, for example, wore brown habits and girts with knotted cords, while Dominicans wore black cloaks and hoods over white gowns. The Benedictines wore all black and the Cistercians white.[20]

In addition, each secular profession and occupation had its distinctive dress, too, such as specific gowns for professors and schoolmasters.[21] The various guilds also adopted dress codes specific to their professions.[22] In fact, dress and color prescriptions covered the entire occupational and social scale. News carriers and other persons employed in communications were to wear special garments "so that they could be distinguished from others."[23] Servants, doorkeepers and porters were required to wear clothing of the same color.[24] Even Frankfurt's executioners were set apart. As of 1534 they had to wear three stripes on their clothing—red, white, and green—so that they could easily be discerned from honorable people.[25] Thus, if special garments could not be prescribed, most likely for financial reasons, Frankfurt's city council resorted to cheaper visual symbols, such as stripes.

A financial motivation can also be advanced with regard to pauper badges. As early as 1476 the city council had required the local poor to wear them. Only

---

18 Hans Körner, *Frankfurter Patrizier* (Munich: Ernst Vogel, 1971); Franz Lerner, *Die Frankfurter Patriziergesellschaft Alten Limburg und ihre Stiftungen* (Frankfurt am Main: Verlag Waldemar Kramer, 1902).

19 Römer-Büchner, "Wohlleben," p. 81.

20 Dorothy Hartley, *Medieval Costume and Life* (London: B.T. Batsford, 1931), p. 49.

21 Friedrich Hottenroth, *Altfrankfurter Trachten* (Frankfurt am Main: Heinrich Keller, 1912), p. 388.

22 C. Williams-Mitchell, *Dressed for the Job: The Story of Occupational Costume*, illustrated by Jeffrey J. Burn (Poole: Blandford, 1982).

23 Hottenroth, *Altfrankfurter*, pp. 73, 388.

24 Some areas even prescribed braided hair for female servants: see Renate Dürr, "Die Ehre der Mägde zwischen Selbstdefinition und Fremdbestimmung," in Sibylle Backmann et al., *Ehrkonzepte in der Frühen Neuzeit: Identitäten und Abgrenzungen* (Berlin: Akademie Verlag, 1998), pp. 170–84, p. 176.

25 Albrecht Keller, *Der Scharfrichter in der deutschen Kulturgeschichte* (Leipzig: Kurt Schroeder, 1921), p. 121; Richard van Dülmen, *Theater des Schreckens: Gerichtspraxis und Strafrituale in der frühen Neuzeit* (Munich: C.H. Beck, 1985), p. 94.

they were entitled to receive municipal support and to beg, and the badges were to set them apart from the non-resident poor.[26] To reinforce the policy, Frankfurt hired two *Bettelvögte*, beadles, who supervised the local poor and tried to oust foreign beggars.[27] Visual symbols, in the absence of alternative policing methods, greatly facilitated the task. However, the pauper badges were so unpopular that even the city council considered abandoning them. Yet they remained in use until the end of the seventeenth century.[28]

Easily identifiable symbols thus worked in two ways. They enhanced the status of some while adding insult to the already injured. And Frankfurt's Jews were similarly denigrated. They had to wear yellow rings "so that they could be easily distinguished from Christians." They were the only religious group marked by badges.[29] Even Jewish doctors, who were held in high esteem even among Gentiles, were not excluded from wearing the signs, as a petition to be released from this ordinance clearly documents.[30]

By contrast, contemporary soldiers, or Landsknechte as they were called until the end of the sixteenth century, followed their own dress codes. They initiated and chose to wear elaborate, colorful and conspicuous costumes—thus deliberately drawing attention to themselves. Frequently, their extravagant clothing was made of the finest material such as velvet and silk in open defiance of dress ordinances.[31]

---

[26] Werner Moritz, *Die bürgerlichen Fürsorgeanstalten der Reichsstadt Frankfurt am Main im späten Mittelalter*, Studien zur Frankfurter Geschichte 14 (Frankfurt am Main: Verlag Waldemar Kramer, 1981), p. 111.

[27] Georg Ludwig Kriegk, *Deutsches Bürgertum im Mittelalter: Nach urkundlichen Forschungen und mit besonderer Beziehung auf Frankfurt* (2 vols, 1868; repr. Frankfurt am Main: Sauer & Auvermann, 1969), vol. 1, p. 144.

[28] Hans-Otto Schembs, *Der Allgemeine Almostenkasten in Frankfurt am Main, 1531–1981* (Frankfurt am Main: Verlag Waldemar Kramer, 1981), p. 37.

[29] Johann Conradin Beyerbach, ed., *Sammlung der Verordnungen der Reichsstadt Frankfurt* (6 vols, Frankfurt am Main: Hermann, 1798), vol. 1, p. 1261; see also Diane Owen Hughes, "Distinguishing Signs: Earrings, Jews, and Franciscan Rhetoric in the Italian Renaissance City," *Past and Present*, 112 (1986): 3–59.

[30] Dietrich Andernacht, *Regesten zur Geschichte der Juden in der Reichsstadt Frankfurt am Main von 1520–1616*, ed. Helga Andernacht, in Verbindung mit dem Institut für Stadtgeschichte Frankfurt und dem Arye Maimon-Institut für die Geschichte der Juden an der Universität Trier (2 vols, Hanover: Hahnsche Buchhandlung, 2007), vol. 2 October 8, 1566, p. 384, item 1683.

[31] The first to write about the costumes of soldiers was J.R. Hale, "The Soldier in Germanic Graphic Art of the Rainaissance," *Journal of Interdisciplinary History*, 17/1 (1986): 85–114. See also Matthias Rogg, "'Zerhauen und zerschnitten, nach adelichen Sitten': Herkunft, Entwicklung und Funktion soldatischer Tracht des 16. Jahrhunderts im Spiegel zeitgenössischer Kunst," in Bernhard R. Kroener and Ralf Pröve, eds, *Krieg und Frieden: Militär*

Dress regulations also applied to Frankfurt's female population. Not surprisingly, the dress ordinances of "reputable" women closely followed their husbands' and fathers', based primarily on social status, honor, and wealth.[32] Frequently an additional color scheme was used to indicate a woman's marital status. Generally, the color red indicated young and single women, and blue and green, married women. Old age was accentuated with gray and black.[33] Virgins were subjected to further labels. In 1483, for example, a young girl was arrested on suspicion of theft, partly because she falsely claimed virginity by wearing the customary "Bändchen im Haar," ribbon in her hair.[34]

Women's sexual status was thus publicly exhibited, and women were punished if they camouflaged it. Needless to say, the same applied to prostitutes. Treated with equanimity until the end of the fifteenth century, they were now subjected to increasingly discriminatory dress regulations, a trend which culminated in the criminalization of prostitution in 1576.[35]

To the potpourri of local dress, color schemes, and badges one must add the variety in regional dress. Like Frankfurt, every other city in the Holy Roman Empire had specific dress codes. In addition to this "bewildering mass of municipal costumes," each region had a specific costume, often referred to as a "Tracht."[36] In Switzerland regional costumes differed not only from canton to canton but also from valley to valley.[37] Thus everyone walking Frankfurt's streets could be clearly identified simply by his or her dress or other visual signs. Frankfurt's ordinances specifically stated that such regulations had been

---

und Gesellschaft in der Frühen Neuzeit (Paderborn: Ferdinand Schöningh, 1996), pp. 109–37; Gundula Wolter, *Die Verpackung des männlichen Geschlechts: Eine illustrierte Kulturgeschichte der Hose* (Marburg: Jonas, 1991), pp. 57–69, 88; Erika Thiel, *Geschichte des Kostüms: Die europäische Mode von den Anfängen bis zur Gegenwart* (Wilhelmshaven: Heinrichshofen, 1980), pp. 156–8; Rainer und Trudi Wohlfeil, "Landsknechte im Bild. Überlegungen zur 'Historische Bildkunde,'" in Peter Blickle, ed., *Bauer, Reich und Reformation: Festschrift für* Günter Franz *zum 80. Geburtstag* (Stuttgart: Ulmer, 1982), pp. 104–19.

32 *CLF*, vol. 1, p. 52.

33 Mathilde Hain, "Die Volkstracht," in Wolfgang Stammler, ed., *Deutsche Philologie im Aufriss*, 2nd ed. (Berlin: Erich Schmidt, 1979), pp. 2889–99.

34 Ferdinand Rau, *Beiträge zum Kriminalrecht der freien Reichsstadt Frankfurt am Main im Mittelalteer bis 1532* (Potsdam: Kramer, 1916), p. 171.

35 Kriegk, *Bürgertum*, vol. 1, p. 323; vol. 2, p. 302; see also Chapter 1.

36 Max von Boehn, *Modes and Manners, vol. 2: The Sixteenth Century*, trans. Joan Joshua (Philadelphia: J.B. Lippincott, 1932), p. 108.

37 Julie Heierli, *Die Schweizer Trachten vom 17. zum 19. Jahrhundert* (Zurich: Polygraphisches Institut, 1896–1900).

introduced "so daß ein jeder in seinem Stand unterschiedlich erkannt werden möge," so that everyone might be easily identified by their rank.[38]

But why did people have to be easily identified? The answer is contained in the full name of the dress codes: *Policeyordnungen*, police ordinances. Thus the codes' most important role lay in regulation and supervision, functions which became important elements in a society where, in the absence of a police force, the policing had to be done by everyone. It was imperative for effective operation of the criminal justice system that the whole population cooperated, and for that reason easily identifiable signs and symbols were introduced so that they could be easily understood by everyone. There was no mistaking a patrician for a Jew, a Jew for a Christian, or a pauper for a councilman. In early modern Frankfurt one could not blend anonymously into a crowd. The principle of anonymity developed much later, with the disappearance of dress codes after 1731 when they and "other outward appearance markers gradually lost their policing significance."[39] Most remarkably it was then that the role of dress in policing reversed itself: uniformed police replaced uniformed crowds.

Personal Data of Convicts

Frankfurt's criminal records also testify to the importance contemporaries attached to visible descriptions. Frequently they include the nicknames of suspects, which mainly depicted their physical attributes or deformities, such as "long Martin" or "fat Valentin." Physical descriptions were even added to a criminal's occupational background, as in "Paul, the little tailor."[40] Frankfurt was not exceptional in recording physical attributes among its criminal data. Similar methods were used in France, where local registers frequently listed physical behaviors as well, such as a suspect walking "with a nimble step."[41]

Surprisingly, Frankfurt's records contained few citations of the religious affiliation of the suspects. Given the religious fervor of the age and the city's

---

38 *CLF*, vol. 1, p. 52.

39 Maria R. Boes, "Unwanted Travellers: The Tightening of City Borders in Early Modern Germany," in Thomas Betteridge, ed., *Borders and Travellers in Early Modern Europe* (Aldershot: Ashgate, 2007), pp. 87–111, p. 110.

40 ST October 9, 1579; October 22, 1579; April 19. 1586; April 7, 1592; June 17, 1615.

41 Nicole Castan, "Summary Justice," in Robert Forster and Orest Ranum, eds, *Deviants and the Abandoned in French Society*, trans. Elborg Foster and Patricia M. Ranum. Selections from the Annales: Economies, Societies, Civilisations, no. 4 (Baltimore: Johns Hopkins University Press, 1978), pp. 111–56, p. 119.

heterogeneous population of Lutherans, Calvinists, Catholics, and Jews, one would expect to find a criminal's religion recorded on a regular basis. It was, however, always entered for Jewish suspects, a policy which was reflected if not reinforced by the city council's promise of monetary rewards to those who turned in Jewish people who had illicit sexual relations with Christians.[42] Obviously, the easily identified yellow rings on the clothing of Jewish people greatly facilitated selective crime reporting.[43]

Frankfurt's patricians, on the other hand, were not even listed and thus were not sentenced for any criminal acts during the 134-year period between 1562 and 1696. This is, of course, a highly unlikely scenario. One might argue that patricians, representing two-thirds of the sentencing body, simply refrained from convicting their social equals, the more so since many councilors were interrelated and/or had family ties to local patrician families. But it is also conceivable that the transgressions of patricians were simply not reported by the people, who would not readily accuse those who daily sat in judgment of them or were related to others who did. One has to bear in mind that no independent judiciary, police force, or prosecutor like a district attorney existed in Frankfurt. That local inhabitants might not have recognized suspect patricians also has to be dismissed, since they were easily identified by sight and sound.

Female convicts carried the most detailed personal information in the criminal records. Their first names were always followed by their marital status and even widowhood was recorded regularly. Since male convicts were described as either single or married only in isolated cases, marital status was considered unimportant for them, whereas for women it was the outstanding identifying characteristic. This method of recording criminals is, of course, reminiscent of Frankfurt's dress symbols by which single women were visibly distinguished from married ones, unlike their male counterparts.

In addition, female suspects were subjected to more intense visual scrutiny than men. Visual evidence stimulated rumors that led to arrest and conviction, as clearly recorded for many female convicts. Allegations of pregnancy were among the most frequently cited reasons for their arrest for sex crimes and infanticide. A swollen belly, especially in single women, caused gossip and eventually was considered a reliable indicator of sexual transgression. The criminal records often read "zu hafft kommen—Schwangerung verdächtigt,"

---

[42] *CLF*, vol. 1, p. 26.

[43] Maria R. Boes, "Jews in the Criminal-Justice System of Frankfurt am Main," *Journal of Interdisciplinary History*, 30/3 (Winter 1999): 407–35.

arrested—suspected of pregnancy.[44] In fact, many women convicted of fornication were pregnant and single.[45]

Frankfurt's sentences for infanticide exhibit the same pattern: 15 of 16 convicts were single women alleged to have been pregnant earlier. The pattern is startling, especially since an additional five unmarried women received the *Verdachtstrafe* for infanticide. Single women also received the only two *Verdachtstrafen* for abortions, based on similar allegations.[46] Singleness thus seems to have been damning evidence. While infanticide could also occur within the family setting, there it was easier to hide.[47] Even many incest convictions were based on reports of unmarried pregnancy, as in seven cases involving stepfathers and stepdaughters.[48]All of these cases clearly point to visibility as the crime-reporting factor that eventually led to criminal indictments and sentencing.

Prostitution convictions follow a similar pattern. Out of 35 convicts, 32 were women and only three were men. That the city council, as the judiciary, might be solely responsible for this pattern seems highly unlikely, considering that many of the women had been arrested simply for being "Hurerei verdächtig," suspected of prostitution. No such criminal arrest recordings were ever listed for men. That women were more likely to be suspected of prostitution than men is, again, largely attributable to public appearances. Prostitutes, especially soliciting prostitutes, were easily identified by their attire and visual behavior; not so their male partners. Detailed studies on prostitutes and courtesans of Italian cities reveal striking similarities. There, as in Frankfurt, public attire could and did lead to criminal indictments.[49]

Thus visible criteria, in the form of physical deformities, badges, swollen bellies, and special attire facilitated criminal accusations, often very selectively. While no direct entries link Frankfurt's people to selective crime reports, the city's arrest descriptions, often based on vague, visually stimulated rumors, strongly allude to the suggestibility and prejudices of the population at large.

---

44 BB May 25, 1641; ST December 21, 1680; ST April 14, 1681.

45 See also Jan Sundin, "Sinful Sex: Legal Prosecution of Extramarital Sex in Preindustrial Sweden," *Social Science History*, 16/1 (1992): 99–128.

46 ST February 9, 1648 and ST January 30, 1681.

47 R.W. England, "Investigating Homicide in Northern England," in L.A. Knafla, ed., *Criminal Justice History: An International Annual*, vol. 6 (New York: Crime and Justice History Group, 1985), pp. 105–25, p. 119.

48 ST November 11, 1588; ST October 23, 1589; ST December 19, 1618; ST December 31, 1623; ST November 12, 1662; ST February 20, 1685; ST March 21, 1685.

49 Lynne Lawner, *Lives of Courtesans* (New York: Rizzoli, 1987), pp. 17, 19; John K. Brackett, "The Florentine Onesta and the Control of Prostitution, 1403–1680," *Sixteenth Century Journal*, 24 (1993): 273–300, pp. 279, 296.

Penal Structure

The penal structure also points to the importance of visible aids for policing. Much has been written about early modern punishments, especially the public nature of executions. Explanations by numerous scholars as to why capital penalties were carried out in public range from stresses on the significance of the "spectacle of suffering" to the "theater of horror" and the correlated "symbols of state power."[50] However, a caveat is warranted. The almost exclusive concentration on the death penalty cited in conjunction with these interpretations is belied by the number of actual death sentences. In Frankfurt, only 25 percent of 1,338 sentenced criminals during the period 1562 to 1696 were executed.[51] And similar ratios can be observed for other German towns, such as Augsburg and Nuremberg.[52] While the ceremonies may have reflected elements of state formation, it should be added that the public nature of executions was also part and parcel of the community's mutual surveillance system. A publicly executed criminal cast a public punitive stigma on his or her relatives and friends, especially in relatively small urban settings. The longer the corpse was exposed, the longer the public might "police" it. A swift execution by the sword, followed by immediate burial, was the least dishonoring for all, and the often ardent pleas that the convict be buried right away testify to this most clearly. And so does the fact that sometimes corpses were even secretly removed from the gallows at night.[53]

The public nature of non-capital sentences sheds additional if not more substantial light on the underlying reasons for public "ceremonies": future policing. Corporal punishments, shaming sentences, and banishments were meted out almost exclusively in public; and besides humiliating the culprit,

---

50 Michel Foucault, *Discipline and Punish: The Birth of the Prison*, trans. Alan Sheridan (New York: Random House, 1979), pp. 43, 46, 47; Jim Sharpe, *Judicial Punishment in England* (London: Faber & Faber 1990); and Pieter Spierenburg, *The Spectacle of Suffering: Executions and the Evolution of Repression from a Preindustrial Metropolis to the European Experience* (Cambridge: Cambridge University Press, 1984) echo the theme of the importance of staged execution, as do Randall McGowen, "The Body and Punishment," *Journal of Modern History*, 59 (1987): 651–79 and van Dülmen, *Theater*; meanwhile Thomas W. Laqueur, "Crowds, Carnival and the State in English Executions, 1604–1868," in A.L. Beier et al. eds, *The First Modern Society: Essays in English History in Honor of Lawrence Stone* (Cambridge: Cambridge University Press, 1989), pp. 305–55, p. 309, still focusing on the theatricality of public executions, disputes the all-powerful role of the state and concentrates instead on "The crowd, and particularly the carnivalesque crowd, was the central actor in English executions."

51 Based on entries in the Strafenbuch.

52 Van Dülmen, *Theater*, pp. 113–14.

53 ST January 15, 1662.

these penalties served the important communal function of exposure, which, again, facilitated surveillance of the culprit and the community later.

Out of 320 corporal and 204 shaming sentences, 90 percent of the culprits were subsequently banished from Frankfurt. If one adds in the 460 banishment sentences, then 95 percent of non-capital punishments included banishment from town. Obviously, the community tried to rid itself of the criminal element, a clear testimony that public welfare was the central motive for the banishing sentences. What, however, would prevent an ousted criminal from returning and being recognized in the absence of a regular police force? It had to be a communal effort. Everyone had to be vigilant about protecting the community. But the people could only act to prevent and/or report the illegal return of ousted criminals if they recognized them. And, to state the obvious, in order to do so they had to be informed of the criminals' identities so they could recognize them. This was achieved by publicly exposing the culprits during their punishments. For this reason a criminal might be pilloried "damit ihn jedermann kennen lernte," so that everyone got to know him, or displayed in the marketplace or paraded through the streets, and afterward "öffentlich hinaus geführt," publicly escorted out.[54] Thus, as long as contemporaries subscribed to banishing offenders from the community, the public nature of punishment had to be an integral part of the penal structure.

Public exposure could even take the form of "Schandbilder," defaming pictures. In Germany they mainly depicted debtors, while in Renaissance Florence they exposed various lawbreakers who had escaped from the authorities.[55] Defaming pictures thus served as punishment in absentia. But, most importantly, they also served an implicit policing function by exposing an absent culprit to a large audience. In most cases the pictures appeared on buildings, city gates, or church doors.[56] No less an artist than Sandro Botticelli was commissioned to draw them.[57] Should the subject return, he or she would be recognized and possibly handed over to the authorities.

Even the Catholic Church publicly exposed sinners for punitive and identification purposes. One only has to think of penitential garments such as

---

54 Kriegk, *Bürgertum*, vol. 1, p. 258; the Strafenbuch contains numerous examples such as ST January 10, 1613; ST October 24, 1618; ST September 4, 1619; ST January 28, 1620; ST April 29, 1671; ST December 20, 1681.

55 Wolfgang Brückner, *Bildnis und Brauch* (Berlin: Erich Schmidt, 1913), pp. 514–20; Samuel Y. Edgerton, *Pictures and Punishment: Art and Criminal Prosecution during the Florentine Renaissance* (Ithaca, NY: Cornell University Press, 1985).

56 Guido Kisch, "Ehrenschelte und Schandgemälde," *Zeitschrift der Savigny-Stiftung für Rechtsgeschichte* (1913): 514–20, p.519; Edgerton, *Pictures*, p. 72.

57 Edgerton, *Pictures*, p. 106.

the *habitello*, used by the Roman Inquisition, and the *sanbenito*, a yellow garment used by the Spanish Inquisition. Such garments had to be worn by heretics and other sinners for periods from a few months to life.[58]

In Frankfurt's case the emphasis on the public nature of punishment increased over the years. While until 1617 corporal punishments were listed only by name—such as pillorying, whipping or banishment—case descriptions afterward routinely mentioned their public character, such as "öffentlich ins Halseisen," publicly put into the pillory.[59] That the multiplication of explicit references to public penalties coincided with the proliferation of dress ordinances was no historical accident but, rather, proof of the use of visual aids for diverse social functions, including public policing. Public penalties had a lasting effect both on the culprits and on those who observed him or her on display. Public punishments served as visual aids for future criminal policing. They became a visible database.

The efficacy of such a system greatly depended on the capacity of the people to memorize the physiognomy of an offender. Two factors contributed to that end. Rampant disease often left disfigurements, from goiter to the loss of limbs. Even syphilis seems to have "maimed far more victims than it killed."[60] Deformities called attention to themselves and, as noted above, were registered in the form of nicknames. Visual aids also enhanced one's powers of retention. Francis Yates stresses the importance of visual memory devices and asserts that in a predominantly illiterate society, where knowledge was preserved primarily by memorization and oral transmission, "remarkable feats of memory were achieved."[61]

Books on the memory arts multiplied despite the advent of the printing press, which, "as an agent of change," it was suggested, "altered the system of data collection and data storage."[62] However, the "immense consequences of the preservative powers of the print" were felt only much later.[63] During the

---

58 Henry Kamen, *The Spanish Inquisition* (London: Weidenfeld & Nicolson, 1965), pp. 185–6.

59 ST March 23, 1617; ST November 22, 1617 (two entries); ST December 13, 1617; ST April 29, 1618; ST May, 27, 1618; ST June 20, 1618.

60 J.R. Hale, *Renaissance Europe* (Berkeley: University of California Press, 1977), p. 25.

61 Francis Yates, *The Art of Memory* (Chicago: University of Chicago Press, 1974), p. 126; see also Mary J. Carruthers, *The Book of Memory: A Study of Memory in Medieval Culture* (New York: Cambridge University Press, 1990).

62 Elizabeth L. Eisenstein, *The Printing Press as an Agent of Change: Communications and Cultural Transformation in Early Modern Europe* (2 vols, Cambridge: Cambridge University Press, 1979). vol. 1, p. 125.

63 Ibid., p. 182.

sixteenth and seventeenth centuries "the value of the efficacy of visual resources was unquestioned" and hence "individuals of the Baroque thus knew that direct vision of things was important beyond measure."[64]

Nothing shows the power of visual imagery better than the "unprecedented increase in images" in churches during the late fifteenth and early sixteenth centuries.[65] The trend to depict religious concepts visually continued through the Reformation. Catholics and even Protestants made ample use of images, without which, Martin Luther claimed, "we can neither think nor understand."[66]

That visual imagery worked successfully in the administration of criminal justice is demonstrated by frequent sentences for breach of the banishment oath. The Strafenbuch lists 70 such cases. Some offenders tried repeatedly to return to Frankfurt: on April 14, 1604 one was banished for the third time, and on 20 June 1690 another was banished for the fourth time.[67] Culprits were even recognized years after they had been banished: a thief ousted in 1668 returned in 1680 but was promptly rebanished. No other crime category relied so heavily on the people's capacity to recognize the offender.

Contemporary topography further facilitated such policing. Despite its numerical and social growth, Frankfurt occupied a relatively small area throughout the sixteenth and seventeenth centuries.[68] Long after it had expanded its city walls in 1628, the new section remained sparsely populated. Thus the people lived near one another, which encouraged daily contact, rumors and supervision.

---

[64] José Antonio Maravall, *Culture of the Baroque: Analysis of a Historical Structure*, trans. Terry Cochran (Minneapolis: University of Minnesota Press, 1986), pp. 252–3.

[65] J. Wirth, "Against the Acculturation Thesis," trans. John Burke, in Kaspar Greyerz, ed., *Religion and Society in Early Modern Europe, 1500–1800* (London: Allen and Unwin, 1984), pp. 66–78, p. 75.

[66] Robert W. Scribner, *For the Sake of Simple Folk: Popular Propaganda for the German Reformation* (Cambridge: Cambridge University Press, 1981), p. 249; J. Wirth, "Le dogme en image: Luther et l'iconographie," *Revue de l'Art*, 52 (1981): 9–23; Peter Burke, *Popular Culture in Early Modern Europe* (New York: New York University Press, 1978), p. 231.

[67] ST November 17, 1576; ST April 10, 1583; ST April 19, 1586; ST August 23, 1587; ST February 10, 1602; ST June 19, 1605; ST August 13, 1608; ST November 18, 1609; ST April 19, 1615; ST July 19, 1615; ST July 6, 1616; ST March 22, 1617; ST September 25, 1619; ST August 13, 1624; ST August 18, 1624; ST May 12, 1675; ST July 7, 1675; ST February 27, 1679; ST October 6, 1685.

[68] Werner Gley, *Grundriss und Wachstum der Stadt Frankfurt am Main: Eine stadtgeographische und statistische Untersuchung* (Frankfurt am Main: Ludwig Ravenstein, n.d.), pp. 60–70; Heinz Stoob, "Stadtformen und städtisches Leben im späten Mittelalter," in Heinz Stoob, ed., *Die Stadt: Gestalt und Wandel bis zum industriellen Zeitalter* (Cologne: Böhlau, 1985), pp. 151–94.

Summary

With a change of legal practices, especially with the use of eyewitnesses, the population at large was drawn into the criminal adjudicatory process; the people became policing agents. The introduction and proliferation of dress ordinances, the public nature of punishment, and highly developed visual-retentive capacities greatly facilitated recognition. Visual symbols permeated life; from birth to death the life cycle was not only mirrored in but regulated by appearances. Dress codes mandated clearly discernible signs of social status, wealth, religious affiliation for Jewish people, occupation and, for women, marital status and age. Frankfurt's population could thus easily tell a patrician from an artisan, an artisan from a Jew, a Jew from a Christian, a prostitute from an "honorable" woman. Visible signs not only helped in mutual policing but made crime reporting easier. Yet they also encouraged selective crime reporting. A burgher who might think little of reporting social inferiors might think twice about reporting a patrician.

Thus the visual social identification system served a double purpose, namely, to protect the upper echelon of society and to expose the lower. But the system could function only with the cooperation of the people. Neither Frankfurt's city councilors, who had the final say in criminal adjudication, nor its average citizens can be absolved of bias. In the absence of an independent police force they all exercised selectivity when reporting suspects. Here visual insignia had a direct, frequently prejudicial bearing on the accusatorial stage of criminal proceedings, as the following chapters will clearly demonstrate.

PART III
Cultural and Religious/Racial Impediments

Chapter 4

On Cultural Crossroads: Gypsies on Trial

The history of Gypsies, especially for the early modern German period, is still rather fragmented. One might want to blame the lack of scholarly interest for this void—it was only recently that scholars started to publish monographs on their lives—but this line of argument does not fully explain the gap in historical research. One of the major stumbling blocks is the difficulty in locating relevant source material, or, indeed, the lack thereof. While for the more recent period written data, supplemented by oral transmissions, is becoming more accessible this is, unfortunately, not the case for the early modern era. Here, the historian has to be rather lucky, if such a term might be used in the context of historical scholarship, to find some traces of Gypsy lives.[1]

Fortunately, four sets of such relevant documentation could be located in the municipal archives of Frankfurt am Main dating from the years 1685, 1687,

[1] Of great help is the 2005 established Forum Tsiganologische Forschung (FTF) in Leipzig and the Gypsy Lore Society and its journal. See also Thomas Fricke, *Zigeuner im Zeitalter des Absolutismus: Bilanz einer einseitigen Überlieferung. Eine sozialgeschichtliche Untersuchung anhand südwestdeutscher Quellen* (Pfaffenweiler: Centaurus-Verlagsgesellschaft, 1996); Jacqueline Gier, ed., *Die gesellschaftliche Konstruktion des Zigeuners: Zur Genese eines Vorurteils* (Frankfurt am Main: Campus, 1966); Reimer Gronemeyer, *Zigeuner im Spiegel früher Chroniken und Abhandlungen: Quellen vom 15. bis zum 18. Jahrhundert* (Giessen: Focus, 1987); Joachim Stephan Hohmann, *Neue deutsche Zigeunerbibliographie* (Frankfurt am Main, 1992); Joachim Stephan Hohmann, *Verfolgte ohne Heimat: Geschichte der Zigeuner in Deutschland* (Frankfurt am Main: P. Lang, 1990); Leo Lucassen, "Zigeuner im frühneuzeitlichen Deutschland: Neue Forschungsergebnisse, -probleme und -vorschläge," in Karl Härter, ed., *Policey und frühneuzeitliche Gesellschaft* (Frankfurt am Main: Klostermann, 2000), pp. 235–62; Wulf D. Hund, ed., *Zigeuner: Geschichte und Struktur einer rassistischen Konstruktion* (Duisburg: DISS, 1996); Claudia Beerger, *Ortlosigkeit des Fremdend. "Zigeunerinnen" und "Zigeuner" in der deutschsprachigen Literatur* (Cologne: Böhlau, 1998); Martin Rheinheimer, "'In die Erde können sie nicht kriechen': Zigeunerverfolgung im frühneuzeitlichen Schleswig-Holstein," *Historischen Anthropologie*, 4 (1996): 330–58. For France see Francois de Vaux de Foletier, *Les Tsiganes dans l'ancienne France* (Paris, 1961); for Portugal Bill M. Donovan, "Changing Perceptions of Social Deviance: Gypsies in Early Modern Portugal and Brazil," *Journal of Social History*, 26/1 (Autumn 1992): 33–53. In general see Angus Fraser, *The Gypsies* (Oxford: Blackwell, 1995); Ian Hancock, *The Pariah Syndrome: An Account of Gypsy Slavery and Persecution* (Ann Arbor, MI: Karoma, 1987); A.L. Beier, *Masterless Men: The Vagrancy Problem in England, 1560–1640* (London/New York: Methuen, 1985).

1690 and 1696. Unfortunately, these documents consist of criminal dossiers covering Gypsies accused of and sentenced for criminal deeds.[2] Although at first glance a negative find, criminal dossiers do not entirely warrant such a gloomy assessment. True, they implicate the suspects and thus immediately shed a negative light on Gypsy behavior patterns. However, an in-depth analysis discloses intriguing socio-cultural and religious patterns and a notable resilience on the part of the accused, traits possibly reflective of the wider Gypsy community. Most important, a careful reading of the criminal documents also exposes contemporary negative legal, judicial, and religious labeling mechanisms applied to Gypsies.

Brief Historical Background

When exactly Gypsies arrived in the Holy Roman Empire is still unclear, but many scholars tentatively point to the end of the fourteenth century.[3] Initially, Gypsies were well received, even being granted imperial letters of protection or safe conduct.[4] However, this general benevolent attitude had vanished by the end of the century, a development clearly demonstrated on the local, such as in Frankfurt, as well as the imperial level.

When Gypsies briefly appeared for the first time in Frankfurt in June of 1418, they were believed to be pilgrims who had come from "cleynen Egypten," little Egypt, and as such they received gifts from the local city council.[5] Upon their return in 1434, the locals extended their compassion and gave them

[2] Criminalia (hereafter CR)—1666 of 1685; CR 1724 of 1687; CR 1856 of 1690; and CR 2084 of 1696. These sources were supplemented by entries in Frankfurt's Strafenbuch (ST), Book of Punishments, covering every sentenced criminal from 1562 to 1696, including personal descriptions, legal details and penal repercussions. In addition, entries in the Bürgermeisterbücher (BB), minutes of the mayors' meetings and Ratsprotokolle (RP), minutes of the city council meetings, were consulted.

[3] Fraser, *The Gypsies*, pp. 61–5. Arno Herzig, "Die Fremden im frühmodernen Staat," in Gier, *Konstruktion des Zigeuners*, p. 33 refers to a chronicle by Herman Cornerus of Lübeck citing their existence for that year. See also Sebastian Münster's Cosmographia of 1550; Reimer Gronemeyer and Georgia A. Rakelmann, *Die Zigeuner: Reisende in Europa. Roma, Sinti, Manouches, Gitanos, Gypsies, Kalderasch, Vlach und andere* (Cologne: DuMont Buchverlag, 1988); and Karl Härter, "Zigeuner," in *Handwörterbuch zur deutschen Rechtsgeschichte*, vol. 5 (Berlin: Schmidt, 1998, [1699–1701]), pp. 23–36.

[4] Fraser, *The Gypsies*, pp. 64–5.

[5] Gerhard Ludwig Kriegk, *Deutsches Bürgertum im Mittelalter: Nach urkundlichen Forschungen und mit besonderer Beziehung auf Frankfurt am Main* (2 vols, 1868; repr. Frankfurt am Main: Sauer & Auvermann, 1969), vol. 2, p. 149.

money in order to buy bread, meat, and straw for their animals.[6] In 1446, a Gypsy even acquired local citizen status.[7] This evidently benevolent mentality, however—starting with their third visit in 1449—underwent decisive changes for reasons as yet not clearly defined primarily because of the lack of exact archival documents. In that year, it ended at the city gates.[8] Gypsies were no longer welcome in town. When two years later some Gypsies managed to gain access to town, Frankfurt's authorities had them promptly removed. On two similar occasions, in 1454 and 1458, Frankfurt resorted to the use of force to oust them. Six years later, arriving Gypsies were again stopped at the city wall. True, in 1466, Frankfurt eased its tough stance by giving money to the Gypsies' leader, the "Herzog von Egypten," the Duke of Egypt, as he was described in the records, but this proved to be an exceptional measure.[9] Frankfurt remained adamantly opposed to Gypsies, a pattern that continued through the remainder of the fifteenth century.

This mentality was also reflected at the imperial level. During the 1498 Diet in Freiburg, it was decreed that Gypsies were to be expelled from the realm on the grounds of being spies for the Turks, although scholars attribute the demise of Gypsies to other reasons as well such as ethnic, economic, social, and cultural aspects.[10] Seemingly ineffective, it was renewed in 1500, with a strict time line for their expulsion, after which it would no longer be considered a crime to take violent action against them: Gypsies had turned into outlaws. Again, while these imperial stipulations were very harsh, they were difficult to enforce, and as a result, there was no general exodus of Gypsies, or any general widespread attack on their lives.[11]

Yet this general development did not preclude any local action. On the contrary, one might argue that the stipulations of these imperial mandates were implemented on a local level, as is documented in the case of Frankfurt am Main. A scenario from 1561 clearly demonstrates this trend.[12] A Gypsy leader,

---

6 Ibid., vol. 2, pp. 149–51.

7 Konrad Bund, "Frankfurt am Main im Spätmittelalter 1311–1519," in *Frankfurt am Main: Die Geschichte der Stadt in neun Beiträgen* (Sigmaringen: Frankfurter Historische Kommission, 1991), p. 131.

8 Kriegk, *Bürgertum*, vol. 2, p. 150.

9 Friedrich Bothe, *Geschichte der Stadt Frankfurt am Main* (1913; repr. Frankfurt am Main: Sauer & Auvermann, 1966), p. 245.

10 Ernst Schubert, *Fahrendes Volk im Mittelalter* (Bielefeld: Verlag für Regionalgeschichte, 1995), p. 363; Zoltan Barany, "The East European Gypsies in the Imperial Age," *Ethnic and Racial Studies*, 24/1 (January 2001): 50–63.

11 Fraser, *The Gypsies*, p. 89.

12 Kriegk, *Bürgertum*, vol. 2, pp. 150–51.

Hans von Löwenburg, as he was recorded in the archives, submitted a request to Frankfurt's city council asking for permission to let him and his people come to town in order to buy goods they sorely needed, but his request was denied.[13] Two days after this group rejection, two Gypsies dared to enter, only to be promptly arrested. They were released on condition that they swear never to set foot inside Frankfurt again, on pain of flogging. Even more telling was a case from 1571, when Frankfurt's city council, in its capacity as the criminal judiciary, did not prosecute the son of a peasant from one of Frankfurt's suburbs who had stabbed a Gypsy to death. The culprit was let go unpunished. Frankfurt's city council based this decision on the 1500 imperial legislation stipulating that violent acts committed against Gypsies were not punishable.[14]

Coming to Town

Given this abbreviated but nonetheless telling historical backdrop, and Frankfurt's strictly off-limits attitude toward Gypsies, it is surprising to find even Gypsies on trial in Frankfurt. Two factors are worth pondering in this connection. First, since Frankfurt was entitled to sentence culprits who had committed their crimes elsewhere, this legal category might apply to the five Gypsies to be discussed in this chapter. But this was not the case. All had committed their alleged crimes either in one of Frankfurt's suburbs or directly in town. Second, it is noticeable that there were no men among the accused, only one boy and four women. This fact is all the more conspicuous because during the previous centuries, only Gypsy men had gained access to Frankfurt legally or illegally. Their absence thus raises various questions, such as whether they were unavailable, or whether the Gypsy boy and the four Gypsy women were now more suited than the men to gain access to town and, if so, how they succeeded in these obvious trespassing maneuvers.

While the absence of Gypsy men will be discussed in the text below and the Gypsy boy's alleged crime occurred in one of Frankfurt's suburbs, the immediate and most tantalizing question concerns the women's success in gaining town entry. Frankfurt had neither relaxed its anti-Gypsy stance nor made special allowances for Gypsy women to be welcome in town. On the contrary, Frankfurt intensified town-entry controls by promulgating a series of strict dress codes, which, among other factors, helped to identify everyone coming to and moving about town. Dress codes served mutual policing purposes and were

---

13 Reimar Gilsenbach, *Weltchronik der Zigeuner, vol. I: From the Beginnings to 1599* (Frankfurt am Main: Lang, 1994), p. 179.

14 Kriegk, *Bürgertum*, vol. 2, p. 151.

generally very effective.[15] Hence, how did Gypsy women, who might easily be recognized by their colorful attire if not by their skin, and possibly hair color, gain access? Obviously, the accused had found a way to bypass Frankfurt's strict municipal mandates.

Frankfurt's authorities seemed to have been puzzled, if not irked, by this issue, for the interrogators repeatedly approached the topic of town entry during their criminal examinations. Especially troublesome seems to have been the fact that the four women had been able to enter town without being recognized at the guarded city gates. A house servant, the main witness of the 1687 incidence, was the first to expose the Gypsies' method. Pointing to the obvious, in his initial description to the authorities, the servant described how the two suspects whom—he called "Zigeunerinnen," Gypsy women—had entered his employer's house: disguised as peasant women. While, unfortunately, the records do not disclose how this witness immediately knew them to be Gypsies, his description of the concealing outfits prompted the interrogators to pursue this lead with vigor.

One of the first questions posed to the suspects centered on their peasant disguises. The "kleine Zigeunerin," the little Gypsy, as she was described in the documents, was asked where she had obtained her peasant gear. She replied that she had owned it for several years. Obviously concerned about her easy access to town, the authorities now questioned her about which gate she had used to enter. Her reply was vague; she claimed that she did not know its name since she had not come by herself but with another Gypsy woman. When questioned as to what she was doing in town, she claimed that the devil had instigated her to come there, asserting that she had never been in town before.

Her accomplice, described as "older and stronger," had to answer almost identical questions, but with a stronger emphasis on possible previous town entries. She denied these allegations vehemently, stating, "never during my life, except for this time."

A similar scene took place in the 1690 case. One of the initial questions centered again on how the suspect had managed to get into town. Like the previous two Gypsy women, she admitted that she had gained access dressed as a peasant woman. Unlike the previous two suspects, however, she disclosed the point of entry as the Eschenheimer gate and readily admitted to having come to Frankfurt in order to steal. She, too, was questioned as to whether or not she had been in town before, something she emphatically denied.

Her disguised town entry spread fast among the locals. Several other claimants came forward and contacted the authorities with alleged crime

---

15 See Chapter 3.

observations. One of these accusers based her claim on local rumors circulating that a Zigeunerin in disguise was in town.

Equally, if not more, revealing were the questions and answers raised and exchanged during the third Gypsy interrogation, in 1696. Method of entry was again one of the leading queries. When asked how she had got into Frankfurt, the Gypsy woman disclosed that she had come in the company of three other peasant women whom she knew personally and that they had entered via the Bockenheimer gate an hour before she was apprehended. She revealed that she had put her hair in a sleeping bonnet, which she had carried with her for this particular purpose. Asked if they had been questioned at the gate as to their identity and where they had come from, she replied, no, certainly not. She, in contrast to the former suspect, denied allegations that she had come to town to steal but asserted instead that she wanted to beg for bread for her children. Questioned as to any previous visits, she stated that this was her first stay in town.

These various exchanges reveal that the Gypsy women must have known about the strict impediments to coming to town. They must also have been aware of Frankfurt's dress codes, and based on this insider knowledge, they figured out a method to outwit the local authorities. They arrived in peasant disguises. And they were successful, at least initially, bypassing the various inspection points at the gates and thus gaining access to town.

Equally revealing is the fact that one Gypsy woman admitted having come to town in the company of three other peasant women whom she knew. While at first glance this disclosure might seem a trivial detail, it is an indication that Gypsies, at least Gypsy women, had interactions with non-Gypsies. These contacts might not have been in-depth or everyday occurrences, but they do exhibit some form of positive rural communication between peasants and Gypsies, a deduction that will be further substantiated by findings disclosed during the ongoing trial procedures as shown below. Suffice it to state here that this initial disclosure raises doubts about the existence of frequently cited strict barriers between Gypsies and non-Gypsies.

While the Gypsy women's recourse to peasant camouflage in order to gain successful entry to town is remarkable, an equally important question has to be addressed: what prompted these women in the first place to risk coming to an off-limit city where, if discovered and exposed, they would possibly have to face severe punishments? Was it a question of dire personal circumstances coupled with personal strength, or was it—as so frequently alluded to in rather stereotypical fashion—an adventurous spirit at the root of their daring entries?

Personal Characteristics of the Suspects

At the beginning of each trial, Frankfurt authorities asked the suspects some seemingly routine questions pertaining to their name, age and, in the case of women, their marital status. In most instances name queries did not cause any problems. Accused offenders knew their names. And so did the young boy of the 1685 case, who readily stated his name as Daniel Rauch. By contrast, some confusion, if not obfuscation, occurred when the four Gypsy women were questioned. In the 1687 case of the two accomplices, the "little" Gypsy told the authorities that her name was Cathrin but immediately added "and nothing else." Most remarkably, however, she disclosed voluntarily that in "her language" her name was Palantin. Similarly, when asked about the name of a fellow Gypsy—an old widower unrelated to the crime—she revealed it as Petur in "their language." When she was questioned about his surname, she replied that they did not have last names. She gave the name of her accomplice as Margareth, adding, after some initial hesitation, Praniti.

When her accomplice was interrogated, she contradicted the "little" Gypsy's name assertions by stating that her own name was actually Cathrina, not Margareth. Questioned as to her last name, she passionately replied that even if "one killed her she would not know," and neither could she remember her father's name. But soon thereafter she conceded that her father's name was La Croix. She subsequently revealed her husband's name as Johannes but did not know of "wie er mehr heisse," any additional names. Pressed further to cite her real name, she now told the authorities that it was Anna Catharina, conceding that her accomplice called her by a different name because she did not know her well. When asked about the names of other Gypsies who stayed with them at their residence site, she answered that she did not know, since, so her argument went, she was "not present when they were being baptized."

In contrast to the difficulties in extracting various names from these two accomplices, the female Gypsy accused three years later disclosed her own without ado as Anna Elsa. As her last name she stated that she had her father's, namely La Fortune. But there was some hesitation on her part regarding her husband's name, which she eventually revealed as Johannes without, however, citing his last name. She stated that she did not know his surname for they would not call each other by their last but only by their baptized names.

The fourth Gypsy arraignment, in 1696, echoed the theme of baptized names. While she volunteered her name as Maria Bitterlin, and offered her husband's name as Veltin, she stressed that her youngest child had been baptized "im Hessenland," in Hesse, the area surrounding Frankfurt, and that his name was Johannes Christ.

While the hesitation on the part of some of the accused to disclose their own and their relatives' names might be interpreted as a protective mechanism, the information eventually ceded, however, offers a glimpse into Gypsies' religious and cultural patterns. Three themes emerge: first, almost all of their first names were of a Christian nature; second, at least one Gypsy woman disclosed names in "their language"; and third, last names were not uniformly used. Some vehemently denied even their existence, while others disclosed mainly French surnames.

Unfortunately, the study of names—in particular first names, or Christian names as they were called until recently—has not received enough scholarly attention, especially for the early modern period.[16] The notion that Christian, in particular saints', names were to bestow the saint's protective power over his or her namesake has been all but ignored by historians, although it was of paramount importance to contemporaries. Even Martin Luther was said to have issued a list of names his followers were to use.[17]

Therefore, the Gypsies' use of Christian names would not be surprising given this widespread tradition were it not for allegations by many contemporaries that Gypsies were not Christians but "Heiden," heathens. The German term *Zigeuner* for Gypsy, a derivative of the Greek *athinganos*, referring to a heathen sect, bears clear witness to this attitude.[18] Undergoing a linguistic twist equating Zigeuner to heathen, this label was used in Frankfurt dating back to 1434. But Frankfurt was no exception. This denigrating religious stereotype was used by many for many years, including religious dignitaries such as Martin Luther, who

---

16 Maria R. Boes addressed this problem in her paper "Judicial Dialogues: An Historical/Cultural Perspective" presented at the Fourth International Conference on the Dialogical Self, June 1–3, 2006 at the University of Minho, Portugal. See also W.G. Naphy, "Baptisms, Church Riots and Social Unrest in Calvin's Geneva," *Sixteenth Century Journal*, 26/1 (1995): 87–97, where he stresses the "dispute over baptismal names," p. 87. For more general comments see Joel T. Rosenthal's emphasis that "Historians have been slow to embrace the field of onomastics," in his reviews in *Journal of Interdisciplinary History*, 36/1 (Summer 2005): 57–62, covering David Postles, ed., *Naming, Society and Regional Identity: Papers Presented at a Symposium Jointly Arranged by Marc Fitch Fund and the Department of Local History* (Oxford: Leopard's Head Press, 2002); and Della Hooke and David Postles, eds, *Names, Times and Place: Essays in Memory of Richard McKinley* (Oxford: Leopard's Head Press, 2003).

17 Martin Luther's "Namen-Büchlein" (Wittenberg, 1537), although it has been questioned whether he was the actual author; frequently the work is attributed to John Carion.

18 Donald Kenrick, *The Romani World: A Historical Dictionary of the Gypsies* (Hatfield: University of Hertfordshire Press, 2004); see also Gier's linguistic reference of the German *Zigeuner* to the Greek term *athinganoi* in *Konstruktion des Zigeuners*, p. 16.

was not a friend of the Gypsies.[19] Voicing his discontent, he issued a virulent statement against them and Jewish people, urging in 1543 that both be put in stables "so that they learn that they are not masters in our land."[20]

Thus, a cynical interpretation of the Gypsies' use of Christian names might attribute it to their adroitness in pretending to be Christians in order to superficially fit into a predominantly Christian society and/or an attempt to bring the religious blessings of the protective powers of saints to their own children, relatives and friends. Nevertheless, such a condescending construal would, at its worst, reveal an effort on the Gypsies' part to partake in contemporary society; or, at best, point to a sign of sincere religiosity on their part and thus a religious acculturation, especially given their own frequent references to Christian baptisms in conjunction with their names.[21]

Yet neither Christian names nor the Gypsies' own declaration of their religious affiliations impressed Frankfurt's authorities. They continued to harbor deep-seated religious prejudices against them. Anna's case clearly documents this reigning mentality. While, unlike most other suspects, with the exception of Jewish people, religious entries or questions were very rare in Frankfurt's criminal records—even in the case of a murdered Catholic priest of 1678 the suspects were not questioned about their religious affiliation—Anna was asked about her religion, which she disclosed as "catholisch," Catholic.[22] Her answer had no effect whatsoever on the authorities. The criminal documents prove that she was being labeled a "Heidin" and "Zigeuner," a heathen and Gypsy, starting with the first sentence on the first page, a pattern which continued throughout her entire criminal dossier and, thus, her entire trial.[23]

While one might argue that Frankfurt, a predominantly Lutheran town, was irked by the Gypsy's Catholic affiliation, such a mental reservation can be easily put to rest for two reasons. First, in other criminal sentencing, the Catholic faith of suspects did not entail harsher judicial or penal treatment. In one incident,

---

19 Kriegk, *Bürgertum*, vol. 2, p. 150.

20 Martin Luther, *On the Jews and Their Lies* (1543), Article 301; see also Fraser, *The Gypsies*, p. 185 and Wolfgang Wippermann, *'Wie die Zigeuner': Antisemitismus und Antiziganismus im Vergleich* (Berlin: Elefanten Press, 1997).

21 These references to baptism seem to contradict findings for Portugal by Donovan, "Changing Perceptions," p. 35; see also Fraser, *The Gypsies*, who stated that "baptism became popular among them," p. 313.

22 Maria R. Boes, "Jews in the Criminal-Justice System of Early Modern Germany," *Journal of Interdisciplinary History*, 30/3 (Winter 1999): 407–35.

23 Fraser, *The Gypsies*, p. 312, who confirmed that "they have tended to accept the religions of the countries in which they have lived for some time. Thus there are Catholic Gypsies, various types of Protestant and Orthodox Gypsies."

the culprit was even accorded a Catholic priest.[24] Second, the statement of Dr. Johann Heinrich Gabler, one of Frankfurt's municipal advocates in Anna's case, is very clear. In his legal brief on Anna, he took an all-encompassing religious view of Gypsies, calling them the "gottlose Zigeunervolk," godless bunch of Gypsies, a mentality that existed not only just in Frankfurt but also in many regions in Europe, and for many centuries.

Jewish people were treated in a similar way. The few among them who had converted and were baptized were still being recorded as Jews, albeit "getaufter Jude," baptized Jew; and, similarly, one of Frankfurt's advocates, Dr. Anton Glock, also labeled them as "godless Jewish hoodlums."[25]

Apart from these religious name-related disclosures, two other name-related factors are worth analyzing. One points to the geographical range of Gypsies' travels. Two suspects had cited their fathers' last names, which were of French origin, pointing, as some scholars have suggested, to a possible Gypsy flight from France, where they were subjected to harsh persecution during Louis XIV's reign.[26]

Culturally more insightful were some of the Gypsies' references to names in "their language." True, citing two apparently indigenous Gypsy names seems to contradict Anna's claim that they only used baptized names, unless, of course, Palantin and Petur were synonyms for Christian names. But the disclosure of and reference to names in "her" and "their own language"—without, unfortunately, yielding any further insights as to language specifics—clearly show that Gypsies, contrary to assertions advanced by some scholars, had a deep sense of belonging to their cultural linguistic heritage: why else use the possessive?[27]

Yet, most remarkably, the Gypsy suspects also spoke fluent German. After all, the trials' question and answer sessions were conducted in the German language, and the accused did not seem to have any difficulties understanding

---

24 ST August 11, 1626.

25 Boes, "Jews in the Criminal-Justice System," p. 420 and Chapter 6; CR 1585, 1683.

26 Bernd Roeck, *Aussenseiter, Randgruppen, Minderheiten: Fremde in Deutschland der frühen Neuzeit* (Göttingen: Vandenhoeck & Ruprecht, 1993), p. 89, suggests that the frequent appearance of French Gypsy names in the archives of the Holy Roman Empire is connected to their flight from France to escape harsh persecution under Louis XIV; see also Hancock, *Pariah Syndrome*, where he stresses the Gypsies' plight during the reign of Louis XIV, pp. 55, 57.

27 By contrast, some scholars argue that "Zigeuner" were not an independent cultural group but rather the product of a labeling process from above, that is, the ruling authorities; see, in this connection, Leo Lucassen, *Zigeuner: Die Geschichte eines polizeilichen Ordnungsbegriffes in Deutschland 1700–1945* (Cologne: Böhlau, 1996) and Wim Willems, "Aussenbilder von Sinti und Roma in der frühen Zigeunerforschung," in Gier, *Konstruktion des Zigeuner*, pp. 87–108.

the questions.[28] On the contrary, their respective answers to the interrogators were given in at times passionate and colloquial tones; at times even with legal finesse, as will be demonstrated below.

Therefore, based on the Gypsies' familiarity with and use of Christian names, their belonging to the Christian faith, and their knowledge of the German language, it is safe to advance that they must have had friendly interactions with at least some of their German contemporaries. How else would they have found out about the various societal/religious intricacies? In the absence of widespread literacy, the only way to learn about the various cultural patterns was via verbal exchanges and, hence, personal contacts. Gypsies thus made serious efforts to garner local knowledge, which they proved they mastered impressively. While they retained their own cultural heritage, they found themselves at cultural crossroads and became cultural pioneers, forerunners of bi- if not multicultural approaches and mentalities.

The five Gypsies were also questioned with regard to their age, an approach Frankfurt's authorities applied to all other suspects. The Gypsies' age-related answers were vague, not an unusual phenomenon for the times. Either they did not know their age or they were not sure, such as when the young boy cited an age range of 16 to 19 or even 20. Similarly, the "little" Gypsy admitted that she did not know how old she was but put her age at approximately 30, while her partner in crime was seemingly not even asked but was simply listed as older. The accused in the 1690 incident stated her age as 26, while in the 1696 case the suspect also admitted that she really did not know but believed herself to be approximately 22 years old.

As they did with other female offenders, Frankfurt's authorities also questioned the four Gypsy women about their marital status. By contrast, the young man stated that he was single without even being asked. The four women were married and had children. These familial disclosures seemingly enticed the local authorities to ask for more family-related details, a path of inquiry that deviated from Frankfurt's general judicial pattern, in which questions regarding close relatives were hardly ever posed. The young Gypsy was subjected to a rather pejorative question about how he had "ended up" among the Gypsies. His answer was simple and frank: his mother and father were Gypsies. He even disclosed their whereabouts. His parents, together with his father's sister and her husband, stayed not too far from Bornheim (near Frankfurt), close to a bridge under the trees.

---

28 Roeck, *Aussenseiter*, p. 87, quotes the statement of a contemporary, Sebastian Münster, who observed that they "kan vil Sprachen," know many languages.

The "little" Gypsy told Frankfurt's authorities that she had two small children and that her husband was in Hungary. She explained that he had to leave because the master of "ihrem Völklein," their people, had sent some of them to the Emperor to be with "Prinz Manfeldern," as she put it. Questioned about the whereabouts of her children, she stated "across the water"—obviously meaning the local river Main—claiming that she did not know the name of the place. Eventually, however, she referred to it as Bockenheim (a place in Frankfurt's vicinity), adding a more specific description of their residence location: "under the willow trees."

This disclosure raised the interest of the interrogators even further. Asked who else resided with them at this location, she replied vaguely "women and children, three or five, and many small children." Questioned as to what they were doing, she replied "traveling around." Obviously not satisfied with this vague information, the authorities pressed her into disclosing how many men stayed with them. "One old man, a widower, without children, and nobody else," was her answer.

The older Gypsy, her accomplice, told the authorities that she had four little children, the youngest being eight days old. Like the "little" Gypsy she stated that her husband was in Hungary. But she volunteered more information by disclosing that "Graff Mansfelden" had sent 400 men of "ihrem Völklein," their people, down there. When asked how many more people were in her company outside of Frankfurt, she replied, in contrast to her accomplice, that three or four men stayed with them. This new information immediately prompted the authorities to re-question the "little" Gypsy as to how many men were actually in their company across the river. She conceded that her accomplice's disclosure, three or four men, was correct and asked the authorities for forgiveness for her earlier misstatement.

The third suspect also stated Bockenheim as her present residence, adding that she had come by herself to Frankfurt, leaving behind her two small children, who were sick. The last suspect disclosed that she had been married for several years and had four children, the youngest barely six months old. The children were with other Gypsies in Bockenheim while her husband served in the Hessian military.

Obviously, the four Gypsy women's familial patterns were very similar. They were all married with small children. The children were in the company of other Gypsies, mainly women, while their mothers had ventured to Frankfurt. Except for the young man, all four women described Bockenheim as the location of their residential site. Their disclosure of Bockenheim could hardly have been a surprise to Frankfurt's authorities, since non-Gypsies knew about it. One of the alleged additional victims in the 1690 case disclosed her knowledge—and prejudice—in her allegations by referring to the Gypsies as the "Gesindel sich in Bockenheim aufgehalten," hoodlums having stayed in Bockenheim. And so did one of Frankfurt's advocates in his legal brief in the same case, stating that Gypsies had stayed in Bockenheim for an extended period of time.

Why the Gypsies selected Bockenheim, a predominantly rural site in Frankfurt's vicinity, as their site of domicile is difficult to ascertain. It is also almost impossible to assert whether they stayed there throughout the period assessed in this chapter, that is from 1685 to 1696, or whether they returned to this location periodically and, if so, why. Despite various attempts to locate pertinent information, no historical data or archival entries could be found.

This lack of historical backup material might be interpreted in two ways: Gypsies were not important enough to be registered; or, in a more positive fashion, their stay did not cause any negative ripple effects in that location. At least in Bockenheim they were not registered for alleged misbehaviors, the registry frequently, if not exclusively, constituting the only existing written source material available. It is thus safe to conclude that the people of Bockenheim must have been at least somewhat positively inclined toward Gypsies, for why else would they have stayed and/or returned to that location repeatedly?[29]

Equally elusive, yet enticing to pursue, are some of the suspects' references to trees at their residence site. The young boy pointed it out and so did the "little" Gypsy. While their statements might have been insignificant, in that trees might have merely served as location markers, the fact, however, that the "little" Gypsy described them in greater detail as willow trees suggests they are possibly culturally significant, a deduction confirmed by various Gypsy folkloric traditions, such as the festival of Green George, where a willow tree is the center of festivities.[30] Jacques Callot's 1622 engraving *Gypsy Camp* and the recent video *Latcho Dron* (1993), produced by Gypsies depicting their cultural heritage and

---

29 E. Schubert, *Arme Leute: Bettler und Gauner im Franken des 18. Jahrhunderts* (Neustadt a.d. Aisch: Degener, 1983), p. 137 similarly demonstrates that the local population was not always unfavorably inclined toward Gypsies; and so does Alfred Höck, "Recht auch für Zigeuner? Ein Kapitel Minderheitenforschung nach hessischen Archivalien," in Konrad Köstlin and Kai Detlev Sievers, eds, *Des Recht der kleinen Leute: Beiträge zur rechtlichen Volkskunde* (Berlin: E. Schmidt, 1976), pp. 77–8.

30 Various Gypsy songs refer to willow trees, such as "Little Willow Tree" and the "Gypsy Lament.". Also, the Gypsy saying for a person deeply in love points to that tree, namely, "willow-bound." See James George Frazer, *The Golden Bough: A Study in Magic and Religion* (London: Macmillan, 1917), p. 126, which points to the importance of the willow tree for the Gypsies of Transylvania and Romania, who celebrate the festival of Green George, some of them on Easter Monday, others on St. George's Day, April 23; see also, Othmar Keel, *The Symbolism of the Biblical World* (New York: Seabury Press 1977), pp. 135–8.

traditions, are further evidence of this cultural phenomenon.[31] While the origins and dissemination of such cultural developments are beyond the scope of this chapter, they, nevertheless, demonstrate again that Gypsies cherished their own cultural heritage.

Equally, if not more, revealing than their place of residence was the Gypsy women's disclosure of their husbands' whereabouts. They did not live with them, at least not at the time of their arrests in Frankfurt; all four suspects' husbands were engaged in military service. They were not fighting their own battles, but instead almost all of them were in Hungary for the defense of the Christian realm and one was described vaguely as fighting in Hesse, the area surrounding Frankfurt. It thus seems more than paradoxical that while the Gypsies were labeled as "godless rogues," they often risked their lives to defend Christianity.

The Gypsies' military service could not have gone unnoticed. There is ample documentation available to prove it; in fact, it was "üblich und selbstverständlich," common and taken as a matter of fact.[32]

This might explain why Frankfurt's authorities did not question the Gypsy women any further with regard to their husbands' whereabouts. They must have been aware that Gypsy soldiers were actively and honorably engaged in military service, ranging from the Thirty Years War to the wars against the Turks, starting in 1663, and the French wars, by 1688.[33] In fact, recent scholarship has confirmed that being a soldier was the most frequent occupation exercised by Gypsies,

---

31 Heather Robbins deserves credit for introducing me to the video Latcho Dron.

32 Fricke, *Zigeuner im Zeitalter*, is one of the first historians to pay close attention to their military service. Stefan Kroll, "Kursächsisches Militär und Ländliche Randgruppen im 18. Jahrhundert," in Stefan Kroll and Kersten Krüger, eds, *Militär und ländliche Gesellschaft in der frühen Neuzeit: Herrschaft und Soziale Systeme*. Herausgegeben vom Arbeitskreis Militär und Gesellschaft in der Frühen Neuzeit e.V. Band 1 (Hamburg: LIT, 2000), p. 288 points to the early knowledge of their military service; on p. 291 he also points to their widespread military service proliferation. See also Joachim S. Hohmann, Geschichte der Zigeunerverfolgung in Deutschland (Frankfurt am Main/New York: Campus Verlag, 1981), pp. 19–21; for France see Francois de Vaux de Foletier, "Gypsy Captains in Provence and the Rhone Valley in the 16th and 17th Centuries," *Journal of the Gypsy Lore Society*, 3/41 (1962): 3–10; and his "Wovon leben sie eigentlich," in Karl Rinderknecht, ed., *Zigeuner: Geheimnisvolle Nomaden* (Lausanne: Mondo-Verlag, 1973) demonstrates that many Gypsies served French regiments under Louis XIV and Louis XV, p. 71. Fraser, *The Gypsies*, pp. 152, 180 dedicates a few rather vague sentences to that topic. See also Andrew Morrall, "Soldiers and Gypsies: Outsiders and Their Families in Early Sixteenth Century German Art," in Pia Cuneo, ed., *Artful Armies, Beautiful Battles: Art and Warfare in Early Modern Europe* (Leiden: Brill, 2001), p. 159–80, describing/analyzing various paintings and sketches containing Gypsy women shown with soldiers, although the author is in somewhat vague territory regarding the identities of the soldiers who actually might be Gypsy military men, pp. 174–5, 178.

33 Fricke, *Zigeuner im Zeitalter*, pp. 20, 42.

and not, as has often been claimed, horse-trader, bear-leader, musician, healer or fortune-teller.[34] Also, Gypsy soldiers were not pressed into military service. Many joined "aus eigenem Antrieb und oft mit gefragten Kopetenzen," on their own and frequently offering desired skills, a statement implicitly confirmed by one of the Gypsy women's reference to 400 men.[35] It would be very difficult, if not impossible, to impress, let alone forcefully keep 400 men in military service, given the high desertion rate at the time.[36]

Thus, their husbands' military service seemed to have prompted the four Gypsy women on trial to disclose their husbands' whereabouts without any vagueness or cover-up maneuvers. In fact, a certain element of pride might be detected in the women's assertions in not only knowing the name of the commander under whom their husbands exercised their military service but also, and more important, in describing their soldier-husbands as belonging to their "Völklein," theirs: the Gypsy people.

Obviously, these facts also meant that quite a number of Gypsy women were left alone in charge of their families. One might wonder if this state of affairs did not prompt some of them to take the rare and risky step of coming to an off-limit town such as Frankfurt in order to seek sustenance for their children.[37]

Trial Procedures

While an argument for need-induced illegal town entry could be advanced for the four Gypsy women, as will be discussed below in more detail, the case of the young Gypsy boy disclosed a rather minor crime involvement on his part. He described the unfolding of his crime association by explaining how a stranger, identified in the criminal file as "Blaurock," blue coat, had approached him at his Gypsy residential site the evening before his arrest, asking him for help. Blaurock told him that a prostitute had stolen money from his brother-in-law,

[34] Ibid., p. 443. For an enumeration of the alleged traditional occupations see ibid., p. 67 as well as Peter Burke, *Popular Culture in Early Modern Europe*, revised reprint (Aldershot: Ashgate 2002), p. 49; Frazer, *Golden Bough*, p. 125.

[35] Ulrich Friedrich Opfermann, "Zur Situation der 'Zigeuner' in den Territorialstaaten zwischen Main, Lahn und Sieg in der ersten Hälfte des 18. Jahrhunderts. Drei Fälle im Vergleich," in Udo Engbring-Romang und Wilhelm Solms, eds, *"Diebstahl im Blick?" Zur Kriminalisierung der "Zigeuner" im Auftrag der Gesellschaft für Antiziganismusforschung e.V.*, vol. 3 (Seeheim, 2005), p. 96.

[36] Peter Burschel, "Zur Sozialgeschichte innermilitärischer Disziplinierung im 16. und 17. Jahrhundert," *Zeitschrift für Geschichtswissenschaft*, 11 (1994), 42. Jahrgang, p. 977.

[37] How rare such a move was is further documented by Fricke, *Zigeuner im Zeitalter*, p. 479.

which he was entitled to reclaim by the permission from the local Schultheiss, bailiff, a statement that later proved to be a lie. Hesitant to follow the stranger immediately, he was again approached by Blaurock the following morning, and this time he went with him to get the money. But the alleged prostitute put up considerable resistance, leading Blaurock to threaten that he would cut her throat if she resisted any further. He subsequently tore off her purse and threw it to his supposed helper, who, however, threw it back to the victim.

Evidently a believable description, for a Pro Nota scribble on the legal document stipulated that the Zigeuner had rendered his account "offenherzig," candidly/frankly. The two crime observers rendered a similar appraisal. The victim, the alleged prostitute who had filed charges against Blaurock, verified the young Gypsy's account. She also stressed, and was ready to back up her disclosure with an oath, that at no time had the young Gypsy threatened her. The Schultheiss, who had belatedly appeared on the crime scene, gave his rendition of the crime event. He, too, stressed that the Gypsy boy had been innocent. Obviously having been in touch with the boy's mother, he relayed her feelings, asserting that she "would stab herself" if the boy were not released immediately. But all to no avail, both the Gypsy boy and Blaurock were transferred to a local prison to wait for the outcome of Frankfurt's advocates' legal suggestions and for the final sentences to be pronounced by Frankfurt's city council.

Unlike the Gypsy boy, the four Gypsy women came on their own volition, and they were all caught in flagrante delicto. In the 1687 case, a male house servant initiated the criminal proceedings by reporting to the authorities that two Gypsies in disguise as peasant women had secretly entered his master's house, a tavern, and had stolen stockings and shoes, broken a lock to a chest and taken additional items such as rugs, blankets, a man's coat, a pair of pants and a shirt. He alleged that they had stuffed these items into two bags, which they hid in the stable with the intent to return to the house, but he caught them in the act.

The "little" Gypsy was questioned first. While not denying her present intent to steal, she refuted emphatically having stolen anything previously in Frankfurt. She admitted to having taken "ein bisslein Essenspeis," a bit of food, elsewhere for her small children. When questioned as to how she had entered the house, how she had opened the chamber and the chest, and if she had broken any locks, she replied that all the doors had been open and that she and her fellow Gypsy had broken no locks. When she was shown the broken lock to the chest, she adjusted her statement, conceding that the other Gypsy had opened it with her bare hands. She stressed, however, that they had nothing on them—no instruments—to pry open the lock.

When the "older" Gypsy was interrogated she vehemently denied having pried open the chest by force, avowing to stand by her statement "even if you kill me." Similar to her accomplice's rendition, she admitted that while not having stolen anything in Frankfurt prior to this incidence, she had taken chicken and geese elsewhere.

Another accuser, a woman, now launched an accusation claiming that several days before—last Friday as she put it—the "little" Gypsy had entered a house and had stolen a ring, a silver belt, and other items, which were, however, returned to the rightful owner. The accuser asserted that she had seen the suspect walking across the market and that she had worn a red cap. When confronted with this accuser, the "little" Gypsy woman reasserted her previous statement that she had never been in town before.

Both Gypsy women pleaded for mercy. The "older" one implored Frankfurt's authorities to release her for the sake of her four small children, the youngest being only eight days old, and arguing that if she were arrested and had to stay overnight, the child would die. She begged them to have mercy and urged them to think of "den lieben Gott," our dear Lord. The "little" Gypsy argued in her plea for clemency that other people had committed far more serious deeds and been shown mercy. She and her accomplice had not committed anything big, as she put it; and by contrast, she argued, Jews had committed far more horrible deeds against our "lieben Hergott." They were both arrested.

The following two cases exhibit noticeable similarities. The Catholic Gypsy, labeled as heathen in the files, was also accused of theft. Initially she denied these charges, asserting that a maid had come to the front door of the house and handed her the items. She also denied the existence of any collaborators and that she had ever previously been arrested in Frankfurt for theft. Instead, she asked to be released for the sake of her little children, who were sick. She was imprisoned instead.

Once arrested, two additional charges were launched against her. Both accusations emanated from local women. The first, a burgher woman, alleged that various linen pieces had been stolen from the bleaching ground and, "since she heard from the neighbors that a Gypsy be in town who stole from people," she was requesting that the suspect be subjected to "scharff," severe, interrogation (possibly with torture). The second claimant launched a similar accusation, asserting that several pieces of cloth had been stolen from the bleaching ground. She held a strong suspicion toward the Gypsy woman because "in the neighborhood they were saying that Gypsies who were in disguise had committed various thefts." She, too, asked the authorities to conduct "scharff" examinations.

In a relatively small community like Frankfurt, neighborhood gossip and malicious rumors thus not only made the rounds very quickly but also incited people to file criminal charges. In the case of the Gypsy under indictment, this rumor-mill method met with obvious success, for she was subjected to additional questioning. While she, again, denied all charges, she eventually, after having been "herb zugesprochen," subjected to stern talk, admitted to the original allegation. She conceded having stolen the various items but said that she had returned all of them. Similar to the earlier two suspects, she stressed that she had entered the house because the door had been open. Asked if the door to the room from where she had taken the clothing had been locked, she said no, and in reply to a follow-up question, she retorted that she had neither used a "Diebsschlüssel," thief's key, to enter the house nor opened a chest with a "Diebsschlüssel." She denied, however, the additional theft charges brought against her by the two women. Falling to her knees, she invoked God's mercy and asked the authorities to let her go for the sake of her children.

Instead she had to undergo two physical examinations: one for pregnancy and one for signs of previous flogging. The first was based on her own claim that she was pregnant, an assertion which was refuted by Frankfurt's municipal midwife and counter-challenged by the Gypsy woman, who stated that she knew better. The second was based on Frankfurt's suspicion that she might have been previously flogged for a crime, a suspicion they could not, however, sustain. There were no flogging marks.

A maid was the main witness in the 1696 case. She asserted that a Gypsy woman had entered her employer's house at 11 am. While the door to the house was open, she claimed that the Gypsy proceeded to climb two flights of stairs, where she unlocked a room, from where she entered another, stealing "four of the very best men's shirts and bed linen." When the Gypsy woman was descending the stairs, they caught her. The Gypsy, per the maid, immediately fell to her knees, asking for forgiveness for her theft, which she said she had committed out of great poverty and for the sake of her four children, adding that the goods had been restored.

Based on this account, the Gypsy woman was now interrogated. She claimed she had found out about the open house from a beggar woman, whose name she did not know. She admitted having entered the house and gone upstairs, even to the third floor, but stressed that she had not broken any locks in the process. Falling to her knees in front of the interrogators, she pleaded for mercy, repeating her earlier claim that she had done it out of poverty and for the sake of her children. She was arrested pending sentencing.

What their various statements communicate—beyond their obvious plea for mercy—is the Gypsies' comprehensive and thorough knowledge of the contemporary legal system and religious sentiment. They demonstrated that they were fully aware of the legal and penal implications of the act of breaking into a house or prying open a chest with an instrument with the intent to steal, by stressing that the doors to the houses had been unlocked and that they had not pried open any doors or locks with utensils. Forceful entries would entail far more serious punishments. Also, almost all appealed to the "liebe Gott" in their pleas for mercy. The "little" Gypsy topped these religious forays by accusing Jews of having committed far more serious crimes, especially toward Christ, a remarkable statement for an alleged heathen. Quite obviously she tapped into prevalent anti-Jewish sentiments, which she tried to exploit in order to receive a milder punishment.[38] Thus, as pointed out earlier in this chapter, the Gypsy women's adroit statements demonstrate that they did not live in a social vacuum bereft of any contact with the local non-Gypsy population. Had they lived entirely on the societal outskirts they would neither have learned about nor been able to deliver such cogent legal arguments.

While their legal finesse and religious sense are quite evident, an additional and crucial point needs to be stressed: all four Gypsy women were extremely daring. They risked entering an off-limit town, exposing themselves to a hostile environment where the ill repute that preceded their arrival was so clearly demonstrated by the additional and unfounded charges against them. They even risked entering houses—in one instance even climbing to the third floor—where they could be, and actually were, easily recognized and apprehended.

The motivational force behind their behavior was, in their own words, poverty and concern for their children. Even the most circumspect analyst must at least contemplate the possibility that these four women actually spoke the truth. Given their familial situation—the absence of their husbands, in military service — concern for their children might very well have prompted them to dare these risky moves, facing grave personal ramifications if caught. And the penal ramifications were, indeed, severe.

Punishments

The first case, the 1685 adjudication of the Gypsy boy, was indicative of Frankfurt's selective penal approach, setting the stage for the penalties meted out to the four women. It was, in particular, Frankfurt's advocates, who, in their legal opinions, disclosed at times harsh, biased attitudes toward Gypsies. In the Gypsy boy's case, they obfuscated his involvement in a crime which had been initiated and carried out by a non-Gypsy. While Dr. Johann Brandes, who wrote the initial and influential legal opinion, argued that the "young Gypsy was considerably more innocent than the other, that the victim herself had defended him and that he had returned the goods to her," he, nevertheless, ought to be

---

[38] See Boes, "Jews in the Criminal-Justice System," and Chapter 6.

punished and banished for life, though without being flogged. In a postscript to his legal brief, he made a sweeping assessment of Gypsies in general, describing them as rascals who roamed around in Christian land, and that these "Canaille," as he called them, harmed rural folks with thefts and robberies. And, supporting his claim, he cited the 1500 imperial mandate, which stipulated that everyone could take action against Gypsies without incurring any punishment. Drs. Georg Schuster, Martin Rasor and Anton Glock concurred.

This was a very harsh punishment for two reasons. In their legal assessments, the advocates did not refer to the fact that the young man was in fact lured into participating in a crime by an adult, a non-Gypsy, and that enticing youngsters to participate in a crime was in itself a serious felony. But, more important, they disregarded Frankfurt's general juvenile penal policy. During the sixteenth and seventeenth centuries, possibly even before, youngsters had their punishments reduced due to their age, as regularly stipulated in records.[39] Shielding youngsters from public exposure was one of the leading principles for this lenient trend, a concern that obviously did not apply to the Gypsy boy. His public exposure in the pillory was thus not a reflection of his wrongdoings but a reflection of contemporary legal contempt for Gypsy "Canailles."

The four female offenders met with similar fates. While to Frankfurt's credit the additional charges filed by several women based on rumors were apparently not given credence, there was, however, no reference as to extenuating circumstances, such as the return of or the low value of the stolen goods, or the suffering of a suspect's young children, which generally entailed a much milder punishment.

It was again one of Frankfurt's advocates, Dr. Heinrich Gabler, who laid the base for the harsh punishments. He delivered a scorching legal opinion to the city council in which he, paradoxically, listed the very same extenuating circumstances advanced by one of the Gypsy women. He argued that while the merchandise had been returned in perfect condition and the Gypsy woman had not used a key to enter, she had, nevertheless, come to town in "dangerous disguise" with the intent to steal. He continued his legal argument with a diatribe against Gypsies in general, calling them a "godless bunch," who were "prone to stealing, robbing, lying and cheating," and as such they were to be set apart from other thieves and hence ought to be punished more severely. He submitted, however, that the city council might choose a middle way and only punish her with the pillory. No mercy was granted: she was flogged, put into the pillory, and banished for life.

---

39 See Maria R. Boes "The Treatment of Juvenile Delinquents in Early Modern Germany: A Case Study," *Continuity and Change*, 2/1 (1996): 43–60.

In the case of the two accomplices, he argued first in general terms that theft had become too widespread, and then resorted to a more targeted approach that in order to "abschrecken ihrer Geselinnen," scare their fellow Gypsy women, they were to be put into the pillory and flogged. Even the third Gypsy's direct and explicit plea for a milder punishment because of the return of the goods did not lead to a milder sentence.

The fourth Gypsy woman, sentenced in 1696, was not flogged: she was put into the pillory and banished. But an explanatory remark entered into the Strafenbuch the day after her punishment recognizes the lack of legal parity for Gypsies, conveying an almost regretful admission of a disproportionately severe punishment, stating that "she was put into the pillory despite the fact that the merchandise she stole was of little value." Even more remarkable was another addendum describing the actual punishment scene: "she was put into the pillory holding in her arms her singing little child, which she claimed was only half a year old."[40]

Not even Gypsy children could induce Frankfurt's authorities to commute their mothers' sentences, in contrast to some non-Gypsy offenders who had their punishments reduced because of their small children. For example, in 1664 a father who was convicted of various nightly break-ins — far more serious crimes than those committed by the Gypsy women—received a reduced punishment "because of his five small children"; and in 1688 a female offender was granted a milder punishment for a similar reason.[41]

Whether these harsh sentences reflect a general hardening of criminal prosecutions of Gypsies during the latter part of the seventeenth century, as has frequently been claimed, is difficult to confirm because of the lack of comparative criminal records for the earlier period.[42] On the other hand, it might just be that lack of criminal prosecutions would support this claim. Also, if the sentencing trend of another minority, Jewish people, might serve as a lead, then this argument seems very plausible.[43]

Summary

The trials of the five Gypsies sentenced in Frankfurt disclose valuable insights into their cultural patterns and religious affiliations. They spoke of "their" language and referred to "ihrem Völklein," their people, thus clearly establishing their own group identity. Yet they were also open to "other" or outside influences, such as

40 ST February 5, 1696.

41 BB November 8, 1664; BB August 30, 1688.

42 Fricke, *Zigeuner im Zeitalter*, pp. 78–83; Härter, *Zigeuner*, pp. 72–81.

43 Boes, "Jews in the Criminal-Justice System."

speaking the language of the people around them: German. All five suspects, even the boy, understood, spoke, and cogently expressed their thoughts in German, a fact that might serve as an indicator that other Gypsies did so as well. They were Christians—Catholic in one instance—and had Christian first names, while seemingly retaining names in their own birth language, at least in two cases. They selected one particular area as the site of their residence, either coming or going or remaining there for any length of time, attesting to, if not a good, then at least a somewhat favorable relationship with the rural people surrounding them. All points considered, they were truly bi-, if not multicultural.

Any doubts as to this deduction must fade in light of the fact that many Gypsy men opted to serve in the military defending the realm, the Holy Roman Empire, risking death or maiming, and leaving their wives to at least partially fend for themselves while they fought. Yet, despite all these adaptations on their part, Gypsies were shunned and looked upon with derision, attitudes arguably worse in city environments, as demonstrated by Frankfurt's trial and penal procedures.

While the Gypsy boy experienced two disheartening situations, neither of his own doing—one by a criminal seducer who came to the Gypsy site to recruit him, the other by an undeserved and excessive punishment on the part of the legal authorities—the four Gypsy women deliberately entered into their situations by coming to town. By their own admission, they gained access while in disguise as peasant women, a camouflage that might have offered them one of the few opportunities they had to be admitted. Their desire to come to town was not unusual, for, as is well known, contemporary cities acted as magnets for many, not only Gypsies. But what was unusual in their case was the courage they exhibited in doing so, since Gypsies were strictly barred from Frankfurt, facing serious ramifications if caught, as they would, indeed, experience. True, most entered houses, one even up to the third floor, with criminal intent—that is, to steal—but they did not forcefully open any doors or locks, and the merchandise was restored to the original owners.

Despite these generally penalty-reducing factors, the four Gypsy women were not granted any mercy.[44] It was above all the learned advocates who were intransigent, arguing that the "gottlose Zigeunervolk" ought not to be judged like other thieves but should receive more severe punishments. And they did receive harsher punishments. The mother holding her little baby in her arms while standing in the pillory must be considered the symbol of divergent punishments: it was the only such case in Frankfurt's sentencing history during the 1562 to 1696 period.

[44] This penal development is unlike the argument advanced by Härter, *Zigeuner*, p. 72, that Gypsy women could convince investigating agents of their innocence.

Chapter 5

Targeted Twice: Jews as Individual Criminal and Judicial Victims

Historians to date have concentrated primarily on large-scale attacks on Jewish people during the early modern German period, such as the sack of the Judengasse, the Jewish street, in Frankfurt am Main during the Fettmilch Uprising in 1614.[1] While such studies are important, assessments of individual attacks and/or crimes against Jewish people serve an equally and arguably even more important function, especially if the culprits were caught and brought to justice. Assessments of individual criminal case descriptions reveal with greater accuracy personal motivations for the crime as well as the criminal circumstances. Most importantly, they also disclose in greater detail how the judiciary dealt with both the perpetrators and the victims.

Eleven crime sentences adjudicated in the city of Frankfurt am Main during the 1562 to 1696 period serve to help fill this scholarly gap. While these cases were extracted from Frankfurt's Strafenbuch, the Book of Punishments, which records every criminal sentenced, they do not purport to be quantitatively all-inclusive.[2] In fact, many more crimes were committed against Jewish people but the perpetrators were either released on monetary fines or with just a simple warning.[3] Thus it has to be stressed at the outset that the focus of this chapter is primarily a qualitative, in-depth analysis aimed at establishing individual criminal motivations, patterns of victimology, judicial practices, and possible

---

1 For an in-depth account of the various interpretations of the Fettmilch Uprising see Christopher R. Friedrich, "Politics or Pogrom? The Fettmilch Uprising in German and Jewish History," *Central European History*, 19 (1986): 186–228. See also Alfred Haverkamp, "Die Judenverfolgung zur Zeit des schwarzen Todes im Gesellschaftsgefüge deutscher Städte," in Alfred Haverkamp, ed., *Zur Geschichte der Juden in Deutschland des späten Mittelalters und der frühen Neuzeit* (Stuttgart: Hiersemann, 1981). For a discussion of the terms "ghetto" and "Jewish quarter" see Alfred Haverkamp, "The Jewish Quarters in German Towns During the Late Middle Ages," in R. Po-Chia Hsia and Hartmut, Lehmann, eds, *In and Out of the Ghetto: Jewish–Gentile Relations in Late Medieval and Early Modern Germany* (Cambridge/New York: Cambridge University Press, 1995), pp. 13–15.

2 The Strafenbuch (ST) is located in Frankfurt's Municipal Archives.

3 Dietrich Andernacht, Regesten zur Geschichte der Juden in der Reichsstadt Frankfurt am Main von 1520–1616, ed. Helga Andernacht, in *Verbindung mit dem Institut für Stadtgeschichte Frankfurt und dem Arye Maimon-Instituts für Geschichte der Juden an der Universität Trier* (2 vols, Hanover: Hahnsche Buchhandlung, 2007), vol. 2, pp. 447–1069.

changes over time, in addition to including comparative aspects to the treatment of Gentiles similarly situated.[4]

Individual criminal dossiers, Frankfurt's *Criminalia*, serve as the main source for this study. They contain witness accounts, legal briefs by local advocates, letters by judicial authorities from other towns, Jewish intercessions, barber/medical reports, written personal pleas and, lastly and most importantly, the legal opinions and penal deliberations by Frankfurt's advocates. While, unfortunately, complete folders do not exist for all cases, the fragmentary ones can be supplemented by judicial entries in Frankfurt's Ratsprotokolle (RP), the minutes of the council meetings, and the Bürgermeisterbücher (BB), the minutes of the mayors' meetings.[5]

Victim Identification and Arrest Procedures

The general population played an important role at the initial stage of the judicial prosecution. They acted as crime-reporting and sometimes even arresting agents in addition to serving as witnesses, as clearly documented in seven of the 11 cases under review here. In three of these instances, the Jewish victims, one of them a woman, initiated legal proceedings and in a fourth, the brother of the victim pressed charges.[6] Since in all these cases the suspects were arrested and put on trial, it seems safe to suggest that Jewish people had recourse to Frankfurt's criminal justice system.

The direct accusatorial input of Gentiles can, unfortunately, only be assessed in three cases due to the lack of pertinent data. But despite this shortfall, their respective accounts point to surprising similarities in their observations and actions. In the 1599 murderous attack on a Jewish man in the town of Heidelberg, whose assailant was tried in Frankfurt four years later, all witnesses immediately described the victim as being Jewish.[7] Several of them tried to help the injured, either by lifting him off the ground or by administering wine to him after he had been struck.

Similarly, in an attempted murder of a Jewish man in 1610, four men hearing a "jammerlich Geschrei," heartbreaking scream, rushed to the crime scene.[8] The

[4] The 11 cases are: ST October 16, 1568; ST April 30, 1585; ST April 20, 1592; ST April 18, 1601; ST October 25, 1603; ST July 26, 1610; ST December 23, 1614; ST April 20, 1615; ST July 19, 1649; ST November 17, 1664; ST May 23, 1679.

[5] Criminalia (CR) 137; CR 389; CR 641; CR 745; CR 1113; CR 1268; CR 1430.

[6] ST October 16, 1568; ST November 17, 1664; ST May 23, 1679; ST April 30, 1585.

[7] CR 389.

[8] CR 641.

first on the scene stated that upon arrival, he saw the suspect sitting on top of a Jew. The second witness reported that he found a seriously injured Jew lying on the ground with a man sitting at his side. The third and fourth witnesses gave almost identical renditions in that they described finding a seriously injured Jew lying on the ground. All witnesses stated that they immediately intervened, apprehended the assailant, and brought him to the authorities.

Thirty-nine years later, in a 1649 manslaughter case, witnesses delivered an almost identical descriptive pattern and reported immediate intervention on their part. Over 10 witnesses, after hearing a shot being fired, rushed into the street toward the victims, whom they immediately identified as Jewish. They all tried to help them and in the process apprehended the suspect.[9] One of the witnesses stated that when he reached the scene of the crime, he saw a "Jud uff der Gasse gelegen," a Jew lying in the street, bleeding heavily. Another reported that he found a Jew lying on the ground and that he helped him get up. A third witness added that he helped him up to sit on a bench.

These various witness renditions disclose two remarkable patterns. First, it is rather striking that almost all witnesses immediately recognized the victims as being Jewish, a fact they clearly stated in their depositions. Only one witness reported in the 1610 case that when he reached the crime scene he was not sure whether the victim "was a Christian or a Jew." But the latter's statement of uncertainty only underlines the obvious: the witnesses attached considerable importance to the identity of the victims as being Jewish; otherwise they would surely not have bothered to state it. Second, despite their obvious descriptive emphasis on setting the Jewish victims apart from Gentiles, none of the witnesses hesitated in rendering immediate assistance to the Jewish victims.

This spontaneous, unquestioning help on the part of Gentiles might seem surprising, especially given the fact that in Frankfurt Jews had to live in separate quarters from Christians, in the infamous Judengasse. But, as these examples demonstrate, physical discriminatory segregation did not in all instances translate into individual apathy. Even during the Fettmilch Uprising, some locals tried to protect Jewish people. When the threat of attack on the Judengasse was imminent, "several Jewish families fled in time to the homes of befriended Christians."[10] In one instance, "one city councilor took in approximately 60 Jewish people, among them 10 women who had just given birth."[11] Some of Frankfurt's inhabitants thus not only befriended Jewish people but also shielded

---

9 CR 1113.

10 Isidor Kracauer, *Geschichte der Juden in Frankfurt am Main, 1150–1824* (2 vols, Frankfurt am Main: Kauffman, 1925), vol. 1, p. 386.

11 Ibid.

them in times of serious troubles, an often-neglected aspect of the multifaceted question of contemporary social interaction between the two groups.[12]

While more scholarly research needs to be done to unravel this complex picture, the quandary as to how contemporaries, especially the various witnesses, were able to immediately identify the victims as being Jewish is less opaque. Visual personal insignia played the decisive role. By the end of the fifteenth century, Frankfurt, similar to many other areas in the Holy Roman Empire, started to promulgate dress codes and/or visible insignia to be worn by everyone in society. Specifically tailored to the socio-economic and religious status of the individual, these visual symbols covered the entire spectrum of society, ranging from the local poor to Frankfurt's patricians.[13] These visible signs affected everyone. Jews, however, were the only religious group that had to wear religious identity markers, thus setting them visually apart from Christians. As such, they were easily identifiable, as the above witness renditions clearly demonstrate.

Quite obviously, visual insignia work in two ways. They either protect or negatively single out the bearer. Unfortunately, the latter scenario increasingly, as time went on, bore itself out with regard to Jewish people, as is amply demonstrated by an analysis of Frankfurt's criminal records.[14]

Crimes Committed Against Jews

Conspicuously, but not aberrantly, the perpetrators in eight of the 11 cases sought general economic gains from their Jewish victims. This pattern conformed to the general trend at the time in that most criminals were sentenced for property crimes in Frankfurt during the period in question. However, any possible notion of criminal conformity is immediately punctured by the fact that in four of the eight property crimes the perpetrators also resorted to physically assaulting their Jewish victims. If one adds to these four violent property crimes the two counts of murder and the one murderous assault, a different criminal pattern emerges.

As nine of the 11 crime descriptions demonstrate, this trend was not the result of haphazard actions but rather was based on targeted decisions by the perpetrators. They deliberately selected Jews as their victims. In a 1568 embezzlement incident, two local citizens who were related sought out a local

[12] Robert Jütte touches on the personal relations between the two groups in his "Contacts at the Bedside: Jewish Physicians and their Christian Patients," in Po-Chia Hsia and Lehmann, *In and Out of the Ghetto*, pp. 137–50.

[13] See Chapter 3.

[14] Maria R. Boes, "Jews in the Criminal-Justice System of Early Modern Germany," *Journal of Interdisciplinary History*, 303 (Winter 1999): 407–35.

Jewish man, whom they tied up, beat and forced to write a debtor's note saying that he owed them a huge sum of money. The two local collaborators had carefully selected a local Jew as their victim.

And so had the three perpetrators who robbed and brutally murdered three Jewish merchants near Strasbourg in 1583.[15] Their intent to select Jews becomes evident from the judicial records of one of the assailants put on trial in Frankfurt a year after the attack. The records contain a statement issued by the bishop of Strasbourg shortly before the murderous hold-up of the three Jewish men. The bishop had alerted "his Jews" to be careful since street robbers were roaming about. Quite obviously, based on the bishop's selective warning to "his Jews," Jews were the prime targets of marauding highway robbers.

The six culprits in the December 1614 case exhibit similar motivations.[16] All of them had not only participated in the attack on the Judengasse during the Fettmilch Uprising, but they had also returned to the Jewish street at a later date, breaking into houses during nighttime. The location of the crime scene leaves no doubt about their targets: Jewish people.

More explicit was a local soldier's statement in the 1615 incident. He and his fellows proceeded with their robbery and assault only once they realized that the possible victim was a "Jud."[17] Another even more explicitly targeted operation occurred in 1679.[18] A goldsmith and seal-maker from out of town headed to Frankfurt's Judengasse, where he approached a Jewish woman to have her exchange some of his ducats of Dutch imprint. The Jewish woman, immediately recognizing the coins as forgeries, filed an official complaint, leading to the arrest of the suspect. The accused bluntly asserted to Frankfurt's authorities that he had wanted to exchange the faulty coins only to Jews and that, therefore, no harm was done.[19]

Similar intentions but with a twist were disclosed in the 1664 case.[20] This time both the victim and the perpetrators were Jewish. A local Jewish "medico" complained about the theft of a large sum of money as well as expensive jewelry out of his house in the Judengasse. He pointed to several Jewish men, one of whom had stayed in the victim's house for a week as a guest and had thus become familiar with the crime scene,[21] hence a perfectly targeted operation to steal

---

15 CR 137.

16 ST December 23, 1614.

17 CR 745.

18 ST May 23, 1679 and CR 1430.

19 CR 1430.

20 ST November 11, 1664.

21 CR 1268.

from a fellow Jew. While the main culprits escaped successfully, "Itzig, Jud von Prague," as the records describe him, became the judicial fall guy.

Physical assaults against Jewish people disclose a similarly selective trend on the part of the perpetrators. Of the murderous assault on a Jewish man in the town of Heidelberg, the four eyewitnesses gave almost identical renditions of the unfolding of the event. A citizen of Frankfurt, who had been standing quietly beside a stove in a local tavern suddenly took a big stick, walked over to the Jewish man and hit him over the head so vigorously that he fell to the ground and died.[22] According to the witnesses the victim had not given the attacker any reason or cause for his assault. Indeed, the Jewish man had minded his own business and appeared to have been very happy and jovial and humming a tune. Since no theft or robbery had taken place and the attacker had not acted in self-defense, this unprovoked murderous attack occurred solely because the victim was Jewish.

Two additional assault cases corroborate this selective, unprovoked victimization pattern. In June of 1610, a Jewish man was attacked "uff offener Strass," in the street.[23] According to the victim, the assailant started physically assaulting him, which he initially mistook as an attempt to rob him. But when he threw the attacker his purse, the assailant disregarded the gesture and attacked him even more ferociously, first with a pike, then with his knife. The various witnesses, who ran to the scene after hearing the "jämmerlich Geschrei," dreadful screams, had the following to say. Two witnesses who helped subdue the offender testified that the culprit had voiced his intention of killing the Jew and leaving him at the spot of the deed. A third witness reported that the perpetrator had told him that he wanted to beat the Jew to death. A fourth repeated a similar outburst on the part of the offender, who screamed "ich hät ihn todt geschmissen," I would have beaten him to death. Most startling, however, was the testimony of a fifth witness. He had questioned the culprit at the scene of the crime as to the motivation for his murderous assault on the Jewish man. The attacker admitted that the "Jud" had done him no harm. But he continued to assert that he had hoped "to kill the highly defenseless Jew."

From the various witnesses' accounts and the culprit's own admission one cannot conclude that this was a robbery in progress. Money was not the issue here. What triggered the attack was obviously the fact that the victim was Jewish. An added "incentive" for the attack was delivered in the assailant's own words stressing the defenselessness of the Jew. He must have been aware of the

22 CR 389.

23 CR 641.

fact that Jews were not allowed to bear arms, which quite obviously made them more vulnerable to attacks.[24] They could and did become easy prey.

Equally defenseless were the three Jewish men walking in town prior to being shot at by a soldier, leaving one dead and another seriously injured.[25] Based on the testimonies of the various witnesses, the following picture emerged in this 1649 incident. A soldier, who had been drinking with other soldiers in a local tavern, went to the house where he was a lodger, fetched his rifle, cleaned it and shot at three Jewish men who were walking by, killing one of them and seriously injuring another. Many locals who heard the shot and the screams of the Jews ran to the crime scene. But none of them had actually observed the entire unfolding of the assault. Only the victims did and one of them was able to speak up. But his account contradicted that of the soldier.

While the soldier claimed repeatedly that he had not been aware of the approaching Jews and that they must have run into the shots, the Jewish witness who had been in the company of the two who were shot stated that he saw the soldier aiming at them and that he screamed at him to lower his gun. It was only because he, the witness, immediately jumped back that he saved his own life. Eventually, the soldier, caught up in his own contradictions, admitted that at approximately eight feet away from him he had seen the "Jews coming around the corner."

Most perplexingly, and in stark contrast to these predominantly violent physical attacks on Jewish people, no Jewish person was ever convicted in Frankfurt for having committed murder, manslaughter or murder and robbery during the time period under discussion.[26] This disquieting picture only highlights the selective nature of assaults on Jews. While contemporaries did not have a linguistic legal expression for such targeted discriminatory crimes, their nature is quite obvious: hate. Hate crimes thus have a much longer history than has generally been acknowledged. They extend back far beyond the official inception of this designated legal term coined and put into practice only toward the end of the twentieth century.

Frankfurt's authorities were aware of targeted attacks on Jewish people. They were also cognizant of the fact that soldiers and artisans were the main perpetrators. By openly admonishing soldiers to refrain from antagonizing Jewish people they showed their concern.[27] And by issuing similar exhortations

---

24 Guido Kisch, *Forschungen zur Rechts- und Sozialgeschichte der Juden in Deutschland während des Mittelalters* (Sigmaringen: Thorbecke, 1978), pp. 33–40.

25 CR 1113.

26 Boes, "Jews in the Criminal-Justice System," p. 425.

27 RP July 5, 1683, p 24.

to local artisans they acknowledged another group of agitators.[28] But such admonitions have far wider ramifications. They testify to the fact that individual physical attacks on Jewish people occurred much more frequently than officially reported and/or judicially prosecuted.

These findings, in turn, raise the momentous question as to how Frankfurt adjudicated those who were actually brought to justice. How did this apparent and widely known Jewish victimology pattern translate into judicial/penal actions? This question is worth serious consideration since pre-selecting a crime victim fell into the category of premeditated criminal acts, which were to entail serious penal consequences.

Judicial and Penal Practices

Most interestingly, Frankfurt's judicial authorities did, in fact, increasingly resort to focusing their legal and penal deliberations on Jewish aspects when dealing with Jewish victims and/or Jewish witnesses. And so did the suspected criminals. This trend started to emerge by the end of the sixteenth century and reached unprecedented proportions by the mid- to late seventeenth. But it was not a positive pattern for Jews in the criminal justice system. On the contrary, the case descriptions disclose progressively heightened negative religious and racial attitudes toward Jewish crime victims and Jewish witnesses expressed by both the authorities and the suspects.

While the trial procedures and penalty meted out in the 1568 case of the beating of a Jewish man and forcing him to write an IOU corresponded to general contemporary patterns, the subsequent 1583 incident discloses a slightly different trend. In the 1568 incident, the authorities arrested the suspects two days after the Jewish victim had initiated legal proceedings against them. They debated the case during nine sessions, consulted with two of their municipal advocates and subjected the suspects to judicial torture. And, as was common practice at the time, they also heard pleas for milder punishments from two of the suspects' relatives. After two months of incarceration—a lengthy prison stay—Frankfurt's city council sentenced the culprits to the pillory, in addition to having to wear a special hat depicting their crimes. Subsequently, they were banished for life.[29] Since the culprits were citizens of Frankfurt, being publicly ridiculed and exposed to their fellow burghers and being banished from town must be considered a severe sentence.

---

[28] Kracauer, *Geschichte der Juden*, p. 397.

[29] ST October 16, 1568.

The 1583 case of the robbery and murder of three Jewish tradesmen near Strasbourg, while exhibiting similar trial procedures, demonstrates considerable penal changes.[30] Based on the accusation of the brother of one of the murdered victims, a soldier was arrested in Frankfurt. The suspect refused to admit his involvement despite having been additionally and most seriously incriminated in a written witness report by one of the other participants in the crime. His constant refusal led Frankfurt's city council to subject him to judicial torture. He did not confess. The councilors, still harboring doubt as to his innocence, had him tortured again two months later. Again, the suspect refused to plead guilty.[31] Not satisfied with this outcome, the city council continued to detain him the "entire winter in prison," whereupon he "lastly confessed."

Yet despite his heinous crime, robbery and participation in a murderous attack—cutting the throats of the three Jewish merchants—Frankfurt's city council sentenced him to execution by the sword. While a capital sentence is under any circumstances the ultimate punishment, other culprits who had committed similar crimes received punishments exceeding the harsh method of this form of execution. In a case from 1575, for example, Frankfurt's authorities resorted to breaking the culprit on the wheel.[32]

Arguably this 1583 sentence might still be interpreted as somewhat of an aberration; but no such reservations can be voiced for the remaining nine cases. Not only did the Jewish identity of both victims and witnesses increasingly take a negative center stage but also in eight of these cases the culprits received a banishment sentence only, blatantly disregarding the severity of the crimes they had committed. Most tellingly, the only exception where the suspect was meted out a stiff sentence was that of a Jewish culprit.

In the 1592 case when the culprit cheated a Jewish man by exchanging stones for good money, he was handed down a banishment sentence only. Similarly and even more troubling were the banishment sentences meted out to the two soldiers who in 1601 attacked several Jews on the open road. Banishment sentences were also meted out to the six men who had not only participated in the plundering of the Jewish street during the Fettmilch Uprising but who had also later returned there to carry out further break-ins.[33] The soldier who had participated in the robbery of a Jewish man also received a mild punishment, banishment, by Frankfurt's city council, although the two municipal advocates,

---

30 CR 137.

31 RP March 30, 1585, p. 80.

32 ST July 15, 1575.

33 RP March 24, 1601, p. 84; April 16, 1601, p. 89; BB April 16, 1601, p. 290;and ST April 18, 1601. ST December 23, 1614; RP November 10, 1614, p. 52; January 13, 1614, p. 59; December 20, 1614, p. 61; BB December 20, 1614, p. 202.

Drs. Christoph Kellner and Caspar Gabriel Rasor, had suggested he at least be put into the pillory and subsequently banished.[34]

Murder and murderous assaults selectively perpetrated against Jews are equally if not more indicative of this softening penal trend, such as the 1603 case involving a local burgher who had killed a Jewish man in Heidelberg for no apparent reason other than that he was Jewish and was banished only. Although Frankfurt's three advocates realized the premeditated nature of the crime, they subsequently softened their stance. Dr. Johann Baptist Caesar, who three years later would write and publish the anti-Jewish tract "Der Judenspiegel," the Jewish mirror, which eventually led to his dismissal as Frankfurt's advocate, opted for a legal loophole in this particular case. He stated that since the culprit had not been arrested after the deed and since nobody had accused him legally—knowledge of the deed emerged during another indictment—one ought to show mercy and banish him and have him fight the Turks for several years. Dr. Caspar Schacher, who would be accused of corruption in 1612 during the Fettmilch Uprising and quietly removed from office, declared that since the victim was a "Jud who had mingled too frivolously with Christians," the suspect should be shown mercy—a move backed by the third advocate, Dr. Christoph Kellner. Frankfurt's city councilors sentenced him to lifelong banishment because, as explicitly stated, they wanted to spare his life "out of mercy."[35] This was the only case during the 1562 to 1696 period in which a murderer literally got away with murder.[36]

The 1610 local murderous attack on a Jewish man evidences similar features. True, the victim survived the very serious assault, but according to the culprit's own repeated admissions he wanted to kill the defenseless Jew for no other reason than his being Jewish. This particular incidence greatly disturbed the local Jewish community. The Baumeister sent a written petition to Frankfurt's city council citing the concerns of the Jewish community, stressing the criminal's checkered past and, most importantly, the suspect's repeated statements of intent to kill the Jewish man. In separate pleas, both he and the victim asked for a strict sentence, referring to the premeditated nature of the murderous attack and their fear that similar attacks might happen on fellow Jews unless a severe sentence were meted out.[37]

Frankfurt's city councilors, seemingly taking this case very seriously, initiated various medical reports by local barber-surgeons and inquired about the seriousness of the wounds, which proved to be of a severe nature. They also

34 CR 745 and ST April 20, 1615.

35 BB October 25, 1603, p. 142.

36 CR 389.

37 CR 641.

contacted the authorities of the offender's previous place of residence to inquire about his past conduct. But instead of being informed of the offender's troubled past as stipulated by the Baumeister, they were told that the suspect had been a pious and decent man all his life. It was, so they were informed, without a doubt the Jew who had enticed the suspect to this action.[38] Frankfurt's three advocates, Drs. Caspar Schacher, Christoph Kellner and Caspar Gabriel Rasor, while mentioning the backhandedness of this murderous assault with the intent to kill, nevertheless recommended that the murderous assailant be handed down a banishment sentence.

Absurdly suggesting that the Jewish victim had caused his own demise was a curious but not isolated twist. The soldier who shot two Jewish men, killing one and severely injuring the other, advanced a similar self-infliction theme by alleging that the victims had walked into the shots he fired. Yet he eventually got caught up in his own statements and had to rescind his initial denial of even having seen the approaching Jewish men, a contradiction which raised the concern of Frankfurt's advocates. They now proceeded to carefully compare the culprit's testimony to the one presented by the third, unharmed, Jew who had asserted that the suspect had not only aimed at them but also that he, the witness, had warned him to put down the gun. The Jewish witness's statement, however, did not seem to greatly impress them. The advocate Dr. Maximilian Faust von Aschaffenburg, adding a highly disparaging parenthetical remark in his legal deposition, claimed that the Jewish witness "als ein Jud einem Christen nicht glaubhaft genug zu achten ist," as a Jew is not to be trusted as much as a Christian—a remark which was not challenged or questioned further by the other two advocates, Drs. Jacob Schütz and Lucas Kupferschmidt.[39]

This, in the literal sense prejudicial legal comment against Jewish people is astonishing, all the more so since no such denigrating references are contained in the official criminal code for the Holy Roman Empire, the *Constitutio Criminalis Carolina*.[40] To Frankfurt's credit, despite the advocate's biased judicial note, the authorities continued with their legal pursuit. They even subjected the suspect to judicial torture. However, the accused did not confess to having deliberately shot the Jewish men. He also denied that he had just tried to scare them. And, as if to stress the latter point, he asserted, without having been questioned to that effect, that he had no "Feindschaft uff der Juden," no animosity toward Jews. The suspect's wife did not share this sentiment. In her plea to the city council to release her husband, she added a different perspective, turning Jewish-specific

38 Ibid.

39 CR 1113.

40 Johann Christoph Koch, ed., *Hals- oder peinliche Gerichtsordnung Kaiser Carls V* (Goldbach: Keip, 1996).

rhetoric into distinctive religiously tainted allegations. She argued that her innocent husband should not be condemned because of such "abergläubischen Juden," heretical Jews.

Quite obviously the unfolding of this trial demonstrates a noticeable increase in negative references to *Jewishness* as a judicial issue. This change in the judicial climate seemed to have been noticed in the Jewish community as well, for friends, the brother and brother-in-law of the two Jewish victims sent petitions to the city council stressing Jewish–Christian interactions. They emphasized that regardless of whether the victims be "Juden oder Christen," Jews or Christians, innocent blood should not be spilled in vain and such heinous deeds should not go unpunished. All three of Frankfurt's advocates took up the theme of innocent blood, and they also seem to have concurred with the Jewish community's assessment of the seriousness of the case. Yet, Dr. Johann Jacob Schütz digressed in his legal brief by asserting that the victim "was only a Jew," an argument implicitly bolstered by Dr. Lucas Kupferschmidt's repeated references to Christian mercy for the accused.

By contrast to these religious insinuations, the advocates, in their final legal and penal suggestion, advanced purely legal reasons. They argued that the suspect had been "purgirt," purged, because he had not admitted, even under torture, to having shot the Jews intentionally. Therefore, he ought to be banished only, a verdict the city council accepted.

The 1664 trial of "Itzig Jud von Prague" echoes this negative judicial and penal selectivity but in a reverse context.[41] Itzig was allegedly implicated in a theft which had taken place in Abraham's home in the Judengasse. The victim himself reported the crime but had to back his claim by swearing an oath specially designed for Jewish people, the Judeneid. As a consequence, Itzig was arrested. After answering some initial identification queries, such as that he was from Poland, he asserted that he had not participated in this theft, that no one had given him any merchandise and that nothing had been found on him upon his arrest. He explained that a Jewish man by the name of Daniel had asked him to do him a favor and carry a bag from the Judengasse to his friend Liebermann in Bornheim, one of Frankfurt's suburbs, which he had done. Itzig asserted that he had no knowledge of the contents of this bag and that, after this transaction, they parted company without any further verbal exchange. Partly based on the fact that Frankfurt's authorities were not satisfied with his answers, and partly based on advocate Dr. Anton Glock's remark that the "incarcerated Jew is a Pole," Itzig was to confront one of Abraham's witnesses.

---

41 CR 1268.

This Jewish–Polish theme resurfaced during the actual confrontation. But this time the suspect initiated it. Itzig refuted the witness's claim of having taken a purse full of money out of his, Itzig's, trousers. He also denied that he was about to flee when the witness apprehended him and brought him to the authorities. Instead he argued that he had very little money in his purse, that he did not try to escape but that, instead, the witness had beaten him severely for "he as a Polish Jew was very much hated by German Jews."

Eventually, however, Itzig confessed that he had a lot of money in his purse. Yet he continually asserted that he was at a loss to understand how it got there. Frankfurt's advocates, Drs. Anton Glock and Martin Rasor, seemed to be in a quandary. Two other suspects, one of whom had lodged with the victim for a week, seemed to be the main culprits. But both had escaped. In addition, they were uncertain about Itzig's role in this scheme. They decided to have Itzig subjected to judicial torture either via the leg- and/or thumbscrew.

Prior to the actual application of the torture instruments, Itzig was asked additional personal questions, such as why he had come to Frankfurt. He replied that being a poor Jew he came there to receive alms. When questioned as to why he did not remain in Poland he answered that he no longer could support himself there since everything was decayed. He also told the interrogators that for six years he had been a children's instructor to two Jewish families in nearby Mayence. When asked why he did not stay there, he replied that they did not need a teacher anymore.

He now also explained his earlier refusal to admit that he had a large sum of money in his purse. He claimed that he originally had denied this out of fear since one of the Jewish suspects had given him the money. But he again refuted having had any knowledge of the crime. Not satisfied with his explanations, the interrogators decided to apply the thumbscrew, which was "soweit als möglich zugeschraubt," tightened as much as possible. However, Itzig still did not confess. As a consequence, he now was subjected to the application of the leg screws as well. It was only when he "screamed very loudly and behaved strangely" that the interrogators, realizing that "no further news could be extricated from him, and (that) he appeared very weak, and (that) since he repeatedly asserted during his screams that he had said everything he knew," stopped the torturous procedure.

During the advocates' ensuing penal deliberations, none of them stated that since Itzig had not confessed even under the most severe torture that he was "purgirt." On the contrary, the argument was advanced that stealing "auch bei den Juden," also among the Jews—especially "the Polish ones"—was becoming too common. While Dr. Rasor suggested Itzig be put in the pillory and banished, Dr. Glock was much more adamant. He suggested that Itzig be branded on a "sichtbaren Ort," a visible spot, and subsequently either flogged or put into the pillory and banished. Consequently, Itzig was branded on his right cheek with an F, standing for "furti," theft, in addition to being put into the pillory and banished.

Itzig's case discloses flagrant judicial and penal disparities both when compared to the 1649 case of the soldier who killed a Jewish man and wounded another, and with branding penalties in general. The soldier was "purgirt" after he withstood torture; Itzig was not, although he had been subjected to far harsher torture procedures than the soldier, a not uncommon practice with regard to Jewish suspects.[42] The soldier was sentenced to banishment. Itzig was branded on the face. While branding in itself is an extremely severe punishment, in Itzig's case it must be regarded as even more so since branding had not been in use in Frankfurt since 1568. Most tellingly, when it was reintroduced in 1664, it was almost exclusively applied to Jews. Out of the seven culprits who were subjected to branding, six were Jews and, while "the non-Jewish culprit was branded on his neck, all six Jews were branded on their faces."[43]

By the mid-seventeenth century being Jewish had thus become a conspicuous issue in contemporary trials. And no case demonstrates this better than the 1676–77 trial which exposed not only flagrant negative religious allegations but also a new element: strong racial overtones.

An astute Frankfurt Jewish woman launched this 1676 trial by reporting that a goldsmith had asked her to exchange coins of Dutch mint, which she immediately recognized as counterfeits. The suspect was arrested and questioned but refused to admit that it was he who had contacted the Jewish woman. Instead he argued that she erred because, as he claimed, one person resembled another. During several follow-up interrogations he repeated these assertions, arguing that the Jewish woman was mistaken.

In the meantime, three Jewish men from out of town accused the same suspect of the same crime of having exchanged faulty coins with them in their respective towns. The accused, similar to his earlier argument, stated that the three Jewish men erred and that it was not he who had exchanged the coins. But the three Jewish men remained adamant in their claims, which they eventually substantiated by swearing the Judeneid, the Jewish oath. The accused, however, while still steadfastly refusing his involvement with the three Jewish men, finally admitted that he had, indeed, tried to exchange faulty coins with the Jewish woman. As a justification for his deceitful action he claimed that since he had

---

42 Boes, "Jews in the Criminal-Justice System," pp. 418–19 clearly demonstrates this pattern. See also Otto Ulbricht, "Criminality and Punishment of the Jews in the Early Modern Period," in Po-Chia Hsia and Lehmann, *In and Out of the Ghetto*, p. 68, who stated that "jurists demanded that torture be used with less restraint against Jews."

43 Boes, "Jews in the Criminal-Justice System," pp. 432–3.

only wanted to conduct this exchange with Jews, it should not have any dire consequences.

This condescending, if not reckless, attitude toward Jewish people emerged as the central theme for the entire trial, as clearly evidenced by the over 600 pages of trial documentation.[44] The suspect, while in his initial defense had claimed that the Jewish accusers were mistaken, soon turned the charges against him upside down by putting the blame on the accusers simply because they were Jewish.

Increasingly anti-Jewish arguments emerged ranging from religious invectives to strong racially denigrating arguments, obviously in the hopes of achieving a milder punishment if not a dismissal of all charges against him, an initiative carefully orchestrated by a jurist, whom the suspect and his staunchest defenders, his wife and his brother, had hired. He not only wrote vehement pleas for his clients but also laced them, in contemporary judicial fashion, with Latin phrases.

The first targeted legal indication of the suspect's about-face occurred during a follow-up interrogation. He now proceeded to portray Jewish people in general as liars, obviously with the aim of discrediting and thus derailing the Jewish accusers' claims. He tried to buttress this claim with a religious assertion by labeling Jews as foes of Christians. The introduction of this new religious theme proved to be a successful legal avenue, for it led to the opening of a veritable religious-legal floodgate which was to dominate the remainder of the trial.

The suspect's wife took up this lead in her numerous pleas to the city council but she, in turn, added another novel feature, racial insinuations, by asserting that all Jews were "by nature cheating usurers."[45] The suspect's brother intensified the religious allegations in his plea. He argued that the "Jews wrongly accused our redeemer and savior, lied to him and cheated him, lashed him and tortured him and finally nailed him to the cross," and declared they are "up to today the mortal foes of Christians." He concluded his plea with the legal claim that Jewish "unchristians" were not to be admitted as witnesses against Christians. The suspect's and his entourage's objective was thus clearly stated. According to them

---

44 CR 1430.

45 The origin of the "by nature" argument seems to be still somewhat elusive to historians. While R. Po-Chia Hsia, "The Usurious Jew: Economic Structure and Religious Presentations in an Anti-Semitic Discourse," in Po-Chia Hsia and Lehmann, *In and Out of the Ghetto*, pp. 169–70, cogently argues that it originated with the Protestant Reformation "born of the evangelical movement, which identified an innate, racial character," Henry Kamen, *The Spanish Inquisition* (London: Weidenfeld & Nicolson, 1965), pp. 123–9, points to similar occurrences in Catholic Spain, especially what he calls the "racialist movement" of the Limpieza de Sangre.

there was no basis for a trial in the first place since all the witnesses, who were also the accusers, were anti-Christian Jewish liars and as such their statements were not to be trusted; they had forfeited their legal prosecutorial rights.

This carefully thought out religious-legal finesse had been prepared by a jurist the family had consulted and it presented the prosecution with a thorny problem, with implications exceeding this particular case. If taken seriously it would send a dangerous message to everyone in society that it was all right to cheat and attack Jewish people because, while Jewish people could file legal charges against their tormentors, the accusations would be dismissed in court as unsustainable. Frankfurt's city councilors and advocates were thus faced with a case of potentially serious legal and societal repercussions.

While to Frankfurt's city councilors credit, they did not cave in to these legal allegations, their three municipal advocates, Drs. Georg Schuster, Martin Rasor and Anton Glock, were not quite as steadfast in their approach. And their hesitation should not come as a surprise. Recall that it was one of Frankfurt's own advocates, Dr. Maximilian Faust von Aschaffenburg, whose 1649 parenthetical remark had offered a watered-down version of this very same theme when he suggested that Jewish witnesses were less trustworthy than Christians.

Seemingly cornered by the religious-legal anti-Jewish line of argumentation, Frankfurt's advocates, yielding, now tried to locate a Christian witness who would back up the Jewish witnesses' claims. They were successful. A "Christian" witness, as the record explicitly state, was located. It was a maid who had observed one of the incidents, and she confirmed the Jewish witnesses' stance. But her statement was obviously not entirely satisfactory, for she was subsequently also confronted with the suspect.

Even this confrontation turned into a quasi-religious drama. The suspect, who had to put on his coat for identification purposes, used this opportunity to compare this procedure to the "suffering of Christ who had to put on his clothes, then remove them, and Jews were witnessing." He then accused the maid, who had recognized him and confirmed her earlier report, of having been instructed by Jews to say so, an allegation she vehemently denied.

But the allegations discrediting Jewish people did not stop. Underscoring this religious line of defense, but adding, again, a racial overtone, the suspect's wife, in yet another plea to the city council, repeated the allegations that Jews were not to serve as witnesses since they were by nature the foe of Christians. Again this repeat-line of defense proved to be successful. Frankfurt's advocates recontacted the authorities of one of the towns where one of the Jewish witnesses had given his testimony; they not only requested that he be requestioned under the "Judeneid" but they also inquired whether there were other, Christian, witnesses. When they learned that the Jewish witness had reconfirmed his earlier statement and that there were no other Christian witnesses, Frankfurt's city council, refusing to concede to the defense's claims, decided to seek outside legal help. They sent the entire dossier to the legal faculty of the University of Tübingen.

Obviously, Frankfurt's advocates did not take a definite legal stance, appearing unsure, intimidated or possibly clandestinely in agreement with the religious-legal claim. The suspect had succeeded in making legal inroads. However, in sharp contrast to their soft religious-legal stance, the advocates strongly opposed another of the suspect's claims: to be accorded an official defensor, defender, of his choice. Early on in the trial the suspect and his family wanted the writer of their personal pleas as their defensor, a request turned down by Dr. Martin Rasor, who claimed that if a defensor were to be admitted he had to be a person of good standing who would not bring bad repute to the authorities—an interesting statement implicitly questioning the integrity of at least some fellow jurists. Various repeated claims, and even the suggestion of another defensor, Dr. Bader, were turned down by Frankfurt's advocates, while Frankfurt's city council was more amenable to this request and so was the University of Tübingen.

In their reply, the law faculty of Tübingen suggested admitting a defensor, although they did not see any problems with this case. They argued that the suspect had knowingly and deliberately tried to pass counterfeit ducats to a Jewish woman, a deed aggravated by the fact that the suspect had initially refused to admit his intent. They also declared that the Jewish accusers were reliable witnesses since they had not only given their testimonies under the special Jewish oath, but also that their testimonies had been consistent throughout. As to the suspect's anti-Jewish argumentation, Tübingen's faculty announced that he, the suspect, "pretends that the Jews are the foe of Christians."

But not even this clear-cut legal decision settled the case. Frankfurt's city council and its advocates did not sentence the suspect. On the contrary, when they eventually approved the suspect's alternate choice of legal defensor, Dr. Bader, it did little to settle the cases. On the contrary, this defensor—who, as the advocate Dr. Glock perceptively pointed out, "pretends to be so religious"—intensified the religious coaching of the suspect and his family, who deluged Frankfurt's authorities with letters of sweeping denigrating generalizations about Jewish people. Reasserting that they, the Jews, had "falsely accused our redeemer and savior"; that they "lied and cheated, flogged him and tortured him and finally nailed him to the cross"; and that—again stressing the racial element—they are "by nature and up to today the mortal enemy of the Christians," the accused and his family concluded again that because of these traits they are not to be admitted as witnesses against a Christian. In one striking analogy the suspect's brother even compared the behavior of the Jews "in Jerusalem" at the time of Christ's trial to the "present case against my brother."

Not surprisingly, the suspect's over 20-page long "Summarische Defension Schrift," Summary Defense Document, prepared by their legal advisor, was again replete with anti-Jewish statements focusing on the alleged evil nature and behavior of all Jewish people against Christians. Jews were repeatedly portrayed as "persecutors of Christians," as "cheating by nature" and as "lazy people who lived off Christians' sweat and blood," especially by exchanging "gold and silver." Hence, repeating their frequent previous legal allegations, Jews could not be witnesses against Christians.

The jurist who had provided the suspect and his entourage with legal advice was thus not only well versed in legal matters but also in contemporary theological/religious anti-Jewish exegeses and he used this combination to intimidate and/or convince their legal opponents, Frankfurt's advocates, as well as the city council. Even a most cursory reading of the numerous anti-Jewish allegations contained in the various pleas and in the Summary Defense Document exhibit undeniable similarities to Martin Luther in his *On the Jews and Their Lies*. The central theme of portraying Jewish people as liars is the most obvious and clearly reflects Luther's tract, in which he relentlessly pounds on this argument. Even the various linguistic expressions used in the pleas resemble Luther's own words too precisely to have been accidently chosen. Words such as "Faulenzer," lazy person, "Schweiss und Blut," sweat and blood, are replicas taken directly out of Luther's tract, particularly Articles 293, 310, 312 and 359. The defensor's approach thus attests not only to a heightened anti-Jewish sentiment but also to the continuation, if not intensification, of religious, particular Lutheran, impetus in the judicial process—a process discounted by some scholars.[46]

Frankfurt's city councilors, who had shown a remarkable resistance to the suspect's anti-Jewish legal arguments, nevertheless, failed to sentence him to a corporal or capital punishment frequently meted out to persons who had committed a similar crime. True, they kept the suspect incarcerated for close to 40 weeks and thus had taken a stoic stance, but they ignored the university's legal opinion, yielding instead to their own advocates' advice, who, in turn, had exhibited a less than stellar legal consistency during the trial. They repeatedly gave in to anti-Jewish legal claims, a tendency most clearly demonstrated by their final penal suggestion by opting for a 10-year banishment sentence, which, so they argued, was based on the fact that this case had not only turned into a cause célèbre, news of which had spread around Frankfurt's neighborhood and

[46] Such as Michael Stolleis, "Grundzüge der Beamtenethik (1500–1650)," in Roman Schnur, ed., *Die Rolle der Juristen bei der Entstehung des modernen Staates* (Berlin: Duncker & Humblot, 1986).

throughout the Holy Roman Empire, but also that the suspect had received numerous pleas and that he had endured a long incarceration.

This opinion exhibits a seemingly pragmatic approach, especially by circumventing the central religious anti-Jewish legal arguments advanced by the opposition. However, it was just the omission of not addressing this topic, and of not rebutting any of the numerous religious-legal claims of the opposition, which turned the advocates' legal opinion into a legal surrender. Frankfurt's advocates as well as the city councilors surrendered to the anti-Jewish legal-religious arguments. On July 10, 1677 the city council banished the culprit for 10 years.

As if to give this trial a last special last twist, a written note on one of the documents states that the suspect was executed by sword in the nearby town of Hanau on February 6, 1701. His crime: the exchange of faulty coins.

Summary

This last trial leaves no doubt that Jews were deliberately selected as crime victims in the hopes that by increasingly exposing if not subjecting them to religious and racially denigrating treatment during the judicial process, their credibility as accusers and witnesses would be undermined. This reverse legal criminal psychology turned victims into alleged criminal instigators if not outright offenders.

Thus, being Jewish had not only taken center stage in criminal trials by the late seventeenth century but also was seriously and negatively affecting the outcome of the trials. It was a slowly evolving process in which Frankfurt's own advocates played a decisive part. It can be traced to one of their 1649 remarks questioning the validity of Jewish witnesses as compared to their Christian counterparts and their denigrating if not dismissive description of a Jewish murder victim as "only a Jew." Frankfurt's city council contributed its share by consistently lowering the penal threshold for those who had robbed, attacked and murdered Jewish victims while increasing it for the Jewish perpetrator.[47]

In a small community like Frankfurt such penal patterns could hardly go unnoticed. This might explain why the suspects selected Jews as their victims and why the various suspects and their families increasingly founded their defense on religious and racial anti-Jewish polemics. While there existed beacons of hope, such as the spontaneous and unsolicited helpful actions of Gentile crime witnesses, especially in cases of murderous assaults, Jewish crime victims were

---

[47] As demonstrated for Frankfurt by Boes, "Jews in the Criminal-Justice System," p. 434.

increasingly bereft of substantive legal recourse. True, Jewish plaintiffs could and did start legal criminal proceedings against their attackers, but they were not successful in achieving the same results as Gentiles.

This development parallels the substantial increase of Jewish criminal suspects by the late seventeenth century, when "public anti-Jewish outbursts such as the 1614 Fettmilch Uprising were replaced by more 'refined' judicial attacks."[48] Thus, Jewish people were not only increasingly targeted as crime, frequently hate crime, victims but also as judicial victims and "the court system served as a veiled discriminatory weapon."[49]

[48] Ibid., p. 435; and this development should not come as a surprise given the general tenor of anti-Jewish backlash especially towards the 1650s to 1670s which was most clearly exemplified by the expelling action initiated by the nearby town of Fulda, which decided in 1677 "to drive out the bulk of the Jews" despite the fact that it had been "one of the most ancient communities in Germany." Jonathan I. Israel, *European Jewry in the Age of Mercantilism, 1550–1750*, 2nd ed. (Oxford: Clarendon, 1989,) pp. 146–7.

[49] Boes, "Jews in the Criminal Justice System," p. 435.

Chapter 6

Enough is Enough: Two Jewish Resistance Trials

In two different instances, and one year apart, Jewish men were sentenced for fighting back over insults and injustices they felt they had endured. Both cases occurred during the last decades of the seventeenth century, that is, at a time when Jews were increasingly and disproportionally sentenced for crimes, especially under the infamous Verdachtstrafe, a punishment for being suspicious. Out of a total of 26 such sentences 13 were handed down to Jews—as clearly documented.[1] It was also during the same period that Jews experienced increasingly unfair judicial treatments as crime victims, as so clearly demonstrated in the previous chapter. Their living conditions in the segregated and cramped Judengasse, the Jewish street, could only have accentuated their desperation. Possible pent-up anger, turned inward for too long, might partly explain the highly emotional character of these two cases of Jewish physical and verbal reactions.

The first incident occurred in 1683 and involved an alleged physical assault by several Jewish men on a soldier; the second, of 1684, constituted the crime of lese-majesty, in this particular case an alleged insulting verbal outburst against one of Frankfurt's mayors by the son of a local Jewish man. Both incidents took place in the Judengasse in the presence of witnesses and, most tellingly, both involved soldiers, the very group which had repeatedly been admonished by Frankfurt's city council to abstain from harassing Jewish people.

The 1683 Case

This complex criminal trial was based on a total of 14 witness accounts, the statements of three suspects and the victim's testimony. Medical reports, personal pleas and, in particular, Frankfurt's advocates' legal opinions served to elucidate the judicial handling of the case. Also, apart from these criminal and judicial procedures, the various documents, especially the witnesses' renditions, disclosed cultural aspects difficult to extract from other sources of a predominantly oral society.[2]

[1] Maria R. Boes, "Jews in the Criminal-Justice System of Early Modern Germany," *Journal of Interdisciplinary History*, 30/3 (Winter 1999): 407–35.

[2] Criminalia (CR) 1585.

The answers to who saw what were diligently recorded during the various interrogations, and so were several confrontations between the accused and the witnesses. The unfolding of the trial began with the questioning of two Judenbaumeister, Jewish lay officials, who were asked about their knowledge of what had transpired during a physical assault on a soldier close to the gate to the Judengasse allegedly carried out by several Jewish men. Both assured Frankfurt's authorities that they did not know anything about the incident. But they took this opportunity to complain about a Bierhaus, tavern, whose back door opened onto the Judengasse, and from where rowdy drunks exited, causing consternation and broken windows in the Jewish community.

While nobody was implicated by this disclosure, Frankfurt's authorities took up their complaint and asked the gate-keeper to verify these allegations, which he did—confirming that during the evenings many fights erupted at the exit of the tavern. Asked whether he knew anything about this specific case, he denied it, stating that he had not been present at the beginning of the assault. He had been in the company of servants and a shoe repairer in the bleaching garden. However, he did hear a commotion, which prompted him to run to the gate where he found a good 100 people standing in front of it. When he opened the door, he saw a guy lying on the ground proclaimed dead by various surrounding people. But, he inserted, he had heard from others that the guy on the ground had been very drunk and that someone had taken his sword.

Frankfurt's authorities immediately pursued this after-the-fact account by questioning the said shoe repairer, who was readily available. He declared, similar to the gate-keeper, that he had not witnessed the unfolding of events. Instead, when he arrived at the scene, military security personnel had already been there and a military adjutant screamed in the ear of the guy on the ground asking him who had beaten him, to which the beaten guy answered, the "kraussköpfige Jud," the Jew with the curly hair. While this witness also failed to describe what had transpired, he, nevertheless, documented that the victim was conscious and responded immediately, pointing to the alleged wrongdoer.

The third witness was a woman from the bleaching garden. She reported that when she heard noises, she immediately ran toward the source of the commotion and saw Jews hovering over a soldier and beating him. She asserted that she could not identify the Jewish attackers since it was somewhat dark, and, as if to confirm her statement, she said that she had already eaten dinner. But then she continued her account by claiming that she did recognize the one Jew who had beaten the victim the most, a "fremder Jud," foreign Jew, with curly hair.

While the records do not disclose how the Jewish man she claimed to be the perpetrator—Bonnum, a Jewish man from Rödelheim, an out-of-towner—had been caught and arrested so swiftly, Frankfurt's authorities arranged for a confrontation during which she, again, insisted that she had seen him hitting the victim. Bonnum initially denied her charges, but eventually conceded, explaining that when he arrived at the scene, other Jewish men had already beaten the soldier, disclosing further that one Amsel had taken the sword away from the soldier. Subsequently, the soldier had attacked him, Bonnum, and pulled him down.

Amsel could not be interrogated because he was missing, which led the authorities to focus on his brother David, who also asserted that he did not know what had transpired because he had arrived late. He conceded, however, that he had seen Amsel, having taken the soldier's sword, walking away toward the Judengasse. David stressed that the soldier had as yet not been seriously beaten and that it was the soldier who had attacked Bonnum. Questioned as to why his brother Amsel had taken the sword, and where his brother was, David answered he did not know.

A musketeer was the next witness to be interrogated. He stated that he had left the aforementioned tavern with his comrade through the back door, when he heard a woman scream that someone was being beaten to death. He ran toward the scene and saw several Jewish men, four of whom he knew, hovering over a soldier and beating him. They had sticks in their hands, which he claimed he took away from them and deposited at the tavern, without, however, disclosing how he was able to do this without encountering any resistance. He conceded that he had not been present at the beginning of the event but he was able to reveal the identity of a witness who had been there from the start.

The musketeer's comrade, who was questioned next, confirmed this account. Moreover, he added a new element by asserting that some Jewish people had thrown stones but he could not identify who they were; he had only seen Jewish women in houses high up in the Judengasse.

The introduction of sticks led the authorities to have the first musketeer confront David and subsequently Bonnum. David vehemently denied the allegation that he had had a stick in his hand: they "could cut off his head and hand if he had had one." The musketeer contradicted him, insisting that he did have one and that he had taken it from him by the door where one enters the bleaching garden from the Judenmauer, the Jewish Wall. David again denied it. Bonnum was now escorted into the interrogation room, and he contradicted David's statement, but not with regard to the sticks, but rather to the beating sequence of the soldier. While Bonnum claimed that the soldier had already been beaten, David asserted the opposite.

With great swiftness—partly due to Frankfurt's relatively small size, where sound traveled fast and witnesses were readily available, especially for public brawls—another witness, a burgher, was questioned. He turned out to be the first full-fledged eyewitness, having observed the unfolding of the attack from beginning to end. Similar to accounts given by previous witnesses, he mixed personal intentions with actual events by declaring that he had wanted to walk behind the Judenmauer to the Wollgraben, but on his way, when he reached the Judenkirchhof, Jewish cemetery,[3] he heard some Jewish boys yelling "Mä, Mä" (an untranslatable sound, possibly imitating the cry of sheep) after a soldier who had also come over to the Wollgraben. This sound seemed to have agitated the soldier, who had obviously been drinking, because when the Jewish boys followed the soldier to the gate of the cemetery, the soldier picked up a stone and threw it at them, which caused the boys to retreat somewhat.

The witness, continuing his account, described the soldier as having a sword under his arm, but it was in its case. Then, according to the witness, a tall Jewish man approached, talked to the soldier and took his sword but left the case under the soldier's arm. As if to give an explanation for this rather strange, peaceful disarmament of the soldier by an unarmed Jewish man, the witness claimed that the Jewish man had conducted himself like a Christian and further opined that the soldier must have thought the same.

After the removal of the sword the Jewish man, according to the witness, immediately took the soldier by the throat and threw him to the ground. Seemingly apologetic toward the interrogators, the witness claimed that as he was alone he could not do anything to help. He added, however, that he knew the name of the Jewish attacker, Amsel, who had thrown the soldier to the ground. Subsequently, so the witness continued with his account, two Jewish men appeared, one tall and the other short, and one of them took the soldier by the hair while the other beat him. Then a fat Jewish man appeared—the witness thought his name was Schmutz—who held the soldier's feet. He claimed to know them all by sight, but not by their names.

Continuing with his account and seemingly changing his theme of "being alone without help," the witness now claimed that he had approached the Jewish men and asked them what they were doing, whereupon Amsel, holding the sword in his hand, called him names, among others "you dog, what do you want," whereupon the soldier got up and walked away. A Jewish man with curly hair, however, immediately followed him and grabbed the soldier by his hair, hit his head against the wall, threw him to the ground, knelt on him and beat him heavily. At this juncture, other Jewish men arrived and beat the soldier. Subsequently, he, the witness, saw the curly-haired Jewish man run toward the Judengasse while the soldier lay on the ground as if dead. Other burghers now arrived—he cited several

[3] Judenkirchhof literally translated means Jewish churchyard, a remarkable description for a Jewish cemetery.

by name—all of whom went to the Judengasse questioning the Jewish men as to what they had done. The Jewish men, according to the witness, stood there with sticks in their hands till two musketeers arrived and took the sticks away from them. When they went to look after the man on the ground, Jewish people threw stones at them from their houses so that they had to leave.

This seemingly breathlessly rendered account raises, of course, several questions. Why was the soldier so irritated by kids whose only remarks were "Mä, Mä?" Why did the soldier threaten the kids by throwing stones? Why was it so easy for a non-armed Jewish man to disarm a soldier even if he behaved "like a Christian"?

The ensuing confrontation between this eyewitness and Bonnum and David did not even address these issues. Instead, it focused on who had started the beating. The witness claimed it was Bonnum; Bonnum alleged it was the soldier, while David denied having participated in any beating. The witness who asserted that he had been there from the very beginning to the end, contradicted David's account but conceded that he could not say what David had actually done. Nevertheless, this statement did not prevent him from asserting* that all of them had beaten the soldier "like a dog."

One of the burghers who had arrived somewhat later at the crime scene was the next to be questioned. He stated that between 7 and 8 in the evening he had walked over the Wollgraben when he saw Jewish men with sticks, but did not know what all the commotion was about. Continuing with his vague account, he reported that stones were thrown, that he almost got hit and that he heard a woman scream that a dead man was lying on the ground. Subsequently, somebody had taken the sticks away from the Jewish men. He asserted that he could not identify any of the Jewish men, except for one who was very tall with curly hair, and that "there was also a little one." When he, the witness, tried to talk to them they had used "very bad words." He finished his rendition by reiterating that he was not there at the beginning of the event.

After this fractional eyewitness account, Frankfurt's authorities proceeded to question another burgher and a Jewish man. The burgher had nothing to add, while the Jewish witness gave a detailed account of what he had observed. He began telling the authorities that he had been walking with another Jewish man and two children on the Wollgraben in the evening, as they usually did, when a soldier arrived swinging his sword, which was still in its case. This scene led him, the witness, to turn to his companion and say "this could lead to something bad," especially since they were defenseless. When they subsequently turned and walked away toward the Judengasse, they saw the foreign Jew acting in an agitated manner toward the soldier. They, the witness and his companion, however, continued to walk to the Judengasse and did not know what had happened. He asserted that he could procure hundreds of Jewish people as his witness.

The interrogators, obviously not content with his version, persisted in questioning him further, such as to whether Amsel had been there, which he claimed he did not know, but ultimately conceded that yes, it was Amsel who had taken the sword from the soldier and ran with it toward the Judengasse. He also stated that the soldier had drawn his sword and hit out at Amsel, who had to defend himself. Asked whether other Jewish men had been there, he answered that many had come running. This obviously very reluctant witness explained further that he had seen the soldier joking with young Jewish girls, and that he had drawn his sword, without, however, doing any harm to anyone. When questioned about how Amsel had taken the sword from the soldier, he stated he could not tell because they had already been in the Judengasse, when Amsel ran with the sword toward the same. But he added that Bonnum was the first to have engaged with the soldier.

After this, the second full eyewitness account, Frankfurt's authorities recontacted the Jewish Baumeister and asked them about other Jewish men who might have been involved in this incidence, but without much success. They were told that one of the alleged suspects was not even in town, playing music at a wedding at another location, and that the others were foreign Jews who had left town.

The assertion that Jewish men had left town prompted the authorities to focus on another theme: the importance of the wall encircling the Judengasse, the Judenmauer as it was called, as a possible escape route for Jews. The Judenmauer, the symbolic and physical reality of confinement, became the center of the inquiry with a burgher, a dyer, who was questioned as to whether he had seen a Jewish man being lowered from a house in the Judengasse to the outside of the wall. In a detailed rendition he explained that because of the intense heat he was still sitting outside at 10 in the evening when he saw a person walking up and down the wall, obviously on the non-Jewish side, across from him. He thought him to be a Christian, maybe a soldier, who had a leaping pole in his hand, possibly, according to the witness's interpretation, to guard against Jewish people starting unrest. He, the witness, then went back to his house and, when he was about to undress, his female neighbor, the carpenter's wife, arrived to question him about the tumult she had heard. Walking immediately back to the wall, he saw someone being lowered on a rope from the top of the wall, jumping to the ground, releasing the rope and running toward the Allerheiligengass, a nearby street. Although the moon was bright, he did not feel like running after him. The other man with the leaping pole had also left. When he, the witness, said goodnight to his neighbor, she asserted that the jumper had been a Jewish man. And, yes, he remembered exactly the spot from where the man had jumped —a spot subsequently marked by the municipal guard.

Two women were now questioned with regard to the wall-jumping incident. The first, the carpenter's wife, admitted that she had heard something falling off the wall, but since she had been standing at the door of her house with a child, she could not pursue it further. The second witness was more precise, asserting that between 10 and 11 in the evening she heard something at the wall like sliding and falling down as if it had been a sack. She ran toward the source of the noise and, although the moon was bright, she could not identify whether the person she spotted was a Christian or a Jewish person.

The wife of a local sergeant also reported on the incidence, which, according to her statement, occurred between 9 and 10 in the evening when she saw a Jew with a big leaping pole pacing up and down the wall close to the windmill. He wished her a good evening and then walked toward the Allerheiligentor, a city gate. The witness stated that "when the Jewish man thought that it was quiet and nobody was in the street" he scratched the wall with his jumping pole and made the sound of a crow. All of a sudden a Jewish man with a rope around his waist was lowered from the wall close to the fat schoolmaster's house. Originally she thought it to be a ghost but she then identified the person as a Jewish man with a common coat on his arm, running toward the Allerheiligengass. She thought him to be the son of the fat schoolmaster.

While obviously her account includes a personal assumption about the identity of the wall-jumper, the incident per se reported by four witnesses, nevertheless, sheds light on how some daring Jewish people literally surmounted the obstacle of the Judenmauer, possibly using it as an escape route. This particular incident was not an isolated occurence. Already in 1572 a Jewish man had to pay a heavy monetary fine for having climbed over the Judenmauer together with several foreign Jewish men.[4]

Finally the authorities located Amsel, who was promptly arrested and questioned. His lengthy deposition began with the Sabbath evening, when he was sitting at the table asking the woman in the house where he was a lodging to bring him some wine. The woman, distressed, told him that there was a big tumult on the Wollgraben with a soldier who was swinging his sword. She begged him, Amsel, to go and see how her children were doing, who were walking on the Wollgraben. He, Amsel, went but assured Frankfurt's interrogators that he did not know what the soldier had originally done there but that upon his arrival the

---

[4] Dietrich Andernacht, *Regesten zur Geschichte der Juden in der Reichststadt Frankfurt am Main von 1520–1616*, ed. Helga Andernacht, Institut für Stadtgeschichte Frankfurt und dem Arye Maimon-Institut für Geschichte der Juden an der Universität Trier (2 vols, Hanover: Hahnsche Buchhandlung, 2007), vol. 1, p. 547, item 2227.

soldier hurled invectives at him and charged at him with his sword, which was half out of its case under his arm. He, Amsel, took the sword from the soldier and, while assuring the interrogators that he had not hit the soldier, ran with the sword toward the Judengasse. After his retreat into the Judengasse, he admitted having first hid behind a tree and subsequently behind the baking house; then he had stayed behind closed doors. He admitted that he was hiding out of fear of being accused of having participated in the assault. Questioned as to why he was so afraid and who scared him so much, he simply replied "by nature," especially because he did not have a father or a mother, only his brother David.

A confrontation between the key witness and Amsel followed. Amsel was questioned about whether he had insulted the key witness on the crime scene, to which he replied "on the contrary," it was the witness who had praised him for having behaved like an honest man by taking the sword away from the soldier. By contrast, the key witness asserted that after Amsel had taken the sword from the soldier, he had hit the soldier and had called him, the witness, a dog. Amsel refuted both accusations, but his assertions were not enough. He was escorted back to prison.

While out of the total of 14 witnesses only two had actually observed the event from start to finish, their accounts and the statements by the suspects concurred that a soldier had been beaten by Jewish men, although the unfolding of events and who had actually hit the soldier remained somewhat nebulous. Also, while some witnesses included personal interpretations in their accounts, it was remarkable that none of them resorted to any anti-Jewish verbal attacks, polemics, which would have been recorded in the write-up of their accounts. Equally noteworthy are the statements by those who commented on the jumping over the Judenmauer. The three women reported the incident matter-of-factly without any derogatory statements and the male witness, in similar fashion, did not even consider it offensive enough to run after the suspects. This lax interpersonal attitude was also demonstrated by the various disclosures that both Jewish people and Christians enjoyed promenading on the Wollgraben, and this in perfect harmony before the arrival of the soldier. The soldier thus triggered the event and his disclosure added another puzzle to the case.

Contrary to the more common practice of rendering verbal statements, the procedure followed in all of the above reports, the soldier submitted his version in writing. This was done intentionally. He had hired someone cognizant not only of reading and writing but also of the complexities and legal advantages, as became very obvious. The soldier claimed that after leaving the Wacht, the military headquarters, at 3 p.m. he had walked over to the Wollgraben of "sober and of good mind," where he saw several Jewish girls standing together. He approached them "with good words" several times and, in return, he received polite replies. While he was thus engaged talking to the Jewish girls, a boy 16 or 17 years old, who had stood close by, started without special cause to yell at him in "his Hebrew language and cursing him wishing the bad disease on him, which our dear God should prevent men from contracting." He, the soldier, answered back wishing him the same and reprimanding him that such a disgusting thing should not even be wished on a dog, whereupon the Jewish boy called him a dirty dog. When he tried to grab the boy with his hands, he failed to reach him, whereupon he took the sword out of its case and ran after him to beat him, but again failed to reach him.

At this juncture, according to the soldier, many Jewish men ran toward them trying to kill him. They ignored his explanations, conducting themselves "like mad-men, and fanatical enemies of Christians." He ran away and when he finally reached the door of the bleaching ground where he hoped to find the protection of "Christians and burghers," the "duplicitous Jew Amsel" tackled him from the back by his hair, threw him to the ground, and hit him with stones and fists. Other Jewish men arrived with sticks and hit him on the head and body, kneeling and sitting on him and kicking him so that in the end he was taken away as dead. Various burghers, whom he identified by name in the letter, and two soldiers arrived who took the sticks away from the Jewish men.

He concluded that because the "Jud Amsel" had attacked him in such a murderous way, inflicting serious health problems, he was forced to abandon his military service and, in Dr. Sultern's medical opinion, he would remain a sick man for the rest of his life. He was, therefore, asking the city council to instruct Amsel and his fellows to pay for all medical and other expenses incurred, including the composition and writing fees for this very letter. He also insisted on the payment of 50 Thaler for his pain and suffering.

The soldier's letter is startling for several reasons. Conspicuously absent is the fact, and all witnesses concurred on this point, that a Jewish man had peacefully disarmed him, a fact he obviously considered shameful and against his military honor. Also, in contrast to the above so-called "Christian" witnesses, who did not resort to anti-Jewish allegations, the soldier did, and this in a letter prepared by someone cognizant of legal angles.

Legal finesse also points to his claim to monetary punitive compensation. Two legal interpretations might be offered to address this monetary demand. Either the former Germanic concept of compensatio or Wergeld, payment to the injured party, was still in existence and operative on various subterfuge levels or it was the beginning of a new plaintiff legal mentality claiming monetary payments for physical damages by using a doctor's expertise, a trend all too familiar to modern legal claims. What had been conducted so far as a criminal case now seemed to merge criminal and civil charges.

Frankfurt's municipal doctor and barbers, who had submitted their findings on the soldier's health condition, did not agree with the soldier's private doctor. Citing head, shoulder and swelling wounds, they did not consider his health to be in special danger; but they recommended he be observed further, especially because of his breathing problems, which they stated would normally be called emphysema.

Frankfurt's four advocates evaluated the case as requested by the city council. Their statements range from partly succinct to elusive to stunning biases. Dr. Friedrich Binder, in a lengthy legal opinion, was the first to comment, and he did so by immediately questioning the accuracy of the soldier's claim of having been sober, and having come directly from the Wacht. Had that been the case, so Dr. Binder's argument went, he would have been armed differently, not carrying his sword under his arm, and he would not have exchanged pleasantries with Jewish girls. However, despite these credibility reservations, he proceeded to argue that the soldier had not insulted anyone and had not contributed to the assault on him. Instead, he put the blame on the Jewish kids who had yelled at him dishonorably and on the Jewish boy's Hebrew curse, all the while questioning and thus inherently contradicting himself as to how the soldier could possibly have understood it since it was exclaimed in Hebrew.

While in contrast to the soldier Dr. Binder addressed the incident of the peaceful sword removal, he did so, however, without questioning the soldier's omission of this incident. Instead he claimed that Amsel had removed the sword from the soldier "vermutlich," most likely, only when he saw that many other Jewish men were arriving. As to Bonnum's action, he concluded that he had not acted in self-defense and, therefore, he had had no viable cause for attacking the soldier. He simply reduced Bonnum's behavior to the "Jud boshaftes Gemüt," the Jew's evil disposition.

Dr. Binder, in his penal suggestions, questioned another of the soldier's claim, namely that he would remain an unhealthy person for the rest of his life and, therefore, needed a sizable sum of money. While agreeing with the soldier's claim for the reimbursement of medical and writing fees to be paid by Amsel and Bonnum, he only awarded him 25 Thaler in punitive damages, buttressing his stance on the findings of the municipal medics and barbers. As a consequence, Bonnum was to pay the soldier a certain amount, after which he should be banished. Amsel was to be incarcerated for four weeks or given the option to reduce this penalty by paying 50 Thaler. David, although Dr. Binder conceded that it could not be established whether he had actually hit the victim and that in general he had inflicted the least amount of harm, ought, nevertheless, to be imprisoned for eight days.

Individual punishments were not enough for Dr. Binder. Assessing the whole event as scandalous—which could entail very harmful consequences, especially since the public was highly insulted—he held Frankfurt's entire Jewish community in contempt. He proposed to have a sharp and intimidating warning issued to "sämtliche Judenschaft," all Jews. By threatening corporal or capital punishments he intended to instill fear in them and thus prevent, as he put it, "Jews from beating Christians."

This, the first of four legal opinions, is, obviously, riddled with contradictions, omissions and unsustainable allegations. While Dr. Binder voiced serious reservations about the soldier's statements, discrediting him on various accounts, he proceeds to ignore his own caveats. He mentions Amsel's removal of the sword, in contrast to the soldier, but he does not give him any credit for doing so. Peacefully disarming a soldier with a drawn sword is a heroic act under any circumstances. In Amsel's case it is even more so since he was unarmed. Instead, Dr. Binder injects a "most likely" assertion in his arguments as a disclaimer for Amsel's action, an astoundingly unprofessional legal declaration devoid of any evidence.

Thus failing to recognize the physically threatening move on the part of the soldier swirling his sword and running after a Jewish boy, which might have prompted Jewish men to come to his rescue, he argued instead that the mockery by a few Jewish kids had caused the assault, an abysmal legal response resembling the equally abysmal emotional reaction of the armed soldier toward the Jewish boy.

On his part, the second advocate, Dr. Georg Schuster, issued a very short legal opinion, basically agreeing with Dr. Binder's assessment, but he added that since approximately 50 Jewish men had been involved, the inquiry ought to be expanded. Dr. Martin Rasor, the third advocate, asserts in his legal brief that the three main delinquents be punished and adds that an inquiry be conducted to ascertain from which houses the stones were thrown. But he distances himself from Dr. Binder by arguing that a threatening decree against Frankfurt's Jewish population was unwarranted.

In stark contrast to Dr. Rasor's restraint toward the Jewish population, the fourth advocate, Dr. Anton Glock, advanced most virulent anti-Jewish claims in his legal opinion. He stated that he was saddened that the soldier had to suffer verbal and physical injuries, and that he had to cope with medical problems for the rest of his life because of the "verfluchten Judengesindel," damned Jewish hoodlums. Therefore, the soldier's claim for 50 Thaler was not too excessive, although, he conceded, that if a Christian had beaten him, the amount could be reduced. But for these "gottlosen Judengesindel," godless Jewish hoodlums, it was not too excessive. Continuing in this anti-Jewish vein,

Dr. Glock expressed his reservations about the promenading of Christians and Jews on the Wollgraben, which, he argued, would lead Christian youth to be too exposed to Jews. What had been the place and scene of peaceful cultural interactions was scorned from above by an advocate.

Noticeably, none of the four advocates addressed the beneficial act of removing the sword from the soldier because this admission would have amounted to conceding to a serious military dishonor on the part of an unarmed Jewish man, a concept the advocates did not want to touch on or admit to, and so they ignored it.[5]

The soldier's mother now entered the litigation by claiming, citing the same doctor's physical assessment, that her son would no longer be able to work and that he ought to be awarded 500 Thaler. She stated in a written plea, obviously also prepared by a legally cognizant person, that the "Jews as foes of Christians" had beaten her son so severely that he had been carried away as dead and could not use his mind for three days. Her claim was, however, immediately struck down by Dr. Binder, followed by Dr. Schuster and Dr. Rasor who, pointedly added that while her son had only asked for 50 Thaler, she now wanted 500.

Various pleas now emanated from the suspects and their friends. Bonnum, as an out-of-town Schutzjude, protected by the count of Rödelheim, contacted the count to effect his release from prison, stressing his innocence and the welfare of his wife and children. The count immediately contacted Frankfurt's city council pressing for the release of this Jewish man who was under his special princely protection. Frankfurt responded by arguing that Bonnum had been one of the prime assailants in the dangerous beating of the soldier, an accusation which was promptly questioned by the count, who stressed the defensive nature of Bonnum's action, citing the aggressive behavior of soldiers against Jewish people, and that Bonnum had committed neither murder nor manslaughter and that for the sake of his wife and children he be released from prison. Frankfurt's city council, obviously unimpressed by the count's argument, countered that the soldier had been close to death because of the beating he had received, a statement they repeated twice in the same letter.

Bonnum now addressed Frankfurt's city council directly, asking for a mild sentence and his release from prison, an ordeal, as he put it, he had endured for four weeks already. He asked that his extended prison stay be credited toward a milder punishment. Bonnum's plea to have his extensive prison stay taken into consideration was not an individual aberration but a frequently applied penal consideration. And Amsel, the other detainee, knew about it as well, for he too submitted a plea to Frankfurt's city council to have his five weeks' detention

---

[5] See Chapter 11 on Frankfurt's advocates' judicial treatment of soldiers.

count toward a milder sentence; and he stressed that by removing the sword from the soldier he had contributed to the safety of many.

A third plea was sent to the city council. It originated from the leaders of the Jewish community, who addressed an ordinance from the city council which stipulated that if those involved in the beating of the soldier were not financially able to pay the punitive damages of 150 Thaler, the entire Jewish community was to share in remitting the expenses. This demand implicitly turned every Jewish person into a criminal contributor, and as such exceeded general criminal contemporary judicial practices. A community of people regardless of denomination or cultural composition did not have to pay for the crime of one or several of its members. When a Catholic committed a crime, not all Catholics had to share the burden; when a soldier committed a crime, not all soldiers had to share the burden. Unfortunately, the available documents do not disclose whether or not the Jewish community actually paid this amount.

Eventually, as the entry in Frankfurt's Strafenbuch of July 5 states, both Amsel and Bonnum were sentenced to banishment. There is no mention of any financial penalties to be paid by the two Jewish men, which is not surprising because the Strafenbuch only lists criminal corporal, including shaming, and capital punishments. The financial payback came, however, to light in Bonnum's additional plea to the city council when he asked to be readmitted to town to conduct his business. He stated that he had not only suffered six weeks of incarceration but had also paid the harsh monetary fine and that the soldier, who received a lot of his money, was not sick but spent his money eating and drinking to excess. Bonnum's plea was denied.

Summarizing, one can assert that it was without a doubt true that the soldier was beaten, but doubtful are the circumstances leading to this beating and the severity of the beating. Doubtful are also the prosecutorial approaches by Frankfurt's advocates exhibiting various irregularities, omissions, personal projections and biases, reaching their crescendo in Dr. Glock's outspoken anti-Jewish legal opinion. The soldier had initiated the anti-Jewish process in his legally prepared statement, and most of Frankfurt's advocates, with the notable exception of Dr. Rasor, followed that lead. Their behavior was in stark contrast to Frankfurt's witnesses, none of whom voiced such anti-Jewish sentiments. The inflammatory remarks, if not attitudes, emanated from the men in charge of justice.

It is also quite obvious that many in the Jewish community had perceived the soldier as a threat, for, in the words of one witness, "many of them came running" and rallied immediately to take defensive action by collecting sticks, possibly even stones and, most importantly, by taking away the soldier's sword. This spontaneous attack on the soldier in what one might call a group-self-defensive mode prompted by the soldier's own admission of having drawn his sword and running after a Jewish youngster was, however, ultimately rooted in and motivated by a deep-seated fear stemming from the long history of soldiers' menacing and selective aggression toward them.

Despite multiple exhortations to soldiers, promulgated over many years by Frankfurt's authorities, to refrain from harassing Jews, these repeated warnings did not stop their destructive and selective behavior toward them, a pattern which was neither explained nor addressed by the advocates in this case. Most curiously, even at the time when the two Jewish men were sentenced in this trial, soldiers were reprimanded to seriously curtail their bad comportment toward Jews.[6]

Despite these drawbacks, the witnesses' reports disclose some positive shared cultural patterns. Many Christian witnesses either knew the names of Jewish people or stated that they recognized them, implying that they had seen them prior to the event. This name and face recognition points to at least some interaction between the two groups. A more unambiguous example, and obviously a very popular cultural phenomenon shared by Jews and Christians, was taking a stroll on the Wollgraben. Both Christians and Jews, even with their children, promenaded there during the same early evening hours in seeming harmony. The Wollgraben literally and symbolically was their shared common ground, obviously a thorn in the side of Dr. Glock, who wanted to prevent such communality for the sake of "Christian youth."

This mutual promenading on the Wollgraben also demonstrates that Frankfurt's population did not fear any physical attacks from Jewish people, and this with good reason. Jewish people had the lowest pattern of aggressive behavior of all those sentenced during the 1562 to 1696 period. No Jewish person was convicted for murder, murder and robbery or manslaughter, while soldiers' sentences demonstrate the opposite trend.[7]

But as this and the following 1684 case clearly demonstrate, Jewish people could not be endlessly pushed around, and while no attack on another person should ever be condoned, some Jews took defensive action by hitting back: enough was enough.

The 1684 Trial of Aaron

A considerably less complex but equally telling trial of 1684 concerned the actions of a Jewish son in response to a municipal functionary's invasion and destruction

6 Bürgermeisterbücher (BB) July 5, 1683, p. 24.

7 Boes, "Jews in the Criminal-Justice System," p. 425.

of his father's house. It began with the arrest of Aaron Luria on March 3, 1684 for having hurled "atrocissimus injuries" against one of the mayor.[8]

A plea from Aaron to the city council, submitted a week after his arrest, is the first pertinent document of the trial found in the criminal dossier. In it, Aaron asked for his release from prison, outlining his version of the unfolding of events which had led to his arrest. He cites a report by the Richter (the city's municipal enforcement agent)—not contained in the criminal folder—in which the latter claimed that Aaron's exclamation of offensive words against one of Frankfurt's mayors was the cause for his arrest. Aaron denied these allegations by giving his version of what transpired. He stated that on the fateful day, when he entered his father's house he encountered the Richter who had just slashed and destroyed everything inside the home. When he questioned him to explain why he had done such damage and who had ordered him to do so, the Richter had replied that it was the mayor who had ordered it, adding that if his, Aaron's father, had paid his debts, this would not have happened.

Aaron admitted in his plea that in his utter consternation at this incident he had called out that if he—without giving a name—paid his own debt as well as paying my father, this would not have happened. Aaron conceded that his exclamation could lead to misunderstanding and he asked the city council not to misinterpret it, especially because he had been absent from Frankfurt for a long time.

Accusingly, Aaron continued in his plea that the Richter, once he had arrested him, let him stand for a quarter of an hour in front of the town hall close to the soldiers' quarters where he mocked him, proclaiming that he, the Richter, would have to put a red coat around him to honor Aaron. Even on the way to the town center, Aaron asserted, the Richter had mistreated him and showed no concern whatsoever about the destruction he had caused. Aaron pleaded with the councilors to release him from prison so that he could help his father pay his debts and that he had uttered those—undefined—words "aus Passion," out of passion.

Aaron's plea led the city council to question the Richter as well as several soldiers who had been in his company during the destructive event. Subsequently, the witnesses' statements were submitted to the advocates for their legal advice. In their initial assessment, Drs. Martin Rasor, Georg Schuster and Anton Glock agreed with Dr. Friedrich Binder's findings that because of "dieses Juden grosse Bosheit," this Jew's great malice, to have him interrogated and confronted with the witnesses.

---

8 CR 1611; Ratsprotokolle (RP) 1683, p. 37.

After almost two weeks' imprisonment, the witnesses' interrogation process began. The first to be questioned was a soldier stationed in Frankfurt serving in a local military company. He stated that he had been at the house, standing "one or three steps" lower than where the Richter was standing, when Aaron arrived asking who had ordered the use of force in his house. The Richter replied that the younger mayor had instructed him to do so. "Der Jud," the Jew, according to the soldier, made a remark about the mayor paying his debts and snapped his fingers, whereupon the Richter shouted to the Notary, who was standing at the bottom step of the house, that he should listen to what "der Jud" was saying. But when the Notary arrived, "der Jud" left and was quiet. But, so the soldier reported, the Richter informed the Notary of what had transpired.

Questioned next, the Richter, confirmed that he had been standing high up on the steps by the house talking to a Jewish woman. He did not know whether it was Aaron's sister, and when she started to cry he tried to appease her saying that everything would be all right. It was then that "der Jud" came up the steps and asked who ordered you—using the informal German "du"—to carry out such destruction in my house? He, the Richter, claimed to have been startled that "der Jud" had assailed him so fast and vehemently and he answered back that he had "not guarded the pigs with him for him to address him on a first name basis." Aaron, according to the Richter, repeated who had ordered him to use such force, to which he, the Richter, replied that he had not used any force but only carried out what the mayor had told him to do and that soldiers had helped remove things from the house. When "der Jud" asked again who had ordered him to use such force, he replied again the mayor, whereupon "der Jud" snapped his fingers and said he should pay his debts.

This exclamation, according to the Richter, prompted him to call down to the Notary, who had been standing at the lower part of the house and who had already been informed by the soldier of what had transpired. He asked the Notary to have "der Jud" imprisoned. Most curiously, the Richter ended his account that "der Jud" claimed that he, the Richter, had been drunk, but the Notary could testify that this was not the case.

The Notary, who was questioned subsequently, confirmed that he was in the house but that he had not heard anything and, therefore, could only repeat what the Richter had told him: "der Jud" had snapped his fingers and exclaimed that he honored him, the Richter, as much as the mayor and that the latter ought to pay his debts. He confirmed that neither the Richter nor the soldiers had been drunk, but conceded that the Richter had had some pear wine at lunch and that the four soldiers had also had some "Wein."

The Notary's account thus established, somewhat confirming Aaron's claim that the Richter had, indeed, been drinking, but, according to him, not enough to be drunk. In addition, he introduced a more precise account of how many soldiers had been involved, namely four, all of whom had also been drinking; but, again according to the Notary, not enough to be called drunk.

As a consequence, and at the suggestion of all four advocates, Aaron was confronted with the Richter. And it was Aaron, the suspect, who went onto the offensive. He started with a possible legal incongruity by questioning how the Richter could be his accuser and a witness at the same time. The reply was short and swift: he, Aaron, had been accused ex officio, that is by the municipal authorities. In turn, Aaron now challenged the witnesses' allegations, as well as the introduction of a new witness whom he did not know.

Switching to a more emotional approach, Aaron elaborated that when he saw the destruction the Richter had caused in his house he questioned him, with tears in his eyes suggesting that the mayor would not have ordered such damage; neither would he have had the house cleared by the soldiers. Aaron then proceeded to address several omissions in the Richter's statements, such as his failure to disclose that he had wanted money from him, Aaron, to pay for wine, a request he had turned down with the explanation that they were poor people too. Also missing from the account was the incident, Aaron claimed, of when he asked the Richter why he forcefully removed a wooden plank which had been nailed to support a cupboard, the Richter replied that he had been given full powers to do whatever he wanted because the accused had not paid their debt. And when he, Aaron, countered this allegation by saying that by destroying everything they would not be in a position to pay their debt, the Richter threw the loosened wooden plank at him, which left a black and blue mark on his left foot; and to substantiate his claim, Aaron uncovered his foot to show the marks to the interrogators.

Aaron also challenged the Richter's claim of his alleged verbal assault against the mayor, namely that the mayor ought to pay his debts. Instead he countered that when the Richter made this allegation, he, Aaron, had turned immediately to the Notary, saying that the Richter was twisting his words and that, in the presence of the Notary, he informed them that he had been given eight days by both mayors to solve the debt problem. The Richter, Aaron reported, disregarded his assertion and cried out instead that he felt like having soldiers escort him to the military headquarters, the Wacht, a remark which had prompted him to exclaim that he should do so because it was common knowledge that the soldiers themselves borrowed money from them.

Subsequently, Aaron was confronted with a new witness, a soldier. Surprised, he questioned how this was possible since he, the Richter, had not mentioned this witness; and, again going on the offensive, he asked the soldier why he had not immediately contacted the Notary. The soldier replied he had done so but only after the Notary had asked him, posing, in return, the rhetorical question of why he should burden his conscience because of that "Jud." He confirmed, however, that he had heard the exchange. Aaron countered how this was possible since nobody was around at the time of the verbal exchange between him and the Richter. The soldier asserted that he had stood three steps away from the Richter and when Aaron persistently questioned him that the people below should also have heard it, which they did not, the soldier claimed that they had not been that close.

After that confrontation, Aaron's father sent a personal written plea to the mayors and the city council. While he was asking for mercy for his son he also outlined the circumstances which would have "offended Christians and Jews alike," namely that the furniture and other household items were destroyed with force. He explained that when his son, who had been away and did not know anything about the debt situation, saw the destruction caused by the Richter and observed his condescending behavior it did lead to verbal exchanges—words, which, however, did not include any insults against the mayor. And he stressed that nobody could prove otherwise, especially since the soldier could not have heard any of the exchange.

Concluding, Aaron's father explained that while his son was to help him collect outstanding debts so that he could pay his own, he could not do so because he had been imprisoned for four weeks, a devastating incarceration blocking his effort to get the money. Pleading with the city council for his son's release, he asserted that he, an old sick man, did not want to be reduced to begging or dying of hunger.

Aaron was released from prison over a month after his incarceration only to be told that he was sentenced to life-time banishment from Frankfurt. Frankfurt's four advocates had argued in their unanimous legal opinion that since Aaron had spent already a month in prison, he should only be punished by life-time banishment. True, extremely long detentions, such as over four weeks, were painful given the contemporary prison conditions—and other offenders for far more serious crimes frequently had their sentences reduced because of extended imprisonment—but in Aaron's case the advocates' "benevolent" penal suggestion is of a questionable nature given that the documents disclose a rather murky judicial picture at best, showing neither a crime "atrocissimus" nor one which can be fully substantiated.

The advocates did not even bother to fully outline their respective legal stances, and they neglected to question the woman whom the Richter had described as crying. Furthermore, it was never established whether the mayors had actually given full powers to the Richter to carry out this seemingly unreasonable destruction or whether it was due to a deliberate provocation on the part of the overzealous Richter and the soldiers, all of whom had obviously little regard for "der Jud." What should have been a civil trial, the debt problem of Aaron's father, escalated into a criminal one because of lese-majesty allegations—allegations which could not be fully established.

Aaron did not find out the truth, and Frankfurt's four advocates did not help in the process. In fact, their final penal deliberation was very superficial if not flagrantly biased for never taking into consideration Aaron's various points or the destruction inside his father's house. It is quite obvious that the authorities gave more credence to the Richter and the soldiers. They also neglected to address the Richter's personal provocative stance to expose Aaron to a humiliating, deliberate confrontational stance in front of soldiers, the very group who, paradoxically, were frequently admonished by Frankfurt's authorities to stop harassing Jews. And to expose an equally if not more perplexing feature of this trial, soldiers were used as law enforcing agents by Frankfurt's authorities by accompanying and assisting the Richter on his tour. Jews were thus in effect left at the mercy of soldiers.

This trial also showed that the judicial and penal procedures against Jewish people had deteriorated. The advocates ignored Aaron's father's plea; and in a highly unusual move it was decreed not to accept any further pleas on Aaron's behalf, a deliberate judicial incongruity compared to other suspects—especially the treatment of soldiers, as will be discussed in Chapter 11.[9] Also, in an earlier serious case of lese-majesty of 1607, when a Jewish man conducted himself offensively inside the Römer, the mayors' office, and ridiculed the younger mayor in front of people, the suspect was arrested but released eight days later with only a serious warning.[10] Obviously, the judicial climate had changed.

Given the dire judicial circumstances for Jewish people in the criminal justice system, Aaron's immediate stance against the Richter questioning his destruction, as well as his subsequent daring and logical defense, do not show any fear on his part. On the contrary, he was a person fired up by the injustices committed toward his father and himself. He challenged the authorities; he defended his father, their house and himself. And while one will never know whether or not he actually exclaimed the words against the mayor, his comportment made one thing very clear: he, as a Jewish person, was taking a stance.

Summary

Both the 1683 and the 1684 case demonstrate that despite increasingly difficult judicial recourse, Jewish people resisted. While in the 1683 instance it was a

9 BB April 8, 1684, p. 133.

10 Andernacht, *Regesten*, vol. 2, p. 948, item 3734.

Jewish communal defensive effort, in 1684 it was an individual one. Both trials also demonstrate the increasing recourse of advocates to anti-Jewish remarks in their legal opinions and the factual omission of relevant and demonstrable evidence given by the various witnesses. Even the letters prepared by people of legal background, such as the soldier's and his mother's written submissions, evidence an anti-Jewish stance, a trend casting a grave, severely religiously and culturally biased shadow over many officials in the legal profession.

PART IV
Gender Issues

Chapter 7
Women and the Penal System in Frankfurt am Main, 1562–1696

The objective of this chapter is to assess the role and treatment of women in the penal system in Frankfurt am Main from 1562 to 1696. Three distinct subjects will be probed: municipal laws, criminal court proceedings and penal structures. The method consists of both quantitative and qualitative analyses, and comparative data will be furnished throughout in order to compare and contrast patterns of male to female penology.[1]

Judicial Setting

As discussed in Chapter 2, Frankfurt's extensive judicial power resided in its city council, which was divided into three benches. Local patricians occupied the first two benches, while the third bench was composed of representatives of select local guilds. While the first bench represented the civil court, the combined three benches constituted the criminal court.[2] All councilors were men and belonged exclusively to the Lutheran faith.

While on the surface this evidence suggests that all of Frankfurt's women were excluded from any judicial say or influence, such a deduction would be an oversimplification because Frankfurt's women were not a monolithic group. Patrician women, at the apex of the social ladder, were more powerful than wives of artisans or single female servants. In their exalted position they exercised various degrees of influence over their husbands, including those in the city council, a deduction borne out by the fact that none of them, similar to their husbands, was ever sentenced for criminal wrongdoing in Frankfurt

---

[1] Again the source material consists of the Strafenbuch (ST), the Ratsprotokolle (RP) and the Bürgermeisterbücher (BB), together with six volumes of the *Concepta Edictorum* and five volumes of the *Corpus Legum Francofurtensium* (*CLF*). The six volumes of the *Sammlung der Verordnungen der Reichsstadt Frankfurt* represented a further legislative source. The Rathsprotokolle also included many municipal edicts. The records of the guilds, the *Amts-und Zunfturkunden*, were studied in conjunction with social aspects.

[2] Johann Georg Rössing, *Versuch einer kurzen historischen Darstellung der allmählichen Entwicklung der heutigen Gerichtsverfassung der Stadt Frankfurt am Main* (Frankfurt am Main: Mohr, 1810), p. 39.

during the 134-year period under investigation. Obviously, wealth and social status did affect women's criminal adjudication pattern, and the city's municipal legislation partially accounts for that.

An analysis of various local laws reveals the existence of a double standard: the selective influence of wealth and social status on the penal structure. For various categories of crime, in particular prostitution and fornication, monetary fines could be substituted for physical punishment depending, among other factors, on the financial and social status of the offender.[3] While such legal loopholes worked in favor of women of patrician descent, they served men even more frequently for the simple reason that men gained more wealth, influence, status and power in the course of the sixteenth century.

Traditionally, while Frankfurt's women had been excluded from municipal government, they at least were able to join the local guilds.[4] By the mid- to late sixteenth century, however, the city's guilds increasingly barred women from joining their ranks, resulting in lower incomes and the abolition of an alternative life-style for many local women. And Frankfurt as a predominantly Lutheran city with a Lutheran city council seemed to accentuate this occupational gender division. One only has to cite Martin Luther's dictum that "women should remain at home, sit still, keep house, and bear and bring up children."[5] Bearing in mind these economic and social downgrading developments, women could not take advantage of Frankfurt's financial and social loopholes in the laws the same way men could. This is most clearly evidenced by an example from 1618 when an unmarried female servant had sexual relations with her master, a local burgher, and became pregnant. She was charged with fornication and punished by flogging and banishment, while her master had to pay a fine only.[6]

Women and Criminal Court Procedures

Despite partiality in the laws, Frankfurt's women were not completely devoid of judicial influence. They played a decisive role with regard to crime reporting and criminal accusations. One of the most interesting cases dates from the year 1662, when an unmarried burgher's daughter started legal proceedings against

---

3 Johann Conradin Beyerbach, ed., *Sammlung der Verordnungen der Reichsstadt Frankfurt am Main* (6 vols, Frankfurt am Main: Hermann, 1798), vol. 1, pp. 553–5.

4 See Chapter 2.

5 *The Table Talk of Martin Luther*, trans. and ed. William Hazlitt (London, 1857), no. 725.

6 ST February 28, 1618 and BB 1618, p. 168.

a burgher with whom she had had a child.[7] She insisted that he, the father, not only pay for all the expenses incurred but also that he take and rear the child. Frankfurt's women also resorted to indirect criminal accusations—rumors. Local arrest procedures revealed that a number of suspects were brought to trial based on rumors and hearsay.[8] And women, just like men, started and conveyed rumors.

Frankfurt's women played a role even during criminal court proceedings. The city council frequently sought the expertise of women, particularly midwives, to establish or confirm pregnancies in suspects involved in infanticide, incest, and other reproductive-related offenses. But most curiously, by the mid-seventeenth century their advice was less frequently sought. Instead, men were increasingly listed in the archives, such as barbers or "Medicorum, Physicorum and Chirurgis" as they were now frequently referred to.[9] Thus the evidence suggests that an emerging male medical profession was gradually displacing women in the courtroom.

This removal of female experts from criminal court proceedings is even more striking considering that it coincided with the increased employment of advocates or legal advisors by the city council. Advocates were trained in Roman Law and assisted the council in establishing the proper punishment for criminal offenses. Needless to say, no woman was to be found among such advocates. Women were not trained in Roman Law, and had no access to the universities. And, as the various chapters in this study show, the sentences suggested by Frankfurt's advocates were often influenced by social and/or political factors. Numerous soldiers sentenced to death for manslaughter had their sentences mitigated due to the influence of local advocates who suggested they fight the Turks or the French, or be banished.[10] No woman sentenced for infanticide was ever accorded a milder verdict.[11] An emerging male legal profession seemed to identify more closely with the sentencing of male suspects.

Torture

No immediate gender gap existed with regard to the use of torture. The torture patterns for female criminals closely resembled those for men in both

7 BB 1662, p. 219.
8 See Chapter 3.
9 RP 1665, p. 57; RP 1687, p. 9.
10 See Chapter 11.
11 See Chapters 8 and 9.

quantity and quality, especially during the period 1562–94. Fifty-one out of 79 female convicts (64.6 percent) were subjected to torture. The ratio for men during the same period was 286 of 383 (74.7 percent).[12] Qualitatively speaking, women were subjected to the same kind of torture as men, namely either "mit Güte"—which is translated literally (and not ironically) as "with kindness"—or "with pain." The former consisted of a psychological drama by displaying the torture instruments in front of the suspect, while "with pain" quite obviously meant applying them.

Women by no means succumbed to speedy confessions at the mere sight of the torture instruments. Out of a total of 95 women tortured, only 36 confessed at the sight of the torture instruments.[13] Confessions made during the application of torture were valid only once ratified by the suspect a day or two after such an application. If the confession was rescinded, torture could be reapplied. And women were also subjected to frequent torture procedures. Several even withstood torture and did not confess. However, as the case of the collaborative infanticide disclosed (see Chapter 8), Frankfurt's advocates, as a consequence, did subject two of the suspects to extra harsh follow-up torturous procedures. In another unrelated instance, Frankfurt's authorities seemed to have been rather annoyed, for the records read "sie hat ihr Maul schweigen lassen also das man ihr bekanntnis nit hab könne"— she kept her mouth shut so that we could not get her confession.[14] Pregnancy, however, affected the application of torture. Out of three registered cases of pregnant women, two were tortured "with kindness" while the third was subjected to "a little pain."[15]

Punishments

Women, just like men, were subjected to both capital and corporal punishments. But women's capital punishments differed from those of men. Until 1618, capital punishments for women consisted of being thrown into the local Main River from a designated bridge or live burial. Out of the total of 24 women sentenced to death, six were drowned. In contrast, out of 313 executed men, only five were handed down such a penalty.[16] And these five male culprits were not even representative because two were Jews, who were generally

12 Based on entries in the BB and RP series.

13 Ibid.

14 ST November 16, 1625.

15 RP 1573, pp. 52, 78.

16 Based on entries in the ST.

handed harsher punishments than other males. Two of the other men had been banished from Frankfurt under the threat of drowning if they returned, and the fifth was a notorious horse thief. Drowning thus seems to have been predominantly applied to women, as is most clearly demonstrated by an incest case of 1588. The stepfather was decapitated, while his stepdaughter was drowned.[17]

As mentioned above, live burial was also a female death sentence. The only two cases of such a punishment in Frankfurt, one in 1498 and the other in 1585, were given to women.[18] The accused in the latter case had murdered her former employer, and as a punishment was pinched on her arms with hot tongs in front of the house where she had committed the crime. She was then led to and placed in an open grave, her body covered with wooden branches, and a wooden pole rammed through her heart. True, no woman was ever broken on the wheel in Frankfurt, but it is an academic question which punishment was more cruel.

The harshness of the death penalties imposed on women changed in 1618, when the first woman was decapitated in Frankfurt for committing incest. Thereafter, decapitation by sword became the norm. But this milder trend cannot be ascribed to a more lenient treatment of women. It was in keeping with Frankfurt's general trend toward less cruel capital punishments. Compared to other European locations, however, Frankfurt's women received milder punishments, especially after 1618. In Frankfurt no woman was hanged, while in Amsterdam female offenders were hanged until the mid-eighteenth century and in England until the end of that century.[19] While in Frankfurt no woman was broken on the wheel, a woman suffered such a fate in Amsterdam as late as 1746.

As to corporal sentences, women again were not spared harsh physical punishments. Frankfurt's women, like men, were flogged in public, put in the pillory, and banished. Out of a total of 76 women sentenced for simple theft, 30 were flogged, 25 put in the pillory and 21 banished. Unlike Amsterdam, however, none lost an ear, and none was ever branded. In fact, in Amsterdam during the 1730–50 period "a greater proportion of women than men were branded."[20] In France women were also branded until the eighteenth century.[21]

---

17 ST November 8 and November 15, 1588.

18 Ferdinand Rau, *Beiträge zum Kriminalrecht der Freien Reichsstadt Frankfurt am Main im Mittelalter bis 1532* (Potsdam: Kramer, 1916), p. 86; ST June 11, 1585.

19 Pieter Spierenburg, *The Spectacle of Suffering* (Cambridge: Cambridge University Press, 1984), p. 74; J.M. Beattie, *Crime and Courts in England, 1600–1800* (Princeton, NJ: Princeton University Press, 1986), pp. 454, 501, 515, 536–7.

20 Spierenburg, *Spectacle*, pp. 75, 167.

21 Julius Ralph Ruff, *Crime, Justice and Public Order in Old Regime France: The Sénéchaussées of Libourne and Bazas, 1696–1789* (London/Dover, NH: Croom Helm, 1984), pp. 113, 117.

However, Frankfurt's women were sentenced to physical punishments for which their male counterparts were either not convicted at all or received monetary fines only.[22] Prostitution and fornication were primarily women-oriented punishments in that only three men were sentenced for prostitution in contrast to 32 women; in the case of fornication 21 men versus 43 women were sentenced. However, most noticeably, this trend only emerged during the late sixteenth and early seventeenth centuries. While from 1562 to 1594 six men and nine women were sentenced for fornication, this jumped to 21 female versus only five male sentences during the ensuing period, 1595 to 1627. In addition, there exists a considerable qualitative difference between these numbers. Only three men were sentenced for simple fornication, while the rest received corporal punishments only in conjunction with other crimes. Women had a far higher rate of sentencing based on simple fornication and prostitution, a trend closely connected to the guild-induced sexual transvaluation.[23]

Mitigating Factors

There existed, however, various ways to mitigate the punishments. Again, pregnancy could have a moderating effect on the penal structure. Out of 14 verifiable case entries, the earliest in 1573 and the latest in 1662, a total of 12 pregnant women were given a milder sentence, while in two instances the sentences were not changed but carried out after the child was born.[24] This policy was not unique to Frankfurt. In England, for example, "approximately one-half (of all those pardoned) had successfully pleaded pregnancy at assizes."[25] In Frankfurt, the mitigated sentences consisted in seven instances of life banishment and in five of the pillory and banishment.[26] No pregnant woman was flogged in Frankfurt.

Yet one cannot help but wonder about the so-called leniency in these cases. Although the sentences were mitigated, the punishments—especially banishment sentences—were still harsh when one realizes that in almost all cases

---

22 BB 1607, p. 23; BB 1618, p. 168; BB 1668, p. 212; ST April 2, 1668.

23 See Chapter 1; the data is based on entries in ST.

24 BB 1636, p. 148; BB 1662, p. 87.

25 James C. Oldham, "On Pleading the Belly: A History of the Jury of Matrons," *Criminal Justice History*, 6 (1985): 1–64; Beattie, *Crime*, p. 431; R.A. Sharpe, *Judicial Punishment in England* (London: Faber & Faber, 1990), p. 41.

26 ST December 23, 1573; ST February 11, 1574; ST February 28, 1582; ST October 14, 1607; ST May 19, 1609; ST October 26, 1615; ST January 10, 1618; ST April 9, 1618; ST October 24, 1618; ST December 8, 1619; ST Macy 17, 1625; ST December 7, 1633.

the woman was single and would have to care for her baby outside the protection of the city walls. In one very moving case description of a decapitation for infanticide, the female culprit even stated that she preferred the death sentence over banishment.[27]

Other mitigating factors were disease, religious conversion, extended imprisonment prior to the actual sentencing, the reimbursement of stolen goods, or young age. For these categories, there was no noticeable gender gap. But when it came to rape, the gender gap was flagrant. Most noticeably, there were only two rape cases. In both instances stepfathers had coerced their 14-year-old stepdaughters. True, the stepdaughters received a milder punishment due to their young age, but they were punished, nevertheless, in that both were banished from Frankfurt.[28] These sentences raise, of course, the question whether the fairy-tale notion of the bad stepmother is a fully adequate representation. Stepfathers contributed their own share to making the lives of stepchildren unbearable.

However, arguably the most biased gender-related punishment consisted of sentencing women who had committed no crime whatsoever but whose husbands had been convicted of criminal offenses. In six cases women were banished simply because they were perceived as suspicious for no apparent reason other than being married to a convicted criminal.[29] An additional 18 women, some with their children, were ousted from Frankfurt when their husbands received the banishment sentence. In such cases, entries in the archives almost nonchalantly stated that the offender was "to have his wife" or "his wife and children to follow him."[30] These extremely unjust punishments deprived innocent women and children of the security of the town in addition to depicting wives as mere appendages of men with no personal freedom whatsoever.

This sentencing pattern is in sharp contrast to eighteenth-century English female criminals, who "were not held responsible for illegal acts done in the company of their husbands."[31] It also is in clear distinction to Languedoc, France,

27 ST January 19, 1659.

28 ST November 22, 1604; ST December 31, 1623.

29 ST May 5, 1585; ST May 7, 1585; ST April 7, 1592; ST October 14, 1594; ST October 24, 1618; ST May 13, 1659.

30 BB 1568, p. 89; BB 1586, p. 134; BB 1587, p. 201; BB 1588, p. 130; ST March 26, 1590; BB 1595, p. 248; ST April 20, 1596; BB 1606, p. 35; ST May 19, 1609; ST October 9, 1613; ST November 4, 1616; ST November 14, 1618; ST August 11, 1627; ST April 22, 1635; BB 1634, p. 157; BB 1664, p. 129; BB 1674, p. 40; BB 1696, p. 13.

31 J.M. Beattie, "The Criminality of Women in Eighteenth Century England," *Journal of Social History*, 8 (Summer 1975): 85–97, pp. 95–6.

were allegedly married women were better protected.[32] For Frankfurt, no such assertions can be maintained.

In contrast, when it came to pleading for milder criminal punishments, Frankfurt's women had more leeway. The goal of private pleas or intercessions was to achieve a mitigation of the sentence. Commutations of sentences could take various forms, such as changing death by hanging to the milder version of decapitation in addition to a speedy burial. It could even entail the acquittal of a culprit, as demonstrated by various case entries.[33] While traditional historiography has it that in the majority of cases pleas were voiced and submitted by persons of high social or political standing, this was not the case in Frankfurt.[34] Here, the vast majority of supplications originated with family members or friends of the accused.

Most remarkably, it was Frankfurt's women who played the decisive role in entering intercessions throughout the 1562–1696 period. They constituted the largest group of plea bargainers, with 43 such pleas. Wives of suspects led this list with 23 pleas followed by 10 mothers. In contrast, fathers petitioned for a milder sentence in 17 instances, relatives in general in 16, children of suspects in 13 and friends in 13 cases.

The high representation of women among plea bargainers seems somewhat paradoxical if one considers that very few intercessions were voiced on their behalf, namely 19 compared to 83 for men (see Table 7.1). Who, for example, would plead for a prostitute? But the most striking aspect of this trend is the fact that many wives, who were asking for milder punishments for their husbands, happened to be the prime victims of their husbands' criminal behavior.[35] It surely does not make sense that women whose husbands had betrayed them through incestuous relations with their own daughters or sisters would afterwards turn around and plead for milder punishments. The answer to this riddle lies in the nature of contemporary penal structures and the socio-economic status of women. Almost all punishments, whether capital or corporal, were meted out in public. In addition, most corporal punishments entailed banishment as well. Public exposure of the culprit entailed public exposure of the culprit's family, and male banishments often entailed the banishment of a convict's wife and children. Both the implicit punishment of the relatives via public exposure and

---

32 Nicole Castan, *Les criminels de Languedoc: Les exigences d'ordre et les voies du resentiment dans une societe prerevolutionnaire, 1750–1790* (Toulouse: L'Université de Toulouse-le-Mirail, 1980), p. 29.

33 BB 1574, p. 188; BB 1566, p. 281; BB 1593, p. 117.

34 Beattie, *Crime*, p. 431; Ruff, *Crime*, pp. 48, 62.

35 BB 1611, p. 178; RP 1643, pp. 40, 138; RP 1646, p. 33; RP 1662, p. 24; BB 1662, p. 87.

the explicit punishment by sharing the banishment sentences prompted many wives to plead for their criminal husbands.

Contemporary women could not just leave the scene, or their husbands or the community. Once women were turned out of the guilds they became increasingly dependent on their husbands. Therefore, while emotional reasons surely played a role in petitioning for milder sentences, women interceded out of practical concerns. They were pleading for themselves.

The large number of granted requests demonstrates the effectiveness of such private supplications (Table 7.1). Considering that a suspect had no recourse to a court of appeal, the submission of private pleas was of prime significance. It offered an accused access to indirect channels of appeals. Thus intercessions constituted an important extrajudicial means of reducing penalties throughout the period, and women were the most ardent and most successful of all plea bargainers.

Table 7.1 Distribution of pleas per gender, 1562–1689

	1562–1594		**1595–1627**		**1628–1660**		**1661–1689**		**Total**	
Outcome	M	F	M	F	M	F	M	F	M	F
Requests granted	10	1	10	2	10	3	15	7	45	13
Requests ignored	11	1	9	2	1	1	2	0	23	4
Outcome unclear	5	0	4	0	1	1	5	1	15	2
Total	26	2	23	4	12	5	22	8	83	19

Source: Bürgermeisterbücher (BB) 1562–1625, 1627, 1629–46; Rathsprotokolle (PR) 1562–1625, 1627, 1629–89.

Conclusion

In conclusion, while Frankfurt's partial laws allowed for preferential treatment of local patrician women, such loopholes were far more advantageous for men in general. True, while women retained a surprising amount of leeway with regard to crime reporting, their influence waned considerably in criminal court procedures. Commensurate with their general socio-economic decline, Frankfurt's female court experts, usually midwives, were slowly phased out starting from the mid-seventeenth century. Instead, male doctors were consulted. This trend coincided with the increased use of male legal advisors, the advocates. Reminiscent of Frankfurt's partial laws, Frankfurt's advocates exhibited social and political biases expressed in partial punishments such as for soldiers and infanticides. True, pregnancy had a mitigating effect on the general penal structure. However, women were given physical punishments for crimes their male counterparts paid for with monetary fines. Most noticeably, they were even punished simply for having been married to criminal husbands. It should, therefore, not come as a surprise that women ranked among the most ardent plea bargainers in this early modern German society. They were implicitly pleading for themselves.

Chapter 8

Women Bonding: Collaborative Infanticide

Most historical studies disclose infanticide as the crime of lone, unwed mothers, primarily female servants.[1] While an unwed female servant was also at the center of the 1645/46 incident, Frankfurt's authorities indicted two additional women, both married, and leveled conspiracy charges against them of having helped the servant in her efforts to abort and subsequently kill her newborn. Eventually even the husbands of the servant's sister and her friend were questioned. The five comprehensive and at times overlapping trial documents reveal in relentless and at times breathtaking and harrowing detail the various legal and emotional twists and turns, beginning with the discovery of an unburned baby corpse in an oven followed by steadily intensifying engagements on the part of the legal and judicial authorities.[2]

Arrest and Initial Interrogations

Not surprisingly, as was frequently the case in contemporary small towns, the initial inquiry was prompted by a rumor, which eventually led to the arrest of

---

1 Ulinka Rublack, *The Crimes of Women in Early Modern Germany* (Oxford: Clarendon Press, 1999), chapter 5 and her "The Public Body: Policing Abortion in Early Modern Germany," in Lynn Abrams and Elizabeth Harvey, *Gender Relations in German History: Power, Agency, and Experience from the Sixteenth to the Twentieth Century* (London: University College London Press, 1996), pp. 57–81; Otto Ulbricht, "Kindesmord in der Frühen Neuzeit," in Ute Gerhard, ed., *Frauen in der Geschichte des Rechts: Von der Frühen Neuzeit bis zur Gegenwart* (Munich: Beck, 1997); Keith Wrightson, "Infanticide in European History," *Criminal Justice History: An International Annual*, 3 (1982); Peter C. Hoffer and N.E.H. Hull, *Murdering Mothers: Infanticide in England and New England, 1558–1803* (New York: New York University Press, 1981). See also Cornelia Hughes Dayton, "Taking the Trade: Abortion and Gender Relations in an Eighteenth-Century New England Village," *The William and Mary Quarterly*, 3rd series, 48/1 (1991): 19–49. Richard van Dülmen, *Frauen vor Gericht: Kindesmord in der frühen Neuzeit* (Frankfurt am Main: Fischer Taschenbuch, 1991); Susanna Burgharts, "Jungfräulichkeit oder Reinheit? Zur Änderung von Argumentationsmuster vor dem Baseler Ehegericht im 16. und 17. Jahrhundert," in Richard van Dülmen, ed., *Dynamik der Tradition* (Frankfurt am Main: Fischer Taschenbuch, 1992).

2 Criminalia (CR) 1080; the lack of detailed footnotes is due to erroneous/missing page numbers.

the maid Agnes Schönin on December 11, 1645. On the day of her arrest, six of Frankfurt's "medici" and barbers submitted their written report after they had examined the dead child. They found its nose bent sideways, the left eye damaged and markings on its head, and they concluded that these injuries had occurred as a result of heavy pressure having been exerted on the child's throat.

Immediately after receiving this report, Frankfurt's authorities, the city councilors, sent two municipal midwives—Mutter, mother, Catharina, and Mutter, mother, Christine, as the midwives were referred to in the documents—to question and physically examine the arrested maid. They reported back that Agnes had initially refused to have her breasts examined, and had denied allegations of having given birth. However, when they eventually succeeded in convincing her to submit to an examination they "discovered milk oozing from her nipples," which prompted them to put the dead child in her lap. While it is unclear how they had obtained the body, the midwives continued with their rendition asserting that this gesture led the servant to provide them with an explanation.

Agnes, giving her account in a staccato-style version, claimed to have been sexually abused by two soldiers, but that she had been unaware of her pregnancy. Because of her swelling belly, she had consulted a Jewish doctor, who found her to be "verstopft," constipated, in addition to retaining a lot of water. He had prescribed a remedy consisting of a long list of herbs to be put together by the apothecary. She stated that she had consulted another, foreign, doctor, who had come to see her twice and who had given her the same diagnosis of constipation. Also, another midwife, called the Wormser Anna, had visited her and she, too, had concurred with the doctors' findings that she was not pregnant.

After hearing this account from the midwives, Frankfurt's authorities, most remarkably, did not proceed to question the doctors but instead interrogated the Wormser Anna. She readily confirmed her visit to Agnes, which, she stated, had been initiated by the wife of a soldier, whom she knew. Upon arrival, based on a smell she perceived, she had jokingly exclaimed, whom she should help to deliver a child, an exclamation which elicited a shriek from Agnes' sister Elizabeth, who also had been in the room. She shouted "God help us, do you think that we have prostitutes or pregnant women among us?" Not waiting for an answer, the sisters asked her for advice on how to help Agnes' constipation. They handed her a powdery substance prepared by the foreign doctor, which she tasted and found very bitter and sharp.

After this verbal exchange, according to the Wormser Anna, she proceeded to examine Agnes' belly, after which she told the sisters that if she, Agnes, were married, she would think her to be pregnant.

Again, her statement caused an immediate verbal outburst, this time from both sisters that this was impossible as she had not seen a man on a regular basis.

They suggested instead that Agnes must have had something bad to drink during the recent harvest. Before leaving, so the Wormser Anna continued her account, she had handed Agnes a Blutstein, bloodstone, a hematite for healing purposes.

But her visit had not ended peacefully. The midwife added that she had been mistreated verbally and physically by Agnes' brother-in-law, Elizabeth's husband, who, so she alleged, must have overheard some of the verbal exchanges, for he pushed her down the stairs accompanied by a barrage of insulting words.

After evaluating these reports, the city council decided to question Agnes, the suspect. At the beginning of this, her first of many interrogations, she was asked routine questions such as her name and her age, to which she replied Agnes Schönin, approximately 20 years old. While this seemingly harmless exchange appeared to be devoid of any judicial bias, the first glimpse of a not so above-board attitude presented itself in a parenthetical entry in the document stating that, based on her appearance, she looked more like 30.

Follow-up questions now concentrated on the topic of her arrest and the charges levied against her. Asked whether she knew why she had been arrested, she answered candidly: because of the child she had borne. Being a single maid, the identity of the father now entered the picture. Questioned as to who he was, she reconfirmed her statement given to the two midwives, that she had been sexually forced against her will (raped) by two foreign soldiers. Obviously not content with this explanation, the interrogators countered that they had heard different allegations, to which she replied God be her witness, she had not had any other sexual encounters. And, in line with her earlier statement to the midwives, she denied having had any knowledge of her pregnancy.

More detailed questioning followed. Queried about her menstruation, she admitted that it had stopped, adding that she had told the Jewish doctor who, not suspecting her of being pregnant, ascribed it to serious constipation. Asked whether she did not feel the child move, she conceded that there were rumblings in her belly like nuts, a symptom she had also described to the foreign doctor whom she had consulted. He too thought of her condition as constipation.

Urged to disclose the unfolding of the birth, she described the following scenario. On the Thursday prior to giving birth she had asked her sister to have the Wormser Anna visit her for medical assistance. Upon touching her belly she, similar to the doctors, had also found her to be suffering from "böse Verstopfung," serious constipation. The next day, Agnes continued, she had felt better, but on the Saturday it turned considerably worse.

Adding to her stress, so she pointed out, was the fact that quite a number of people had been present at the time in the house where she lived, such as her father, her brother and brother-in-law, her sister, a woman residing close by and another woman. When they left on Sunday she felt better. On Monday morning she had the foreign doctor come to visit her again. He informed her that the constipation was easing but that she should cleanse herself. Following his instructions, she asked her sister to take a bucket of water to the doctor's house so that he could mix in some medication. While her sister was gone, the pain increased dramatically and, standing up, she gave birth to a dead child who fell to the floor.

After this detailed rendition she was questioned to explain the markings on the child. She exclaimed, calling God her witness, that the child had been dead at birth and that she had not done anything wrong. Questioned as to what she did after the delivery, she said that she had gone downstairs because someone had knocked at the door. Since nobody was at home she opened the door and saw a female beggar standing there, to whom she gave the bundle to hide it. The bundle, she explained, contained the dead child wrapped in some cloth together with the umbilical cord. She denied having known this person, strengthening her argument with the exclamation "even if she had to suffer instant death." When questioned as to what the woman was wearing, she replied she could not remember. Lastly, when asked why she did not have the child publicly buried she replied that since she had given birth secretly and alone, and because she had kept her forced sexual encounter and following pregnancy secretive as well, she did not want now to resort to a public burial.

While this extensive rendition on the part of Agnes did not convince Frankfurt's authorities of her innocence and they proceeded with further legal steps, her initial judicial trial-oriented statements disclosed, nevertheless, some remarkable contemporary medical cultural practices. It was in particular the custom of smells as conveyors of diagnostic guidelines that stood out. Wormser Anna "smelled" Agnes' pregnancy, a diagnostic procedure obviously medically more precise than those offered by the doctors Agnes had consulted. Also, while the doctors prescribed various powders, the Wormser Anna relied on the medical healing powers of a stone, the hematite. And since the documents do not disclose any adverse reaction to her statement, one might conclude that this procedure was a generally accepted cultural healing tradition.

Torture, Friendship and an Informer

Frankfurt's authorities, obviously disbelieving Agnes' statement now consulted their three advocates for legal advice on how to proceed. Drs. Maximilian Faust von Aschaffenburg, Zacharias Strenglin, and Lucas Kupferschmidt submitted a joint written legal opinion in which they argued, referring to the *Constitutio Criminalis Carolina*, the law code of 1532 promulgated under the Catholic

Emperor Charles V, that when a woman keeps her pregnancy secret and gives birth in secrecy without the help of others, her subsequent statements are not to be trusted. Also, they projected, without any proof, that because the maid had "invented" the unfolding of the murder of the child in an "unchristian" way, she ought to be questioned under torture. Finding her to be "extremely stubborn," they suggested she ought first to be subjected to the thumbscrew and if that did not yield the desired result, the leg screw in order "to elicit the truth with pain." Toward that end, they prepared a 37-item questionnaire, based on the various items disclosed during the preceding interrogations.

At the start of this procedure, when the interrogators had barely reached the fourth question, namely why she had not realized that she was pregnant, a claim she defended, she was subjected to the thumbscrew. Even under terrible pain Agnes did not change her answer. She also stuck with her statement that she had only observed some rumblings in her belly like nuts, a reply which resulted in the thumbscrews being tightened. Obviously not content with her refusal to admit to any wrongdoing, the interrogators applied the leg screw, which they subsequently tightened. But again, even under this heightened excruciating pain, being tortured four times in a row, Agnes did not alter her earlier statements—to the obvious consternation, if not frustration, of the interrogators, for they left a little note at the bottom of the documents stating that she had not even shed a single tear throughout the whole ordeal.

While in many other instances suspects who withstood torture without confessing were "purgirt," cleared, and released from prison—often accompanied with a banishment sentence—Agnes' case took a different turn, possibly caused in part by her fear and concern for two other women. After having withstood this torturous ordeal she beseeched a woman in the hospital where she was held prisoner to contact her sister Elizabeth and another woman, the wife of a soldier, "for the sake of the Last Judgment" and tell them to go away or leave town.

As she would later admit, she resorted to this desperate mechanism to warn the two women because she doubted whether she could withstand another painful interrogation without implicating them. Her action offered the first glimpse not only of her deep concern for the other two women but also of proof of the existence of a shared and deep sense of mutual understanding and assistance among contemporary women, attitudes which came to the fore in greater detail during the further unfolding of this trial.

Unfortunately, this "united front" was not shared by the woman in whom Agnes had confided and put her trust to warn the others. Instead of relaying Agnes' message, she contacted the authorities. This informer's betrayal caused the authorities to act very fast. They immediately re-questioned the suspect, who now admitted to the involvement of two other women, her sister Elizabeth and

Catharina, a soldier's wife. She also revised her earlier statement, now admitting that she could not tell whether the child had been dead or alive because of the intense birthing pain. Also contrary to her earlier statement she now declared that the dead child had remained in the house overnight and that Catharina had carried it away only the next day.

Additional Suspects and a Disappearance

Frankfurt's authorities now tried to question Catharina, but they could not find her: the soldier's wife had disappeared. Her disappearance prompted an even more rigorous pursuit in that Frankfurt's two mayors now got involved and questioned the husband of the missing woman, Andreas Kintzbach, who served as a local soldier. After posing some routine questions he was asked where they lived, to which he answered in the same house as Agnes and Elizabeth and her husband.

Questioned about the disappearance of his wife Catharina, he readily stated that she had left to visit her very sick father in the town of Wetzlar, her place of origin. He denied, however, having known that his wife had carried the dead child out of Agnes' lodging. Obviously still not believing Agnes' rape claim, the authorities now pursued a different angle by questioning the soldier as to whether he had not "sensed" that Agnes' brother-in-law, Michael Buchmüller, the owner of the house where they all lived, had had an affair with the arrested Agnes. Again the soldier pleaded ignorance.

The mayors had their own version of the disappearance of the soldier's wife and treated it as a "flight." Consequently, based on their advocates' advice, they sent a letter to the town of Wetzlar to track her down.

In the meantime the suspect's sister and her husband were subjected to a series of questions. Michael stated that he had not been aware of his sister-in-law's pregnancy, elaborating further that he found out about the birth only after she had been arrested. He also asserted he did not know the identity of the father of the child, but admitted that he heard of two soldiers having raped her. When confronted with town rumors that he loved his sister-in-law Agnes more than his own wife and that he had sexual relations with her, he exclaimed "God should protect him from that," asserting that he loved the accused like a good friend. But his deposition did not prevent him from being arrested.

Elizabeth, his wife, repeated Agnes' allegation of her sexual assault by two soldiers and asserted that she had not known about her sister's pregnancy until approximately one week prior to the birth. She admitted that she had brewed some special drinks for her sister, but only those prescribed by the Jewish doctor.

She also confirmed that the foreign doctor, who had visited Agnes a few days prior to the birth, diagnosed her condition as serious by asserting that her entire belly was "rotten." Her statements with regard to the unfolding of the birth confirmed her sister's second, adjusted rendition. Questioned as to how long the child was alive she repeated her sister's claim that it had been stillborn, so "God be her witness." She added, however, that she had wrapped the dead child in clothes and given it to Catharina to carry to a cemetery or somewhere else. She also stated that the soldier himself had not been aware of his wife's involvement. Similar to her husband, she was arrested but her young child joined her, because it still depended on the mother's milk.

From the various questions raised and answers given, the spatial setting of the alleged crime scene begins to crystallize. All of the suspects together with their various children lived in the same house and seemingly they all had a friendly relationship with each other. The various follow-up interrogations would disclose, however, that it was the three women who shared the closest bond and mutual concern.

Caring Sisters

Testing their caring relationship, Frankfurt's authorities had Agnes confront her sister Elizabeth. The two sisters declared that they were unaware of any injuries to the child but Agnes admitted that during birth she had hit the child with her legs, a declaration immediately followed by her assertion that this had not been done on purpose. The two sisters reiterated that the child had been born dead and that it was only once the child had been born that the soldier's wife arrived and agreed to take it away. They also asserted that the very morning of the birth the doctor had given Agnes seven pills, which she took, and these, according to Elizabeth, must have hastened the birth.

Agnes now also conceded that she had confided in her sister about her pregnancy, but only toward the end. By contrast, she had told the soldier's wife, Catharina, early on, namely six weeks after the sexual incident. Catharina had immediately consoled her not to worry; she would brew her a drink made of beer and bay leaves, which would "loosen everything in a woman's body." She, Catharina, had added—obviously trying to reassure Agnes—that she had given the same drink to another local woman who feared she would give birth prior to nine months after marriage. The drink had aborted the child, and the woman in question was now a respectable person in town.

Agnes also mentioned that she followed several of Catharina's other recommendations, such as the bleeding of her feet; using some herbs and taking a special bath, the "content of which was to kill everything in a human's and animal's body within hours"; and not to tell anyone about the pregnancy, and that she would carry the child away later. Questioned as to why she had kept her pregnancy and birth secret, Agnes answered out of concern for her sister and her three young children, who might otherwise be subjected to ill repute.

Agnes thus described Catharina, the soldier's wife, as a close woman friend who was ready to help her at every turn, especially coping with her anxieties over her pregnancy. But then Agnes made a stunning revelation. She now conceded that she had had two sexual encounters with the very same married soldier whose wife, Catharina, had tried to help her abort and shield her pregnancy. She admitted that it had happened once in the barn and the other time close to the well when no one was around, and that she had kept it secret in order to protect her friend the soldier's wife, her sister and their children.

This twist of events only thickened the suspicion of the authorities. They proceeded to arrest the soldier, who faced immediate questioning. But he only had to answer eight questions, with the focus on whether he knew who the father of Agnes' child might be. He claimed ignorance. Once confronted with Agnes' earlier admission, he did yield. He denied, however, having had any knowledge of the planned abortion or of his wife's involvement in carrying the child away.

By now four people—Agnes and her sister Elizabeth, the latter's husband and the soldier—had been arrested, while Catharina, the soldier's wife, was still missing. Flagrantly absent in the various documents, however, was any mention of questioning the doctors who had diagnosed Agnes' condition as constipation. Instead, Frankfurt extended its legal search by contacting the preacher of a nearby suburb where Agnes had resided. He informed them that he knew of her involvement with another soldier who, however, subsequently married a woman in another town. While he asserted that he was not aware that she had been pregnant, he did attest to her cheery nature.

Extradition and Strong Female Bonds

Frankfurt's authorities now started to tighten the legal surroundings of the soldier's wife, Catharina. They contacted the mayor of Wetzlar, Catharina's home town, where she allegedly had sought refuge and asked him to have her arrested, questioned based on a questionnaire Frankfurt had submitted, and have her answers sent back to Frankfurt. They also stressed not to release her until further notice.

The town of Wetzlar promptly responded. But its authorities had a problem. After a thorough search of her father's house as well as looking for her in town, they were not able to find her. Two days later, they were, however, successful. They informed Frankfurt that Catharina had appeared with a very small child and that they had promptly arrested her for questioning. When Catharina's answers finally arrived, they did not meet with local approval. It was especially her claim not to have known about Agnes' pregnancy that increased Frankfurt's authorities' suspicion of a possible collaboration among the three women. Hence, so they decided, Catharina had to be extradited to Frankfurt in order to be confronted with Agnes and Elizabeth.

But this intended transfer proved to be very difficult to carry out. It was a legally complex and dangerous proposition because Catharina would have to pass through three different independent regional territories, and this while the Thirty Years War was still raging. It would entail a lot of coordination, in addition to hiring soldiers to protect Catharina and her small child en route.

Frankfurt's authorities were adamant about her extradition. They challenged the town of Wetzlar—which was very reluctant to release her, pointing to the dangers she would have to face on the way to Frankfurt—by contacting various other places with judicial leverage, as well as those territories through which Catharina would have to pass. In a series of letters exchanged with numerous authorities, Frankfurt's city councilors stressed that Catharina was sought for abortion and complicity in the murder of a child, and the promise that they would pay for all costs, including all expenses accrued for the hiring of soldiers who had to accompany her and guarantee her safe journey. Eventually Frankfurt's efforts yielded the desired result. Catharina was released from Wetzlar prison, and she arrived safely in Frankfurt heavily guarded by 40 musketeers accompanied by a very high transfer bill.

Arrested on the spot, Catharina was subjected to intense questioning. After she stated her age to be 50, she was charged with abortion. But she denied these allegations, referring instead to the "Christian and Jewish" doctors whom Agnes had consulted and who had prescribed purgatives. When asked about the unfolding of the actual birth she explained that Elizabeth had come to her while her husband and children were in church and told her that Agnes had given birth to a dead child and that she should help. When she, Catharina, suggested to Elizabeth to have the child buried similar to other "children of prostitutes," Elizabeth exclaimed that this would entail a disastrous dishonor.

Obviously sensing an opening in their examination, the interrogators now focused on the burial of the dead child by using a suggestive questioning technique. They asked Catharina why she had let herself be used by the two other women to carry the dead child out of the house. But Catharina, not falling for this trap, answered: they all lived in the house together and they all got along extremely well.

Her positive account of the living conditions did not, however, include her husband, for she explained that she had fled to Wetzlar because she was afraid of him. She described him as having a violent temper, and if he had found out that she had carried the dead child out of the house, he would have severely beaten her. But she was not spared a similar fate when she arrived in Wetzlar, where her father beat her so severely that she left him abruptly, only to be arrested by the local authorities.

Her confessed strong cooperative bond to the two sisters was, however, stretched to the limits when she was told that it was actually her own husband who had impregnated Agnes. Remarkably, she did not break down or turn on her friends. She only exclaimed in tears that she had been unaware of it.

While one can only hypothesize about the reasons for Catharina's amazing composure at finding out about her husband's infidelity with her close friend, her fear of her husband's physical abuse—what one would now call domestic violence—might have been a contributing factor in why she bonded with the women. As the follow-up interrogations would demonstrate, Agnes and Elizabeth stated similar misgivings. Thus, the women, apart from sharing a common trepidation over shame caused by giving birth to an illegitimate child, also shared the fear of becoming victims of physical violence and abuse by the men in their lives. And these apprehensions surely contributed to their forging strong supportive ties.

Judicial Tightening

Not content with Catharina's account, Agnes was now confronted with Catharina. Catharina detailed the unfolding of the birth scenario as she had perceived it. She explained that while Agnes was in labor she was sitting next door with Elizabeth and her husband as well as Agnes' father and the children. Elizabeth then asked the men and children to leave the room, which they did, unaware of what transpired next door. Subsequently, Elizabeth went to help her sister during childbirth. When the various family members returned, they were told that a clump of blood had oozed out of Agnes, a cover-up account which seemed to have worked, at least temporarily. Finalizing her account, Catharina asserted that she had offered her services and help to Agnes "as if she were her sister."

The interrogators now focused on Agnes, who was pressed into releasing more information about her sexual relationships with other men, including references to her brother-in-law. She conceded that apart from having had sex twice with Catharina's husband, she had also had sex three times with another soldier several years earlier. She, however, vehemently denied again having had any sexual relations with her sister's husband, a denial which prompted the interrogators—as disclosed by an off-hand note on the transcript—to proceed with putting the torture instruments on Agnes "to frighten her." While steadfastly denying these allegations, she exclaimed that if her brother-in-law had known she was pregnant he would have "beaten me half to death."

Seemingly testing the women's bond further, the theme of who administered what drinks to Agnes resurfaced. Agnes restated that Catharina had given her one made of beer and bay leaves and a green copper drink to abort the child, in addition to suggesting she take a bath and have bloodletting procedures conducted on her feet. She also stated that Catharina had told her about a woman in one of Frankfurt's little streets who had taken a drink infused with saffron, which had led to abortive results.

Catharina defended her action that she only carried out what the Jewish doctor had prescribed; and, while she admitted having administered a drink made of beer and bay leaves, she asserted that this did not cause any harm since she was drinking it herself. She restated that she had offered to help Agnes because she was very close to her, as close as if she were her sister, and that it was done as a good-will gesture.

Also, somewhat more assertively, Catharina now claimed that her husband must have been aware of both Agnes' pregnancy and that he was the father of the child. However, her allegations were not taken seriously and the topic did not resurface again. Instead, Frankfurt's authorities refocused on the drinks Catharina had suggested by contacting their local "medici."

The doctors' findings were unmitigated assertions: the medications suggested were not only to open up constipation blockages but would also serve to abort the "Frucht," fruit. While bay leaves, so their argument went, were not in a "classe fortissimorium," when absorbed in great quantities they would move the "fruit." Also, wine used together with airborne "Spanish green" (patina) was strictly forbidden for pregnant woman, and they cited a contemporary saying—"Siebengrün und Spangrün macht unzüchtige Mägde kühn," seven green and Spanish green renders lewd maids keen—as sufficient evidence of their claim.[3] They also listed the abortive side effects of three more herbal drinks: one derived from Rheinblume, the others from Siebenbaum and saffron. While they stated that the bleeding of the feet was entirely unacceptable to perform on pregnant women, taking a bath was not quite as debilitating; but it should, nevertheless, be avoided. In their overall conclusion they asserted that whatever Agnes had drunk or had done was strictly off-limits for pregnant women.

[3] The color green was believed to have magical and powerful values; see Lyndy Abraham, *A Dictionary of Alchemical Imagery* (Cambridge: Cambridge University Press, 1998).

A subsequent follow-up confrontation uniting the three suspects shed little additional light on the matter, except that Elizabeth now gave more details regarding the birth by disclosing that when the child's shoulders appeared out of the womb, she pulled it with her hands but she did not injure it; nor did she feel any life in the child. Agnes again stressed that her hitting the child with her feet had occurred accidentally.

In the meantime various personal pleas had been submitted to the authorities aimed at the immediate release of Catharina and her husband for the sake of their children and for Elizabeth's husband. Absent, however, were any personal interventions for the sake of Agnes and Elizabeth. Instead, the sisters, at the recommendation of two of Frankfurt's advocates, Drs. Maximilian von Aschaffenburg and Lucas Kupferschmidt, were again to be confronted with each other; and because Agnes, so they claimed, had leaped from "one lie to the next," they ought to be questioned under the repeated application of torture.

The sisters, under torture, had to answer questions resembling those raised before. However, Agnes now repeatedly contradicted her sister's disclosures. When Elizabeth stated that she only pulled the child's head after it had appeared out of the womb but not with the intention to kill it, her sister contradicted her, asserting that the child was still in her when she pulled. Elizabeth replied she had felt the head and pulled it possibly too hard, reiterating she had done this without bad intentions. Agnes contradicted her again and implored Elizabeth to tell the truth. When both were asked whether the child's throat was pressed close, Agnes said she had not done anything. And it was Elizabeth who confirmed her sister's statement, asserting that Agnes had not touched the child. Consequently when both were asked whether the procedure they employed during birth was to kill the child, Agnes replied yes, Elizabeth no, asserting that she had assumed the child was dead already since she did not feel any life, blaming this lifelessness on the various drinks and other means administered during Agnes' pregnancy. In the end, and now centering on premeditation, Agnes readily admitted that her sister Elizabeth had strangled the child deliberately and that both had intended to kill it. Elizabeth now confirmed this statement.

As mentioned earlier, for confessions extracted under torture to be legitimate, they had to be reconfirmed by the suspects, in this case both sisters, at a later date while not under torture. A day later Elizabeth adamantly withdrew her admission and asserted that she had had no intention to throttle the child during birth but admitted that they tried to have it removed prior to its birth. She also stated that her sister Agnes had given her no indication that the child was alive. Agnes now confirmed her sister's answer, thus leaving the authorities without confessions of guilt.

Far from abandoning this case, the authorities re-questioned Catharina and her soldier-husband. Catharina's husband merely reiterated that he had had sexual relations with Agnes twice, adding that he had forgotten exactly when it happened. He also stated that he was not aware that he was the father of the child, in contrast to his wife's previous allegations. Frankfurt's authorities believed the soldier-husband and ignored his wife's claim. They did not subject him to intense questioning or threaten him with or subject him to torture.

Catharina reconfirmed the bond the three women shared by reaffirming that she had carried the dead child out of the house without asking for or receiving any compensation. On the contrary, she stressed having done it out of gratitude because Agnes had always been very good to her own children and, thus, when Agnes came to her worried about her pregnancy she readily tried to help her.

Since obviously Catharina's statements did not shed additional light on the issue, the sisters were subjected to yet another confrontation and again under torture. Agnes, somewhat reversing her earlier report, now conceded that the child had moved during birth—a fact she had withheld from her sister Elizabeth. Elizabeth confirmed her previous statement that she had not known that the child was alive. Agnes, asked why she had not told her sister earlier about her pregnancy, replied she had concealed it out of fear of their father and Elizabeth's husband. Taking up the fear theme, the interrogators now wanted to know whether the sisters, out of fear of both men, had not resorted to killing it. Agnes conceded but stressed that both she and her sister had done it to keep her reputation intact. Under further pressure, Elizabeth now admitted that she had in fact entered the womb, throttled the throat of the child and thus killed it. Agnes repeated her concern about her honorable reputation, a claim her sister Elizabeth confirmed, namely that it had been their prime objective to keep her sister's good reputation intact.

The sisters' proclaimed anxieties about shame and loss of honor were, however, not unique or case-specific, as was disclosed a few days later when they were yet again confronted with Catharina, and under a renewed threat of torture. While Catharina repeated her former statements that she had prepared the various abortive drinks because of her fondness of Agnes and the latter's kindness toward her children, the sisters now stated that Catharina had helped another maiden in a similar dilemma, by advising her to eat the lungs of a fox cooked in vinegar. Agnes and Elizabeth also reiterated their previous statement that Catharina had helped another, now married, woman. This time they stressed that the woman in question had feared very much for her husband's wellbeing in that his career to become a master would be seriously jeopardized if not halted altogether if she gave birth "too early."

While Catharina again denied these allegations, the very fact that the sisters described such a detailed scenario attests to a circulating if not prevalent fear by male guild members of having their careers shattered in the guild system by the premature birth of a child. And this concern should not come as a surprise. With increased ferocity, the guilds had closed their ranks by the latter part of the sixteenth century, excluding women and anyone born out of wedlock. They even extended their net of exclusion to married fathers if their child were born prior to the regular nine-month period after marriage, which was obviously the scene described above when the wife feared that an early birth would ruin her husband and, of course, herself and the future of her child.

With the guilds' barring of women and illegitimates, even excluding the parents of those conceived before the official wedding day, they turned previously widely accepted cohabitation patterns upside down, leading to a transvaluation of former acceptable pre-marital sexual patterns. Sex before marriage now turned into an officially generated and socially enforced loss of honor, with its concomitant feature of shame lest a child be conceived and/or born outside guild-mandated marriage.[4]

The repeated statements by the three suspects citing shame as the cause for hiding the pregnancy, the secret abortive intents and the secret birth attest to the power of shame. It not only engulfed the single maid but also her sister and a close friend and many more judged by the various disclosures. Shame-generated fear even led them to ponder infanticide.

And they were not the only ones increasingly resorting to such thoughts and measures. It was during and shortly after the guilds' barring of illegitimates that infanticides were recorded in increasing numbers, and this was no historical coincidence. While up to the mid-fifteen century infanticides were rarely if ever mentioned in general secular, criminal or religious archival documents—and obviously children born out of wedlock had access to the guilds and other amenities—infanticide listings increased dramatically by the latter part of the sixteenth. And this criminal trial, with its clear exposure of the women's anxieties over shame and loss of honor over giving birth to an illegitimate child, clearly attests to these concerns and connections.[5] It also clearly documents that societal

---

4 For a detailed analysis of this development see Maria R. Boes, "'Dishonourable' Youth, Guild, and the Changed World View of Sex, Illegitimacy, and Women in Late-Sixteenth-Century Germany," *Continuity and Change*, 18/3 (2003): 345–72.

5 Yet there are historians who discard shame as the motivational force—such as Regina Schulte, "Kindesmörderinnen auf dem Lande," in Hans Medick and David Warren Sabean, eds, *Emotionen und materielle Interessen: Sozialanthropologische und historische Beiträge zur Familienforschung* (Göttingen: Vandenhoeck & Ruprecht, 1984), pp. 113–47, 124—claiming that maids did not feel shame or loss of honor since they belonged to the

threats led them to forge strong bonds of solidarity as a defense mechanism, a topic rarely discussed by scholars.[6]

The Advocates' Verdicts

Frankfurt's three advocates, Drs. Maximilian von Aschaffenburg, Zacharias Stenglin and Thomas Kupferschmidt, exhibited little understanding or sympathy in their legal opinions. On the contrary, while they subjected the women, especially Agnes and Elizabeth, to repeated torture, none of the males were subjected to this painful procedure. The soldier did not have to solidify his statement under torture that he was not aware of Agnes' pregnancy or that he did not participate in any of the procedures. He was also not asked about further sexual encounters/adulteries; and neither was Agnes' brother in-law, in stark contrast to Agnes, who was questioned under torture as to whether they, she and her brother-in-law, had a sexual encounter.

Instead, the advocates argued that since Agnes on two occasions had confessed that she sought first to abort and then to destroy her living child deliberately and had willingly agreed to have it strangled, she should be punished either by being buried alive and having a pole rammed through her heart or drowned. However, since such punishments were no longer commonly practiced and might ignite undue public resentments, they suggested she should be decapitated by sword instead.

For Catharina the advocates suggested she be flogged and banished for her bad intentions to help abort the child. By contrast, the advocates praised her husband, the soldier, for admitting his sexual encounter and adulterous behavior with Agnes and for not contesting, so they claimed, being the father of the dead child. He was banished for life. Elizabeth's husband was to be released since he did not commit any wrong, but his wife's penal fate was as yet undecided because

---

lower echelons of society. Sabean also asserts that illegitimacy was not accompanied by any "Schuld- or Schamgefühl," feeling of shame or guilt, in his "Unehelichkeit: ein Aspekt sozialer Reproduktion kleinbürgerlicher Produzenten: Zu einer Analyze dörflicher Quellen um 1800," in Robert M. Berdahl et al., *Klassen und Kultur: Sozialanthropologische Perspektiven in der Geschichtsschreibung* (Frankfurt am Main: Syndikat, 1982), pp. 54–73, 64. Rublack, *Crimes of Women*, p. 195, while giving some examples on shame, nevertheless states that "the prospect of poverty" was the main motive for infanticide.

[6] Except for Amy Leonard, *Nails in the Wall: Catholic Nuns in Reformation* Germany (Chicago: University of Chicago Press, 2005), p. 146, who traces the nuns of Strasbourg's strong "communal solidarity (which) supported the women through the hard times of the Reformation and gave them the strength to resist dissolution and extinction."

of claims she might be pregnant. She was kept in custody for a while longer to be examined by midwives.

When subsequently Frankfurt's two municipal midwives visited and examined Elizabeth, they did not find her be to pregnant, adding that even if she had been pregnant the "fruit" would surely have left her body because of the terrifying fear she was experiencing of her impending execution. The midwives made, however, another, more tangible, discovery. They reported that they found a long cord lying beside Elizabeth, who, when questioned about its purpose, readily admitted that she had made it out of one of her garments. She had wanted to escape so that she could be with her young children.

The young children were also one of the main topics of her husband's plea to Frankfurt's authorities to have her released from prison. In a moving letter he begged them to be merciful in view of their three young children and Elizabeth's three-month incarceration, motives which Frankfurt's authorities had frequently taken into consideration as valid arguments for reducing other criminal penalties. But instead of making any concessions, Frankfurt's city council submitted these latest documents to their advocates for penal advice. And their advice was fast in coming and flagrant in content and tenor. While at first they referred to Elizabeth's husband's plea for mercy positively by conceding that mercy was always preferable to harshness, especially in cases of "holy matrimony" such as this one, they quickly reversed this benevolent religious argument by citing various other religious examples to prove the opposite.

Most stunningly, they proceeded by claiming in their legal opinion that they were following "göttlichem Befehl," God's instructions/order. While other advocates had more generally referred to "göttlichem Recht," divine law, in their legal briefs, the use of the linguistic term "Befehl" was quite exceptional, if not startling. Equally exceptional were their subsequent citations of and references to biblical sources, predominantly the Old Testament, to buttress their penal suggestion, such as Genesis 9, Leviticus 24, Apocalypse 13 and Deuteronomy 13:8, all passages advocating the death penalty.

Apart from questioning why Frankfurt's advocates cited arguably some of the harshest biblical references to justify their capital punishment claims in this particular trial and in a secular court, the very fact that they even knew about these passages raises equally challenging questions: were Lutheran legal advocates also theological advocates and what differentiated them from Catholic ecclesiastical proponents?

Whether Frankfurt's city council had second thoughts about these citations does not become evident from the sources. However, they re-questioned Elizabeth and even had one of Frankfurt's two mayors interrogate her. Elizabeth's statements during these follow-up interrogations differed from her confession given under torture of having strangled the child during birth. She now referred to an earlier statement, which she gave when she was not under torture, asserting that she thought the child to be dead at birth due to the various drinks and bath her sister had taken. She restated that what she had done was "to protect her sister's honor" and not to upset her old father.

Most revealing, when, as a consequence of her latest statement, she was again threatened with torture she exclaimed that she would confess to having killed the child deliberately rather than suffering such excruciating pain again. Her exclamation proves beyond reasonable doubt that under torture suspects had been—and still are—confessing to crimes they did not commit.[7]

Even her intense plea to the mayor to spare her life out of mercy for the sake of her children went unheeded. Instead, Frankfurt's three advocates were again consulted and they delivered their last legal brief in this case. They argued that while Elizabeth during her last interrogation had withdrawn her earlier confession of the "murder of the child" she had given under torture she, nevertheless, conceded that she tried to kill it with drinks and baths. Hence she had demonstrated the will and intent to kill and, therefore, deserved to be made an example of and be buried alive and have a pole run through her chest or be drowned. But, similar to the argument they used for her sister Agnes, they stated that since such punishments might cause unrest, she should be decapitated.

The advocates thus suggested identical punishments for Agnes and Elizabeth, and they were startling for several reasons. Citing former extremely harsh punishments, such as live burials and drowning, leaves one to ponder why the advocates mentioned such harsh punishments in the first place. True, live burials had been meted out in Frankfurt, but only twice—in 1498 and 1585—and most tellingly they were solely applied to women, a fact which could not have escaped the advocates' knowledge.[8] In the 1585 case, the woman, sentenced for the murder of her former employer, was placed in an open grave, had her body covered with wooden branches and subsequently had a wooden pole rammed through her heart.

Drowning might also be considered a typical female punishment in Frankfurt because out of 24 women who received the death penalty during the 1562 to 1696 period, six were drowned; meanwhile out of 313 males executed only five were handed a similar penalty, two of which were meted out to Jewish men, who were generally handed harsher punishments.[9] It was only in 1618 that

---

7 See in this connection David K. Shipler's article, "'I Confess!' Why Do People Admit to Things They Haven't Done?" *New York Times*, February 23, 2012.

8 Ferdinand Rau, *Beiträge zum Kriminalrecht der Freien Reichsstadt Frankfurt am Main im Mittelalter bis 1532* (Potsdam: Kramer, 1916), p. 86; ST June 11, 1585.

9 See Frankfurt's Strafenbuch.

these cruel capital punishments for women changed when the first woman was decapitated in Frankfurt.[10]

The advocates' claim that because of a possible outcry the punishment of burying alive ought not to be applied does not testify to their own inclination to mete out milder punishments. Had it not been for a changed mentality of public opinion, they would have subjected both women to this cruel punishment. Hence, in Frankfurt's case, the people must be credited with the emergence of a milder trend for capital punishments, and not legal professionals as claimed by some scholars.[11]

Even the advocates' concession to public pressure should not be overrated, bearing in mind their remarkable legal comment that any additional mercy to spare Elizabeth's life would go against God's explicit command and as such did not reside in the powers of the authorities to adjudicate. Thus, Frankfurt's advocates took the right to punish out of the hands of Frankfurt's secular authorities and, instead, they turned themselves into the instrument of God's wrath with the implied message that he had vested in them the power to punish. This was an astounding legal stance to take, clearly reflecting the advocates' usurpation of legal/penal prerogatives, based on religious exegesis.

And they continued with this legal/penal approach. Three years later, two of the same advocates, Dr. Lucas Kupferschmidt backed by Dr. Maximilian Faust von Aschaffenburg, stressed again religious arguments. But this time they opted for a milder punishment, insisting that mercy was always preferable to harshness, explicitly basing their legal opinion on Christian principles. As a consequence the culprit, a soldier sentenced for the killing of a Jewish man and injuring another, had his penalty reduced to corporal instead of capital punishment.[12] His life was spared based on Christian principles, but not Elizabeth's. She was decapitated based on religious arguments.[13]

---

[10] In contrast to other European locations such as Amsterdam where women were hanged until the mid-eighteenth century, and one even broken on the wheel in 1746. See Thorsten Sellin and Wolfgang E. Marvin, *The Measurement of Delinquency* (New York: Wiley, 1964), p. 5 and Pieter Spierenburg, *The Spectacle of Suffering* (Cambridge: Cambridge University Press, 1984); burning also continued to be practiced there until 1696, pp. 74, 75. In England, it continued until the mid-eighteenth century, J.J. Tobias, *Crime and Industrial Society in the Nineteenth Century* (New York: Schocken Books, 1967), p. 145.

[11] See in particular John H. Langbein, *Torture and the Law of Proof: Europe and England in the Ancien* Régime (Chicago: University of Chicago Press, 2006), p. 57, who asserts that "They [professionalized judiciary, judges] may also have been motivated by humanitarian grounds ... to decrease the use of both the blood punishment and of torture."

[12] CR 1113 – Chapter 5.

[13] Thus, religious principles were still very much used, in contrast to allegations to the opposite such as by Michael Stolleis, "The Legitimation of Law through God, Tradition,

Summary

These detailed and intrinsically connected trials offer remarkable insights into contemporary legal and penal practices by disclosing the workings of Frankfurt's advocates, in addition to revealing cultural and societal patterns, especially the networking and bonding of women. While on the surface the three advocates pursued different aims than the three women suspects, they, nevertheless, had something in common: both feared public outcry. The advocates feared it if they insisted on meting out very harsh punishments; the women feared it for having to face public dishonor. And each group fought with all the means they had at their disposal to prevent this exposure from occurring. Thus, by the mid-seventeenth century, public opinion was definitely a prime mover.

Among the most instructive judicial approaches were Frankfurt's three advocates' legal and penal opinions. They tried, almost obsessively, with the repeated application of torture to have Agnes and Elizabeth confess to infanticide. But they failed in establishing with certainty that the women had actually strangled the child at birth. The only verbal confession they obtained was that the sisters had intended to do so, and on this basis they were decapitated.

In contrast to their harsh judicial treatment of the women, the advocates' omission to apply the same standards to men—such as pursuing and posing strict follow-up questioning to Elizabeth's husband and the soldier—points to an obvious judicial gender divide, a deduction substantiated by their neglect to follow up on the women's complaints about their fear of and actual beating by the men in their lives.

Their recommendations for sentencing further corroborate this judicial gender divide. It was the advocates' fear of a public outcry, and not any benevolent attitude on their part, that prevented them from handing down the extremely cruel pre-1618 female punishments. They also precluded Frankfurt's authorities from remediating the capital punishment for the women by taking recourse to citing explicit harsh, biblical death penalty references and by warning them that if they showed mercy, they would be acting against God's will. Obviously, the means Frankfurt's advocates used were all too familiar: references to religious citations to subjugate women. Lutheran advocates well into the seventeenth century did not differ from their Catholic predecessors regarding the legal/penal treatment of women. But the advocates' religious claims point to an additional facet, one that exceeds the gender divide, namely their quest to abrogate judicial power to themselves not only as the interpreters of secular law but also as the

Will, Nature and the Constitution," in Lorraine Daston and Michael Stolleis, eds, *Natural Law and Laws of Nature in Early Modern Europe: Jurisprudence, Theology, Moral and Natural Philosophy* (Farnham: Ashgate, 2008), pp. 45–56.

harbingers of God's will. By taking recourse to a higher power they solidified their own.

By contrast, the three women in the trial had no recourse to any legal help. Even their fear of public exposure was of a completely different nature and intensity than those of the advocates. They were gripped by the fear of shame and societal ostracism if they were to give birth to an out-of-wedlock or prematurely delivered child. Exclusionary guild policies thus entailed a destructive exclusionary social climate, one in which single mothers bore the main brunt suffering from the all-engulfing sentiment of shame.

However, this trial also demonstrates the women's strength in fighting back despite the lack of judicial means. They not only contemplated, mulled over or lamented this shaming climate with others, but also actively generated networks of support and solidarity. Women found support among other women. And while such networking trends are difficult to trace because of the clandestine nature of their bonding and the lack of written records in a predominantly oral society where women ranked among the most illiterate, historians do get some glimpses from trial records, which, despite their negative connotations, do shed some light on otherwise extinguished trends.

Unfortunately, in this particular case, despite the three women's supportive bonding and networking, they were no match for the advocates who, in their quest for the power to adjudicate, not only subjected them to repeated torture applications in the name of secular laws, but also cited God's will in subjecting them to the death penalty—although it was never clearly established that they actually had committed infanticide. Not surprisingly, some single pregnant women, who might have been bereft of some bonding networks, chose self-inflicted death rather than suffer the excruciating pain of public shame, as the next chapter will demonstrate.

Chapter 9

Choosing Death Over Shame: Unwed Mothers and Infanticide

In recent years, historians have increasingly focused their research on the judicial treatment of infanticides as well as suicides.[1] However, few, if any, have concentrated on assessing possible interconnections between these two dramatic occurrences. It is the objective of this chapter to focus on this phenomenon by means of two cases adjudicated in Frankfurt, one in 1690, the other in 1695. In both instances there exist criminal dossiers, which contain witness reports, barber/surgeon and midwife statements, and, for the 1690 incident, legal briefs by Frankfurt's municipal advocates, as well as statements by the deceased for the 1695 suicide.[2]

A brief explanation is warranted with regard to the selection of these two cases, and general terminology. Out of 16 women sentenced for infanticide and an additional seven suspected of the deed, these two cases constitute the only suicide/infanticide recorded entries in Frankfurt's Strafenbuch, Book of Punishment, which lists all crime sentences during the 1595 to 1696 period. Single female servants were at the center of these two investigations, one of whom was Jewish, the other a Gentile.

As to terminology, English scholars have used the term "suicide" since the mid-seventeenth century and their French counterparts since the mid-eighteenth century. By contrast, in Germany scholars only started to use it very recently. Prior to the acceptance of this somewhat more neutral-sounding term, the criminally charged terms "Selbstmord," self-murder, and "Selbstmörder," self-murderer, were in circulation. While Chapter 12 deals with a more detailed assessment of the historical background of the negative, and criminal aspects of suicide, a short legal, historical synopsis is, nevertheless, warranted at the outset of this assessment.

Obviously, since both infanticides and suicides were contained in Frankfurt's Strafenbuch, both acts were considered criminal deeds. Yet this interpretation did not always exist. Infanticide only appeared in German criminal records toward the mid-sixteenth century, and suicide was not considered a "taboo" among Early Germans. With the development of Christianity, attitudes toward suicide

---

1 See Chapters 8 and 12 for historiographical references.

2 Criminalia (CR) 1858 and 2036.

hardened considerably; and this, most curiously, despite the fact that neither the Old nor the New Testament contains any such condemning references.

For Catholics, suicide became a grave sin, and was eventually criminalized, entailing posthumous punishments on the corpse. None of the later Protestant reformers challenged or abandoned their Catholic predecessors' religious and punitive stance on suicide. But they slightly changed the interpretive outlook: the devil now took center stage. Martin Luther was among the first to put a heavier emphasis on demonic temptation without, however, relaxing any of the previously introduced punitive measures on mutilating the corpse of a suicide.

In 1532 Emperor Charles V included the act of suicide in his criminal code, the *Constitutio Criminalis Carolina*. Article 135, the "Straff eygner tödtung," punishment for self-killing, distinguishes in remarkable, modern-sounding gradations between those who commit such acts out of fear of punishment for their own misbehavior and those who are suffering from diseases such as melancholy, madness and other similar mental afflictions.[3] The mental and/or emotional status of the suicide thus was to play a decisive role in assessing punitive actions. Sadly, however, these provisions played no role whatsoever in the judicial assessment of the two cases analyzed here. On the contrary, the emotional state of the suicides was not mentioned at all.

The 1690 Case of Anna Catharina Carlin

This trial opens with a report by one of Frankfurt's municipal midwives, who relayed to Frankfurt's authorities that a local woman had contacted her to come to look at her female servant, whom she had found lying in a big puddle of blood. Upon arrival, she examined the maid and, after having touched her belly, asked her "Who was with you?" At first, according to the midwife, the servant was very reluctant to answer the question, expressing fear that if she did, the "whole thing would be disclosed," as she had put it. However, after much trepidation, and especially after her, the midwife's insistence, the servant conceded "the heavy stable-servant with frizzy hair working for the neighbor was with me."

After this exclamation, so the midwife continued her account, she and the servant's mistress implored her to tell them "what has left your body," whereupon, in a silent response, the servant led them to the corner, where she had been found lying in a big puddle of blood for several hours. There, she pointed to something on the floor which resembled "a piece of meat." Both the mistress and she, the

[3] Johann Christoph Koch, ed., *Hals- oder peinliche Gerichtsordnung Kaiser Carls V* (Goldbach: Keip, 1996), pp. 67–8.

midwife, now begged the servant "in the name of God" to open her heart and tell them what had transpired. But instead of answering, the servant suddenly opened the door to the outside and jumped into the nearby local well.

Horrifying additional details as to how the servant had sought her death were recorded in Frankfurt's Strafenbuch. She had jumped into the well head first and when efforts were undertaken to pull her out she deliberately submerged her head and drowned. Her corpse was subsequently removed and an investigation launched into the causes of her actions, followed by deliberations as to what to do with her corpse.[4]

At the request of Frankfurt's city council, six medical experts submitted their findings with great speed on the day of the incident, followed by another report by the midwife. The medical experts, after they had inspected what had resembled "a piece of meat," as well as the corpse of the servant, reported to have found a baby boy whose umbilical cord was still attached and whose neck showed string markings. These markings, so they concluded, were signs that the child had been strangled by a cord.

In their reports they further disclosed that the servant's corpse still had a linen cloth wrapped around the lower part of her body and the belly button, "as women do monthly," and that it had been soaked in blood. The midwife added that the abdomen of the servant's corpse had been wide open and that her nipples released a few drops of milk. Based on these findings, they concluded that the maid had been pregnant and was the mother of the dead baby.

With astonishing speed, the same day the city council proceeded to interrogate the implicated neighboring stable-servant. After initial identification questions such as how old he was, to which he replied that he was approximately 24 years old, but was not really sure, he was asked about his religion and his years of service. He was Lutheran and had been in service with several employers, whose names he cited. Questioned as to whether he had known the young woman, for how long, where they would meet and whether he had impregnated her, he affirmed that they had met regularly in the stable belonging to his master, located adjacent to the maid's employer's stables. He also admitted that he had known her for three years, but he denied having impregnated her. Asked when he saw her last, he replied "yesterday morning about seven" when, so he reported further, she had asked him to give her a bundle of straw, a request he could not fulfill for lack of time.

The query now focused on his possible involvement, such as whether he had been present when she gave birth and whether he had assisted her in strangling the child. He denied both incriminating questions, asserting that he did not

4 Strafenbuch (ST) September 17, 1690.

have any knowledge of the incident. Not even the allegation that the midwife had told the authorities that the young woman had implicated him unsettled him. Stressing his point that he had nothing to do with her, he asserted that if he had impregnated her, she would surely not have caused him the misfortune in which he presently found himself. Despite his denials, he was arrested.

The mere fact that the stable-servant was subjected to such detailed and incriminating questions points to a general awareness on the part of the judiciary of the existence of similar cases where male-servants did force unmarried women to kill their newborns.[5] By contrast, marriage-related questions such as whether the stable-servant had broken his wedding promise to the servant were absent from Frankfurt's interrogation possibly signaling the authorities' knowledge that male servants rarely proceeded to marry female servants whom they had impregnated.[6]

The following day, however, Frankfurt's authorities did focus on the stable-servant's attitude toward women. They proceeded to question three people possibly acquainted with his comportment. The first, a woman from the stable-servant's previous employer stated that he had always been "very fond of all women." By contrast, his present employer could not say much on this topic and the deceased servant's employer did not know whether the two had had a relationship.

Most astoundingly, before questioning additional witnesses, who might have pointed to the servant's innocence, or possible accomplices, or even another culprit altogether, the deceased young woman was found guilty of infanticide based on rather vague circumstantial evidence. There were no eyewitnesses; nor had the deceased made a confession. This judicial lapse raises the obvious question whether Frankfurt's city council interpreted her suicidal act as a statement of guilt. The punishment inflicted on her corpse the following day is a clear affirmative to that query: her corpse was dragged to the gallows where her head was severed and put on a pike and her body put on a wheel covered with straw. The severity of this posthumous punishment is startling. It becomes even more conspicuous compared to other suicides as discussed in Chapter 12.

Most curiously, this penal procedure did not close the case. Seven days after this gruesome penalty had been carried out the city councilors proceeded to conduct further interrogations by questioning a fellow female servant of the

---

[5] See Ulinka Rublack, *The Crimes of Women in Early Modern Germany* (Oxford: Clarendon Press, 1999), p. 163, who in footnote 3 lists several cases.

[6] As documented by Renate Dürr, "Die Ehre der Mägde zwischen Selbstdifinition und Fremdbestimmung," in Sybille Backmann et al., *Ehrkonzepte in der Frühen Neuzeit: Identitäten und Abgrenzungen*, Institut für Europäische Kulturgeschichte der Universität Augsburg, Colloquia Augustana, vol. 8 (Berlin: Akademie Verlag, 1998), pp. 170–84, p. 174.

deceased. This latest witness told the interrogators that she was 27 years old and belonged to the Reformed religion. When asked whether the "drowned servant" had been going to church regularly, she stated that occasionally she had been slacking off. Questioned as to whether she had seen the stable-servant and "the drowned," as she was now referred to in the documents, talk, she replied in the affirmative, but was unable to give further details. By contrast, she strongly refuted "with a good conscience" that "the drowned" had gone for walks with other men on Sunday afternoons—obviously the only free time accorded to servants; and she also denied having had any knowledge of her pregnancy.

On the eighth day after "the drowned's" posthumous punishment, the authorities subjected the stable-servant to further questioning. This time, the tenor of the interrogations differed in that the interrogators started with a religious plea and subsequently used a more emotional approach. They urged the stable-servant to tell the truth "in God's name," an exhortation he seemingly took as a thematic lead, for he now cited God in all his ensuing answers. Questioned again as to whether he had not impregnated "the drowned," he denied it "as true as God had created him"; and he also denied that she had confided in him anything about a pregnancy, "as true as God is alive." Most curiously, and in stark contrast to the posthumous religious inquiry about "the drowned's" church-going pattern, the interrogators did not ask the stable-servant whether he attended church regularly.

Focusing on his conscience, the interrogators repeatedly appealed to him, using intense and emotional but surprisingly non-threatening questions, such as whether his conscience had not acted up when he heard that she had drowned herself or when he saw her corpse being pulled through Frankfurt's streets to the gallows. Obviously not moved, the stable-servant replied each time: "not the least since I had nothing to do with her." He denied having been present during the birth, and he denied having helped or given her advice on how to kill the newborn.

Two days after this interrogation, Frankfurt received a report from another of the stable-servant's previous employers. It not only confirmed his womanizing tendencies as disclosed by a previously questioned employer; but also this last revelation contained much stronger implicating terms, asserting that he, the stable-servant, had pressured every servant to become his sexual partner.

Twelve days after the punishment had been meted out on the corpse of "the drowned," Frankfurt's three advocates filed their reports. The first striking element was their word choice: all three, Drs. Georg Schuster, Johann Brandes, and Johann Heinrich Gabler, referred to the deceased as the "Selbstmörderin," self-murderess, whereas in all previous records she was described as "the drowned." Obviously, their word choice was indicative of the legal stance they were taking: guilty of self-murder.

Second, while they expressed doubts with regard to the stable-servant's comportment—especially his womanizing habits, his daily encounters with the "Selbstmörderin," as well as the fact that her physical description of him being heavy with frizzy hair fit his physical appearance—they, nevertheless, disregarded their own reservations and declared that another person most likely had impregnated her. They also blatantly ignored the fellow female servant's fervent statement that she was not aware of "the drowned" seeing other men.

Ignoring the fellow servant's statement was not the only gender bias exhibited by the advocates. In his legal opinion—most curiously written in a different hand but signed by Dr. Georg Schuster—he admitted that there existed "several doubts" about the stable-servant's involvement. However, he immediately counteracted his own doubts by labeling the deceased a "self-murderess" and by suggesting that the stable-servant be released from prison.

Dr. Johann Brandes, while stressing such implicating circumstances as the "Selbstmörderin" and the stable-servant's daily meetings in the barn, her identification and fitting physical description of the stable-servant, and, most perceptively, the stable-servant's curious statement that if he had impregnated her "she would certainly not have caused me the misfortune I am in right now," ignored his own caveats. Instead, he suggested that there was no need to subject the stable-servant to torture for further questioning and that he be released from prison without further ado.

The legal opinion of Dr. Johann Heinrich Gabler was even more gender biased. While praising the stable-servant's various references to God during his last interrogation, even paraphrasing some of them in his legal opinion, he totally discredited the statement given by the midwife. He argued that only the midwife had heard the "Selbstmörderin's" finger-pointing and descriptive remarks implicating the stable-servant and that she had not even been under oath when she repeated these assertions. He continued his assertion by claiming that the mistress of the house had not confirmed the midwife's allegations, a most astonishing deduction since the authorities had failed to interrogate the mistress of the house. And he made no amends in either direction: he did not suggest a legal interrogative follow-up by questioning the mistress of the house; neither did he suggest having the midwife confirm her statements under oath, as was frequently done in other cases.

Instead, he concluded that since the "Selbstmörderin" had murdered her child before even talking to the midwife, she had "allowed the evil spirit to guide her to kill herself," which for him was "enough testimony to the fact that nothing would stop her from also implicating an innocent person," obviously referring to the stable-servant. In his religiously laced legal opinion, Dr. Gabler thus accused the deceased of a calculated criminal plan without any proof, totally ignoring her emotional and physical state of just having given birth to an illegitimate child—one of, if not the most shaming events a single woman had to endure in early modern society.[7]

At the behest of the three advocates, Frankfurt's authorities released the stable-servant from prison without any follow-up or punitive action. Neither the advocates nor the city council pursued this case any further, such as by requestioning the servant under the threat of torture as to whether, among other things, he had abandoned his promise to marry her—a broken promise which was not only considered a crime but also might have contributed to the young woman's desperate act of suicide. They also did not look for another culprit or a possible doppelgänger. For them the case was closed.

This trial, especially the advocates' legal opinions, reveals various omissions and unfounded personal allegations as well as selective, gender-biased religious implications. One of the most obvious omissions was their lack of producing legal evidence connecting the servant's suicide to her admission of guilt of infanticide. She had not confessed and there were no eyewitnesses testifying to her actions, and circumstantial evidence was not to lead to sentencing.

Also, while they cited religious concepts, they did so selectively, if not discriminatorily. They questioned the "Selbstmörderin's" church-going pattern, but never queried the stable-servant on this topic. Dr. Gabler was the most outspoken religious advocate. He favorably and repeatedly referred to the stable-servant's religious, God-centered references, especially during his second testimony, but alleged, without any proof or direct citations from the "Selbstmörderin," that she had been consumed by the evil spirit, the devil, leading her to commit atrocious acts. Lutheran advocates thus served a double function, as legal advisors and religious exegetes reminiscent of their Catholic predecessors' practices and as such demonstrating the continuation of a theological-judicial albeit gender-biased approach.

Equally disturbing was the advocates' biased assessment of testimonies. They considered the stable-servant's testimony more trustworthy than those given by the "Selbstmörderin" and the midwife. And they failed to address the deceased young woman's fear and anxiety that "the whole thing will come out," as she put it. The desperate voice of the single female suicide transmitted by another woman was not heard by those entrusted to seek truth and justice.

---

[7] Maria R. Boes, "'Dishonourable' Youth, Guilds, and the Changed World View of Sex, Illegitimacy, and Women in Late-Sixteenth-Century Germany," *Continuity and Change*, 18/3 (2003): 345–72; see also Chapter 8; Dürr, "Ehre der Mägde."

Yet, most curiously, while citing the advocates' claim of the devil's instigation leading to her demise, Frankfurt's medical establishment did not shy away from wanting her body. They pleaded with the city council for the release of her corpse in order to pursue its dissection for the medical benefit of the "weiblichen Geschlecht," the female gender.

The 1695 Incident of Jüdin Bölle

The emotional anguish experienced by a single pregnant servant so blatantly ignored by Frankfurt's advocates in the 1690 trial comes clearly to the fore in this 1695 case. The incident involving "Jüdin Bölle," Jewess Bölle, as she was listed in the documents, occurred in the Judengasse, and it discloses with great clarity the emotional suffering of a single pregnant woman leading her to the desperate act of taking her own life. Various witness reports detail the unfolding of this tragedy.

The report by a corporal opened the trial. He proceeded to explain to the interrogators that he had been asked by the mayor early in the morning of May 31 to go to the house of Simon Moses to find out what had transpired there—obviously military personnel also served as municipal investigating agents. When he arrived, he found the female servant of the house lying in a puddle of blood. In a very weak and broken voice she told him that the previous night, after her employer had already retired to bed, she had fallen asleep sitting at the living room table, when she was awoken by a knock at the door, which she opened. A man standing at the door insisted that he talk to the Jewish lodger on the upper floor, but she refused to let him go upstairs. A scuffle between the two ensued during which the intruder, firmly holding both the servant's hands, stabbed her in the throat with a cut-throat razor. She fell to the floor, and the intruder left precipitously. After she had recovered somewhat, she went upstairs and knocked at the Jewish lodger's door. When she did not get a reply, she descended the stairs, and fell to the ground.

Questioned by the corporal as to the identity of the intruder, she replied that he was a foreign Jewish man. When, he, the corporal, asked her how she could be sure of that, the servant answered that he had asked her in Yiddish. She added she could tell very little about his physical appearance because it was around 11 at night and dark, but that he was a man of tall stature.

As if to back up the corporal's report, the municipal clerk who had transcribed the corporal's verbal statement wrote a little note at the bottom of the report confirming that "the house, where it happened, is so dark that even during bright daylight one can hardly see anything, not to mention during the night."

The next witness to be questioned was "Meyer Jud," the lodger whom the intruder had wanted to see. He stated that he heard someone come up the stairs, knock on his door and cry. However, since he was afraid to open the door, so he told the interrogators, he shouted to his neighbor, who, in turn, woke up a corporal on watch duty that night. When both the neighbor and the corporal came to the house, he, Meyer Jud, went downstairs, where they found the servant lying in the blood.

The interrogators now focused on this second corporal for further details. He had, however, little to say. He stated very briefly that when he arrived, the door to the house had been open and that he had found the maid lying in blood in close proximity to a cut-throat razor. Again, a note was scribbled at the end of this corporal's statement: "close to the entry door there was an object lying in blood and there was a lot of blood close to the steps."

Unfortunately, the documents do not disclose the identity of the person who subsequently questioned the injured servant, but the records list the following exchange. The first question centered on whether she had had quarrels or arguments with anyone, which she denied. Her marital status became the next focus of attention. Asked whether she was engaged to someone and, if so, to whom, she replied, no, to no one. The question of the identity of the attacker resurfaced, and again the maid stated that he was Jewish and that he spoke Yiddish "the way Jews from Prague talk," and that, no, she had not recognized him. She asserted that she could not disclose further details because it was dark.

The authorities then proceeded to question her employer, Simon Moses. He stated that he was 22 years old and married. Asked about his servant, he confirmed her name and that she had been in his employ for eight weeks. Disclosing the name of her previous employer, he added that he could not complain about her and neither did he know anything bad about her. When asked whether she or he himself had any quarrels or enemies "with Jews or Christians," he replied no, not his maid, not himself, and neither his wife nor his mother. As to the unfolding of events, he admitted that he could not contribute much because not only had he gone to bed around nine or 10 but also because his bedroom faced the back of the house, which prevented him from hearing anything. He added, however, that Meyer, his lodger, might know more about the incident.

For the second time, the interrogators questioned Meyer. This time he disclosed more personal information, namely that he was 28 years old and that he was married. Confirming his previous account, he restated that he heard someone knock at his door and, because he was afraid, had called to his neighbor David, who later appeared and told him that something had happened to the servant. He was unable to report more because he had gone to bed at eight; but he stressed, being questioned on this topic, that neither he nor the maid had had quarrels with anyone, that he could not say anything bad about her and that he had no knowledge of her being engaged. He confirmed that she was still single.

In the meantime, so the documents disclose, the cut-throat razor with which the stab wounds had been inflicted had been found and brought to the authorities who, in turn, handed it to the municipal medical experts and surgeons, and subsequently included it in the trial documents. Most surprisingly, it was never removed from the files and thus still exists today, a copy of which is reproduced at the end of this chapter (Figure 9.1, p. 180).

With astonishing speed, the same day, May 31, five municipal medical experts who had examined the injured servant submitted their findings. In their written medical report they drew attention to the considerable length and depth of the wound: a finger-long cut and a deeply penetrating stab to the throat. They concluded that these wounds had led to serious "Hemorrhia," which had caused the maid to lose a lot of blood, intensified by the fact, so they reported, that she had been lying unattended for three hours and without any bandages around her throat. When they found her, so the report disclosed, she was unconscious and half dead. However, she recovered somewhat after they had tended to her wounds so that she became fully cognizant and of "a clear mind." The prognosis for recovery was, however, extremely poor.

All these reports describe a horrible scene with the Jewish servant found lying in a puddle of blood, close to dying from a long and very deep wound to her throat inflicted by an intruder.

However, on June 2, an event turned this picture upside down. Another medical report, this time filed by eight of Frankfurt's medical experts, disclosed that the very same day, June 2, between 10 and 11 o'clock the maid had given birth: a momentous, if not bizarre, revelation by Frankfurt's medical experts, who only two days earlier had examined her without finding her to be pregnant. While they did not explain how they had missed her pregnancy two days earlier, they now clarified that one of them had inspected the maid at 10 o'clock on the morning of June 2 and had found her to be pregnant. But from the time of his discovery to his alerting the mayor of this new fact, the birth had taken place.

After inspecting the baby, they, the medical experts, found it to be dead—although they asserted that it had been in a "natural condition," without any signs of force on the body. Being very cautious, they admitted that they could not determine how the birth had actually happened and whether or not the child had been born alive, especially because nobody had heard any screams or cries coming from the child. The midwife, who had finally been contacted to attend to the servant, had told the medical experts that when she arrived the dead baby had been lying between the legs of the maid underneath her clothes, which could point to her having suffocated it. But to the medical experts' credit, they refrained from establishing this as a fact in their report.

This unexpected and sudden discovery of a seemingly stillborn baby turned the inquiry into the servant's attack on its head. Instead of focusing on an outside attacker, as she had indicated, she now became the target. It was a phenomenal development of tragic proportions, implying that the servant herself might have inflicted the deep stab wounds to her throat by using a cut-throat razor, leading her to suffer terrible pain, in addition to giving birth under such grim circumstances.

Frankfurt's authorities indeed became suspicious of "Jüdin Bölle," as she was now referred to in the records. They proceeded to solicit information from anyone who had recently been in contact with her. The first to be questioned was a local soldier who had been assigned to guard the house of the alleged attack on Jüdin Bölle and where she was still staying. The authorities wanted to know whether he had been privy to a conversation between the "Christian" midwife who had been sent to help Jüdin Bölle and the latter. They asked the soldier point-blank whether the midwife had approached Jüdin Bölle with the question as to whether she, herself, had not inflicted the cuts to her throat. But the soldier could not confirm this question because, as he stated, he had not heard anything to that effect.

Self-inflicted death, "Selbstmord," now became the lead question in all subsequent inquiries. On June 5, the authorities questioned another contact, the "Warthefraw," a 50-year old municipal female helper of the sick who had also been sent to take care of Jüdin Bölle the day after she had given birth. The Warthefraw disclosed that she and the municipal midwife had repeatedly asked Jüdin Bölle to speak the truth. Both of them, so the witness reported, urged her to admit that she, herself, had inflicted the wounds to her throat out of fear of the shame she would have to endure if her pregnancy were discovered and her old mother found out about it. But "Bölle"—as she was now referred to in the documents—just answered "es ist geschehen," it has happened, followed by "was soll ich tun, es ist geschen," what should I do, it has happened. But, according to the Warthefraw, Bölle did not admit to any wrongdoing.

Continuing with her account, the Warthefraw stated that after the midwife had left, Bölle intensified her cries—"oh weh, what should I do," and "oh weh, what a dishonor"—raising her hands in agony and despair and repeating "what should I do?" The Warthefraw, as she said, tried to calm her, but failed to do so. Around nine last evening Bölle moved to the left side of her bed and complained about intense pain on her right side, whereupon she, the Warthefraw, took her hand and held it; but the pain, which had now moved to Bölle's breast, was so intense that she began to whimper terribly and tried to rip off the bandage around her neck in order to breathe better.

This is when she, the Warthefraw, called for the barber, who appeared immediately together with a soldier who threatened Bölle that if she did not remove her hands from her bandage, he would do something else—a non-specific threat that, however, so frightened Bölle that she removed her hands. Soon thereafter two more medical persons arrived and prescribed some medication. But Bölle died shortly thereafter.

The Warthefraw's report was followed by the statement of another woman who had also been in attendance assisting Bölle in her sickness. She reported that she had frequently tried to talk to her and question her, but that Bölle had only exclaimed over and over again "My poor mother, what did I do?" When asked whether Bölle had not admitted to having inflicted the stab wounds herself, the witness said no, reiterating that Bölle only had exclaimed repeatedly "Ach, my poor mother, what did I do?"

Subsequently, another soldier, who was standing guard in Bölle's house, was asked whether he had heard her say anything relating to her stab wounds. But he reiterated the previous woman's statement, that Bölle had only exclaimed "Ach weh, my poor mother, what did I do?"

Lastly, the interrogators questioned the midwife. She reported that she had been with Bölle shortly before she died. Upon arriving, she first had asked her how she was feeling, to which she replied very poorly. She then asked Bölle why she had kept her pregnancy secret, to which she replied that she had been unaware of it. Finally, the midwife reported that when she asked Bölle why she had inflicted the stab wound herself, she exclaimed "Oh weh, dies Schand war gar gross" and "diese Schimpf ist gar gross," this infamy was too great; this shame is too great. Thus it was only a few minutes before dying that Bölle admitted to her self-inflicted death. These, her last short, verbal exclamations, need no further explanation.

An entry in the Strafenbuch, documents that she had disclosed the name of a local Jewish man as the father of her child and that Frankfurt's authorities concurred that the child had been stillborn. It also stated that because she had ended her life in a murderous way out of fear of shame and punishment for having given birth to an illegitimate child, she was sentenced posthumously to a dishonorable interment below the gallows reserved for "Selbstmörder," self-murderers.[8]

That nobody from the Jewish community claimed her body for burial is not surprising. "Jüdin Bölle" was sentenced like a criminal and as such fell under the

[8] ST June 6, 1695.

jurisdictional authority of Frankfurt's city council. Missing from the documents are any entries or actual endeavors to convert the maid to Christianity, in contrast to almost all other sentenced Jewish criminals, who were subjected to intense proselytizing efforts.[9]

Equally if not more noticeably absent from the trial documents are any references to Jewish doctors, who had an excellent reputation even among Frankfurt's Gentiles. Also, not a single Jewish midwife was listed or cross-referenced in the documents. However, this possible lack of Jewish medical assistance should not be interpreted as a non-caring attitude by the local Jewish community or Frankfurt's city council. Had Frankfurt's authorities exhibited a total lack of concern for the Jewish maid they surely would not have sent a "Christian" midwife, as the documents read, to her; nor would they have sent two additional women to assist her, one of whom was called the "Warthefraw" in the records; and nor would they have guarded the house with soldiers.

The deployment of soldiers in the service of the judiciary is clearly depicted here. Frankfurt's city council sent several soldiers to investigate the case and report back their findings, operations which might be regarded as precursors to later policemen and their functions. Also, and to further substantiate this deduction, Frankfurt used its own military to protect its inhabitants, including its Jewish residents, from possible criminal assaults within the community, thus exceeding the traditional role and objective of the military to protect the community against attacks from outside enemies. Several soldiers, as the documents clearly show, had to stand guard at the house where Jüdin Bölle lived in order to avert another attack—prior to the discovery that she herself had caused the assault—obviously a protective measure suggestive of a preventive police patrol. It is noteworthy, though hard to explain why in this particular case, soldiers exhibited a remarkable restraint in contrast to their general excessive conduct toward Jews.

Summary

Comparing the 1690 and 1695 cases, it becomes evident that they share a core feature: shame of giving birth as the impetus for the single female servants' desperate acts. Although the records do not disclose when exactly Jüdin Bölle had discovered her pregnancy, the very fact that she did obviously had a devastating impact on her, as this highly emotional and heart-wrenching case

[9] Maria R. Boes, "Jews in the Criminal-Justice System of Early Modern Germany," *Journal of Interdisciplinary History*, 30/3 (Winter 1999): 407–35, especially pp. 430–32.

testifies. Fear and anxiety over the shame she would have to endure for giving birth to an illegitimate child so overwhelmed her that she resorted to an intense cover-up story and cut her throat with a razor, leading to terrible physical suffering and ultimately death. In the 1690 incident, the maid sought a terrible death by drowning. Internalized shame thus turned into a most powerful self-destructive weapon.

What made such shame-associated fears and anxieties even more terrifying was the fact that they were not only known to single pregnant women: it was common knowledge, which, in turn, compounded and increased societal pressure. Midwives and other women such as those attending to Jüdin Bölle knew about it; and so did Frankfurt's authorities, otherwise they would not have raised shame-related questions in their inquiries and nor would they have suggested shame as a motive for suicide. However, their perceptive insight did not induce them to make any judicial allowances for the servants' emotional state of mind by granting them milder posthumous punishments. Neither did they—in both the 1690 and 1695 cases—make any serious effort to pursue the identity of the fathers of the children and their possible collaboration. Shame was sufficient evidence in their judicial pursuit.

This mentality raises, of course, a seemingly academic question: why should anyone be ashamed to give birth, causing some mothers to take their own lives? Frankfurt's pre-sixteenth century suicide documents reveal an earlier different attitude toward illegitimacy. Not surprisingly, none of the female suicides documented there relate to illegitimate pregnancy and shame.[10] During the latter part of the sixteenth century, however, a transvaluation of sexual mores had taken place which led to a serious denigration of single pregnant woman, who felt increasingly isolated and subject to stringent legal and "moral" pressure.

The emotional impact of being single and pregnant was thus so profound as to drive two women to most painful, self-inflicted deaths. Unfortunately, there are some historians today who fail to acknowledge gendered shame as a motivational force, and others who claim that women committed fewer suicides during the early modern period because they were less subject to social pressure.[11]

---

10 Ferdinand Rau, *Beiträge zum Kriminalrecht der Freien Reichsstadt Frankfurt am Main im Mittelalter bis 1532* (Potsdam: Kramer, 1916), p. 93, n. 310.

11 Such as Alain Joblin, "Le suicide à l'époque modern: Un exemple dans la France du nord-ouest: à Boulogne-sur-Mer," *Revue Historique*, 291/1 (1994): 103—"Juridiquement et socialement mineurs, sans doute furent-elles moins soumises a la pression sociale qui pesait sur l'homme de l'epoque." Also Jeffrey R. Watt, *Choosing Death: Suicide and Calvinism in Early Modern Geneva*, Sixteenth Century Essays and Studies Series (Kirksville, MO: Truman State University Press, 2001): "The fact that women had lower expectations for earnings is another reason that poverty and financial concerns were less likely to be motives for suicide

Rarely did shame apply to fathers who did not care much about their illegitimate offspring: rather like the philosopher Jean-Jacques Rousseau, who admitted that he had "not kept a note of their dates of births, so little did I expect to see them again" after he had abandoned them to foundling hospitals.[12]

among women," p. 207; and since "men enjoyed far more opportunities for economic success than women, they accordingly had many more reasons to feel like failures." Hence, so he continues to argue, "As a result, work failure and job loss generally have not produced the same feelings of failure as they do for men," p. 209.

12 As quoted by Jean Meyer in "Illegitimates and Foundlings in Pre-Industrial France," in Peter Laslett, Karla Oosterveen and Richard Smith, eds, *Bastardy and its Comparative History* (London: Edward Arnold, 1980), p. 259, n. 40 (Correspondence general, vol. VI, p. 146, lettre du 12 Juin 1761 de J.J. Rousseau a la marechale de Luxembourg).

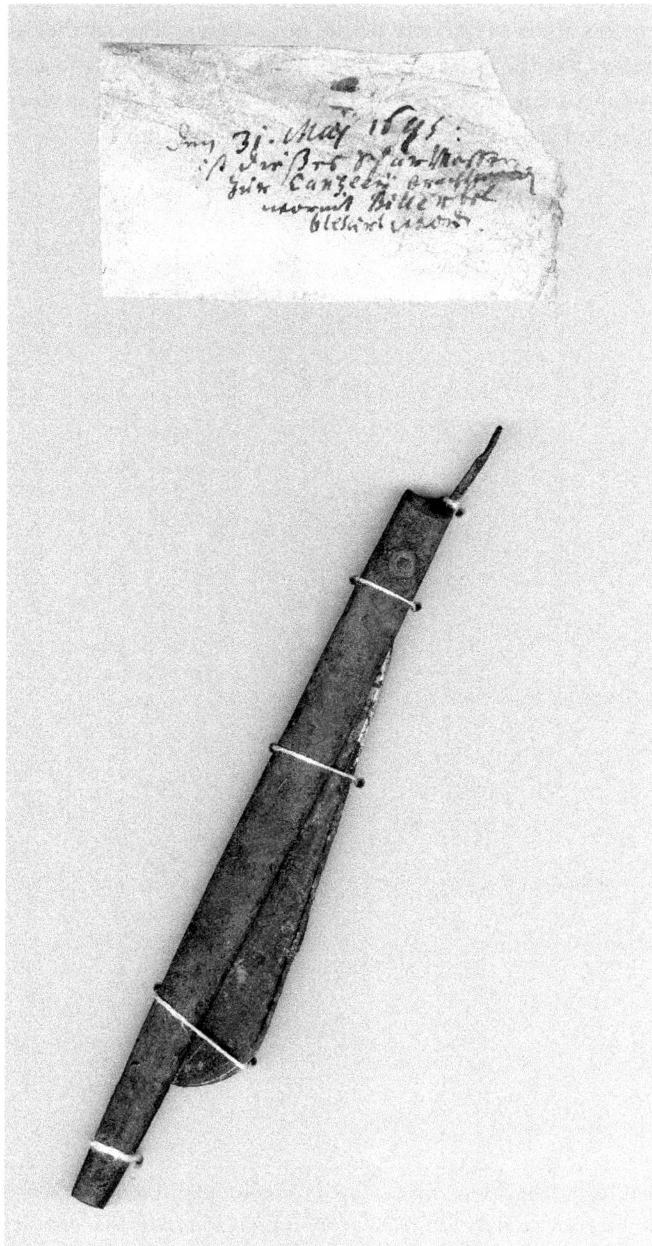

Figure 9.1 Razor used by "Jüdin Bölle" in her 1695 suicide (Criminalia 2036). Photo: Michel Schmidt © Institut für Stadtgeschichte, Frankfurt am Main.

PART V
Sexual Behavior

Chapter 10

On Trial for Sodomy in Early Modern Germany*

During the last 40 years an unprecedented number of suits have been filed in European and North American courts aimed at abolishing homosexual judicial and social exclusionary policies. Increasingly, acts of violence or harassment perpetrated against homosexuals are entering the legal category of hate crimes. In this recent quest for emancipation and social justice, the courts can serve as liberating agents.[1]

The opposite occurred in many parts of Europe during the early modern period.[2] Secular courts increasingly served as discriminating and often eliminating agents. Between 1459 and 1502 convictions for sodomy in Florence "nearly quadrupled to a yearly average of 48."[3] In Venice they jumped from 11 between 1348 and 1369 to 110 between 1448 and 1469.[4] In Aragon more than 150 men were sentenced to death during the period 1570 to 1630, and in Geneva 15 received the same sentence during the period 1561 to 1610, while many others in these areas were subjected to severe corporal punishments.[5] Yet, while

---

* This chapter is dedicated to the memory of my cousin, Karl-Heinz Harnischfeger.

1 The July 1969 Stonewall riot in Greenwich Village, New York, when gay people fought the police for two consecutive nights and days, turned into the most decisive impetus towards liberation.

2 John Boswell, *Christianity, Social Tolerance, and Homosexuality: Gay People in Western Europe from the Beginning of the Christian Era to the Fourteenth Century* (Chicago: University of Chicago Press, 1980) and *Same-Sex Unions in Premodern Europe* (New York: Villard Books, 1994); for England see David F. Greenberg, *The Construction of Homosexuality* (Chicago/London: University of Chicago Press, 1988), p. 274.

3 Michael Rocke, *Forbidden Friendships: Homosexuality and Male Culture in Renaissance Florence* (New York: Oxford University Press, 1996), p. 60; see also pp. 4, 26–7, 57.

4 Guido Ruggiero, *The Boundaries of Eros: Sex, Crime and Sexuality in Renaissance Venice* (New York: Oxford University Press, 1985), p. 127.

5 E. William Monter, *Frontiers of Heresy: The Spanish Inquisition from the Basque Lands to Sicily*; reprinted as "Sodomy: The Fateful Accident," in Wayne R. Dynes and Stephen Donaldson, eds, *History of Homosexuality in Europe and America* (New York: Garland), pp. 192–215, pp. 204–5, although a caveat must be added in that Monter's numbers might include bestiality cases; E. William Monter, "Sodomy and Heresy in Early Modern Switzerland," in S.J. Licata and R.P. Petersen, eds, *Historical Perspectives on Homosexuality*, special issue of *Journal of Homosexuality*, 6/1–2 (Fall/Winter 1980–81): 41–55. See also Mary Elizabeth Perry, *Gender and Disorder in Early Modern Seville* (Princeton, NJ:

by the mid-sixteenth century, same-sex relations had become a criminal offense in most European areas, this "explosion of prosecutions" did not manifest itself uniformly.[6] In fact, there were noticeable exceptions. One of them constituted the city of Frankfurt am Main, where only two men were sentenced from 1562 to 1696.[7]

Princeton University Press, 1990), pp. 119, 123–4, who states that "male homosexuality appeared so dangerous that men accused of it were isolated from others in the Royal Prison of Seville, their deviance regarded as a contagion that could easily infect others." Randolph Trumbach, "Sodomitical Subcultures, Sodomitical Roles, and the Gender Revolution of the Eighteenth Century: The Recent Historiography," in Dynes and Donaldson, *Homosexuality in Europe*, p. 389.

[6] Rocke, *Forbidden Friendships*, p. 27; Iwan Bloch, "Die Homosexualität in Köln am Ende des 15. Jahrhunderts," in Dynes and Donaldson, *Homosexuality in Europe*, pp. 2–9, who documents that in 1484 the city councilors decided not to prosecute. Richard van Dülmen, *Theater des Schreckens: Gerichtspraxis und Strafrituale in der frühen Neuzeit* (Munich: Beck, 1985), pp. 192–3, shows only two convictions of sodomy in Nuremberg between 1600 and 1692. Karl Wegert, *Popular Culture, Crime, and Social Control in 18th-Century Württemberg* (Stuttgart: Steiner, 1994), p. 189, asserts that "only one case of actual sodomy (anal intercourse between males) was brought to trial in the eighteenth century." Wolfgang Behringer, "Mörder, Diebe, Ehebrecher: Verbrechen und Strafen in Kurbayern vom 16. bis 18. Jahrhundert," in Richard van Dülmen, ed., *Verbrechen, Strafen und soziale Kontrolle: Studien zur historischen Kulturforschung III* (Frankfurt am Main: Fischer Taschenbuch, 1990), p. 290 n. 85, documents only one case in 1603. For opposite assertions see Richard J. Evans, *Rituals of Retribution: Capital Punishment in Germany 1600–1987* (Oxford: Oxford University Press, 1996), p. 40; for England, see Alan Bray, *Homosexuality in Renaissance England* (London: Gay Men's Press, 1982), p. 74, who states that only "isolated individuals fell foul of the law." J.M. Beattie, *Crime and the Courts in England, 1660–1800* (Princeton, NJ: Princeton University Press, 1986), p. 433, documents only four executions in Surrey between 1660 and 1800, and even that number has to be assessed carefully since the author does not differentiate between bestiality and same-sex crimes; for the Dutch Republic see Pieter Spierenburg, *The Spectacle of Suffering* (Cambridge: Cambridge University Press, 1984), pp. 124–5, who states that "around 1700 the authorities did not care about gay sex," whereas in 1730 a "sudden proliferation of trials" occurred; for France, the picture is somewhat muddled, while Trumbach, "Sodomitical Subcultures," p. 389, states that the Parlement of Paris executed 77 men between 1565 and 1640. Guy Poirier, *L'Homosexualité dans l'imaginaire de la Renaissance* (Paris: Champion, 1996), p. 48, indicates a more muted occurrence; see also Julius R. Ruff, *Crime, Justice and Public Order in Old Regime France* (London/Dover, NH: Croom Helm, 1984), p. 171, who does not list a single case for several regions in France; for Sweden see Jonas Liliequist, "Peasants against Nature: Crossing the Boundaries Between Man and Animal in Eighteenth-Century Sweden," in John C. Fout, ed., *Forbidden History: The State, Society, and the Regulation of Sexuality in Modern Europe* (Chicago: University of Chicago Press, 1992), pointing to the infrequent sentencing of male-to-male sexual behaviour.

[7] Criminalia (CR) 379 and CR 1083.

It is the goal of this chapter to shed light on the underlying reasons behind this apparent divergent judicial norm by analyzing the court records of Frankfurt's two trials. Several factors greatly enhanced this project: first, the nearly complete legal dossiers of the two cases. Located in Frankfurt's municipal archives, they contain statements by the suspects, witness accounts, detailed torture proceedings, legal opinions by the city's advocates, private pleas and summaries of the various judicial meetings. The 47-year time span between the two sentences—1598 to 1645—proved to be advantageous for comparing and contrasting the various findings in the hope of disclosing continuities and/or changes over time.

Laws

The criminalization process of same-sex relations is closely connected to the Roman Catholic Church, with its emphasis on the procreative purpose of sexual relations. Historians differ on the sentencing actions taken by the Church. John Boswell proposes a rather tolerant Church until the fourteenth century, despite restrictive ecclesiastical legislation, while others such as Warren Johansson and William A. Percy suggest the opposite. They stress the harshness of ecclesiastical actions, from Pope Gregory the Great's legislation in the seventh century down to the Church's recommendation of death by burning during the Council of Nablus in 1120; of Thomas Aquinas' input in his *Summa Theologiae*; and Gregory IX's actions against heretics in southern France, which resulted in the correlation of same-sex relations with heresy, thus reinforcing death by fire.[8]

In contrast, secular legislation had a longer germination period. Germanic law codes, with three exceptions, did not cite same-sex relations as a felony.[9] Even the *Sachsenspiegel* of c.1230, one of the many regional codes of the Holy Roman Empire, did not list any same-sex prohibitions.[10] However, with the reception of Roman law, the legal climate began to change, culminating 200 years later in 1532 in Article 116 of the *Constitutio Criminalis Carolina* which criminalized

---

[8] Warren Johansson and William A. Percy, "Homosexuality," in Vern L. Bullough and James A. Brundage, eds, *Handbook of Medieval Sexuality* (New York: Garland, 1996), pp. 165, 168 and 174.

[9] Greenberg, *Construction*, pp. 250, 272–3, cites Visigoth Spain and the Old Norwegian *Gulapingslog* as exceptions; Helmut Blazek, *Rosa Zeiten für rosa Liebe: Geschichte der Homosexualität* (Frankfurt am Main: Fischer Taschenbuch, 1996), p. 37 also includes the Frisian codes.

[10] Günther Gollner, *Homosexualität* (Berlin: Duncker & Humblot, 1974), p. 152.

such acts, including bestiality, as "wider die natur," against nature, warranting death by burning.[11]

The contemporary term "sodomy" thus had a multiple meaning. Depending on the time and place, it also included sex between Christians and Jews, Turks and Saracens.[12] In Frankfurt's case, the records list the term sodomy interchangeably for bestiality and same-sex relations. Although the city sentenced two men for sex with animals during this time frame, this chapter focuses on the two male-to-male sexual convictions only. In compliance with contemporary practice, the term sodomy will be used throughout this chapter.

The Case of Ludwig Boudin

Ludwig Boudin's case unfolded during the months of May through July 1598. Most curiously, the charge was launched by an individual who had no first-hand knowledge of his own allegations, namely sodomy, against the accused, but based them on oral reports of others or on rumors in general. To make the case even more striking the accuser, Thomas de Fuhr, was a French-speaking individual accusing another French-speaking person. Unfortunately, the records do not disclose their place of origin, but it seems most likely that both belonged to the French-speaking group of Calvinist religious refugees from the Netherlands whom the city of Frankfurt had allowed to settle locally.[13] The accused, a citizen of Frankfurt, was in fact a member of the local Reformed Church. Another common denominator between the accused and the accuser was their profession: they were both pastry bakers.

These common traits might have been purely accidental, but not according to the suspect. In a pre-trial summation, he rebutted de Fuhr's charges of sodomy by proposing professional envy rather than sexual misconduct as the underlying reason for the accuser's claim. In a lengthy and detailed statement, the suspect

[11] On the impact of Roman Law, see Michael Goodich, *The Unmentionable Vice: Homosexuality in the Later Medieval Period* (Santa Barbara, CA: Ross-Erikson, 1979), pp. 71, 86; *Constitutio Criminalis Carolina*, p. 58; article 116 was the precursor to the infamous paragraph 175 of the 1871 through the 1960s German penal code which replaced the death penalty with imprisonment and loss of civil rights.

[12] For an explanation of the term buggery or "bougerie," see Greenberg, *Construction*, p. 267; James A. Brundage, "Sex and Canon Law," in Bullough and Brundage, *Handbook*, p. 43; Ruggiero, *Boundaries of Eros*, p. 120. Poirier, *Homosexualité*, pp. 11–12, traces its linguistic connection to Bulgaria, the birthplace of the Albergensian heresy, which, in the Church's interpretation, came to be closely associated with sodomy.

[13] See also Monter, "Sodomy and Heresy," p. 44 documenting that in Geneva almost all defendants were religious refugees from France.

recounted that several years ago de Fuhr's female servant, after having been beaten by her employer, sought employment in his, Boudin's, household. To this he had agreed. As a consequence, the servant had diverted many customers from de Fuhr to her new employer.[14] De Fuhr, greatly upset about this, brought unfair practice charges against the suspect, which were heard and consequently dismissed by the mayor. Boudin claimed that de Fuhr was very angry about the loss of his servant and customers and about the dismissed charges, and had only two things in mind: to prevent him, Boudin, from continuing his trade and to have him removed from Frankfurt. The suspect did, however, concede that he was aware that several years ago a "bös Geschrey," bad rumor, had circulated about him.

The accuser de Fuhr continued with his charges that a "bös Geschrey" had not only existed years ago but was, in fact, still making the rounds, and he pointed to various witnesses. He was successful with his claim because on June 13, 13 witnesses gave their rendition of the case.

At first glance 13 witnesses seems to be an impressive number of people with first-hand knowledge about the case. Upon closer analysis, only six had experienced any direct contact with the accused, while seven reported hearsay. They simply restated what other people, including the accuser, had told them. Yet they served as prosecuting witnesses.

This tendency to give credence to hearsay accounts obviously left the door wide open for judicial misuse. While this witness approach runs counter to modern notions of a fair trial, contemporaries seemed to be less inclined to think so, for Frankfurt's practices did not represent a judicial aberration. On the contrary, hearsay and rumor widely served as warrants of arrest. In a predominantly oral society, where people lived together in condensed areas, and without an organized police force, rumor was used as a means of general and mutual surveillance.

Despite the apparent differences between the hearsay and contact witnesses, they shared common denominators. The time element stood out most conspicuously. In all instances, the age of the witnesses was listed, as were the years of their encounters with the suspect. The witnesses ranged from 18 to 50 years old at the time of the trial, and in many instances an extended period of time had elapsed between their experiences with the accused and the trial. A 46-year-old dated the incident to approximately 20 years ago; a 44-year-old cited a time

---

14 The importance of maids is amply documented by Merry E. Wiesner, "Paternalism in Practice: The Control of Servants and Prostitutes in Early Modern German Cities," in Merry E. Wiesner, ed., *Gender, Church and State in Early Modern Germany* (London and New York: Longman, 1998), p. 99; for France see James R. Farr, *Hands of Honor: Artisans and Their World in Dijon, 1550–1650* (Ithaca/London: Cornell University Press, 1988), p. 166.

frame of approximately four or five years; a 30-old mentioned approximately six years. Only the two 18-year-olds cited a recent encounter with the accused, namely the previous May 31.

These time elements are important for two reasons. First, the ages of the witnesses at the time of their experience with the suspect range from 18 to over 40 years. Presupposing the accuracy of their statements, the suspect thus did not single out young men. This age distribution runs counter to findings from other areas, such as Florence and Venice, where the "classical, age-asymmetrical variant remained dominant" during the fifteenth century and where "many of the male homosexual relations were pederastic."[15] It also differs from findings for Aragon, for which E. William Monter asserts that "as even the most sympathetic historian admits, the nearly invariable pattern of relationships was between older men and adolescents, between dominator and dominated."[16] For Frankfurt, this pattern could not be established in Boudin's case.

The second and arguably even more fascinating aspect of the time element is the prolonged time span—over 20 years—between the witnesses' personal experiences with the accused or, in the case of hearsay witnesses, when they first learned about Boudin's alleged deeds and the actual indictment. Moreover, it is safe to argue that more than 13 people must have been aware of these innuendos given Frankfurt's cramped topography and relatively small demographic size of only 18,000 to 20,000 inhabitants. In fact, it is quite possible that the entire town knew about the rumors, especially considering Boudin's status as a fine pastry baker. The question thus arises why these rumors could circulate for such an extended period of time without any of Frankfurt's inhabitants taking recourse to an official indictment.

Witness Accounts

Uninterrupted by any official questioning, the witnesses told their version of what had transpired. Three of the hearsay witnesses partly confirmed Boudin's rationale for his arrest, namely his competitor's anger at the loss of his servant resulting in financial distress. Strangely enough, they had heard this interpretation directly from the accuser, de Fuhr. Two other hearsay witnesses stated that they had heard rumors about the suspect's alleged difficulties in his "Französiche Kirche," French church, because he had touched boys. They also reported that they were familiar with the secular punishment for sodomy, death by fire.

15 Johansson and Percy, "Homosexuality," p. 159; Greenberg, *Construction*, pp. 309–10; Rocke, *Forbidden Friendships*, p. 13.

16 Monter, "Sodomy," pp. 206, 290.

Given the gossipy attitudes of early modern people, it is reasonably safe to conclude that, if two knew about this harsh penalty, many more were cognizant of it, including the suspect. Yet, for 20 years it did not deter Boudin from continuing his alleged same-sex pursuits; neither did it lead any of the locals to turn him in. The first clue to this riddle is provided by the following two witnesses.

A 46-year-old hearsay witness recounted that approximately 20 years ago a young boy told him that Boudin had had dealings with another boy, implying inappropriate sexual conduct. Rather than pursuing this rumor legally, the witness confronted Boudin directly, who refuted the charges by calling the boy a "bad kid." Another hearsay witness reported a similar verbal confrontational approach. Years ago, he had found a "pasquille," a slanderous note, alluding to Boudin's sodomite behavior. Instead of turning it over to the authorities for an investigation of the writer of this illegal note, and ipso facto alerting the authorities to rumors of Boudin's alleged sexual behavior, he went directly to the suspect and showed him the letter. He admonished Boudin by telling him that he should be ashamed of himself. The suspect, according to the witness, seemed frightened but denied the allegations.

These hearsay witnesses thus preferred to deal with Boudin directly rather than have him legally prosecuted. It is also remarkable that they refrained from any threatening comments and physical assaults on the suspect. There remains, of course, the lingering doubt that these witnesses exhibited such a temperate approach while giving their renditions to the court. However, these reservations are offset by similar statements made by the contact witnesses.

A 36-year-old recounted that approximately 13 years ago on a late-night walk, he had met Boudin who suggested he sleep over in his house, and he did. After he had fallen asleep, Boudin joined him in bed and started to touch him. But since he, the witness, turned around, nothing further could happen. In the morning Boudin got up and lay down beside his own wife—the first documented reference to the suspect's marital status. The witness's closing remarks, that "wisse sonsten nichts," this was all he knew, exhibit a surprisingly matter-of-fact attitude on the part of a witness to sodomy, devoid of hatred, disgust or any other emotional reaction or value judgment.

An 18-year-old witness exhibited a similarly detached attitude. He stated that on May 31, in the year of the indictment, Boudin, pretending to be drunk, had asked him to walk him home. On their way Boudin began to touch him, which he rejected by telling him that he, Boudin, had a wife. The next day the suspect asked him not to talk about the incident, claiming that when he had too much to drink he behaved strangely. To this the young witness simply replied that it did not bother him, it was none of his business—a rather nonchalant attitude for an 18-year-old, unless either the suspect or the issue itself appeared to be non-threatening to him.

A similar approach was evidenced by a 22-year-old who stated that a couple of years ago he had been asked by his master to accompany Boudin to his home. Boudin, according to the witness, pretended to be drunk and touched him, saying "er hab ihn gar lieb," that he loved him. When the suspect repeated his emotional outburst and became sexually more demanding, the witness reproached him, saying that he should be ashamed of himself and that he had a wife. Like the 18-year-old, this young man directed his seducer's sexual advances to his wife, in addition to using shame as a deterrent.

It is also remarkable that Boudin expressed his love for the young man. Not only did this declaration add a new dimension to a seemingly purely sexual trial, it also demonstrated that love between men existed and was verbally expressed.[17] Moreover, it says something about Frankfurt's general atmosphere about sodomy that Boudin felt free enough to express his innermost feelings despite the inherent judicial danger. It points to a divide between legal and popular sentiments toward sodomy.

Only one contact witness expressed anger at Boudin. A 19-year-old reported that, while drinking wine in Boudin's house, the suspect expressed his love for him and became sexually demanding. The witness angrily rejected his advances. His anger was, however, confined to a verbal outburst.

A more sexually descriptive account was delivered by a 30-year-old witness. He admitted that approximately six years ago, during his encounter with Boudin, both engaged in sexual touching, which prompted Boudin to urge him to come home and sleep with him or, "he would get crazy." The witness did not heed Boudin's request. He stated in his closing remarks that during the last 12 years such intense rumors had spread around town, that everyone became aware of Boudin's behavior. The witness's apparent knowledge of the rumors, however, did not deter him from meeting with the suspect let alone engaging in male-to-male sexual touching, unless, of course, he deliberately sought his company for these very reasons.

The statement of a 31-year-old witness, referring to an episode of eight years ago, point in the same direction, namely that despite such rumors, people were neither intimidated by nor frightened to associate with the suspect, or even to engage in close physical contact. The witness reported that one night he met Boudin, who told him about a fight with his wife. As a consequence Boudin ended up staying in the witness's house, where they shared a bed for the night. Once in bed, Boudin touched the witness, who retorted that he should

---

[17] This also confirms Boswell's findings, *Same-Sex Unions*, p. 38.

be ashamed and that "such things belonged to women." Similar to previous witnesses, he brushed off Boudin's advances as sexual missteps, using guilt as the intimidator.

What prompted the witnesses and Frankfurt's people in general to exercise such restraint? The severe penalty for sodomy might have acted as a judicial deterrent, especially since many seemed to have been aware of it. This interpretation, however, has to be seen against the backdrop of general sexual crime sentencing. First, it increased dramatically toward the end of the sixteenth century, totalling 239 during the 134-year period covered in this chapter. Second, it also frequently entailed capital punishment.[18] A break-down by category shows, however, that most of these sentences covered marriage-related offenses.[19] One thus has to expand the judicial deterrent argument to include other factors, such as the suspect's personality and the general local mentality regarding sodomy.

It is reasonably safe to argue, on the basis of the witness accounts, that Boudin was generally liked. Even the accuser's servant sought employment in the suspect's house, and this despite the circulating rumors. She even enticed customers to switch from her previous employer to the suspect. In turn, had the customers shown any abhorrent feelings against Boudin or sodomy, they would surely not have bought his merchandise. Therefore, sodomy was not a deterrent. While the legislative and the judiciary, heavily influenced by Roman Law, took a very punitive stance, popular mentality was different though not indifferent to the question of sodomy.

Judicial Torture

After hearing the witness reports, the city council subjected Boudin to further questioning. He was asked whether he knew why he had been arrested, to which he replied he did not. When his accuser de Fuhr was mentioned, the suspect repeated his earlier allegations that de Fuhr was angry at him for employing his servant and, as a consequence, had started to talk badly about him. The suspect stated that he knew the content of this talk, namely that he was a sodomite. When the interrogator referred to the various witness accounts alleging that he had had contact with younger and older men, Boudin refuted the accusations. While he acknowledged knowing about the content of the slanderous note

---

18 Nine were executed for incest alone according to the Strafenbuch (ST).

19 Frankfurt meted out 64 fornication, 61 adultery, but only 35 prostitution sentences. See also Jean-Louis Flandrin, *Le Sexe and l'occident: Evolution des attitudes and des comportments* (Paris: Seuil, 1981), pp. 256–9, who documents similar findings.

depicting him as a sodomite, he countered that others were mentioned in that note as well.

Not satisfied with his answers, the councilors decided to subject him to judicial torture. Initially, Boudin was shown the torture instruments to intimidate him in the hope of eliciting a confession. But since, again, he denied the accusations, claiming they were based on hatred and jealousy, the interrogators resorted to using the leg screw.

The first question posed under torture was an almost exact replica of a witness account, a pattern maintained throughout all consecutive torture sessions regardless of whether the statements had been made by hearsay or contact witnesses. Boudin, under torture, replied that he would tell the truth if the leg screw were removed, a request the interrogators granted. He now admitted that he had been touching one of the witnesses while lying in bed with him, but had been so drunk that he mistook him for his wife. He answered the second question in a similar fashion, namely that he was too drunk to even remember the incident. Not satisfied, the interrogators reapplied the leg screw even more tightly than the first time, whereupon Boudin screamed in pain, begging to have it removed and saying he would tell them the truth. They complied, but Boudin again did not admit to any wrongdoing, repeatedly saying that he had been drunk and that when he was in this state he was a different person. He conceded, however, that occasionally he had been excessive in his dealings and he asked the city council for forgiveness. Again, not satisfied with his answers, the interrogators led Boudin to the rack and hoisted him. But the suspect was persistent in his denial of sodomite behavior.

Upon hearing Boudin's statements the following day, the city council decided to seek legal advice from its advocates. It was during the same session that the council listened to a plea from the suspect's wife to spare her husband further torture. Ignoring the wife's plea, the advocates concluded, based on the witness accounts and Boudin's own remarks, that he be "genügsam überwiesen," sufficiently proven guilty.[20] Yet, they argued, that since the suspect had refused to confess under torture to any of the allegations, torture ought to be reapplied.

Two days later Boudin was informed that the city council had not been satisfied with his answers and that he was to be interrogated further. Again, he maintained his innocence. Questioned as to whether he was ousted from the French Church because he had had dealings with boys, he replied that these were false accusations; he did admit to having been refused communion.

After this exchange Boudin was hoisted on the rack. He screamed in pain, maintaining his innocence. He was lowered from the rack and questioned further.

20 Unfortunately, the documents do not disclose the names of the advocates.

But since he did not confess, he was hoisted again, and again he screamed in pain. This torturous procedure laced with intermittent questioning was carried out a further nine times, escalating the physical pain after each occurrence, so that all in all Boudin was subjected to 12 consecutive torture applications. Throughout, Boudin was steadfast in negating most of the charges, such as that he had sexually forced young boys. He repeated, however, that several times he had been under the influence of alcohol and when he was drunk he was "ein armer Mensch," a pitiful person. Boudin at one point, screaming in pain, suggested that his accuser be questioned, and at another that if the city council wanted his life, so be it. It was only after he had become very weak that the interrogators had him removed him from the rack.

One cannot help but ponder why the suspect was subjected to this extended series of excruciatingly painful judicial tortures, especially since they were conducted on the advice of Frankfurt's advocates, that is, the same persons who, after Boudin had already been tortured three times, proclaimed the suspect to be guilty based on witness accounts. This issue becomes even more puzzling when, later, Boudin's wife wanted copies of the various witnesses' and her husband's statements made under torture, but the advocates refused to release the documents to her.

Equally disconcerting is the fact that, despite Boudin's constant denial of a confession under torture, the advocates did not change their perceptions but reconfirmed their earlier findings of guilt. They based their assessment on six witness accounts, yet they had subjected the suspect to torture based on all 13. It is also troubling that there is no documentation disclosing the identity of the six witnesses upon whose accounts Boudin was to be convicted. One might attribute this omission to negligent recording were it not for other very detailed renditions of the case, including nota benes scribbled at the end of various documents referring to statements by the advocates.

Even the advocates' ensuing penal deliberations and decision seem perplexing. Conspicuously absent are any considerations of the accuser's motives for taking Boudin to court. Equally absent are deliberations with regard to the lack of proof of sexual body penetrations.[21] At best, one can interpret Boudin's behavior as unwanted touching or sexual overtures. While it is true that the advocates argued that since the suspect had "suffered a lot under torture" he should only be put in the public pillory and banished from Frankfurt for life at a distance of 20 miles, it is surprising that they consequently suggested that he be subjected to further questioning.

---

21 See Gollner, *Homosexualität*, pp. 153–4, on this legal point.

While their consideration of Boudin's intense suffering under torture seems reassuring, one cannot help but wonder whether they did not use torture as an insidious punishment—a concept frequently applied to Jewish suspects—since they had already proclaimed the suspect guilty prior to the most intensive torture application.[22] Also, why did they resort to this pattern of ex post facto questioning? A scribbled nota bene at the end of one of the documents furnishes an insight: one of the advocates had voiced a dissenting opinion proclaiming Boudin de jure innocent.

Yet this did not save Boudin from being exposed to additional verbal and visible judicial intimidation, which included being led to the rack. Reasserting his earlier claims, he ended his deposition by asking a most revealing rhetorical question: why had all these witnesses been quiet for so many years—was it not their duty to report bad deeds to the authorities?

Boudin's perceptive remarks, though most likely intended as a defense strategy, nevertheless confirm the proposition that the witnesses did not harbor a lot of resentment against him or his sodomite behaviour, otherwise they surely would not have bought his products, associated with him in private, and even slept in his house and in his bed. It was only when de Fuhr, out of personal and financial motivations, resorted to officially indicting the suspect that the various people were legally obligated to speak out. And even then they demonstrated remarkable restraint.

Frankfurt's population and thus popular opinion, while not necessarily in favor of sodomite behaviour, nevertheless, seemed to have been rather nonchalant about it. In fact, the suspect seems to have felt secure if not protected by the people's attitude for 20 years. Popular mentality served as a protective shield against judicial intrusion. Forty-seven years later, this protective shield was still intact.

The Case of Heinrich Krafft

Krafft's trial lasted from March 10 to April 17, 1645. The accused, a 39-year-old shopkeeper, was, like Boudin, a citizen and married. Unlike the previous suspect, however, Krafft's wife was pregnant and he had a son and daughter from a previous marriage. Apart from this short biographical sketch, little else is known about him.

---

22 Maria R. Boes, "Jews in the Criminal-Justice System of Early Modern Germany," *Journal of Interdisciplinary History*, 30/3 (Winter 1999): 407–35.

In Krafft's trial, 11 witnesses were interrogated. As in the 1598 case, not all of these were contact witnesses. Two reported only hearsay accounts, which suggests that judicial procedures with regard to prosecuting witnesses had not changed during almost half a century. Unlike in the previous trial, however, none of the witnesses' ages was recorded in the documents. This does not mean that age was less important than in the 1598 case; on the contrary, in Krafft's case, the authorities stressed "Knabenschande," seduction of boys, in their allegations.

Unfortunately, the documents are vague as to what actually led to Krafft's indictment. It seems that a few possible suspects pointed to Krafft out of fear of being implicated. Apparently, rumors about Krafft's sodomite behavior had been circulating for at least 10 years according to the witness reports. Although the extended time span from rumor to actual indictment resembled Boudin's case, most witness accounts exhibit a different tone, frequently stating resentment, anger, even fear of the suspect. A picture of victimization emerges, which had almost been absent in the 1598 case.

The question arises as to whether Krafft's behaviour was actually so provoking as to stir resentment or whether other, possibly judicial, factors were at work. Two witness records disclose, in fact, a different style of judicial questioning. In one instance the witness was asked whether he knew about Krafft's "Übelthat," criminal act, a suggestive inquiry which turned the suspect into a criminal before the verdict and thus left the door wide open for criminal innuendos by the witness. In this particular case, the witness reported that when on a Saturday night he and Krafft went into the suspect's basement and drank wine, Krafft exposed himself and tried to sexually assault him. But since he screamed very loudly, Krafft had to let go of him.

The second suggestive question was more targeted when a witness was asked outright whether the suspect had sexually assaulted him. Circumventing a direct reply, he described his encounter with Krafft from approximately five to six years ago. Similarly to the previous witness account, when he and the accused drank wine in Krafft's basement, the latter exposed himself and became sexually forceful with him. Once Krafft realized, according to the witness, that he could not achieve anything and that someone else had entered the basement, he let go of him. The witness, however, threatened that he would tell Krafft's wife about this incident. But whether he actually did was not disclosed in the documents. The witness finished his report by stating that he never had a drink with Krafft again.

Drinking wine in the suspect's basement emerged as a common theme. Six out of the 11 witnesses referred to it. One such was the witness who recounted his experience with Krafft from four years ago. While they were drinking wine in the suspect's basement, Krafft tried to sexually molest him during a three-hour period. Admitting to having been very scared, the witness asserted, however, that

Krafft "did not achieve what he wanted." Closely connected to this account was the statement of one of the hearsay witnesses who disclosed that this witness, "looking like death from fright," had come to his house, telling him what he just experienced in Krafft's basement.

The three additional witnesses who reported on wine drinking in Krafft's basement differed, however, in their reactions to the suspect's overtures. One stated that he told Krafft that his behavior was dishonorable and dashed to the door; another recounted that he was "shocked to death," and dashed to the door, only to return the next day for a repeat scenario. The third such witness reported on a similar repeat visit to Krafft's basement. On each occasion, they drank wine; and on each occasion the accused tried to sexually assault him. These two consecutive sexual molestations did not deter the witness from reassociating with Krafft. He reported that at a later date, when he and Krafft went for a walk, the suspect led him to another person's basement to drink wine. Again, Krafft tried to sexually corner him, but he freed himself.

These last two witness accounts, while disclosing aggravated sexual assaults on the part of Krafft, nevertheless seem somewhat puzzling. The same two witnesses, after having experienced dramatic sexual assaults, returned and socialized with the suspect. Why would anyone, after having experienced unwanted sexual advances, go back to the same place seeking the company of the attacker? The question thus arises as to whether these witnesses did not greatly exaggerate their accounts under judicial scrutiny, either to cover up their own involvement and thus appear above suspicion or to appease the judiciary since they had failed to report these incidents years ago.

It is equally remarkable that none of the witnesses, despite their frequent expression of anger in their testimonies, resorted to any personal physical retribution or revenge toward the suspect; neither did the local population, many of whom must have known about these incidents.

Judicial Torture

Krafft now had to respond to these allegations. While, as in Boudin's case, many questions resembled the witness accounts, the judiciary in Krafft's case diverged from these accounts by targeting sex with young boys and bestiality. The latter point has to be stressed because none of the witnesses had referred to or uttered any insinuations tying Krafft to sex with animals.

Krafft vehemently denied these two charges. He also reversed some of the witness allegations, asserting that in one instance the witness had started with the physical exposure, while in another it was the witness who initiated the sexual activities by talking about his previous male-to-male sexual encounters in other towns. Krafft, like Boudin, admitted, however, to having been drunk and in this state he might have touched some of the men.

The excessive consumption of alcohol, and Krafft's and Boudin's repeated referrals to drunkenness as a possible excuse for their behavior, should not be interpreted as a sign of sodomite behavior patterns.[23] Heavy drinking was a widespread contemporary cultural phenomenon, as demonstrated by the witnesses themselves. In addition, many of Frankfurt's criminal suspects used drunkenness as an extenuating circumstance in the hope of being acquitted or receiving a milder sentence.[24] Thus alcohol-related excuses were not unique to Boudin or Krafft.

Krafft asked the city council for forgiveness and pleaded to be released with a fine, citing his two children and the pregnancy of his present wife. He suggested donating the money to the poor. As in Boudin's case, an unmoved city council now sought the advice of its advocates. Dr. Maximilian Faust von Aschaffenburg stated that since the accused's confession was not complete and "mit Vieh aber will er nichts zu schaffen gehabt haben," he did not admit to having had anything to do with animals, he should be interrogated further. His colleague, Jacob Schütz, supported this proposition. It was in particular Krafft's denial of bestiality that seems to have irritated the advocates, for they now added four detailed bestiality-related questions: whether he did not keep goats at home and in the countryside; where he kept his animals in the countryside; whether or not he visited a peasant who had had something to do with goats; and the name of the peasant.

These suggestive questions exhibit a fundamental change among Frankfurt's advocates. While it is true that Article 116 of the 1532 *Constitutio Criminalis Carolina* includes sex with animals in the same category as male-to-male sex, Frankfurt's 1598 charges and inquiries were confined to same-sex questions only. Forty-seven years later, however, at the explicit initiative of the advocates, the animal connection was heightened and male-to-male sex became closely correlated with bestiality. This development testifies to a transformation of the advocates' legal mentality, a change not reflected in the witnesses' attitude, for none of them even alluded to bestiality.

A change in the judicial climate can also be observed from a scribbled nota bene at the end of the interrogation questionnaire. The advocates suggested keeping the witnesses' and suspect's statements secret, so that the common man and above all the young should not find out about them lest they be unduly

23 Bray, *Homosexuality in Renaissance England*, p. 41.

24 In the following manslaughter prosecutions, drunkenness was advanced in the hope of a milder punishment: ST August 10, 1570; June 16, 1604; June 8, 1671; April 30, 1672; August 30, 1690. See also Chapter 11.

influenced. Their reasoning for taking recourse to secrecy, in addition to their zealous attempts to equate same-sex with bestiality, testify not only to an increasing influence of the legal profession over the treatment of sodomy, but also to their increasingly patronizing if not condescending attitude toward the people. Both trends exhibit a widening gulf separating popular culture from the legal profession.

Krafft's wife, children and friends, also citing the effect of alcohol on the suspect, pleaded with the city council, as did Krafft himself, again stressing his frequently drunken state in addition to "gehässige Zeugenaussagen," malicious witness accounts. In a follow-up letter he inquired about the content of the witness report, stating that several "so mir gehässig sind," hate me.

None of these pleas had any effect on the advocates or the city council, for Krafft was now interrogated under torture. He was subjected to the leg screw and hoisted on the rack. In line with the advocates' previous allegations, sex with young boys and goats formed the core of the interrogation. Again, the suspect categorically denied these charges. He also repeated his earlier statements that one of the witnesses had not objected to his sexual advances: on the contrary, he had "gern geschehen lassen," enjoyed them, while another had actually initiated them. Even under excruciating pain, having been hoisted on the rack twice, Krafft did not confess to ever having committed sodomy with boys or men. He admitted, however, to having touched men sexually.

Under torture, Krafft thus reconfirmed his earlier statement that he had had at least two willing accomplices. In Boudin's case, a witness account could be interpreted similarly, which indicates that the two suspects were not the only ones in Frankfurt with male-to-male sexual or emotional desires and experiences. Unfortunately, the records do not allow further deductions as to the existence of a local subculture.[25] It was also only in one instance that a witness in Boudin's

---

[25] Historians differ on the existence of a distinct subculture for this period. Among its proponents is Boswell, *Christianity* and *Same-Sex Unions*; Ruggiero, *Boundaries of Eros*, pp. 135, 137–8, 144; Perry, *Gender and Disorder*, p. 126; Monter, *Frontiers*, p. 42. Arguing for its later appearance is Michael Foucault, *Histoire de la sexualité* (3 vols, Paris: Gallimard, 1976–84), esp. vol. 1; Randolph Trumbach, "Erotic Fantasy and Male Libertinism in Enlightenment England," in Lynn Hunt, ed., *The Invention of Pornography: Obscenity and the Origins of Modernity, 1500–1800* (New York: Zone Books, 1993), pp. 252–82; see also his comments in "Sodomitical Subcultures," pp. 388–97; Bryant T. Ragan, Jr, "The Enlightenment Confronts Homosexuality," in Jeffrey Merrick and Bryant T. Ragan Jr, eds, *Homosexuality in Modern France* (New York/Oxford: Oxford University Press, 1996), pp. 8–29, p. 12; Alan Bray, "Homosexuality and the Signs of Male Friendship in Elizabethan England," in John Goldberg, ed., *Queering the Renaissance* (Durham, NC: Duke University Press, 1994), p. 40. On linguistic interpretations of the term "subculture" see Greenberg, *Construction*, pp. 267, 31 and Poirier, *Homosexualité*, pp. 12–22.

case hinted at a special meeting place on the banks of the local River Main.[26] The documents also disclose so little about the suspects' wives that it would be presumptuous to interpret the marital status of both suspects.

The city council, seemingly confused about Krafft, again took legal refuge in their advocates' advice, despite a third plea by the accused to spare him. As in Boudin's case, the advocates took Krafft's judicial torture and long incarceration into consideration for a milder sentence; yet, they diverged from the previous case by stressing penal secrecy rather than public knowledge. In line with their previous argumentation, they considered public flogging to be unwise because of the local youth and suggested instead that Krafft be taken immediately from the prison to the city gates and banished for life at a distance of 20 miles. For once, the city council heeding Krafft's request, interceded and allowed him an additional two weeks to conclude work-related arrangements.

The advocates' decision to conduct secret penal procedures represented not only a judicial aberration from contemporary penal practices where, with the exception of juveniles, criminals were punished in public, but also a decisive volte-face from the 1598 case where public exposure in the pillory was strongly advocated on the grounds "damit er bei jedermann ein abschewn gebe," that he should instill disgust in everyone.[27]

This policy reversal, replacing the intended evocation of disgust with secrecy, might be interpreted as a failure of the earlier policy to have the desired effect on the people. It also points to a growing judicial belief that sodomite behavior was contagious. The people thought differently. They refrained from social stigmatization even in the case of a more aggressive suspect such as Krafft. This reluctance might also explain why the "Haberfeldtreiben," a form of German charivari, included male-to-male sexual encounters as objectionable behavior only after 1833.[28] It took centuries to change popular sensitivity toward male-to-male sex.

This reticence is difficult to explain, but the term "toleration" comes to mind. While it is frequently considered anathema or anachronistic to apply this word or even the concept to the early modern period, recent studies have

---

26 Bernd-Ulrich Hergemöller, *Sodom und Gomorrha: Zur Alltagswirklichkeit und Verfolgung Homosexueller im Mittelalter* (Hamburg: MännerschwarmSkript, 1998), p. 55, cites the existence of special meeting places in many cities.

27 Juveniles were spared such public exposure for reformatory objectives; see Maria R. Boes, "The Treatment of Juvenile Delinquents in Early Modern Germany: A Case Study," *Continuity and Change*, 11/1 (1996): 43–60.

28 Ernst Hinrichs, "Le charivari et les usages de reprimand en Allemagne," in Jacques Le Goff and Jean-Claude Schmitt, eds, *Le Charivari* (Paris: Mouton, 1981), pp. 297–306, p. 302.

shown its existence as far back as the twelfth century.[29] If the comportment of Frankfurt's population is an indication of not attaching social stigma to sodomy and refraining from condemning the suspects as socially aberrant despite official legislation, then the concept of sexual toleration seems to have been grounded in the common people rather than the so-called elite.[30]

The almost total absence of any religious remarks on the part of the witnesses furnishes an additional clue. Only one witness reported that he told Boudin he should be ashamed before God and the world. Quite obviously, many did not consider sodomy a terrible or "the worst of sexual sins."[31] It is, of course, tempting to reduce this to the general lack of pertinent comments by German reformers, including Martin Luther, or assertions that Lutherans were more tolerant of popular traditions than Zwingli and Calvinists.[32] But even years before Frankfurt converted to Lutheranism, there were no local sodomy convictions, a possible argument against contentions that Catholic doctrine shaped "popular consciousness."[33] As these findings suggest, the "common person" seems to have been quite resilient and might have espoused a different moral mentality with regard to same sex than many of their secular or religious leaders. Statements such as the "salient horror of homosexuality characteristic of the West since the fourteenth century" or "the popular abhorrence for homosexuality" have thus to be regionally qualified.[34]

---

[29] Cary J. Nederman and John Christian Laursen, eds, *Difference and Dissent: Theories of Tolerance in Medieval and Early Modern Europe* (Lanham,MD: Rowman & Littlefield, 1996). See also Ole Peter Grell and Bob Scribner, eds, *Tolerance and Intolerance in the European Reformation* (New York: Cambridge University Press, 1996).

[30] Communal restraint is also documented by Arthur E. Imhof, *Lost Worlds: How Our European Ancestors Coped with Everyday Life and Why Life Is So Hard Today*. trans. Thomas Robisheaux (Charlottsville: University Press of Virginia, 1996), p.56, but it applied to bestiality cases only. In contrast, also referring to bestiality cases, see Wegert, *Popular Culture*, p. 189 and Liliequist, "Peasants against Nature," p. 61. For more general argumentation of social restraint, see Behringer, "Mörder, Diebe, Ehebrecher," p.121; see also Bray, *Homosexuality in Renaissance England*, p. 76, who seems to be arguing against the concept of tolerance.

[31] Trumbach, "Sodomitical Subcultures," p. 397; Monter, "Sodomy and Heresy," p. 45 found a strong religious correlation.

[32] Blazek, *Rosa Zeiten*, pp. 48–9; Peter Burke, *Popular Culture in Early Modern Europe* (New York: New York University Press, 1978), pp. 216–18.

[33] Ferdinand Rau, *Beiträge zum Kriminalrecht der Freien Reichsstadt Frankfurt am Main im Mittelalter bis 1532* (Potsdam: Kramer, 1916) does not cite a single male-to-male conviction; Greenberg, *Construction*, p. 291; Boswell, *Same-Sex Unions*, p. 220.

[34] Boswell, *Christianity*, p. xxiii and *Same-Sex Unions*, p. 262; Stephen Haliczer, *Sexuality in the Confessional: A Sacrament Profaned* (Oxford: Oxford University Press, 1996), p. 168.

Conclusion

In Frankfurt's case one can assert that the population did not undergo a metamorphosis with regard to sodomy since the 1598 case, but that the advocates did.[35] Considering the absence of sodomite legal clauses in most Germanic laws one might argue that as protagonists of the new Roman Law, they contributed to a tightening of sodomite prosecutions. In their quest to enhance and solidify their professional position, they became professional hard-liners. Their frequent, if not frivolous, recourse to judicial torture serves as one example. Their attitudinal shift toward secrecy in the 1645 case points to another, deliberately distancing their legal attitude from the "common person", and thereby widening the cultural divide between popular and legal mentalities. The prosecution of sodomy became an affair of the state, albeit of the legal profession and not the people. In the process, advocates turned not only into instruments but increasingly into the source of social control via their increased presence in the courts. This trend, with regard to sodomy, only started to reverse itself at the end of the twentieth century.

[35] Poirier, *Homosexualité*, p. 45, found similar attitudinal changes within the judiciary in France during the seventeenth century.

PART VI
Military Ascendancy

Chapter 11

Judicial Treatment of Soldiers for Killings Unrelated to the Battlefield

For the early modern period, it has been amply documented that soldiers committed homicides that were unrelated to the battlefield.[1] Yet it was only recently that some scholars began focusing on the judicial treatment of criminal soldiers in general.[2] Despite this welcome scholarly advance, an in-depth analysis of judicial processes for soldiers accused of killings unrelated to the battlefield has not been conducted. This study seeks to redress this historical question by probing 34 criminal cases adjudicated in Frankfurt am Main during the late sixteenth through the late seventeenth centuries.

The 34 trials in question, which include those of four former soldiers as well, were not chosen randomly but taken from Frankfurt's Strafenbuch (ST), the Book of Punishment, which lists every sentenced offender together with their crime and punishment during the 1562 to 1696 period. The Strafenbuch thus dictated the time frame of this study, but it was not an exclusive source. The most insightful information was derived from data contained in the individual criminal dossiers. While, unfortunately, only 23 complete dossiers exist, the

---

1 John Theibault, *German Villages in Crisis: Rural Life in Hesse-Kassel and the Thirty Years' War, 1580–1720* (Atlantic Highlands, NJ: Humanities Press, 1995), pp. 153–60; Ann Hughes, *Politics, Society and Civil War in Warwickshire, 1620–1660* (Cambridge: Cambridge University Press, 1987), pp. 202–5, 207–8, 215–16, 218, 234–5; Ronan Bennett, "War and Disorder: Policing Soldiery in Civil War Yorkshire," in Mark Charles Fissel, ed., *War and Government in Britain, 1598–1650* (Manchester: Manchester University Press, 1991), pp. 248–73, p. 250; John A. Lynn, "Soldiers on the Rampage," *MHQ: Quarterly Journal of Military History*, 3/2 (Winter 1991): 92–101, p. 93; Frank Tallett, *War and Society in Early Modern Europe, 1495–1715* (London/New York: Routledge, 1992), p. 49 footnote 3; Quentin Outram, "The Demographic Impact of Early Modern Warfare," *Social Science History*, 26/2 (2002): 245–72, p. 255; J.R. Hale, "The Soldier in Germanic Graphic Art of the Renaissance," *Journal of Interdisciplinary History*, 17/1 (1986): 85–114, p. 96 n. 13. See also Geoffrey Parker, ed., *The Thirty Years' War*, 2nd ed. (London/New York: Routledge, 1997), p. 174.

2 This lack of pertinent scholarship prompted Jutta Nowosadtko and Diethelm Klippel to invite scholars to participate in a conference entitled "Militärrecht in der Frühen Neuzeit," which took place in Thurnau, Germany, from October 4 to 6, 2007 and where sections of this chapter were presented; see also Jutta Nowosadtko, "Militärjustiz im 17. und 18. Jahrhundert am Beispiel des Fürstbistums Münster," in Sylva Kesper-Biermann and Diethelm Klippel, eds, *Kriminalität in Mittelalter und Früher Neuzeit: Soziale, rechtliche, philosophische und literarische Aspekte* (Wiesbaden: Harrassowitz, 2007), pp. 115–40.

remaining 11 were supplemented by the Bürgermeisterbücher (BB), minutes of the mayors' meetings, and the Ratsprotokolle (RP), minutes of the city council meetings, both of which contain judicial entries relating to the administration of criminal justice. The combined sources disclose insights into the unfolding of criminal, judicial, and cultural trends and related changes over time. And so do the various legal opinions written by Frankfurt's advocates, which reveal the real workings of the judicial system.

General Introductory Overview

Frankfurt, similar to many other regions, promulgated rules governing soldiers' behavior, the so-called Kriegsartikel, Articles of War.[3] Of special interest for this study were three articles contained in Frankfurt's 1628 legislation.[4] In Article 1 soldiers are warned not to assault people, especially members of the clergy, old people, pregnant women, women who had just given birth, young (virgin) women and children. Article 20 prohibits drunkenness, threatening that crimes committed while inebriated would be punished more severely than those committed in a sober state, and Article 23 forbids any kind of dice or card game. Frankfurt also issued separate exhortations to soldiers, such as admonishing them to refrain from provoking and assaulting Jews, or after instances when soldiers had committed serious street robbery, to curtail their nightly excursions.[5]

The identification of soldiers as sentenced criminals posed no major problems because they were clearly listed as such in Frankfurt's Strafenbuch. The soldiers' visually distinct appearance, mainly manifested by their at times extravagant clothing, surely helped in this process.[6] It was only in a few cases that

---

3 Tallett, *War and Society*, pp. 123, 125, cites the most influential ones such as Ferdinand of Bohemia and Hungary of 1526; those adopted by the diet of the Holy Roman Empire of 1570; Maurice of Nassau's of 1590; and Gustavus Adolphus' of 1617 and 1630. See also Kersten Krüger, "Kriegsfinanzen und Reichsrecht im 16. und 17. Jahrhundert," in Bernhard Kroener and Ralf Pröve, eds, *Krieg und Frieden: Militär und Gesellschaft in der Frühen Neuzeit* (Paderborn: Schöningh, 1996), pp. 47–58, 49, 50; and Peter Burschel, *Söldner im Nordwestdeutschland des 16. und 17. Jahrhunderts: Sozialgeschichtliche Studien* (Göttingen: Vandenhoeck & Ruprecht, 1994), pp. 130–45.

4 Isidor Kracauer, "Das Militärwesen der Reichsstadt Frankfurt a.M. im XVIII Jahrhundert," *Archiv für Frankfurts Geschichte und Kunst*, 3/12(1920): 1–180, p. 39.

5 BB July 5, 1683; BB September 29, 1683.

6 See Chapter 3, which correlates appearance and dress codes with crime policing and arrest patterns. Hale, "Soldier in Germanic Graphic Art," was the first to publish on the appearance of soldiers. Of special value is Matthias Rogg, "Zerhauen und zerschnitten, nach adelichen Sitten: Herkunft, Entwicklung und Funktion soldatischer Tracht des

the records listed offenders in a somewhat ambiguous manner, entering a double occupational profile such as soldier and baker, bricklayer.[7] In these instances, the soldierly status was given priority in the numerical assessment.

A quantitative assessment revealed that Frankfurt convicted 114 soldiers out of a grand total of 1,338 sentenced criminals during the 1562 to 1696 period. By itself, this number offers only limited insights. If it is to yield any understanding it has to be put into comparative perspective. As all soldiers at the time, to state a truism, were men, their sentences ought first to be compared to men's sentences, which amounted to 1,023. Thus, in the male sentencing category, 11 percent fell to soldiers, which might be interpreted as a small percentage. However, before solidifying this stance, a second desideratum has to be taken into consideration, namely to compare soldiers' sentences to the soldiers' actual numerical representation in town. However, this objective represents a far more difficult task to achieve hampered by the sporadic availability of relevant data and the lack of soldier-specific studies for Frankfurt.[8] Patchy entries exist for a few years, such as for 1613 when 60 mercenaries were at the city's disposal, climbing to 160 in 1618, to 750 in 1620 and possibly reaching an all-time high of 1,200 in 1631. And though it might be tempting to evaluate the 114 convictions against this rather vague numerical backdrop, an additional caveat is warranted: Frankfurt was also entitled to adjudicate on criminals from other areas regardless of where they had committed their crimes. Further complicating this issue is Frankfurt's pattern of not clearly distinguishing outsiders from insiders in its recording of criminals, except for those with burgher status, who were always clearly listed as

---

16. Jahrhunderts im Spiegel zeitgenössischer Kunst," in Kroener and Pröve, *Krieg und Frieden*, pp. 109–36; G. Wolter, *Die Verpackung des männlichen Geschlechts: Eine illustrierte Kulturgeschichte der Hose* (Marburg: Jonas, 1991), p. 57; Peter Burschel, "Zur Sozialgeschichte innermilitärischer Disziplinierung um das 16. und 17. Jahrhundert," *Zeitschrift für Geschichtswissenschaft*, 11 (1994): 973; Ralf Pröve, "Vom Landsknecht zum Soldaten: Krieg und Militär 1500–1800," in Bernd Ulrich Hucker et al., eds, *Niedersächsische Geschichte* (Göttingen: Wallstein, 1997), pp. 255–67, p. 258.

[7] ST April 29, 1584; ST July 17, 1589; ST January 19, 1591; ST August 9, 1599; ST April 13, 1621; ST April 27, 1630; ST December 5, 1634; ST June 10, 1671; ST June 10, 1671; ST April 11, 1674.

[8] Except for Kracauer's mainly eighteenth-century study, *Militärwesen*, there are, unfortunately, no monographs on Frankfurt's soldiers similar to the one for Lübeck by Thomas Schwark, *Lübecks Stadtmilitär im 17. und 18. Jahrhundert: Untersuchungen zur Sozialgeschichte einer reichsstädtischen Berufsgruppe* (Lübeck: Schmidt-Römhild, 1990). Johann Anton Moritz, *Versuch einer Einleitung in die Stadtverfassung der Reichsstadt Frankfurt am Main* (2 vols, Frankfurt am Main: Andräische Buchhandlung, 1786), vol. 1, n. 2, pp. 419–20.

such. It was thus frequently difficult, if not impossible, to disentangle local from outside offenders in these records.

The 114 sentences do, however, yield instructive qualitative data. Most soldiers were sentenced for property-related crimes, a pattern in line with Frankfurt's general sentencing trend for both men and women. Only six soldiers were convicted for actual military crimes, five of which were desertions. The sixth case represents a somewhat nebulous case, where a soldier had allegedly talked a Jewish man into joining the military. But as Jewish people were prohibited from bearing arms and thus could not join the army, this new military recruit convert not only chose a different name for himself but eventually ended up as a Spanish soldier-prisoner in the nearby town of Homburg, where he was said to have disclosed some of Frankfurt's military secrets.[9] He was sentenced to death for treason.[10]

Most perplexing, however, were Frankfurt's soldierly crime sentences in two categories: sexual and violent crimes. While soldiers were handed down only 12 convictions out of a grand total of 239 sexual crimes, the opposite pattern was the case for violent crimes, where 40 soldiers were sentenced out of a total of 180. This disparity gives grounds for serious doubts about the objectivity of such sentencing, especially when one juxtaposes the sexual sentencing of women, who received 134 such convictions to the 12 meted out to soldiers. The dubious quantitative nature of this conviction pattern is further enhanced by the qualitative pattern: only one soldier was sentenced for prostitution and none for rape.

The absence of a single rape conviction is stunning as it was clearly listed as a crime in the *Constitutio Criminalis Carolina*, the criminal code for the Holy Roman Empire, as well as in Frankfurt's own military articles. This omission of course raises the immediate question of selective sentencing given the soldiers' amply documented sexual abuse patterns. Various scholars have described horrendous sexually abusive scenes, such as the one depicting a gruesome case of mass rape during which one young girl, "having been raped by eighty soldiers," died "of fright," reinforced by pictorial representations such as Graf's rendition of an "armless girl," where, as a leading military scholar explains, "the soldiers have first been in her and then at her."[11]

---

9 Guido Kisch, *Forschungen zur Rechts- und Sozialgeschichte der Juden in Deutschland während des Mittelalters* (Sigmaringen: Thorbecke, 1978), pp. 33–40.

10 ST April 8, 1635.

11 Lynn, *Soldiers* (n. 31), pp. 100, 96; Hale, "Soldier in Germanic Graphic Art" (n. 13), p. 100; the same author also refers to the painter Daniel Hopfer, who "in one etching, showed a soldier ... grasping the breasts of a by-no-means readily available young woman," p. 106. See also the study by Bennett, "War and Disorder," pp. 255–7 and the more recent editorial "Sexual Violence and the Military," published in *The New York Times*, March 8,

It is hard to believe that in Frankfurt during a 134-year period soldiers, who were sentenced to almost a quarter of all violent crimes, would refrain from aggressive behavior in the sexual field. And, as the following analyses show, soldiers did commit brutal crimes unrelated to the battlefield.

The Adjudication of Soldiers for Homicide Unrelated to the Battlefield

Methodologically, the 134-year time span during which the 34 cases occurred is partitioned into four time periods: three 33-year periods and a final section comprising 35 years. In addition, each of the four sections is thematically arranged into crimes and penal deliberations. This approach, buttressed by in-depth analyses of the witness reports and the legal opinions by Frankfurt's advocates, facilitates a better assessment of the changes that occurred over time. And, indeed, there were many changes disclosed in the documents. They range from the nature of the crimes, such as the emergence and spread of different motives for the offenses best illustrated by the numerous witness accounts, to the nature of the respective punishments, clearly exposed by Frankfurt's advocates' legal and penal opinions. Even the vocabulary used to describe the culprits underwent a metamorphosis, increasingly resorting to military terminology.

First Period, 1562 to 1594

Unfortunately, only four individual criminal dossiers exist for the 11 trials which took place during this period.[12] The available documents, nevertheless, point to a different, military-related punishment by the end of the period. Most

2012. However, there are also military scholars who totally ignore rape by soldiers. They include Geoffrey Parker, *Empire, War and Faith in Early Modern Europe* (London: Allen Lane, 2002), pp. 144–68, who spent an entire chapter on "The Etiquette of Atrocity: The Laws of War in Early Modern Europe," yet only mentioned the "systematic rape that accompanied the Yugoslav Civil Wars in 1991–2000," p. 165; Ronald G. Asch, *The Thirty Years War: The Holy Roman Empire and Europe 1618–48* (New York: St Martin's Press, 1997), p. 19, while dedicating a chapter to "The Impact of Warfare on the Civilian Population" during the Thirty Years' War, does not mention rape, only that "there were more than enough 'bastards' born to 'whores'"; similarly in Jeremy Black, ed., *War in the Early Modern World, 1450–1815* (London: University College London Press, 1999), not a single entry of rape is to be found.

[12] ST May 20, 1572 and RP pp. 3,6; ST July 10, 1573 and RP p. 21; ST February 26, 1574 and RP p. 79; ST October 4, 1577 and RP pp. 29, 31; ST April 25, 1578 and RP pp. 76, 78–83; ST January 25, 1583 and CR 1583; ST April 28, 1584 and RP pp. 65, 85, 89, 90; ST April 30, 1585 and CR 137; ST May 7, 1583; ST April 14, 1586 and CR 156; ST May 19, 1590 and CR 222.

of the offenses stand out by their utter cruelty, such as when in the first, the 1572 case, two Landsknechte, as they were described, murdered an undisclosed victim "cruelly" in public in the presence of witnesses. A year later another undisclosed victim was shot in a tavern. Robbery was the cause of the killing of a tailor in 1574. Drinking and an ensuing altercation led to a stabbing incident in 1577. By contrast, the 1578 crime unfolded secretly during the night, when two Landsknechte robbed and shot a miller and his wife in their home. Equally if not more ghastly was the 1583 incident when the suspect stabbed his wife 16 times with a dagger and injured his child in the process, a crime which nowadays would be labeled domestic violence. A year later, another young boy became the deadly victim of a Landsknecht. In 1585, the brutal robbery and murder of three Jewish merchants took place near Strasbourg, a trial which is discussed in detail in Chapter 5. During the same year, another Landsknecht killed a shoemaker in a local tavern in front of witnesses, and a similar scenario unfolded in 1586. The last trial of this period occurred in 1590. A Landsknecht was accused of having killed a fellow Landsknecht with a hoe during a brawl 13 years earlier.[13]

A ghastly picture of brutal killings thus emerges. And most of the punishments meted out to the culprits are equally appalling. However, apart from the 1590 case, they do not deviate from those handed down to non-military criminals. Two Landsknechte who had brutally murdered a miller and his wife were broken on the wheel and had their heads put on pikes, and a culprit who had robbed and murdered a tailor was decapitated and had his corpse put on a wheel. By contrast the 1585 accomplice to the robbery and murder of three Jewish merchants was only sentenced to decapitation by sword followed by immediate interment, which, compared to all other death sentences, represented the mildest form. Private pleas by family members and friends could also induce the authorities to lower the penal threshold for both civilians and military culprits, such as in the 1572 case, when 12 fellow military men successfully pleaded for decapitation. Even the culprit who had brutally murdered his wife was granted this milder form of punishment based on the pleas of relatives and friend, as was the 1586 culprit.

Young age also exerted a positive effect on the penal structure. It was Frankfurt's policy to mete out milder punishments for youngsters, and the culprit in the 1590 case was no exception. He was spared the death penalty because he had committed his crime 13 years prior to his incarceration.[14] However, his milder punishment deviated from the norm. Instead of finding immediate and irrevocable death, he was sent to Hungary for six years to fight the Turks, obviously a military-oriented punishment.

---

[13] CR 222.

[14] Maria R. Boes, "The Treatment of Juvenile Delinquents in Early Modern Germany: A Case Study," *Continuity and Change*, 11/1 (1996): 43–60.

Second Period, 1595 to 1627

While only four trials took place during this period, the as yet subtle 1590 military-related outlook became much more obvious starting with the first, the 1600 case. First, a new descriptive version appeared in that the culprit was now described as "ein Soldat," a soldier, in contrast to Landsknecht.[15] This new military terminology is obviously linked to broader military changes, and possibly to what some scholars describe as the "military revolution."[16] Second, the crime victim and the unfolding of the crime also point to a military-related shift in that a fellow soldier became the victim during an argument after the consumption of alcohol and in front of witnesses.[17] The second and better-documented incident of 1603 showed this emerging trend more clearly.[18] Eight witnesses—two bakers, four local burghers, a carpenter and a soldier—reported in almost identical statements that a soldier, the son of a local burgher, stabbed a fellow soldier, also the son of a local burgher, in a local tavern after verbal flare-up.

The 1608 case demonstrates even more military-related input in that the soldier's military service was added, his having served six years in the Netherlands, and, most importantly, that the cause of the actual stabbing related to military machinations. The nine witnesses testified that after an altercation had erupted between the culprit and the victim while drinking wine in a local tavern, they left the place and continued their argument outside in the street, where it eventually ended in the deadly duel. All witnesses agreed that it was the invectives that fueled and eventually triggered the fight, but they differed as to their content. One claimed that the victim had called his opponent a "rag soldier" and two asserted that one of them used the term "Schnark." A third also testified to the word Schnark, but conceded that he did not know the meaning of the word—a question which was not answered

---

15 ST April 3, 1600 and CR 413; ST December 15, 1603 and CR 468; ST July 12, 1608 and CR 560; May 4, 1621 and CR 882.

16 On the disappearance of and changes in the military regarding Landsknechte, see Pröve, "Vom Landsknecht," pp. 255–67; Burschel, *Söldner*, pp. 11, 973. For the military revolution, see Michael Roberts, *The Military Revolution, 1560–1660* (Belfast: Queens University Press, 1956), who originated this interpretation, while a revised version was introduced by Geoffrey Parker, *The Military Revolution: Military Innovation and the Rise of the West, 1500–1800* (Cambridge: Cambridge University Press, 1988); this theme was rejected by Jeremy M. Black, *A Military Revolution? Military Change and European Society, 1550–1800* (London: Macmillan, 1991).

17 CR 413.

18 CR 468.

by the interrogators.[19] Four witnesses, however, insisted that one of the soldiers had called the other a "Schelm."

The term Schelm, here used for the first time in this study, reoccurred like a deadly leitmotif throughout the remainder of this study. Being called a Schelm became the most inflammatory insult and consequently triggered most physical assaults. Unfortunately, it is a rather difficult term to explain let alone to translate into English—possibly its closest linguistic expression is "rogue"—because the word Schelm changed its meaning over the years from depicting a corpse, to a person afflicted with a contagious, fatal disease; to its subsequent meaning of loss of honor due to a crime, culminating in the ultimate symbolic verbal meaning of the loss of military honor.[20]

The 1621 stabbing for which the scant archival material makes it impossible to describe more details, nevertheless, discloses the continuation of the military pattern in that a fellow soldier was again the victim.

The penalties meted out exhibit a similarly military-related trend. Surprisingly, however, the 1600 suggested penalty emanated from private pleas for a milder punishment submitted by family members and the mayor and city council of the suspect's former residency. They requested that the murderous soldier be sent to fight the Turks, thus possibly sparing his life as well as considering it a punishment befitting a soldier. While Frankfurt's city councilors did not heed their suggestion, they granted the soldier the milder punishment of decapitation. In the 1603 trial, it was one of Frankfurt's advocates, Dr. Johann Baptist Caesar, who suggested a milder punishment on the grounds that the soldier was the son of a burgher. That soldier, too, was decapitated.

Frankfurt's advocates became even more outspoken in their 1608 penal deliberations, favoring purely military-related reasons. Dr. Christoph Kellner suggested that as both the culprit and the victim had been soldiers, the culprit be handed down a milder death penalty. Dr. Caspar Schacher, in a similar soldierly vein, argued that as the victim had called the suspect a rag soldier, he had incited the fight. Both opted for a military-related punishment: to have the culprit sent to Hungary to fight the Turks. Although Frankfurt's city council sentenced the offender to decapitation, the two legal inputs are an indication of emerging special military-related legal considerations initiated by local advocates.

In the 1621 case no legal opinions are available, but in an unprecedented legal deployment, the city council suggested a stay of execution for a week in

19 The word Schnark seems to elude precise definition, despite the consultation of various relevant sources such as Jacob and Wilhelm Grimm's *Deutsches Wörterbuch* (16 vols, Leipzig, 1854).

20 The brothers Grimm trace the changing meaning of this word in their *Deutsches Wörterbuch*, vol. 14, rubrics 2506–13.

order to give local soldiers enough time to request special funeral services for the soldier culprit, a request eventually presented by all local soldiers. It was heeded. The culprit was escorted by various musketeers to the place of execution, where he was decapitated "standing upright like a soldier" and "with his honor intact" without being touched by the executioner. Fellow soldiers subsequently put his corpse in a burial cart and escorted him to a non-religious cemetery where he was buried.

Thus, a strikingly different picture emerges. Unlike in the first period, all victims were fellow soldiers who died after the eruption of altercations in public in front of witnesses. While the intake of alcohol fueled the emotional outbursts, it was the hurling of invectives, which by 1608 became more soldier-specific denigrations, that triggered the deadly encounters. The punishments meted out in these four cases mirror this emerging military-related trend. Most noticeably, they were frequently suggested by Frankfurt's advocates.

Third Period, 1628 to 1660

The seven crimes adjudicated during this time span evidence even more changes.[21] In the 1630 shooting of a baker, two soldiers cooperated but only one was sentenced. Five people witnessed the unfolding of the crime, which took place in broad daylight. The first witness reported that two soldiers followed a baker, who was leaving town, and asked him for directions. As the baker was heading in the same direction as they were, he suggested they should walk with him. Along the way, the "little" soldier, according to the witness's account, blamed the baker for leading them astray and started to attack him, which, by way of support, prompted the "long" soldier to ready his gun. The baker, in a quick move, grabbed the gun and rendered both soldiers "wehrlos," defenseless. Returning back to town, as several witnesses concurred in their statements, the baker deposited the gun against a fence, a move observed by the "long" soldier, who grabbed it, charged it, and, according to one witness, "without uttering a word and without any cause," shot the baker, who fell to the ground and died. Another witness, who had been closer to the baker, somewhat adjusted this account, stating that when the "long" soldier retook the gun he yelled to the baker "I feel like shooting you," to which the baker replied, "you do not have the heart to do it," which led the soldier to fire the deadly shot. One of the witnesses then ran to alert the authorities, and shortly thereafter soldiers arrived to arrest the culprits.

[21] ST April 27, 1630 and CR 947; ST June 6, 1634 and CR 994; ST June 28, 1637 and CR 1024; ST October 9, 1658 and CR 1033; ST July 19, 1649 and CR 1113; ST November 28, 1659 and CR 1174; ST November 28, 1659 and CR 1177.

Two soldiers also cooperated in the 1634 stabbing of a fellow soldier, although again only one was charged with homicide. Of the 11 witnesses, the first, a wine tavern owner, reported that the victim and three additional soldiers had come to his place at eight in the morning, where they started drinking till three in the afternoon, when an altercation broke out which eventually ended in the deadly stabbing. However, breaking with previous patterns of witness interrogations, the remaining 10 witnesses had to answer questions solely focusing on the degree of drunkenness of the culprit. And their answers were quite confounding, ranging from total inebriation such as "blind" drunk to drunk but not "completely"; to one suggesting that the culprit only pretended to be drunk; to four who refused to commit themselves, stating that they did not know whether he had been drunk or not.

By contrast, the 1637 incident had little to do with alcohol, but primarily with roaming pigs. A former sergeant in Frankfurt, whose status was entered in the records as being married, was accused of killing the mayor of a nearby suburb. The crime occurred outside Frankfurt's city walls in broad daylight. Four witnesses reported their observations close to the crime scene, while an additional two, who had been drinking with the sergeant prior to the homicide, immediately confirmed that the suspect had not been drunk. Of the four witnesses only one could furnish detailed insights because he not only knew the victim but also had accompanied him on his rounds in Frankfurt. He stated that the sergeant had accosted the mayor once he spotted him in the fields outside town, because of a grudge he held against him over the mayor's pigs. Allegedly, the pigs had dug up and eaten vegetables in the sergeant's garden, which had prompted the sergeant to ask the mayor to prevent the pigs from roaming around again. When his request was not heeded, he shot one pig in the upper leg so that it limped. But not even this incident led the mayor to take further action, which, according to the witness, led the sergeant to attack him that day in broad daylight. The three other witnesses, unaware of this background event, reported that when they heard a commotion in the field, they ran toward the noise and found the deceased with his hunting knife on his side, stabbed to death. One of them immediately called for local soldiers to arrest the culprit, who was still nearby. Upon arriving, the three arresting soldiers later testified, the culprit had beseeched them not to bind him, in addition to asking them to contact the captain for help so that he be spared being sent to a terrible prison.

A year later in 1638 a soldier, who was also listed as being married, stabbed his comrade, who died 21 days later. The victim, while still able to comment on the incident, emphasized immediately that he and the culprit had never had an altercation or a fight before, and that he not only forgave his fellow soldier but also prayed for him. He reported that he and the culprit, after they had already been drinking in one place, proceeded to another where a woman, Elizabeth, was in charge. Elizabeth supplemented his account by stating that when she had finished baking herrings for various soldiers, including the culprit and the victim, she served wine to everyone. All of them stayed together till midnight, when the culprit requested more wine, which she refused to serve, telling him that he had had enough to drink. After her refusal, according to the account of the third witness, the culprit went to his own place and got more; and when he returned an altercation broke out between the culprit and the victim during which they hurled invectives at each other, leading to the fatal stabbing.

By contrast, in the 1649 incident, neither altercations nor invectives were involved. On the contrary, a soldier, married with children, shot two Jewish men who were peacefully walking down one of Frankfurt's streets. He claimed that he shot them by accident, a highly unlikely proposition given the various judicial details, which closely resemble those of what nowadays would be called a hate crime, as discussed in Chapter 5.

Ten years later in 1659 a soldier described as a lieutenant stabbed a Swedish captain who died eight days later. While eight witnesses observed the unfolding of the crime, none of their accounts or the victim's statements are contained in the criminal folder. But the crime scene was a familiar one, a beer house.

Several months later during the same year, a "gefreiter Soldat"—one freed from military watch service—had to stand trial. He had been in military service for 16 years, and was married with four children. He had stabbed another soldier, who died seven hours later. The stabbing took place in front of a beer house, but the root of the problem originated inside the establishment. The scenario was a familiar one, but with a little twist. A local corporal, the first witness, reported that while he was drinking with the suspect in the beer house, the victim walked toward them with a rose in his hand asking the culprit to smell it, proudly explaining that his daughter had given it to him. The suspect, instead of smelling the rose, immediately called the rose-bearer a "prostitute hunter." In response, the rose-bearer, according to five witnesses—a brewer, three butchers and a soldier—had called the suspect a Schelm. One of the butchers added that another soldier further provoked the rose-bearer by yelling at him that "if he were a soldier he ought to act like one," a snide remark which seemingly prompted him to go outside. In front of the beer house, the hurling of invectives continued, as reported by the sixth witness; meanwhile the seventh claimed that he had wanted to separate the two adversaries, but it was too late, a fact confirmed by the eighth witness, who saw the suspect stab the victim in the back.

Apart from the unnerving hate crime, this brief summary documents a victim-related picture similar to the previous period in that soldiers mainly killed fellow soldiers as a result of military-related honor insults—even the baker victim falls into that category for having obviously insulted the soldiers by rendering them "wehrlos," but additional changes took place. Increasing attention was paid to the soldiers' military ranks—such as sergeant, lieutenant, corporal and "gefreiter"—as well as to their years of service, followed by more detailed descriptions of the soldiers' family status, registered as being married in four instances, and in one case even including his four children. Also, the documents disclose that the soldiers' general service now included criminal arresting functions.

While the penalties meted out reflect a similar soldier-oriented, albeit soldier-friendly penal trend, such as when the soldier who was described as having deliberately killed was only handed down a decapitation sentence instead of a far harsher one normally meted out to murderers, a novel feature emerged with the 1634 case. The plea-bargaining applications, two of which were submitted by the culprit and one by all officers and soldiers serving under the local captain, became more legally savvy. They contained passages interspersed with frequent Latin arguments, which exhibited a high degree of legal sophistication, obviously the work of legally cognizant persons. True, Frankfurt's three advocates, Drs. Caspar Gabriel Rasor, Melchior Erasmus and Maximilian Faust von Aschaffenburg, did not absolve the suspect from the death penalty. Yet, they were, nevertheless, receptive to the request for special military honors. The culprit was executed by sword and, similar to the 1621 case, accorded the special honor of not being touched by the executioner, and subsequently wrapped in a burial shroud and carried by fellow soldiers to a non-religious cemetery.

The 1637 stabbing over rummaging pigs showed even more elaborate judicial arguments. The pleas submitted by the culprit's wife, the authorities of his home-town, his father and an impressive 30 of his fellow soldiers exhibited again intricate legal knowledge; and so did the inclusion of lengthy Latin and even Greek passages, suggesting again that they had been prepared by legally cognizant persons. The culprit's father added another military element by stressing his own military service in the hope of reducing his son's sentence.

Frankfurt's advocates, Drs. Maximilian Faust von Aschaffenburg, Melchior Erasmus and Georg Hieronymus Marstaller, presented their case unabated by the suspect's claim of drunkenness, adding instead that he, as a soldier of the town and lodging in one of Frankfurt's suburb, was not even entitled to have his own garden, that none of the gardens in the suburb were fenced in, and that he ought to have contacted the local authorities. They also stressed that the culprit had drawn his long sword, whereas the victim only had a small hunting dagger for his defense. Despite these reservations they granted him his wish of a special soldierly execution of being shot, which he preferred, rather than being decapitated. Again, fellow soldiers put his corpse in a burial shroud and buried him at the same non-religious cemetery as the previous soldier.

Frankfurt's advocates became even more outspokenly military-penal oriented in their 1638 legal opinions. Drs. Maximilian Faust von Aschaffenburg, Johann Jacob Schütz and Zacharias Stenglin suggested that while the victim had survived for 21 days and thus his death might also be attributable to other circumstances, they, nevertheless, in a rare legal admission, considered the culprit's drunken state as an additional excuse. They therefore suggested that he be subjected to a special military punishment either by running the gauntlet or being subjected twice or three times to the ducking stool. The culprit was very fortunate in that he was not only spared having to run the gauntlet but when he was to be dunked a second time the ducking stool fell apart. It had been rotting from within.

While the 1649 trial of the shooting of two Jewish passers-by was covered extensively in Chapter 5, a brief summary of the legal opinions is, nevertheless, warranted as a reminder that they constituted one of the most perturbing legal decisions issued by Frankfurt's advocates. One advocate had claimed that the only witness was a Jew and that "as a Jew was not to be believed as much"; the second admitted that human blood had been spilled, "although it was only that of Jews"; and the third argued that according to Kriegsrecht, military law, the suspect ought to be sentenced to death—legal arguments which resulted in the murderous soldier only being banished for life.

An ever-increasing legal sophistication on the part of the suspects, such as demonstrated again in the 1659 cases, now seemingly led to increasingly annoyed local advocates. When the suspect in the first case demanded a defensor, legal defender, Frankfurt's three advocates—Drs. Anton Glock, Lucas Kupferschmidt and Zacharias Stenglin—showed a definite unwelcoming attitude toward this idea, documented in the 29-page set of arguments exchanged between them and the selected defensor. While the suspect's wish to have a defensor was not turned down immediately, Frankfurt's three advocates set up various barriers to block it. They insisted that prior to his admittance, the defensor ought to swear an oath which also included the provision that he abstain from creating "long dilations" but instead ought to speed up the trial, a proviso which can only be interpreted as Frankfurt's advocates blaming defensors in general for instigating long trials. Regardless of who was in the end responsible for the duration of this trial—one of the longest during the 1562 to 1696 period, lasting from February 1 to November 28—the composite effect was to foreshadow later criminal trials.

However, while Frankfurt's advocates did not spare the culprit from a non-capital punishment, they, nevertheless, granted his wish of being decapitated without being touched by the executioner, rather than being shot. Fellow soldiers wrapped his corpse in a burial shroud and, most astoundingly, subsequently eight soldiers escorted his body under the sign of the cross to the new religious cemetery of St. Peter's, where he was buried. This religiously sanctioned funeral procession and burial represented a highly unusual procedure for a sentenced criminal because religious cemeteries were normally off-limits for criminals.

And the second 1659 trial was almost a mirror image of the first one not only because it also lasted for an extensive period, from June 6 to November 24, but also because of the numerous, highly sophisticated pleas, including a seven-page one by the culprit himself, replete with Latin legal arguments. Claims that the culprit had acted out of self-defense topped the list, followed by statements of his good character attested to by the mayor of his former place of residence. Local neighbors followed suit, also stressing character-positive arguments, and so did, most impressively, all soldiers of the local military company. The suspect was obviously successful in this obfuscating approach: Frankfurt's authorities had his dossier sent to the law faculty of Tübingen for their legal opinions.

While the culprit was not spared the death sentence, the penalty meted out, nevertheless, evidenced again the special treatment accorded to soldiers. He had his wish to be shot rather than decapitated granted, including his choice of the two musketeers who were to carry out the punishment. His corpse was put into a burial shroud by fellow soldiers who subsequently, similar to the previous case, escorted him under the sign of the cross to St. Peter's cemetery, where he was buried beside the other 1659 culprit.

Frankfurt's advocates thus increasingly suggested milder military-related punishments and the accused increasingly resorted to outside legal assistance, submitting pleas which not only increased in size but also, most importantly, in legal sophistry, including Latin and Greek passages only well-versed or legally trained persons would be able to muster. Most astoundingly, a religious element was added to the military punishments, granting two murderous soldiers the benefit of a religious funeral procession and burial in a religious cemetery. They were the only executed culprits during the period 1562 to 1696 who were granted such a privilege. Military religious-laced penal honors thus exceeded those of civilian criminals.

Fourth Period, 1661 to 1696: The Crimes

During this period, Frankfurt sentenced more criminal soldiers, namely 12, than during any preceding time frame. It started with two trials in 1671 that almost read like carbon copies.[22] The culprits in each case were sons of local burghers

22 ST June 10, 1671 and CR 1370; ST June 10, 1671 and CR 1371; ST January 4, 1672 and RP p. 82; ST August 27, 1672 and CR 1387; ST April 11, 1674 and CR 1420; ST June 28, 1678; ST December 9, 1679; ST June 10, 1680 and CR 1494; ST June 23, 1681 and CR 1536; ST February 17, 1688; ST March 19, 1690 and CR 1826; ST April 20, 1693 and CR 1693.

described as former soldiers, the first married with a child. They had committed their killings within two days of each other. The first suspect, as reported by five witnesses, killed a tobacco worker during an altercation which had erupted after drinking. The culprit hit the victim in the neck with a club "like he was hitting a dog," as described by one witness, breaking his neck so that he could not even keep his head up. The second of the 1671 incidences started again in a beer house and the victim was a soldier. Three witnesses—two of whom were women and one a servant in the beer house where the brawl between the two soldiers had started—attested that one had called the other a Schelm; this led to a brawl, which they continued outside in the street where, "in bright sunshine," the culprit stabbed his opponent in the back.

A year later, it was the wife of a former soldier who became his victim. He injured her so seriously that she died nine days later. As the fatal injuries prevented her from testifying, and the only witness, described as a "little man," only observed part of the crime scene, the culprit himself gave his rendition of what he claimed had transpired. He began his account with an exceedingly detailed personal description, starting with his military career of two years as a "gemeiner" soldier, whose basic service included watch responsibilities, followed by one and a half years as a "gefreiter" soldier, promoted and freed from watch duty. In an unprecedented move for the military trials assessed here, he also stated his religion as Lutheran. Claiming that his father had originally sent him to a Latin school, he later trained to become a tailor without, however, finishing his journeyman years. His mother had died 20 years earlier and he did not know whether his father was still alive because he had not heard from him in six months. He added that his grandfather was mayor of another town and was an apothecary by profession.

Subsequently, he offered his version of what had prompted him to act out his aggression. He and his wife had gone for a walk and they drank a beer in a local beer house, after which they returned home. Once at home, he told his wife that he was going out again to the same place, asking her to stay home. However, she wanted to go with him. When he told her that it was "not nice that a wife always followed her husband," she ignored him and followed him anyway. On his way, he allegedly repeatedly asked her to go home, but she refused to do so, which enraged him so much that he picked up a stone and threw it at her; the stone hit her on the head and she fell to the ground. When questioned as to the size and the weight of the stone, he claimed he did not recall; but the witness did, stating that it weighed approximately 3 pounds and hit the woman on the back of her head. The suspect, reversing the obvious allegations, blamed his wife instead, not only for having drunk most of the beer in the tavern, but also for being "a very stubborn woman," adding as an afterthought that he had loved her nonetheless.

The deadly weapon changed from a stone to an eating fork in the 1672 case. Unfortunately, no detailed criminal dossier is available but the scant information, nevertheless, reveals a bizarre setting. A soldier fatally stabbed his new brother-in-law with a fork during his wedding dinner.

By contrast, the documents in the 1674 case clearly portray the culprit as a musketeer, in service locally for one and a half years, and married. Seven people reported on the stabbing incident, which led to the death of a gefreiter soldier between seven and eight in the evening. The first witness, the brewer in whose beer house the two soldiers had been drinking, was honest enough to concede that he could not offer any details as he had not been at home at the time of the incident. A soldier, however, had observed the root of the problem. He testified that when they were playing cards in the beer house, one of the players had ripped up a deck of cards except for one, which the child of the victim picked up and handed to the opposite group where it was mixed in with the remaining cards. The culprit, incensed by this move, addressed the victim, saying that children ought not to be allowed at the tables. His exclamation, according to another witness, resulted in an altercation that led both of them to leave the beer place and meet outside in the street where, as another witness reported, they immediately engaged in a fistfight, but could be separated by friends. Thereafter, a witness disclosed, they initially parted in different directions; but then the culprit turned around, followed the victim and called him a Schelm, a provocation also overheard by another witness. This invective incensed the latter so much that he drew his sword and dashed toward him, a move immediately countered by the suspect who inflicted the mortal wound.

In 1678 a soldier robbed and stabbed a "Pfaff," Catholic priest, as the victim was described in the documents. While the stabbing unfolded during the night and did not pose any judicial intricacies, the background to this incident consists of voluminous documentation of a mixture of numerous rumors and ill repute too complex to be covered in this chapter.[23]

By contrast, the 1679 manslaughter is barely documented and simply recorded as a soldier starting a commotion during which someone died. The deadly incident of a year later had been observed by five witnesses—three of whom were women, one the victim's wife, another their maid—and it unfolded in broad daylight. A soldier randomly crossing fields was requested by the Feldschütz—the watchman in charge of the fields and meadows—to take a different path, which the soldier refused to do. His refusal led to an altercation between the two and the eventual wrestling over the Feldschütz's spade. Obviously successful in appropriating it,

---

[23] It is the topic of a separate paper prepared by this author.

the soldier hit the Feldschütz over the head so hard that despite various attempts he could not even get up, and died 15 days later.

For the 1681 murderous incident, the witness interrogation procedures changed in that instead of the traditional individual and separate questioning, the four witnesses were questioned together as a group. All four, three soldiers and one a non-military bystander, stated that around eight in the evening at the closing of the city gates, the victim, a soldier and his brother-in-law, a local musketeer with a military service spanning over six years and four months, were peacefully bowling together in a local beer house until they started betting, which led to an altercation between the two. The two left the premises peacefully; however, once in the street, the musketeer immediately charged at the victim and stabbed him to death. In 1688, an argument between two soldiers, who had been drinking together, also led to a fatal stabbing for which, unfortunately, no further detailed witness reports are available.

By contrast, the 1690 fatal shooting of a female servant "as a joke and out of boredom," in the culprit's own words, represents one of, if not the single most contemptuous but well-documented cases. Various witnesses reported on the unfolding of the crime, which occurred in the house of the servant's employer where several soldiers had been keeping a routine municipal watch. The first, a gefreiter soldier similar in rank to the culprit, reported that when the soldiers were ready to leave the house, the servant asked the culprit to stay for dinner. He declined the offer and, instead, precipitously shot her in the back so that she died an hour later. The same witness claimed that the servant, while still conscious, immediately forgave the culprit "from the bottom of her heart." His account was contradicted by another soldier, who asserted that the servant had not immediately done so. The third witness, another soldier, shed more light on the actual unfolding of the shooting by asserting that the culprit had confronted the servant with the words "I am going to shoot you soon," pointing his musket at her, and promptly firing. The fourth witness, a woman, in turn contradicted his account, quoting the culprit as saying, "You fat whore, I feel like shooting you," before aiming his musket at the victim and shooting her. Two other witnesses confirmed this rendition of the verbal assault prior to the shooting, while another female servant could not remember anything because she had fainted. The situation took another bizarre turn when two additional soldiers asserted that the culprit's gun had not been loaded a few hours before the incident.

The last case analyzed in this study took place in 1693. It documents, apart from the drinking of wine and beer and an ensuing brawl, a more pronounced soldierly element: the question of recruitment for military service. A 20-year-old sergeant, a Catholic whose mother was still alive, became the center of the 1693 inquiry. Despite his young age, the crime pattern resembled those of his seniors: alcohol and ensuing military-related arguments. In a local beer place he approached a miller's servant with the intent to recruit the servant to become a musketeer. But the servant had no such inclination. As a consequence, according to the brewer who was present, three to four soldiers ended up fighting among themselves over the servant's refusal. In order to quell the fight, the brewer's wife felt compelled to contact the local soldier guards, who came and removed the brawlers. One local soldier witness who had overheard the exchange between the servant and the sergeant stressed that his captain needed a musketeer. By contrast, another soldier, also privy to the conversation, did not agree with the recruiting objective and engaged the young sergeant in a conversation; but they left the beer place peacefully. They met for a drink again the next day, and when the recruiting topic from the previous day resurfaced, the discussion became so intense that it led to the hurling of invectives and to a deadly duel.

Thus, similar to previous crime patterns, most soldiers killed fellow soldiers in emotional outbursts triggered by invectives, in particular the term Schelm. Two killings, however, do stand out for their almost cavalier rendition: one committed by the husband and the other the shooting of a servant "as a joke."

Fourth Period, 1661–1696: The Penalties

Not surprisingly, the penal deliberations of these 12 trials exhibit the continuation if not escalation of previously cited military-related penal leniencies. In the first of the two 1671 cases, the soldier's wife was the first to plead with the authorities on the grounds that in their one and a half years of marriage they had had no fights and that their child was still so young that "it could not tell left from right." All local brewmasters followed her lead in their plea, stressing that he had conducted himself laudably well toward his wife during their marriage; that he was a pious person; that he had not started the fight; and, most curiously, that he had been drunk and, therefore, out of Christian mercy, he ought to be meted out a milder punishment.

Frankfurt's advocates needed two rounds of legal opinions to reach their penal recommendations. Despite their legal wrangling, their briefs have one common denominator: opting for a milder punishment, and this despite the fact that all witnesses and the barber-surgeons who checked the victim stated that the accused had beaten the victim so severely that his neck had been broken so that he could not even hold his head up. In their first round of legal opinions Dr. Martin Rasor, who wrote the lead legal opinion, argued that there was no need to subject the suspect to torture—although he had not confessed. He also asserted that the act had not been premeditated as the suspect had not drawn his sword but had used a club, and that he did not flee. Instead, reflecting the brewer's argument, he attributed the culprit's assault to his severe drunkenness at the time; and therefore, given that he was the son of an honorable father, a local burgher, a milder punishment ought to be recommended.

In their second round of legal briefs, the advocates delivered even more exculpatory and less crime-related arguments. It was especially Dr. Anton Glock who suggested mercy on the grounds that the culprit's grandfather was an old and well-known burgher. In the end, all the advocates, including Zacharias Stenglin, opted for a milder punishment, citing God's command to follow the Holy Scripture to extend mercy. The culprit's life was spared. He was sentenced to fight the Turks for five years. This show of religious mercy is, of course, in flagrant contradiction of the advocates' judgment of the two women accused of infanticide (Chapter 8), when they cited the most horrific passages from the Bible to have them sentenced to death.

In the second 1671 incidence of a former soldier, also the son of a local burgher, it was the father who submitted a lengthy plea, which contained even more legal subtleties in Latin than the 1659 cases. His main defensive argument focused on military honor as the causative element of his son's behavior, by claiming that his son had acted solely in defense of his military honor. In a very lengthy legal opinion, Dr. Rasor stated that the witnesses' accounts were not very clear—two of the three witnesses were women—but that, nevertheless, the culprit had broken the Stadtfrieden, peace of the town, and that others, in similar predicaments, had at least had the decency to duel outside the city gates. Dr. Anton Glock in his legal brief cited as his guideline Article 29 of the 1570 Articulbrief issued by Maximilian II, without, however, referring to Article 50, which addresses drinking problems in the military.[24] He conceded instead that it was not clear who had provoked whom, but as the accused was the son of a Frankfurt burgher and his parents and sisters lived there, a milder punishment ought to be meted out. The culprit was sentenced to three to four years of military service fighting the Turks.

And, as if to substantiate the milder form of punishment, post-sentencing documents in the dossier shed additional light on the unfolding of the punishments which apply to both of the 1671 sentenced culprits. These documents consist of a written exchange between Frankfurt's authorities and the mayor and city council of the town of Tübingen. Frankfurt claimed that the two culprits, instead of serving their sentences to fight the Turks, had been hiding at a brother-in-law's house in Tübingen, thus evading their punishment and breaking the oaths they had taken to carry it out. In a somewhat casual reply

---

24 Ewald Stier, *Die akute Trunkenheit und ihre strafrechtliche Begutachtung mit besonderer Berücksichtigung der militärischen Verhältnisse* (Jena: Fischer, 1907), p. 50.

Tübingen's authorities answered that the offenders had left and that they did not know their whereabouts. Hence, sentences to fight the Turks provided escape loopholes that allowed soldier culprits to dodge their punishments altogether.

Soldiers thus increasingly "escaped" harsh penal repercussions, and the 1672 case was no exception. While again all local soldiers as well as various guild masters from the defendant's former residency submitted pleas, it was the legal opinions by Frankfurt's advocates that disclose astounding penal argument reversals, putting disproportionately heavy blame on the victim. The victim was the wife who had refused to let her soldier husband return to the tavern without her, ignoring his argument that it was not becoming for a wife to always follow her husband. Initially, Frankfurt's advocates had paid close attention to the medical reports, which contained some doubts as to what had actually caused her death: swaying between interpretations that it was the stone hurled at her or the subsequent collapse and fall that landed her head on another stone. However, they soon abandoned this line of medical uncertainty in favor of the suspect's thematic lead of a woman's subordination to her husband.

Dr. Rasor began his legal deliberation by referring to "Göttliche, als Natürlichem oder Völkerrecht"—divine law, natural law and the law of nations—citing that those who spill the blood of others should suffer the same fate and that if someone throws a stone and thereby kills someone, they ought to die from the same cause, even acting as a biblical exegete referring to passages from Exodus 21, 12 and 14. The cited passages refer to capital punishment in case of a killing. However, Dr. Rasor, ignoring his own citations of the Bible, argued instead that the husband had no intention of killing his wife. Even more surprisingly, he based this assertion on pleas from the victim's own mother and stepfather, who both had asserted that the husband had loved his wife dearly and that she, the victim, had been a cantankerous person. Dr. Anton Glock agreed with this legal rationale and stressed that the wife had followed her husband against his will, and that she had generally been spoiling for fights, a legal stance also taken by Dr. Zacharias Stenglin. The soldier's wife thus suffered not only a deadly blow from her husband but also a blow to her reputation, which she had no opportunity to defend. Her husband received a milder punishment because of his wife's allegedly cantankerous disposition. He was spared the death sentence and was sent to a border house in Hungary instead to fight the Turks.

A short nota bene at the bottom of Dr. Rasor's opinion is, however, worth citing. It relates to the quality of the beer. He noted that this drinking incidence, possibly the third within the last two to three years, as well as other great tumults, might be attributable to the beer, which seems to make people crazy. He suggested, as a preventive measure, having the beer tested by the

Medicorum Judiciens to see whether it contained poisonous ingredients. But his suspicion had no effect on his legal opinion.

Little legal knowledge is available for the 1672 incident when a soldier killed his future brother-in-law with an eating fork, other than that he was sentenced to lifelong banishment—which he breached by returning to Frankfurt, only to be promptly ousted again.

In the 1674 case military honor came to the fore again when the culprit argued that he had acted out of self-defense in that the victim charged at him with his sword drawn, and that if he had not reacted, he could no longer be considered a soldier. In a rare occurrence, Frankfurt's advocates, Drs. Martin Rasor and Anton Glock, differed in their legal and penal assessments over the suspect's claim of self-defense, which prompted Frankfurt's city council to have the dossier sent to a law faculty at a university for further legal arbitration. Obviously not happy about this turn of events, the two advocates preempted this move by claiming to have received new information. This new discovery consisted of the culprit's assertion that he had only a rapier at his disposal—whose tip he had greased with earwax—instead of a hewing sword, the weapon drawn by the victim. Citing the use of earwax as a "superstitious means," the two advocates—referring to Articles 29 and 30 of Maximilian II's Articul auf die teutschte Fussknecht of 1570, as well as to Holländisches Kriegsrecht Article 3—agreed that the suspect's comportment had been less than appropriate. They were of the opinion that he could have evaded the fight, thus saving the life of his fellow without endangering his own or hurting himself or losing his honor. Despite their reservations, he was spared the death penalty and only sentenced to a border house for six years to fight the Turks.

The 1678 robbery and murder case of a "Pfaff" shows traces of milder, soldier-oriented penal approaches. Even for this heinous crime all local soldiers appealed for a milder punishment, which the accused was accorded by being sentenced to decapitation. Even Dr. Rasor showed sympathy with the robber and murderer by suggesting an immediate execution in order to help him assuage his anxieties and fears over his impending death.

Unfortunately, for the 1679 case no criminal dossier is available and thus very little information could be marshaled other than that the soldier culprit had asked for a defensor, and that he was sentenced to banishment only for six years.

In the 1680 killing of the Feldschütz with a spade, Frankfurt's advocates, Drs. Martin Rasor, Anton Glock and Georg Schuster, exhibited overt anti-woman sentiments by doubting the testimonies given by the three female witnesses simply because of their gender. While Dr. Rasor asserted that the three accounts submitted by the women were contradictory, Drs. Anton Glock and Georg Schuster were more outspoken by squarely disbarring the women's accounts on the grounds that "women's testimonies are not admissible in such important criminal cases." Ignoring the soldier's previous bad behavioral record, as submitted by the authorities where he had lived prior to arriving in Frankfurt, they granted him the milder sentence of being sent to fight the Turks for seven years.

By contrast, good behavior prior to the deadly incident was the reason cited for a milder sentence meted out in the 1681 case, and this despite the fact that Drs. Anton Glock and Georg Schuster had argued that the culprit could have avoided the fight altogether if he had stayed in the beer house and not followed the victim into the street. The culprit who had killed his brother-in-law, also a soldier, was banished for life—but without infamy or loss of honor, as specifically noted.

While in the 1688 case no criminal dossier is available, the few available data, nevertheless, show that the culprit, who claimed self-defense, was not only granted a defensor but also had his dossier sent to the "impartial law faculty" in Nuremberg, which confirmed the culprit's claim of "serious self-defense" absolving him from any wrongdoing. However, Frankfurt's city council, as the final arbiter, added a penal clause of banishment for life because of the excesses he had committed during his self-defense.

The 1690 "joke and boredom" killing of a female servant entailed two separate rounds of advocates' opinions. During the first, Dr. Heinrich Gabler, while referring to the witness who had overheard the culprit saying to the maid "You fat whore, I feel like shooting you on the spot," followed by his immediate aiming the gun at her, nevertheless, suggested that the shooting had occurred because of an unfortunate gun firing, especially as the culprit had expressed deep remorse thereafter. He concluded that the soldier had acted incautiously and that as a soldier he should have known that one cannot joke around with such a dangerous weapon. Obviously harboring doubts about the killed servant, he also suggested that her previous background be checked. Dr. Georg Schuster echoed this first assessment, adding that such a great injudiciousness had led to the spilling of innocent Christian blood; and, lamenting the fact that this soldier did not know whether his gun had actually been loaded, he urged that this incident should serve as a warning to other soldiers to be more careful. Drs. Johann Brandes and Anton Glock voiced similar opinions.

During the second round of legal briefs, three of the four advocates suggested that although the culprit had uttered threatening words such as "I feel like shooting you," he ought to be accorded a milder sentence based on his prior impeccable and pious conduct. Only Dr. Glock was more judicious, referring to the culprit's most recently submitted excuse that he no longer recalled having said "You fat whore, I feel like shooting you." However, the culprit, spared the death penalty, was sentenced to fight the Turks. Again it was Dr. Glock who voiced doubts, expressing reservations that fighting the Turks no longer represented a punishment, and urging the soldier to be sentenced to fight the French instead. The culprit, who shot a woman to death as a joke, ended up having to fight the French for three years.

Fighting the French was also listed as the punishment for the 1693 incidence of the stabbing of a fellow soldier. Unfortunately, the criminal dossier is incomplete, so no penal deliberations could be retrieved. But, obviously, the penal structure was adjusted to conform to the bellicose situation.

The penal deliberations by Frankfurt's advocates seem at times flippant, if not outright discriminatory. Christian mercy and the wife's insubordinate behavior turned the trial more into an accusation of the victim, while the culprit in the senseless shooting of the servant found mercy because of his prior good behavior. Local burgher status served as an additional penal reducer for two of the soldiers killing fellow soldiers. All murderous soldiers sentenced during that last period received milder punishments. None of the manslaughter perpetrators were executed. Even the soldier convicted of robbery and murder could count on the advocates for a milder punishment.

Conclusion

A multitude of changes can be observed from these archival records. The quantitative fluctuations of the sentencing of murderous soldiers stand out by their seemingly erratic pattern, in that Frankfurt sentenced more soldiers during times of peace and local prosperity, such as from 1562 to 1594, as compared to periods of serious instability such as the Thirty Years War. Equally remarkable is the considerable sentencing increase during the last three decades of the seventeenth century, which, while fending off the bellicose comportment of the French, did not expose Frankfurt to the same perils and calamities as experienced during the Thirty Years War. The amply documented general "dramatic increase in army size" for that period might have led to a concomitant increase in crimes committed; however, in the absence of any direct causal connection between army size and crimes, and the additional obvious lack of a direct connection between crimes committed and crimes sentenced, the black figure, this correlation has to remain a purely hypothetical proposition.[25]

---

[25] With regard to the increase in army size during the seventeenth century, see Parker, *Revolution*, pp. 24, 43; see also Dane Archer and Rosemary Gartner, "Violent Acts and Violent Crimes: A Comparative Approach to Postwar Homicide Rates," *American Sociological Review*, 41 (1972): 937–62.

The nature of the crimes exhibited at a first, superficial glance a similar erratic pattern, which, however, on closer scrutiny, proved to be an increasingly constant and explainable trend over time. The numerous and clearly documented witness reports reveal not only the increasingly public nature of many fatal assaults but also a concomitant stable pattern of the motivations for the crimes. Hate crime and domestic violence crime sentencing remained low, although they constituted some of the most heinous crimes. The sentencing of robbery and murders took place primarily during the last decades of the sixteenth century. Thereafter, a drastic change occurred in that Frankfurt sentenced mainly soldiers for manslaughter.

Two distinct explanations emerge from the witnesses' descriptions of these manslaughter cases. First, they were almost exclusively alcohol related, which obviously led to the diminishing of the soldiers' emotional control. Second, and most importantly, it was the hurling of invectives challenging military-charged honor concepts that triggered fatal causative action. However, the consumption of alcohol was, as the numerous witness reports clearly show, neither a soldierly phenomenon nor an unusual pattern for the people of Frankfurt (see also Chapter 10). They both drank, and they drank together in public drinking places. Soldiers either came alone or with fellow soldiers, and obviously they intermixed with the local civilian population. There was no cultural segregation.[26] And Frankfurt's municipally operated wine and beer bell dispels any further doubts about the habitual and routine nature of social public drinking. This bell not only rang daily to "alert" people of when to expect their last drink but also was seasonally adjusted, ringing at 9 pm from March 25 to October 16 and at 8 pm thereafter.[27] Even the German word "Trinkgeld," or the corresponding French term "pourboire" for that matter, both meaning tip, are traceable to their literal meaning of giving someone money to pay for a drink. Thus the consumption of alcohol in taverns was not just a soldierly phenomenon; neither was it a local one. On the contrary, several historians have documented similar public drinking patterns for other locations, even stressing their social importance. Social drinking was not only widely accepted, but also encouraged.[28]

---

26 As suggested for Augsburg during the 1640s by B. Ann Tlusty, "The Public House and Military Culture in Germany, 1500–1648," in Beat Kümin and B. Ann Tlusty, eds, *The World of the Tavern: Public Houses in Early Modern Europe* (Aldershot: Ashgate, 2002), pp. 136–58, p. 154.

27 Georg Ludwig Kriegk, *Deutsches Bürgertum im Mittelalter: Nach urkundlichen Forschungen und mit besonderer Beziehung auf Frankfurt am Main* (2 vols, 1868; repr. Frankfurt am Main: Sauer & Auvermann, 1969), vol. 2, pp. 330–45.

28 See two important studies on this topic: Beat Kümin, *Drinking Matters: Public Houses and Social Exchange in Early Modern Central Europe* (New York: Palgrave Macmillan,

And soldiers were also not an isolated group resorting to physical assaults stimulated by alcohol and unfolding in taverns.[29] Frequently, and, similar to other alcohol-incited fights, verbal invectives were the first step toward physical assaults, especially diatribes aimed at shaming and humiliating the opponent. Insulting personal honor, in particular male personal honor, was frequently the core stimulant and it proved to be especially provoking when the insults were traded in a public place for many to observe.[30]

While many of Frankfurt's soldierly cases also have honor insults as the core instigator for attacks, they, nevertheless, prove increasingly different. It was the content of the invectives hurled at the opponent that changed dramatically: they became increasingly military honor specific. While previously soldiers exchanged more general, personal insulting verbal attacks, these verbal outbursts became more soldier-specific in focus and escalated to their verbal crescendo in the calling of fellow soldiers Schelm. Being called a Schelm meant the ultimate symbolic verbal depiction of the loss of military honor and thus this became the most inflammatory insult, triggering most physical assaults.

However, for this insult to work, a fundamental change in the very concept of military honor, or lack thereof, had to have been created and internalized: a process, which, judging by the numerous witnesses' reports, gradually took effect replacing previous general, non-military oriented invectives. Soldiers, instead of hurling general personal insults at each other, started to target each other over corporate military honors. Their individual identification thus did not reside with their birth town or country, but increasingly with the military, proof of the emergence and intensification of an *esprit de corps*. While research into the causes of this change would exceed the framework of this study, one scholar suggested the introduction of the military drill by the 1590s as a contributing factor.[31] And nothing corroborates better the efficacy of the absorption of this new military honor mentality than soldiers killing fellow soldiers over the hurling of such a military honor-demeaning insult primarily encapsulated in the word Schelm. It is, indeed, quite remarkable that a change in the meaning of an invective—the power of a word—would entail such noticeable and deadly consequences.

That most of the exchanging of these newly developed military honor invectives and subsequent deadly encounters occurred in public, either in

2007), p. 192; and B. Ann Tlusty, *Bacchus and Civic Order: The Culture of Drink in Early Modern Germany* (Charlottesville: University Press of Virginia, 2001).

29 Tlusty, Bacchus, pp. 126 and 132, where she documents a large number of craftsmen involved in brawls.

30 Kümin, *Drinking Matters*, p. 136; Tlusty, *Bacchus*, pp. 127–8.

31 See William H. McNeill, *Keeping Together in Time: Dance and Drill in Human History* (Cambridge, MA: Harvard University Press, 1995), especially chapter 5.

taverns or outside taverns, adds another significant dimension to their efficacy and spread. Military honor concepts, observed and overheard by many, could proliferate fast and unencumbered, especially in a medium sized community like Frankfurt where word of mouth was still one of the primary news transmitters. Military culture thus could easily find access to mainstream thinking.

However, a caveat is in place. The soldiers caught in Frankfurt's criminal jurisdictional net were not the originators of this military honor concept, and neither were they its most influential distributors. Military institutions initiated its practice, and the impact of Humanism can be clearly traced to that effect.[32] For Frankfurt, nothing corroborates this development better than the city's own penal descriptions of criminal soldiers, such as in 1634 when one of them had his sword broken in two at the gallows, "whereby he was publicly turned into a Schelm."[33] Quite obviously, the penal authoritative public application of the term would spread among soldiers who, in turn, used it to punish fellow soldiers by publicly degrading them. It is thus safe to argue not only for the emergence but also for the expansion of a military culture in which the military honor concept played an escalating role leading to, what one might call, military honor killings.

This military cultural honor principle also affected the victimization pattern. Victims increasingly consisted of fellow soldiers.[34] It was not necessarily a deteriorating relation between soldiers and civilians that formed the base for these interpersonal homicidal attacks, but the heightened intra-corporate military culture. Honor-afflicting military insults emanating from soldiers and hurled at fellow soldiers led to the paradoxical phenomenon of soldiers killing their comrades in non-combat environments over military honor concepts.

Changing and increasingly detailed military descriptions entered in the documents serve as additional proof of this steadily evolving military climate or culture. Quite obviously, Frankfurt's civilian court kept up with military changes when firearm-bearing soldiers using guns and pistols replaced the itinerant Landsknecht, mercenary foot soldier. These increasing citations of soldiers' ranks should not be brushed aside as a recording quirk. On the contrary, these military demarcation recordings testify further to a growing awareness of the importance

---

[32] How humanist rhetoric shapes the ritual of command is a theme discussed by Brian J. Maxson in a paper presented at the Renaissance Society's meeting on March 19, 2009 and included in his forthcoming article "The Ritual of Command: Humanism, Magic, and Liberty in Fifteenth-Century Florence," to appear in Nicholas Scott Baker and Brian Jeffrey Maxson, eds, *After Civic Humanism: Learning and Politics in Renaissance Italy, 1300–1600.*

[33] ST, June 6, 1634.

[34] In contrast to Yorkshire during the Civil War, for which Roman Bennett claims that "drink-related brawls" resulted mainly in civilian victims, in "War and Disorder," p. 261.

of military rank and to a tacit approval of an ever-refining hierarchical military structure, and this in a civilian court.

Judicial and penal deliberations exhibit another if not more important dimension to the ascendancy of this military-corporate identity, a spirit particularly fostered by Frankfurt's advocates. Their legal opinions are riddled with at times astonishing shortcomings in favor of the military. While frequently seemingly carefully weighing the statements of witnesses, and presenting their ever-lengthy legal arguments with increasing linguistic erudition—lacing them with more and more Latin and Greek language explanations; even arguing from various legal sources and perspectives referring to various military laws, even biblical passages—their penal arguments do not attest to an objective and uniform picture of jurisprudence.

Discrediting witnesses attests to one of their shortcomings. While only few women witnesses testified—a fact that might be attributable to the crimes increasingly unfolding in public drinking places or in close proximity to drinking houses where fewer women might have been regular customers—it is, nevertheless, a blatant miscarriage of justice by Frankfurt's advocates to explicitly discredit the few female witnesses simply based on their gender.[35] The exclusively male military hierarchical culture found its replica in the courts. Yet, women frequently submitted pleas to obtain a milder punishment for their husbands, such as in the 1571 case and many others.[36]

Frankfurt's advocates also blatantly lowered the legal credibility of female victims. True, increasingly, though not abundantly, the marital status of soldiers appeared in the judicial documents, which should put to rest the claim that soldiers were not allowed to get married.[37] But these inclusions meant relatively

---

35 For women and public drinking see B. Ann Tlusty "Crossing Gender Boundaries: Women as Drunkards in Early Modern Augsburg," in Sibylle Backmann et al., eds, *Ehrkonzepte in der Frühen Neuzeit: Identitäten und Abgenzungen* (Berlin: Akademie Verlag, 1998), p. 194.

36 For an explanation of this pattern see Chapter 7.

37 As suggested by Dennis Showalter and William J. Astore, *Soldiers' Lives Through History: The Early Modern World* (Westport. CT: Greenwood, 2007), p. 136; Ulinka Rublack, *The Crimes of Women in Early Modern Germany* (Oxford: Clarendon Press, 1999), p.183; and Ulinka Rublack, "Metze und Magd. Krieg und die Bildfunktion des Weiblichen in deutschen Städten der Frühen Neuzeit," in Backman et al., *Ehrkonzepte*, pp. 199–222, pp. 210–11. By contrast, demonstrating that they could get married, see Karen Hagemann, "Militär, Krieg und Geschlechtsverhältnisse: Untersuchungen, Überlegungen und Fragen zur Militärgeschichte der Frühen Neuzeit," in Ralf Pröve, ed., *Klio in Uniform? Probleme und Perspektiven einer modernen Militärgeschichte der Frühen Neuzeit* (Cologne: Böhlau, 1997), pp. 35–88; and Beate Engelen, "Warum heiratete man einen Soldaten? Soldatenfrauen in der ländlichen Gesellschaft Brandenburg-Preussen im 18. Jahrhundert," in Stefan Kroll and

little in the legal domain. On the contrary, as the advocates' argument in the stone-throwing killing incident clearly document, they faulted the wife for her alleged insubordinate behavior toward her husband instead of blaming him squarely as the initiator of the deadly throw that killed her. The female servant shot to death as a "joke and out of boredom" after having been insulted by her murderous soldier as "a fat whore" did not get full legal recognition either. The advocates' extremely mild penal suggestions for the soldier serve not only as another gender-biased example, but also as one in favor of the military.

Frankfurt's advocates treated Jewish people in a similar fashion: discrediting them, as explicitly recorded in the documents, as witnesses in the case of the fatal shooting of one of them by a soldier simply because they were Jewish. And upon the advocates' recommendation, the murderous soldier received a very mild sentence because, as one added, only Jewish blood had been spilled (see Chapter 5). Obviously, in their case religion played a major denigrating role, a deduction backed by the lack of religious entries for non-Jewish witnesses, culprits, and victims in these soldierly cases. The religion of soldierly culprits was documented in only two instances, and this only parenthetically.

However, this lack of religious specificity when describing the witnesses and culprits in these soldierly trials did not prevent Frankfurt's advocates from making selective use of religious citations to bolster their military penal arguments. And, when they chose to do so, they used Christian arguments to justify milder penalties in flagrant contradiction of their religious references and urging harsher punishments on Jews, Gypsies, gays and women.[38]

Religious arguments were not the only criteria affecting the advocates' penal decisions. The actual circumstances leading to the unfolding of a deadly act also received high priority. While to their credit Frankfurt's advocates refused, in most cases, to heed the suspects' legal excuse of having been drunk, they, nevertheless, paid close attention to the hurling of honor-shaming invectives and to who was the first to use them. When the victim was the first to scream military honor invectives at his opposite number, Frankfurt's advocates were more inclined to mete out milder punishments to the one responsible for the fatal stabbing or shooting.

The occupational and civic status of both victims and culprits played another decisive role in their penal deliberations. When a fellow soldier was the victim, the advocates frequently suggested milder sentences. If the culprits were sons of local burghers, they always recommended a milder punishment. Both

---

Kersten Krüger, eds, *Militär und ländliche Gesellschaft in der frühen Neuzeit*, published by Arbeitskreis Militär und Gesellschaft in der frühen Neuzeit, vol. 1 (Hamburg: LIT, 2000), pp. 251–73.

[38] See Chapters 4, 5, 6, 8, 9 and 10.

punishment-reducing stances point to general politically sensitive motivations on the advocates' part. And this should not come as a surprise considering that many of their family members and friends were members of the city council (see Chapter 2). Frankfurt's advocates thus seemed to act in what they must have considered a "politically correct" way. Preventing local upheaval by meting out milder punishments to the soldier sons of local upright citizens and assuaging local hired soldiers seemed pragmatic objectives, especially considering that soldiers were needed to protect the city from military and/or financial misfortunes.

The punishments they suggested clearly corroborate this deduction: increasingly advocating military-sensitive punishments, such as fighting the Turks or the French.[39] When soldiers were needed to fight or ward off dangers or reduce Frankfurt's financial contributions, the Turkish tax, fighting the Turks (and later the French) seemed palatable alternatives to the death sentence for murderous soldiers—a penal approach which stands in stark contrast to the sentencing of women for infanticide, who were all executed. This mentality of an obvious corporate military judicial bifurcation started in 1590 at the latest and thus ran an almost parallel course to the increase in military descriptions in the documents, as well as to the increase in military honor-related crimes. In Frankfurt's civilian court, soldiers were thus not considered the dregs of society.[40] On the contrary, Frankfurt's soldiers were even increasingly deployed for general supervisory and arresting procedures, as clearly evidenced by the various witness reports (see also Chapter 9).

In addition, soldiers resorted to submitting pleas for milder punishments for their comrades, a practice which increased in size and numbers with obvious results. Soldiers were given the privilege of suggesting and even actively participating in the actual penal process, replacing at times the much-dishonored executioner. By being integrated into the penal system, carrying out the execution of sentences of fellow soldiers, they accorded their criminal comrades another measure of military respect.

---

39 Pragmatic penal concessions were also made by other rulers: see above all Ruth Pike, *Penal Servitude in Early Modern Spain* (Madison: Wisconsin University Press, 1983).

40 See Jutta Nowosadtko, "Militärjustiz im 17. und 18. Jahrhundert am Beispiel des Fürstbistums Münster," in Sylvia Kesper-Biermann and Diethelm Klippel, eds, *Kriminalität in Mittelalter und Frühen Neuzeit: Soziale, rechtliche, philosophische und literarische Aspekte* (Wiesbaden: Harrassowitz, 2007), pp. 115–40, who suggests that harsher military punishments were meted out to soldiers (p. 132) and that punishments handed down by military courts did not necessarily deviate from civilian ones (p. 139); see also Bennett, "War and Disorder," p. 264.

The two 1659 burials when soldiers, under the sign of the cross, accompanied their executed comrades to their burial site in a religious cemetery—the *only* two such religious burials for criminals sentenced in Frankfurt during the 1562 to 1696 period—are the most telling testimony to military honors, and this in contrast to soldiers, who, when they "died in action were shoveled into mass graves."[41]

While in 1619 a civilian who had committed manslaughter and was executed by sword was also buried at St. Peter's, he, unlike the two soldiers, had his corpse soon thereafter excavated and reburied in non-religious ground.[42] Murderous soldiers had thus achieved the ultimate civil and military/religious recognition.

This implicit religious benediction was surely not lost on Frankfurt's general population, who observed not only many of the deadly encounters that had unfolded in public but also many of the publicly carried out punishments. What would impart a more convincing impression of the honorable status of soldiers than an official, religiously sanctioned funeral of the very same soldiers who had publicly killed their victims in front of many witnesses? Might many of the locals not—rightfully—conclude that soldiers were accorded preferential judicial and penal treatments demonstrating that they were achieving an ever-increasing exulted status in society, a status possibly to be emulated? Might this public display of horrible killings in defense of military honor and the mild, honorable punishments meted out thereafter not lead to a generally accepted if not admired military culture among civilians? While the lack of actual empirical data precludes the affirmation of such a deduction, other scholars did not shy away from suggesting a similar theme for the influence of the Prussian aristocratic officer-military corps in the nineteenth century, which, they claimed, allegedly led to a social militarization and "German militarism."[43]

One clearly traceable conclusion can be drawn from the existing documents. A newly emerging military honor system affected not only soldiers but also the learned, the advocates who, resembling the much debated "military revolution" of the early modern period, also introduced "revolutionary" albeit discriminatory clauses into the judicial system, with far-reaching consequences.

---

41 Hale, "Soldier in Germanic Graphic Art," p .94.

42 ST June 30, 1619.

43 As claimed by Otto Büsch, Military System and Social Life in Old Regime Prussia, 1713–1807: The Beginning of the Social Militarization of Prusso-German Society, trans. John G. Gafliardo (Atlantic Highlands, NJ: Humanities Press, 1997), although he admits and regrets in his foreword "the absence of a detailed treatment of the urban world," p. xiv. His interpretation has been challenged as too narrow by various scholars such Peter H. Wilson, "Defining Military Culture," Journal of Military History, 72/1 (January 2008): 11–41, especially p. 29.

PART VII
Desperate Acts

Chapter 12

Escapes from Judgment: Self-Inflicted Deaths of Criminal Suspects

In recent years, suicides have gained considerable attention, especially those committed by young people or by those with religio-political or war-like objectives. Yet self-inflicted deaths are not a new phenomenon. They have been practiced for centuries. Despite repeated and persistent occurrences, however, historians have only recently started to focus on such phenomena.[1] While this is a commendable scholarly reorientation, few, if any, of these recent analyses concentrate on those who took their lives either immediately after having committed a crime or while imprisoned awaiting the outcome of their trials: judicial suicides.[2]

---

[1] Ursula Baumann, *Vom Recht auf den eigenen Tod: Die Geschichte des Suizids vom 18. bis zum 20. Jahrhundert* (Weimar: Böhlau, 2001); Ossip Bernstein, *Die Bestrafung des Selbstmords und ihr Ende, Strafrechtliche Abhandlungen*, 78 (Breslau, 1907): 1–60; David Lederer, "The Dishonorable Dead: Perceptions of Suicide in Early Modern Germany," in Sibylle Backmann et al., eds, *Ehrkonzepte in der Frühen Neuzeit: Identitäten und Abgrenzungen* (Berlin: Akademie Verlag, 1998), pp. 349–65; Vera Lind, *Selbstmord in der Frühen Neuzeit: Diskurs, Lebenswelt und kultureller Wandel am Beispiel der Herzogtümer Schleswig und Holstein* (Göttingen: Vandenhoeck & Ruprecht, 1999); Michael MacDonald and Terence R. Murphy, *Sleepless Souls: Suicide in Early Modern England* (Oxford: Clarendon Press, 1990); Erik Midelfort, "Selbstmord im Urteil von Reformation und Gegenreformation," in Wolfgang Reinhard and Heinz Schilling, eds, *Die katholische Konfessionalisierung: Wissenschaftliches Symposium der Gesellschaft zur Heruasgabedes Corpus Catholicorumum und des Vereins fur Reformationsgeschichte* (Gütersloh: Gütersloher Verlagshaus, 1995); Georges Minois, *History of Suicide: Voluntary Death in Western Culture*, trans. Linda G. Cochrane (Baltimore: Johns Hopkins University Press, 1999); Alexander Murray, *Suicide in the Middle Ages*, vol. 1: *The Violent against Themselves* (Oxford: Oxford University Press, 1998) and vol. 2: *The Curse on Self-Murder* (Oxford: Oxford University Press, 2000); Markus Schär, *Seelennöte der Untertanen: Selbstmord, Melancholie und Religion im alten Zürich, 1500–1800* (Zurich: Chronos, 1985); Gabriela Signori, ed., *Trauer, Verzweiflung und Anfechtung: Selbstmord und Selbstmordversuche in mittelalterlichen und frühneuzeitlichen Gesellschaften* (Tübingen: Edition Diskord, 1994); Jeffrey R. Watt, *Choosing Death: Suicide and Calvinism in Early Modern Geneva* (Kirksville, MO: Truman State University Press, 2001); Michael Zell, "Suicide in Pre-Industrial England," Social History, 11/3 (October 1986): 303–17; and Jeffrey R. Watt, ed., *From Sin to Insanity: Suicide in Early Modern Europe* (Ithaca, NY: Cornell University Press, 2004).

[2] Watt, *Choosing Death*, p. 167, allots one paragraph to suicides in prison; see also footnote 48.

This gap in historical scholarship, while deplorable, is, nevertheless, understandable given the fact that even for the twentieth and twenty-first centuries such studies are rare, and as a consequence, "The problem of self-inflicted death in prison suffers from a lack of visibility."[3] It is the objective of this chapter to shed some light on this as yet little-known human/judicial deadly interconnection during the early modern German period by analyzing 14 alleged crime-related suicides and two such attempts in the city of Frankfurt am Main. The very fact that all 16 cases were registered in the local Strafenbuch, Book of Punishment, which contains every criminal sentenced during the 1562 to 1696 period, is indicative of the fact that contemporaries did not take judicial suicides lightly.[4] On the contrary, simply being registered in such a criminally implicating manner points to anything but indifference, a deduction borne out by data contained in the various criminal dossiers such as witness reports, barber/surgeons' and midwives' statements, and the various legal deliberations by local advocates.[5] The inclusion of these 16 cases in the Book of Punishment also set the methodological framework for this study: a comparative analysis. A compare-and-contrast approach of Frankfurt's judicial suicides to the city's general judicial/penal treatment of those who did not resort to taking their own lives promises to disclose insightful quantitative and, more importantly, qualitative understandings. Therefore, whenever possible, the treatment of

---

[3] Diana Medlicott, *Surviving the Prison Place: Narratives of Suicidal Prisoners* (Aldershot: Ashgate, 2001), p. 1; see also the 2006 research project on suicide in prison initiated by Keith Hawton, Center for Suicide Research at the University of Oxford.

[4] The Strafenbuch (ST) is located in the municipal archives of Frankfurt am Main. The 16 cases in question are: ST January 10, 1567; ST July 22, 1571; ST August 15, 1572; ST June 21, 1587; ST June 2, 1588; ST April 15, 1598; ST October 10, 1602; ST August 10, 1611; ST February 12, 1616; ST March 15, 1637; ST February 14, 1651; ST April 14, 1651; ST September 23, 1685; ST September 17, 1690; ST December 12, 1690; ST June 6, 1695.

[5] Frankfurt's Strafenbuch was not the only source used for this analysis. Most helpful were the actual criminal dossiers of the individual judicial suicides containing witness reports, barber/surgeon and midwife statements, and the various legal deliberations by Frankfurt's advocates. Unfortunately, there exist only nine such individual criminal dossiers, but additional data can be derived from adjudication entries in Frankfurt's Ratsprotokolle (RP), minutes of the city council, and Bürgermeisterbücher (BB), mayors' protocols. These two sets cover the criminal deliberations by Frankfurt's city council which was in charge of criminal adjudication. The nine dossiers are labeled Criminalia (CR). The nine cases are: CR 365 covering ST April 15, 1598; CR 440 covering ST October 10, 1602; CR 667 covering ST August 10, 1611; CR 750 covering ST February 12, 1616; CR 1125 covering ST April 14, 1651; CR 1664 covering ST September 23, 1685; CR 1858 covering ST September 17, 1690; CR 1872 covering ST December 12, 1690; CR 2036 covering ST June 6, 1695. The Ratsprotokolle exist for the 1562 to 1689 period, except for the years 1626 and 1628. The Bürgermeisterbücher exist, save for the years 1626 and 1628, for the entire time span.

suicides is compared to the handling of other crime sentences in order to discover similarities and/or discrepancies and possible changes over time.

The close linguistic connection between crime and suicide further warrants a comparative approach. Until recently, Germans, including German scholars, used the criminally charged linguistic terms "Selbstmord," self-murder, and "Selbstmörder" for the person committing the act. Similar to their English or French counterparts, who described both the act and the victim with the somewhat more neutral-sounding word "suicide," Germans now referred to it as either "Selbsttötung," killing oneself, or "Suizid."[6] In order to avoid anachronistic interpretations, the earlier term "Selbstmord" will be used in this study, although, unfortunately, the origin of this word has not been fully established as yet. Some scholars claim that a Catholic priest was the first to use this linguistic self-murder expression in 1514. By 1650 at the latest, however, the term was widely used.[7]

Changing semantics point to changing conceptual trends. A brief analysis of the historical progression of changing suicide mentalities—in particular, those related to alleged crimes and/or imprisonment—seems, therefore, appropriate in order to gain an understanding of underlying legal as well as popular attitudes during the sixteenth and seventeenth centuries.

Brief Historical Background

One of the greatest influences on sixteenth- and seventeenth-century mental attitudes toward "Selbstmörder" originated in the Greco-Roman world. Many of the ideas formulated then, particularly philosophical and legal views, influenced

---

6 England did so since the mid-seventeenth century: Murray, *Suicide Middle Ages*, vol 1, pp. 39–40; Minois, *History of Suicide*, p. 181 referring to Sir Thomas Browne's, *Religio medici*, published in England in 1642. The French adopted the term in 1734: see Watt, *Choosing Death*, p. 105; Minois, *History of Suicide*, p. 182.

7 Lind, *Selbstmord*, p. 19; Andreas Wacke, "Der Selbstmord im römischen Recht und in der Rechtsentwicklung," in *Zeitschrift der Savigny-Stiftung für Rechtsgeschichte*, vol, 97 (Vienna: Böhlau, 1980), pp. 27–77, p. 41; see Andreas Bähr's impressive knowledge and rendition of linguistic developments in *Germany, England and France, Der Richter im Ich: Die Semantik der Selbsttötung in der Aufklärung* (Göttingen: Vandenhoeck & Ruprecht, 2002), pp. 12–13. Prior to that date, and strongly resembling Roman practices, German sources, including those from Frankfurt and many other European regions for that matter, used verbs such as "sich erhängt" (hanged him/herself) or "sich ertränkt" (drowned her/himself) to describe the act: Wacke, "Selbstmord im römischen Recht," p. 42. In France, verbs such as "se tuer soi-meme" or "s'oster la vie" were used; see Alain Joblin, "Le suicide à l'époque modern: Un exemple dans la France du nord-ouest: à Boulogne-sur-Mer," *Revue Historique*, 291/1 (1994): 85–119, p. 86.

Christian thought and Canon Law as well as secular legislation. The growing influence of the Catholic Church eventually led to the spread of philosophical/religious suicide interpretations, and the integration of Roman Law into the Germanic legal system fostered their secular inroads.

While some scholars argue that Greek history is "studded with famous suicides" and the "actual practice seems to have leaned toward indulgence," many influential Greek philosophers actually disapproved of it.[8] Socrates and Plato, for example, rejected suicide except under rare and strenuous circumstances.[9] Both philosophers advocated that certain suicides should not be buried publicly, a stance later echoed by Christian doctrines and prevalently applied during the early modern period.[10]

Similarly, at first glance, Rome "is reputed to have been the most favorable to suicide" because "There was no legal or religious prohibition of suicide for free men."[11] But the stress is on free men: prisoners, soldiers, and slaves were excluded from this concept.[12] In fact, Roman prisoners were carefully supervised in order to prevent them from taking their lives, in addition to being subjected to stringent fiscal parameters depending on their sentencing status.[13] Originally, if a prisoner took his life prior to being sentenced, his property would be passed on in full to his heirs.[14] By contrast, a prisoner sentenced to death or lifelong banishment could not pass on his possessions to his designated heirs. The state confiscated it, save for a small amount set aside for his dependants. Later this fiscal inheritance divide was revised to read that if an accused facing the death penalty committed suicide he not only showed

---

8 Minois, *History of Suicide*, p. 43.

9 Ibid., p. 45; see also Wacke, "Selbstmord im römischen Recht," p.46.

10 Wacke, "Selbstmord im römischen Recht," p. 47; Nicole Zeddies, "Verwirrte oder Verbrecher? Die Beurteilung des Selbstmordes von der Spätantike bis zum 9. Jahrhunder," in Signori, *Traue*, p. 60; Minois, *History of Suicide*, p. 45; Murray, *Suicide Middle Ages*, vol. 2, pp. 123–7. Aristotle condemned suicide outright, branding it an act against oneself and against the city; see Minois, *History of Suicide*, p. 46.

11 Minois, *History of Suicide*, pp. 46, 48; Zeddies, *Verwirrte*, p. 61; Murray, *Suicide Middle Ages*, vol. 2, pp. 526–7. Among the most outspoken proponents of suicide were the Roman Stoics, particularly Seneca, who, in fact, committed suicide himself, although he reserved the right to take one's life only for wise people: see Wacke, "Selbstmord im römischen Recht," p. 46; Lind, *Selbstmord*, p. 25; Watt, *Choosing Death*, p. 70, n. 11. Another famous suicide was Lucretia, who "killed herself with a knife after having been raped," Minois, *History of Suicide*, p. 49.

12 Murray, *Suicide Middle Ages*, vol. 2, p. 180.

13 Wacke, "Selbstmord im römischen Recht," p. 51.

14 Ibid., p. 53.

his fear of the punishment but also his guilt and, therefore, the confiscation of property was warranted in all instances.[15]

With the integration of Roman Law into the traditional German body of law, this fiscal clause entered local legal deliberations, and this despite the fact that early Germans seemed to have been less concerned with fiscal considerations and other degrading suicide ramifications. In fact, there existed no "suicide taboo" and "suicide is sometimes referred to as positively honorable."[16] Consequently, no punishments were attached to the act.[17] Suicides by old people were frequent occurrences, and suicides not prompted by old age or disease were related to insanity.[18] Yet, some scholars claim that there also existed the notion that suicides were unable to find a resting place and, consequently, would roam about after death. These possible "portentous resurgents," in some instances, had a pole rammed through their chest to tie them to the ground.[19]

With the advent of Christianity, attitudes toward suicide hardened in Germany. Suicide became a grave sin and this, most curiously, despite the fact that neither the Old nor the New Testament contains any such condemning references.[20] Early church luminaries such as St. Ambrose and St. Augustine—who "adjusted" the commandment "thou shall not kill" to include "thou shall not kill oneself"—began denouncing suicide, although they did not suggest any posthumous punishments for the corpse.[21] During successive church councils, however, posthumous penal repercussions were gradually introduced.[22]

15 Ibid., p. 55; Zeddies, *Verwirrte*, p. 61.

16 Murray, *Suicide Middle Ages*, vol. 2, p. 565.

17 Ibid. and vol. 1, p. 167.

18 Bernstein, *Bestrafung*, pp. 3, 5; Heinz Holzhauer, "Der Suizid in der Rechtsgeschichte," in *Heinz Holzhauer, Beiträge zur Rechtsgeschichte*, eds., Stefan Chr. Saar and Andreas Roth (Berlin: Schmidt, 2000), p. 62.

19 Dieter Feucht, *Grube und Pfahl: Ein Beitrag zur Geschichte der deutschen Hinrichtungsbräuche* (Tübingen: Mohr, 1967).

20 Watt, *Choosing Death*, p. 76; Murray, *Suicide Middle Ages*, vol. 2, pp. 91, 97. On the contrary, the Old Testament contains a series of suicides of Jewish heroes such as Saul, Ahithopel and Samson, who all received honorary funerals: see Wacke, "Selbstmord im römischen Recht," p. 32; Lind, *Selbstmord*, p. 22; Zeddies, *Verwirrte*, p. 64; see also Pieter Bruegel's depiction of Saul's suicide painted in 1562.

21 St. Ambrose embraced its concept, however only when it applied to women who wanted to end their lives after having been dishonored—raped: see Wacke, "Selbstmord im römischen Recht," p.32; Murray, *Suicide Middle Ages*, vol. 2, pp. 100 and 101–17; Lind, *Selbstmord*, p. 21; Zeddies, *Verwirrte*, p. 67; Zilla Gabrielle Cahn, *Suicide in French Thought from Montesquieu to Cioran* (New York: Lang, 1998), p. 25.

22 Zeddies, *Verwirrte*, pp. 67, 71.

Reminiscent of Plato's and Socrates' advocacy of non-public burials for suicides, the Church focused increasingly on punitive burial procedures.[23]

Suicides were increasingly compared to murderers, and, as such, were to be interred in a similar fashion. This punitive approach escalated from burials without songs to the omission of Christian pleas and culminated in the abrogation of "commemorative offerings and masses for suicides."[24] Such punitive posthumous actions reached their peak during the Council of Nîmes in 1284, when suicides were denied Christian burials altogether. Suicides were not to be buried in sacred ground.[25]

Thomas Aquinas further articulated these condemnatory and punitive attitudes in his *Summa Theologiae*, which was to have an impact on the Catholic Church for the next 500 years. Suicide became "a triple deadly sin."[26] Yet despite these theological/ecclesiastical constraints, and despite the fact that the Catholic Church adhered to its burial exclusions until the *Codex Iuris Canonici* of 1983, leniency was granted in cases of insanity.[27]

Protestant reformers did not reform their predecessors' religious or punitive stances on suicides. They only slightly altered the interpretive focus: demonic forces now took center stage.[28] It was, in particular, Martin Luther who put a heavy emphasis on temptations by the devil. Despite this interpretive shift, he did not, however, speak in favor of relaxing any of the previously established punitive measures.[29] Similar developments took place in Zürich and Geneva. Zwinglian

---

23 This attitude started with the Council of Orleans of 533: Zeddies, *Verwirrte*, p. 68.

24 Lind, *Selbstmord*, p. 26; Holzhauer, "Suizid," p. 66; Minois, *History of Suicide*, p. 30. During the Council of Braga, again suicides share the stage with executed criminals, a theme that was followed up during the Council of Auxerre of 578; see Murray, *Suicide Middle Ages*, vol. 2, p. 184; Minois, *History of Suicide*, p. 30; Lind, *Selbstmord*, p. 26.

25 Lind, *Selbstmord*, p. 26.

26 First, he argued, to kill oneself is against the natural law of self-love and preservation; second, a suicide is not only harming himself but society; and third, human life is a gift from God and hence suicide would mean interfering with God, Minois, *History of Suicide*, p. 32; Lind, *Selbstmord*, p. 28. Quite obviously Aquinas' second proposition was heavily based on Aristotle's interpretation.

27 Wacke, "Selbstmord im römischen Recht," p. 34; Minois, *History of Suicide*, p. 142; Holzhauer, "Suizid," p. 73.

28 While Midelfort, "Selbstmord," p. 301, argues that Luther's stance for the continuation of mutilating the corpse was based on political reasons, Lederer, "Dishonorable Dead," p. 351, suggests that he did so "not only as a deterrent to others, but in response to an increase in demonic activity in recent times."

29 Midelfort, "Selbstmord," pp. 296–310, 300–303; Erik Midelfort, *A History of Madness in Sixteenth Century Germany* (Stanford, CA: Stanford University Press, 1999), p. 77.

interpretations of suicide stressed the workings of demonic forces, and so did Calvin by emphasizing that suicide was "caused by diabolical possession."[30] In England, suicide was also increasingly diabolized.[31] The suicide–devil centricity became primarily a Reformation phenomenon.[32]

Secular legal developments, apart from varying from region to region, exhibit a mixed picture ranging from the total omission of any punitive actions to the confiscation of property and posthumous punishments on the corpse. While in England and France secular courts focused primarily on fiscal aspects such as confiscating the suicides' property for the benefit of the state, such tendencies did not make the same inroads in Germany.[33] The *Sachsenspiegel* of 1225, the *Schwabenspiegel* of 1265, and the *Lübecker Rechtsbuch* of 1254/1370—the three leading German legal codes—do not list suicide as a secular criminal act.[34] But with the integration of Roman Law into the German legal system, completed 300 years later, secular legal outlooks changed considerably. Reminiscent of the previously cited Roman legislation, the *Constitutio Criminalis Bambergensis* of 1507 now stipulated that if a sentenced criminal took his life out of fear of the death penalty, his property was to be confiscated.[35]

The first criminal code for the entire Holy Roman Empire, the *Constitutio Criminalis Carolina*, promulgated in 1532, also addresses the act of suicide. However, most remarkably, it clearly distinguishes in Article 135, in rather modern-sounding gradations, between those who commit suicide because they are suffering from diseases such as "melancholei" (melancholy), "irrer sinn" (madness) and other similar "blödigkeiten" (mental disorders) and those of sound mind.[36] Unfortunately, this article was ignored by contemporary advocates as well as by more recent scholars who attribute the emergence of such psychological mitigation to later periods.[37] Despite this humane outlook,

---

30 Lederer, "Dishonorable Dead," p. 352; Watt, *Choosing Death*, pp. 68–69, 73.

31 Minois, *History of Suicide*, p. 73; MacDonald and Murphy, *Sleepless Souls*, pp. 34, 51.

32 Signori, *Trauer*, p. 18, which led George Minois to label it "The Diabolization of Suicide in the Protestant World," Minois, *History of Suicide*, p. 72.

33 See Signori's excellent rendition, *Trauer*, pp. 26–30.

34 Bernstein, *Bestrafung*, pp. 3–4; Wacke, "Selbstmord im römischen Recht," p. 43; Lind, *Selbstmord*, p. 31; Holzhauer, "Suizid," p.64.

35 Lind, *Selbstmord*, p. 31.

36 Johann Christoph Koch, ed., *Hals- oder peinliche Gerichtsordnung Kaiser Carls V* (Goldbach: Keip Verlag, 1996), pp. 67–8.

37 These sixteenth-century gradations put into question claims for a later date of inception of insanity clauses such as suggested by Jeffrey R. Watt, with his rather infelicitous title choice for his anthology *From Sin to Insanity*, and Kathy Stuart, *Defiled Trades and Social Outcasts: Honor and Ritual Pollution in Early Modern Germany* (Cambridge: Cambridge University Press, 1999), p. 198.

the code, nevertheless, also incorporates the Roman legal concept of equating suicide by a criminal suspect to penal evasion.

Legal perplexities concerning suicide continued to abound throughout Germany. True, part of the confusion might be attributable to the fact that the imperial law code was not strictly enforceable, due to the Salvatory Clause, which guaranteed the continuation of local legal practices and traditions. But flagrant discrepancies existed on many local levels between *de jure* and *de facto* practices on suicide.[38] While cities such as Cologne, in its 1570 and 1571 Statuta, and Hamburg, in its 1603 legislation, do not mention suicide, others, by contrast, cite severe posthumous penalties.[39] The region of Henneberg, in its 1539 decree, stipulates that the corpses of suicides be burnt or, in case of the availability of running water, be put in barrels and thrown into the river.[40] Similarly, in its 1616 decree, the Nassau legal code states that the corpse of a suicide either be interred under the gallows or "burnt to ashes."[41] By contrast, Nuremberg, in its 1481 and 1526 codes, did not cite any legal punitive reference; yet it had the corpses of suicides punished posthumously.[42] And this overarching penal *de facto* over *de jure* situation also existed in Frankfurt.

Frankfurt's Judicial Suicides: Legal and Quantitative Assessment

Frankfurt's 1578 Reformation, as the local law code was called, does not include any suicide clause.[43] Yet, Frankfurt had been meting out posthumous physical punishments on the corpses of suicides as far back as 1391.[44] And it continued

---

[38] Bernstein, *Bestrafung*, p. 17.

[39] Ibid., pp. 4–5.

[40] Ibid., pp. 13–14.

[41] Ibid., p. 11.

[42] Jürgen Dieselhorst, "Die Bestrafung der Selbstmörder im Territorium der Reichsstadt Nürnberg," in *Festschrift des Vereins für Geschichte der Stadt Nürnberg: Mitteilungen des Vereins für die Geschichte der Stadt Nürnberg*, vol. 44 (Nuremberg: Verein, 1953), pp. 58–230.

[43] Bernstein, *Bestrafung*, p. 5. Murray, *Suicide Middle Ages*, vol. 2, pp. 446, 448 claims that Frankfurt's civic statutes "are among the most explicit in saying how a suicide's corpse was to be dealt with" and "Frankfurt just happens to have left behind exceptionally tell-tale evidence of it in its law code and judicial records," without citing any specific law codes.

[44] Rau, *Beiträge*, p. 93, note 310; unfortunately, Harry Kühnel, "Selbstmord im Spätmittelalter," in Karl Hauck et al., eds, *Sprache und Recht: Beiträge zur Kulturgeschichte des Mittelalters* (Berlin: De Gruyter, 1986), pp. 480–81 in his discussion on the frequency of suicides in Frankfurt, based on Rau's study, misses five case entries, two of which involved women, namely from 1403. Rau, *Beiträge*, p. 93, n. 310; 1404, 1488 (woman) and 1522 (woman), pp. 66 and 67 and 1510, 1527 p. 59, n. 204.

to do so well into the seventeenth century, as is amply documented by the 16 case entries in the local Book of Punishment of the 1562 to 1696 period, the base for this study.

But what quantitative significance might one attach to these 16 cases? Quantitative interpretations relating to suicides have to be assessed carefully.[45] While several historians suggest a noticeable general suicide increase during the sixteenth century, such quantitative disclosures cannot be taken at full face value because it was—and still is—at times difficult to disentangle an accident from a suicide.[46] In addition, sixteenth-century increases did not occur uniformly everywhere in Europe; and the frequently posited explanation that these increases were related to the Protestant Reformation does not fully lend itself to a unifying synthesis since Geneva, for example, did not experience a suicide increase trend during the sixteenth and seventeenth centuries.[47] Compared to the total of 1,338 criminals convicted in Frankfurt during the same period, it represents barely 0.11 percent. Thus, in Frankfurt's case one cannot speak of prison-prone suicides.

Establishing quantitative trends for suicides related to crime and punishment is an even more tenuous proposition, since there are no systematic studies available that would lend themselves to quantitative comparisons. On those rare occasions when scholars made some reference to judicial suicides, they were frequently very vague, such as for Lübeck and Hamburg, where "references to

---

[45] Despite Emile Durkheim's claim in his, *Le Suicide or Suicide: A Study in Sociology*, trans. John A. Spaulding and George Simpson (New York: Free Press, 1951); Zell, "Suicide in Pre-Industrial England," p. 307; Minois, *History of Suicide*, pp. 148–9, 179–83. Joblin, "Le suicide," p. 97 is outspokenly against it, arguing that "Une réponse précise et complète est pratiquement impossible à donner car de nombreux suicides nous échappent ... Une étude statistique nous est donc interdite." By contrast, see Murray, *Suicide Middle Ages*, vol. 1 pp. 348–78, who speaks of "absolute numbers"; see also Lind, Selbstmord, p. 18, who gives a clear description of the difficulties of obtaining reliable data on general suicides.

[46] Murray, *Suicide Middle Ages*, vol. 1, pp. 368–9 states that "In the early sixteenth century, in more than one country and more than one type of records, suicide rates appear to rise sharply." S.J. Stevenson also argues for an increase in his "The Rise of Suicide Verdicts in South-East England, 1530–1590: The Legal Process," *Continuity and Change*, 2 (1987): 37–75; and so do MacDonald and Murphy, *Sleepless Souls*.

[47] Schär, *Seelennöte*, attributes it to a cultural change brought about by the Reformed Church. Midelfort, "Selbstmord," p. 306 states that one cannot overlook "die merkwürdige Erhöhung von Selbstmordzahlen in der zweiten Hälfte des (16.) Jahrhunderts" and also connects it to the theme of "die Zunahme von Selbstmord unter den Evangelischen im Zeitalter der Reformation," p. 308. By contrast, Watt, *Choosing Death*, found that "suicide was rare in sixteenth- and seventeenth-century Geneva," pp. 261–2.

suicide (in prison) are not very numerous."[48] Similarly for France, the "class of delinquents (suspected prisoners, accused or condemned) have more inclination toward suicide ... than the ordinary population," or "We read between the lines that prisoner suicides were frequent."[49] For England, similar contentions are being advanced in that "suicides by condemned prisoners were commonplace."[50] Thus, a qualitative assessment such as seeking correlations between the accused and their alleged crimes might have greater explanatory value.

Personal Profiles of Suicides and Their Alleged Crimes

Both the incidence of judicial suicides and the pattern differ when gender is taken into account. Of the 16 cases, four involved women and 12 men. Compared to Frankfurt's general sentencing trend, this gender gap reflects the norm in that out of the total of 1,338 sentences only 315, or 23.5 percent, pertain to women. Unfortunately, there are few detailed studies on women and suicide in general.[51] But even the few general female suicide patterns available document a similar trend: considerably fewer women resorted to taking their lives than did men.[52]

---

48 Pieter Spierenburg, *The Prison Experience: Disciplinary Institutions and Their Inmates in Early Modern Europe* (New Brunswick: Rutgers, 1991), only has one paragraph on the topic, p. 192; Dieselhorst, "Bestrafung der Selbstmörder," pp. 89–90.

49 Henry Morselli, *Suicide: An Essay on Comparative Moral Statistics* (New York: Appleton, 1882), p. 261; Minois, *History of Suicide*, pp. 201, 200.

50 MacDonald and Murphy, *Sleepless Souls*, p. 284.

51 Unfortunately, only a few historians present extensive coverage of women and suicide, such as Lind, *Selbstmord*, pp. 190–203 and Jeffrey Watt, "Suicide, Gender, and Religion: The Case of Geneva," in Watt, *From Sin to Insanity*. By contrast, Schär, MacDonald and Murphy, Murray and Kühnel do not give detailed analyses.

52 See Lind, *Selbstmord*, pp. 190, 192; Minois, *History of Suicide*, states that "Men were three times more likely to kill themselves than women," p. 37; Murray, *Suicide in Middle Ages*, demonstrates "a male predominance of almost exactly 3:1," vol. 1, p. 380; Joblin, *Le suicide*, p. 100: "Les femmes sont moins nombreux à se suicider," and continues "Il y a là une permanence qu'on trouve à travers toute l'histoire du suicide." See also S.J. Stevenson, "Social and Economic Contributions to the Pattern of 'Suicide' in South-East England, 1530–1590," *Continuity and Change*, 2/2 (1987): 225–62, pp. 240–41; Midelfort, "Selbstmord," p. 307; MacDonald and Murphy, *Sleepless Souls*, p. 247; Jeffrey Merrick, "Patterns and Prosecution of Suicide in Eighteenth-Century Paris," *Historical Reflections*, 16/1 (Spring 1989): 1–40, demonstrates that "men outnumbered women in these cases by 77 percent (199) to 22 percent (58)," p. 7. Watt, *Choosing Death*, also demonstrates a sizeable gender gap, but points out that there was a much smaller discrepancy between the numbers of men and women who killed themselves prior to 1750, p. 203; and so does Murray, *Suicide Middle Ages*, vol. 1, p. 379.

Why such a gender gap existed is still being debated. Some historians argue that it is attributable to faulty record keeping.[53] But this stance is not entirely convincing given Frankfurt's—and other German areas' for that matter—diligent recording of local female criminals. The archives list their names and their marital status, including the name of the father in the case of a single woman, the name of the deceased husband in the case of a widow, and the name of the husband if married. In contrast to men, who hardly ever had their marital status listed in the records, women were hardly ever recorded without such a reference. A woman's identity thus was non-existent without a male reference. And this pattern existed for many German areas. Hence, the claim that contemporaries did "fail to distinguish the sex of suicides" cannot be confirmed.[54]

Frankfurt's judicial female personal profiles also mirror general sentencing trends. Similar to female convicts, most of the judicial suicides were single, namely three out of the four. Of the three, one was a widow and two had never been married. Again, reflecting general patterns for female convicts, the two never-married suicides were servants. Servants were always clearly identified as such, in contrast to other women, for whom occupational data was rarely provided. All four female "Selbstmörderinnen," self-murderesses, as they were registered, were accused of crimes relating to family settings and/or values. The married woman was to have "not only participated and enjoyed the theft" committed by her husband, but in turn had allegedly taken a great sum of money from his theft and buried it in the garden in front of her house.[55] By contrast, the widow was accused of having poisoned her husband. She was arrested based on "gemeinen Stadtgeschrei," general town rumors, because her husband had died the "10th day, the apprentice the 14th and the dog in the evening of that

[53] In particular, Olive Anderson, *Suicide in Victorian and Edwardian England* (Oxford: Clarendon Press, 1987), p. 44; Howard I. Kushner, "Women and Suicide in Historical Perspective," *Signs*, 10/3 (1985): 537–52, p. 546; and Howard I. Kushner, "Women and Suicidal Behavior: Epidemiology, Gender and Lethality in Historical Perspective," in Silvia Sara Canetto and David Lester, eds, *Women and Suicidal Behavior* (New York: Springer, 1995), pp. 11–34, in which he states that "the assertions that women are less suicidal than men rests on contested data," p. 11. Stevenson argues that "Some may have been of less interest to local administration because the women were propertyless," "Social and Economic Contributions," p. 241. See also Murray, *Suicide Middle Ages*, vol. 1, p.380; and MacDonald and Murphy, *Sleepless Souls*, who argue somewhat vaguely that "The precise ratio of men to women who were judged suicides in early modern England was thus the result of administrative and cultural factors as well as the actual inclination of each sex to kill themselves," p. 248.

[54] Murray, *Suicide Middle Ages*, vol. 1, p. 383; see also Lind, *Selbstmord*, who doubts that faulty record taking was the basis for such discrepancies, pp. 198, 201.

[55] BB p. 131, March 14, 1637.

day after they had eaten barley soup," which she had prepared.[56] The authorities viewed her with great suspicion since, as explicitly stated in the documents, she had lived with her husband in a state of constant brawls. Neither of these two victims left any notes or hints as to why they wanted to end their lives.

The cases of the two servants are, however, more transparent. Although discussed at great length in Chapter 9, it has to be reiterated here that these two suicides, one was a Gentile the other Jewish, were committed during periods of severe emotional stress. Shame was the central causative force: shame at being single and giving birth to an illegitimate—to use a contemporary term—child. As Frankfurt's two cases demonstrate, some single women resorted to ending their own lives rather than be exposed to ostracizing shame, a desperate act presently called "honor suicide."[57] Yet, there are still some historians who claim that women committed fewer suicides because they were less subject to social pressures.[58]

The 11 male judicial suicides and one such attempt exhibit a different pattern. Unlike the almost non-existent recording of female occupations, eight of these 12 male case descriptions include the occupations of the suicides. Six of them were artisans, namely a butcher, a cooper, a goldsmith, a mason, a soap-boiler and a tailor. Three others were described as a former local night guard, a local forester and a former soldier. Of the remaining three, two were only referred to as out-of-towners, while the third was identified as a "Jud," Jew, from a nearby town.

Apart from this male Jewish suicide—and the above-mentioned servant—religious denominational entries for the remaining suicides are non-existent. It is not surprising that in these two cases the Jewish religious identity of the victims was clearly listed, for, in Frankfurt, Jewish people were negatively singled out in criminal records as well as in the criminal penal system.[59]

---

56 ST February 14, 1637.

57 See the cogent article by Dan Bilefsky, "How to Avoid Honor Killing in Turkey? Honor Suicide," *New York Times*, July 16, 2006, International Section.

58 Such as Joblin, *Le Suicide*, p. 103: "Juridiquement et socialement mineurs, sans doute furent-elles moins soumises à la pression sociale qui pesait sur l'homme de l'époque"; or Watt, *Choosing Death*: "The fact that women had lower expectations for earnings is another reason that poverty and financial concerns were less likely to be motives for suicide among women," p. 207 and since "men enjoyed far more opportunities for economic success than women, they accordingly had many more reasons to feel like failures." Hence, so he continues to argue, "As a result, work failure and job loss generally have not produced the same feelings of failure as they do for men," p. 209.

59 This is not surprising: see Maria R. Boes, "Jews in the Criminal-Justice System of Early Modern Germany," *Journal of Interdisciplinary History*, 30/3 (Winter 1999): 407–35; see also Chapters 5 and 6.

In contrast to the women, the marital status of the 12 male suicides was only disclosed in five instances, and then only because it had a bearing on the actual crime and/or possible punishment. Three out of the six artisans were married with children, as was the former soldier, while the forester seems to have been married without children.

Unfortunately, these rather scant personal descriptions render it difficult, if not impossible, to deduce the existence of a judicial suicide persona or typology. However, comparison with Frankfurt's general sentencing pattern reveals some interesting findings. The fact that out of a total of 103 burghers sentenced during the 134-year period in question only two resorted to taking their lives points to low local judicial suicide incidence. Even more conspicuous is the judicial suicide pattern for Jewish men. Considering that Jewish people were subjected to the most grueling judicial procedures and that a total of 94 Jewish men were sentenced, one suicide represents a remarkably rare occurrence.[60] Possibly even more remarkable are three omissions. First, except for the ex-soldier, no recidivist resorted to taking his life.[61] Second, no member of the local patrician elite was among the judicial suicides. Third, not a single juvenile was among the male judicial suicides. While the low representation of recidivists is difficult to explain, the absence of members of the elite is not. The latter mirrors Frankfurt's general sentencing pattern in that during the 134-year period analyzed in this study not a single patrician was sentenced for criminal wrongdoings.[62]

However, the absence of any references to young people is arguably one of the most, if not the most, conspicuous aspects of Frankfurt's judicial suicides, the more so if one considers that Frankfurt sentenced 69 juveniles during the period in question. This omission is remarkable not only given the present proclivity of young people to resort to suicide, but also that in other areas, in particular England during the sixteenth and seventeenth centuries, frequent juvenile suicides were recorded.[63] Local careless record keeping is not the issue in Frankfurt's omission.

---

60 Ibid.

61 ST April 14, 1651; Lind, *Selbstmord*, describes a similar pattern, p. 262.

62 However, a nobleman was decapitated for manslaughter and his remains put in the local church, where his relatives came to get them: ST October 21, 1618.

63 See Alison Liebling, *Suicide in Prison* (London/New York: Routledge, 1992), p. 18 and Morselli, *Suicide*, p. 263. For the earlier period and general suicides, see Stevenson, "Social and Economic Contributions," which, by contrast, shows "a high proportion of suicides" of youngsters in south-east England during the 1530–90 period, p. 229. See also Terence R. Murphy "'Woful Childe of Parents Rage': Suicide of Children and Adolescents in Early Modern England, 1507–1710," *Sixteenth Century Journal*, 17/3 (Fall 1986): 259–70, who states that "In sixteenth- and seventeenth-century England it was not unusual for children and adolescents to commit suicide," p. 259 and "in sixteenth and seventeenth-century England, suicide was largely a function of age," p. 264.

On the contrary, the local Strafenbuch contains detailed references to young criminals—including in most instances their age. This careful age recording was rooted in the local penal approach, which granted considerable lenience to young people. Youngsters received far milder punishments due to their age, as explicitly stated in the records.[64] Might Frankfurt's juvenile penal considerations thus have had a positive effect on juvenile judicial suicides?

While, quite obviously, this hypothetical question cannot be answered due to the lack of pertinent data, the crimes of the 12 adult male suicides are documented, and, as a consequence, promise to shed some light on relevant judicial suicide information. Surprisingly, the majority of them, that is 10, consisted of alleged property-related offences. Of the remaining two, one suicide had committed several sex offenses, while the other had murdered his wife. The criminal dossier of the sex offender is not very comprehensive, yet it discloses a series of sexual offenses by a local forester. He had not only been charged with fornication, but also, while married, with two adulteries and, most seriously, with incest with the wife of his brother's son.[65]

By contrast, detailed information exists for the spousal murderer. The emerging picture seems strikingly familiar to present-day observers: domestic violence coupled with alcoholism. A series of alcohol-related confrontations had taken place between the suspect, the soap-boiler, and his wife, who wanted to stop him frequenting taverns, a "habit" which had brought her and their seven children to the brink of destitution and her husband repeatedly into the poorhouse. Upon his latest release from the poorhouse, he attacked his wife with a knife and stabbed her three times in the throat. Neighbors, hearing the screams, rushed to the scene, and so did a local guard. But they arrived too late. The wife had already died in the street. Locking himself in a room in his nearby house, the culprit shot himself with a pistol twice through the cheek into the head. Surprisingly, however, he was cognizant enough to open the door to the guard who consequently escorted him to the local prison, where he died.[66]

The 10 property-related incidences reveal a mixed picture ranging from seemingly insignificant to frequent thefts and charges of substantial robberies and counterfeiting. In one instance, theft charges were filed against a former local night guard by one of his neighbors. An out-of-towner was arrested for theft he allegedly had committed during one of Frankfurt's annual fairs. Theft was also the criminal allegation against the Jewish man from a nearby town. However, all of these thefts appear to have been of low value since the records do not list any

---

[64] See Maria R. Boes, "The Treatment of Juvenile Delinquents in Early Modern Germany: A Case Study," *Continuity and Change*, 11/1 (1996): 43–60.

[65] ST October 10, 1602 and CR 440.

[66] ST September 23, 1685 and CR 1664.

pertinent entries normally added to thefts of great significance. By contrast, the tailor from out of town had to face numerous theft charges. This well-documented case disclosed that he had been turned in by one of his former accomplices who had been arrested and tortured elsewhere. This accomplice not only divulged the tailor's involvement in numerous thefts in different towns, but also his hiding place in Frankfurt, where he was promptly apprehended and put on trial.[67]

Theft charges were also leveled against the former soldier, married with children.[68] His situation was aggravated by the fact that he had been spared a harsh criminal punishment on a previous occasion because he was a soldier at the time. The suspect had come to Frankfurt with several sons, all of whom he consequently sent home to his wife, except for one who stayed with him until a day prior to his arrest. They had taken up lodgings with a local widow who rented out rooms. This widow-proprietor became the most detrimental witness against him. She not only questioned the origin of some of the merchandise he displayed in her house, but also his whereabouts, especially during the night. While the suspect originally presented himself as a wine merchant, his nightly absence, leaving his son alone in the widow's lodging, aroused her suspicion. Confronted with this nightly pattern, he argued that, totally inebriated, he had fallen asleep in the street. During further interrogations he disclosed that he had been a soldier until the previous year, serving in the Spanish army, and that he had learned no other craft. When questioned as to how he could feed himself, he replied with the goods he had acquired during the war. He admitted, however, that they were running short.

Another out-of-towner, a goldsmith, was apprehended and charged with counterfeiting, a far more serious allegation.[69] The suspect first identified himself with a different name and a different occupation. While the name change might not have been of major significance, the suspect's claim to be a belt maker while he, in fact, was a goldsmith was more telling. Obviously, by this deceitful occupational maneuvering he tried to thwart Frankfurt's authorities from making an occupational connection to the charges filed against him. When he later admitted to having, in fact, forged the coins, he claimed to have done so out of poverty and great debts. He also stressed that his wife and children had no knowledge of his crime.

Embezzlement was the charge levied against another out-of-towner, who allegedly had forged a letter claiming various pieces of clothing. The butcher from out of town faced counterfeiting and robbery charges.[70] His son, apprehended in

---

67 CR 750.

68 CR 1125.

69 CR 365.

70 CR 667.

another town, implicated him. In the end, both father and son were arrested and interrogated: the son at an out-of-town location, the father in Frankfurt. A son also played a significant role in the charges filed against a cooper and burgher of Frankfurt. Not only was he accused of street robbery but also of having allegedly dragged his son into his criminal activities.[71] But the most bizarre property-related case was that of the mason who drew suspicion upon himself by claiming that he had found treasure in a wall without, however, wanting to disclose its location. What might appear as a hoax given the close relation of the suspect's occupation to the location of the alleged treasure, nevertheless incurred the wrath of Frankfurt's authorities and led to his arrest.

Summarizing, one can establish that the crimes allegedly committed by Frankfurt's judicial suicides disclose several trends. First, there existed a gender–judicial suicide crime gap. Women judicial suicides were mainly accused of family-related crimes—such as the alleged murder of the husband, committing a crime with the husband, being single and allegedly committing infanticide, and giving birth to an illegitimate baby. Second, by contrast, family-related issues only surfaced on the periphery in male judicial suicides. Except for one spousal murder and one series of serious sexual offenses, including incest, the remaining 10 male judicial suicides centered on property, in particular theft crimes.[72] Third and most remarkable was the almost total absence of violent crimes by male judicial suicides—except for the highly emotional domestic violence case—and this despite the fact that a total of 148 such sentences were handed down in Frankfurt. This conspicuous gap does not correspond to assertions that "those guilty of crimes against the person make up more than half of the suicides in prison."[73] Such a violent crime–judicial suicide correlation could not be established for Frankfurt.

While, so far, the various analyses have yielded interesting insights, few, however, point to what might have prompted the suspects to end their lives. Thus, two additional factors are worth exploring: the impact of contemporary adjudication procedures and the suicide methods.

Judicial Procedures and Suicide Methods

Frankfurt's city council in its capacity as the judiciary had adopted, similar to most of Continental Europe, inquisitorial methods to arrive at guilty verdicts. Pivotal

[71] CR 1872.

[72] Lind, *Selbstmord*, finds a similar correlation, namely that most of the crimes in conjunction with judicial suicides were thefts, p. 261.

[73] Morselli, *Suicide*, p. 263.

to any successful inquisitorial trial was the admission of guilt by the accused. If such a plea was not forthcoming after intensive questioning or, in some cases, the account of at least two eyewitnesses, and the authorities continued harboring doubts about the innocence of a suspect, torture could be applied—and, at times, reapplied in the hopes of eliciting a confession. Pain was thus a central feature of contemporary trials. It was also the dominant characteristic of ensuing criminal penalties, which could range for capital punishments from hanging to being broken on the wheel, decapitation or drowning, to name a few; and for corporal ones, flogging, the ducking stool, public exposure, banishment and/or any combination thereof. This array of terrible physical sufferings immediately raises the question as to whether judicial suicides resorted to taking their own lives as preemptive strikes against judicially inflicted pain.

Most perplexingly, however, such a clear-cut connection between judicially inflicted pain and suicide could not be established. One of the most revealing findings, in fact, was that judicial suicides resorted to taking their lives at varying stages during their trials. Two of the four women resorted to suicide only after they had suffered considerably pain. The woman arrested based on widespread general rumors of having poisoned her husband, apprentice and dog resorted to "Selbstmord" only after she had endured a long and painful imprisonment. During her incarceration, she had been interrogated repeatedly, various witnesses had been questioned, and three legal briefs had been filed by Frankfurt's advocates. But the accused continued to assert her innocence. When, as Frankfurt's documents claim, the authorities decided to obtain further information and have her confront additional witnesses, she allegedly "did not want to wait for the outcome."[74] She hanged herself with her hair ribbon in prison. She died without having confessed and prior to being sentenced.

Considerable pain was also endured by the woman accused of having participated in her husband's theft. She tried to commit suicide only after the she had been tortured. What makes this case even more conspicuous is the fact that she tried to end her life while under strict judicial surveillance. The suspect had been escorted to her house to disclose the location of the stolen money, which she allegedly had buried in her garden. The money was not found. On the way back to prison, she managed to distance herself from the guards and jumped into a nearby well. Seriously weakened, she was pulled out just in time. By contrast, the two maids took their lives prior to even being arrested. One jumped into a well, in whose case, as claimed by Dr. Johann Heinrich Gabler, one of Frankfurt's advocates, the "evil spirit" had inspired her to do so, while the Jewish maid slit her throat with a shaving knife.

74 ST February 14, 1651.

Frankfurt's male suicides disclose similarly varied patterns, ranging from an alleged devil-induced suicide to suicides resorting to precipitous self-destruction to those who committed "Selbstmord" only after having suffered severe judicial pain. While in the case of the prisoner charged with embezzlement, no archival entries are available with regard to the application of torture or the length of his prison stay, a rationale for his suicide was, nevertheless, listed in the records. Similar to the maid, the suspect's act had allegedly been instigated by the devil.[75] The accused hanged himself with his own shirt, which he had ripped into four long pieces. The husband who killed his wife took his life immediately after the crime. Similarly, one theft suspect preferred to end his life immediately after his arrest, before he was even questioned, by hanging himself in prison around noon.[76] He had not confessed and he had not been sentenced. By contrast, the former night guard hanged himself in prison during the night. He had only been incarcerated for six days. He died without confessing. In his case, the suicidal rationale advanced by Frankfurt's authorities focused on legal aspects. It was claimed that his suicide was due to the fact that "he was possibly concerned about further questioning."[77]

Another legalistic suicide explanation was recorded in the case of the ex-soldier. Starting with his arrest, he had been subjected to repeated and intense interrogations, once with the torture instruments in plain sight, obviously to frighten him into confessing. Even his youngest son had to testify against him. While his wife consequently tried to mitigate the child's detailed accusatory rendition by pleading for her husband's release, her efforts were in vain, for the soldier hanged himself on the door with the bandages he had been wearing on one of his calves. He had not confessed. The authorities claimed that his self-inflicted death was due to the fact that the suspect was soon to be questioned under torture but "deren er dann nit erwarten wollen," he did not want to wait for that to happen.[78]

While fear of pain might have been the motivating force in this particular instance, six men took their own lives only after having been subjected to torture and/or long periods of incarceration, such as the out-of-town theft suspect who had been imprisoned for a "very long time."[79] He never pleaded guilty but hanged himself in prison. By contrast, the Jewish suspect hanged himself in prison after only three days of incarceration, but he did so only after having been tortured. In his case, Frankfurt's rationale for his "Selbstmord" was that

75 ST June 1, 1588.

76 CR 750 NB. no. 9—ST February 12, 1616.

77 ST January, 10, 1567.

78 ST April 14, 1651.

79 BB 1571, p. 24.

he "did not want to confess to this theft."[80] The alleged thief and counterfeiter suffered even more painful judicial practices before taking his own life. He was not only repeatedly subjected to torture but also incarcerated for two months. His suicide depicts his mental anguish: he performed incredible contortions to strangle himself while kneeling down. He also never confessed.[81] The suspect accused of having found a treasure without disclosing its location also only took his own life after he had been tortured. He also never pleaded guilty, and died several hours after he had stabbed himself in the throat and chest using a little knife he had brought with him when he entered prison.[82] The documents are very precise about this incident. They not only record that the knife was short but also, most importantly, that the guards had left it on the accused out of negligence.

The most complex case pertains to the father who was accused of having committed serious thefts and street robberies himself in addition to having forced his son to participate. The 800-page trial documents disclose that the trial lasted for two months. Frankfurt's advocates—Drs. Johann Brandes, Johann Heinrich Gabler and Esaias Philipp Glock—were faced with possibly the most challenging judicial suicide legal decisions, but this did not seem to intimidate them. On the contrary, they subjected the suspect to physical pain and amazing verbally abusive comments in their various legal opinions. Initially, because the interrogations of the witnesses had not disclosed sufficient incriminating material and the suspect continued to refuse to plead guilty, various pleas were submitted to Frankfurt's authorities to have him released. However, the pleas were ignored. Instead, Drs. Johann Brandes and Johann Heinrich Gabler insisted that the suspect be subjected to torture.[83] Even under the most excruciating pain of being tortured with the application of the leg screw, this procedure mainly elicited screams of anguish from the suspect and a few almost intangible words, which the advocates were quick to interpret as a decoy maneuver on his part. They charged him with pretending not to be of sound mind.

When the accused consequently banged his head so vigorously against a stove located in the prison that he incurred very serious injuries, his self-destructive action was likened to a confession—especially since the stolen merchandise had been recovered in his house. Yet, the legal controversy was far from over. While Dr. Esaias Philipp Glock at the beginning of his legal brief voiced some reservations, conceding that the offender showed signs of insanity, a few paragraphs later he began to refute this interpretation, pointing out that it

80 RP 1572, p. 35.

81 RP 1611, pp. 8, 10, 12, 18, 22; BB August 10, 1611.

82 ST June 21, 1587.

83 CR 1872.

was only after the stolen merchandise had actually been found in the accused's house that he had acted up trying to kill himself. Hence, the suspect "wanted to kill himself in order to escape the public shame associated with his execution."

Despite the advocate's claim, Frankfurt's city councilors, to their credit, continued to be concerned about the mental and physical condition of the suspect. They had him subjected to medical examinations by local *phisici*. Based on their somewhat vague report, Frankfurt's advocates suggested another round of torture, though a milder version. Dr. Johann Brandes argued that despite the suspect's poor physical condition after his self-inflicted attack, the leg screw ought to be applied, but on the "strong leg." During a subsequent visit, Frankfurt's medical experts found that the suspect's eyes had totally sunk in, that he barely lifted them when verbally approached and that he did not respond in any other way. They concluded that they were uncertain how long he would survive in such a weakened condition. Frankfurt's authorities now proceeded to sentence him. He died before the sentence could be carried out.

This case clearly shows the advocates' power to decide whether or not a suicide was influenced by a mental disorder or insanity. This distinction between the two was of paramount importance since insanity was one of the few exceptions entailing a milder punishment or even exoneration for suicidal actions. Even while making allowances for the general rudimentary contemporary understanding of mental and emotional conditions, it is amazing, if not deeply troubling, that advocates should judge the mental state of a suspect, let alone come to the conclusion that he was only pretending not to be in his right mind.

The sex offender sentenced to death based on his confession stabbed himself in the heart with a knife shortly before he was to be led to the execution site, but failed in his suicide attempt because the knife was too short.[84] A fellow inmate had provided him with the potential suicide weapon. By contrast, the goldsmith, who also confessed to his counterfeiting crime, ended his life prior to being sentenced. Similar to the above-mentioned mason, he had consciously planned his own demise in case of arrest: he took arsenic which he "sehr verborgen bei sich gehabt," had on him but very well hidden.[85]

While from all these cases a complex pre- to post-pain related suicide picture emerges, it is, nevertheless, surprising that the majority of both female and male suicides resorted to taking their lives prior to making a confession and hence prior to being sentenced. These findings stand in sharp contrast to assertions advanced for contemporary England, where "Suicides by condemned

---

[84] ST December 10, 1602.

[85] CR 365.

prisoners were commonplace."[86] In Frankfurt, suicides by condemned prisoners were extremely rare. These divergent findings heighten the perplexity of Frankfurt's cases. While suicides by condemned prisoners might more readily be interpreted as the suicide's fear of pain associated with the ensuing mostly public punishments, no such clear-cut deduction can be drawn from pre-confession and/or pre-sentencing suicides. Frankfurt's suspects had still a chance of being released, for, as mentioned earlier, a confession or at least two eyewitnesses were needed for a conviction. True, there existed the infamous Verdachtstrafe, a punishment of suspicion, which was meted out when, despite a suspect's refusal to plead guilty, the authorities continued to harbor doubts about his or her innocence. But such a penalty consisted in almost all instances of a reduced punishment, namely banishment.

The suicidal methods and comments by Frankfurt's authorities shed a little more light on this perplexing phenomenon. While, admittedly, it is in many if not most cases impossible for an outside observer to establish when a suicide decides or plans to end his or her life—did they plan their exits long in advance, did they succumb to on-the-spot impulses or was it a combination of the two?—two of Frankfurt's cases point to deliberate pre-arrest suicide plans. Both victims brought or better still hid their chosen weapons on them: one a small knife, the other arsenic. By contrast, in seven instances the suicidal action seemed, at least on the surface, to have occurred rather spontaneously. The servant jumped into the well precipitously, and the spouse murderer shot himself immediately after the deed. Five in-prison suicides also point to on-the-spot decisions by the suspects. One woman hanged herself with her hair ribbon; another suspect hanged himself after ripping his shirt into four strips; and a third hanged himself with his own calf bandages. The fourth strangled himself while kneeling down, and the fifth hit his head against a stove in prison: desperate methods by desperate people.

In six instances, Frankfurt's documents disclose the authorities' rationale as to why the suspects resorted to ending their lives. One was ascribed to the suspect's fear of further questioning; another to not wanting to confess to theft charges; one to being afraid of impending torture; one to trying to escape the public shame associated with his execution; and two to the instigation of the devil. While the four judicial evasion explanations read more like exculpatory statements on the authorities' part, citing the devil as the instigating force has strong religious overtones. Frankfurt's demon-causative rationale is not surprising. What is astounding, however, is the fact that the local authorities referred to demonic forces in only two instances during a 134-year period.

86 MacDonald and Murphy, *Sleepless Souls*, p. 284.

Allegations of satanic forces were, according to many historians, widespread suicidal motivations in many areas, and this "well into the seventeenth century."[87] Frankfurt thus constitutes an obvious aberration, a fact further highlighted by the non-existence of a devil-suicide/gender gap. One demonic reference pertained to a woman, the other to a man. The local authorities, and most likely large segments of the population, seemed to have been less inclined to heed the devil argument, a deduction backed by the fact that not a single witch, popularly believed to have strong ties to the devil, was ever sentenced to death locally.

While the picture emerging from the assessment of the impact of contemporary judicial procedures on Frankfurt's 16 suicides is not uniform but rather mixed, it, nevertheless, conveys an overriding common denominator: the importance of the personal makeup of the individual. This qualitative deduction is supported by the quantitative fact that the vast majority of Frankfurt's sentenced criminals—1,322—who underwent similar procedures did not resort to killing themselves.[88] Obviously, some suspects had stronger psychological stamina than others to face and endure the grueling judicial procedures and punishments, a causative-interpretative dilemma which has continued to vex researchers to the present day, for even now "The problem of prisoners who commit suicide whilst in prison is a complex one with no simple set of solutions."[89]

---

[87] Quotation in Minois, *History of Suicide*, p. 73; see also Midelfort, *History of Madness*, p. 315, who argues that "the devil seemed even more active in Germany during the seventeenth-century both as the great tempter (to suicide and despair) and as the maddening possessor of body of soul." For a similar conclusion see Vera Lind, "The Suicidal Mind and Body. Examples from North Germany," in Watt, *From Sin to Insanity*, p. 70. For England see MacDonald and Murphy, *Sleepless Souls*, who state that "suicide was interpreted far more often as the result of diabolical temptation than divine retribution ... Satan was above all the Tempter," p. 34 or "The devil was a literal symbol of suicidal despair," p. 35 and the remaining pages to 41; in fact, the authors entitle Chapter 2 "The Instigation of the Devil." Schär, in his study of Zurich, cites the year 1710 as the last case in which a pastor adduces a suicide to the "tempter from hell," while the local population ascribes it to the devil as late as 1788, *Seelennöte*, p. 66–7. See also Midelfort, "Selbstmord," pp. 300–302; by contrast, see Signori, *Trauer*, who finds that suicide was not always attributed to the devil, p. 18.

[88] In Frankfurt, of the total of 1,338 sentenced criminals during the 1562 to 1695 period, 636 were tortured: BB and RP; see Schär, *Seelennöte*, who suggests that in part prisoners committed suicide out of fear of impending punishment, pp. 83–5.

[89] See Diana Medlicott, *Surviving the Prison Place: Narratives of Suicidal Prisoners* (Aldershot: Ashgate, 2001), p. 5, who demonstrates this for the twenty-first century.

Punitive Consequences of Suicide

By contrast, sixteenth- and seventeenth-century penal consequences are more readily accessible. As described in the previous short historical introduction, punitive acts frequently followed a suicide. While exactly when Frankfurt initiated legal steps to punish the corpses of general and/or judicial suicides is still somewhat of an enigma, it can be ascertained that the de facto occurrence of such a penalty runs an almost parallel course to the appearance of harsh capital/corporal criminal punishments in general as well as to the spread of judicial torture.[90] All three punitive principles were established practices in the fourteenth century, with a possible earlier date of inception.[91] Obviously, these parallel developments are no historical accidents and as such underline the desideratum to study judicial and possibly all suicide punishments within the context of general penal procedures.

Such a contextual framework has to include the input of Catholic and Protestant authorities that not only sanctioned all three judicial treatments but, arguably, also compounded their severity by giving them religiously sanctioned status. During the Fourth Lateran Council of 1215, the Catholic Church endorsed the application of physical torture in its own courts in order to elicit confessions, especially in heresy trials. The Church also condoned the use of physical punishments, including the death penalty for heretics and other major sinners. Many of the proceedings of the Inquisition are too well known to be worth repeating here. And the Church, as demonstrated above, initiated posthumous punishment of suicides by refusing to grant them church burials in consecrated ground.

The Protestants did not change any of these punitive practices. They did not relinquish or abolish the Catholics' use of judicial torture, capital or corporal punishments, or postmortem punishments for suicides. There was no religiously induced break in or softening of penal concepts during the Reformation and immediately thereafter in most European areas. In fact, in 1532 Martin Luther "insisted that the magistrates treat these corpses (of suicides) with exemplary

---

90 See Rau, *Beiträge*, pp. 66–7, 75 and Georg Ludwig Kriegk, *Deutsches Bürgertum im Mittelalter: Nach urkundlichen Forschungen und mit besonderer Beziehung auf Frankfurt am Main* (2 vols, 1868; repr. Frankfurt am Main: Sauer & Auvermann, 1969), vol. 2, pp. 219–22. Murray, *Suicide Middle Ages*, vol. 2, pp. 446–7, who bases his statements on these two authors, cites Frankfurt's Rechenbücher, fiscal ledgers, as their base of argumentation for the existence of posthumous local punishments of suicides. While these records furnish proof of the de facto treatment of suicides, they do not establish concrete legal dates of their inception.

91 In Frankfurt, the first mention of the death penalty can be traced to 1297.

harshness, not only as a deterrent to others, but in response to an increase in demonic activity in recent times."[92]

However, Frankfurt's by now exclusive Lutheran city council did not heed Luther's stern admonition. While not abandoning its Catholic predecessors' general judicial and penal policies, including the treatment of judicial suicides, the city did not mete out extra harsh penalties on the corpses of judicial suicides. Reminiscent of the treatment of general criminal suspects, Frankfurt drew a clear line of penal distinction between those judicial suicides found guilty of their crimes and those who had not confessed to their alleged wrongdoings. The guilty ones received far harsher punishments. For example, the husband who in public view had killed his wife and then himself had his corpse publicly dragged through town, passing the scene of his crime, to the place of execution located outside Frankfurt's city walls. There, his head was severed from his corpse and put on a pike, and his corpse put on a wheel. While this extremely harsh posthumous procedure was carried out despite heart-wrenching pleas on the part of the culprit's mother, his seven children, and his sisters and brothers to have his body interred, similar penal procedures were carried out for non-suicide murderers.[93]

The Gentile servant who had killed her newborn and then herself suffered a similar fate. Her body was dragged to the execution place, where her head was severed and put on a pike. Similar to the aforementioned male culprit, her corpse was put on the wheel; however, unlike the male culprit's, it was covered

---

[92] Lederer, "Dishonorable Dead," p. 351; and in fact MacDonald and Murray, Sleepless Souls, demonstrate for England that "The Tudor revolution in religion ... fostered intolerance of suicide," p. 28; and that "The clergy tolerated the rites of desecration as an additional punishment," p. 49. The deployment of physical pain for sinners and criminals remained widespread and, with regional variations, generally accepted until the eighteenth century when secular rulers and/or courts took the initiative to do away with torture and eventually eased first capital then corporal punishments. Frederick II was the first European ruler to abolish the various sanctions against suicides, in 1752, Bernstein, *Bestrafung*, pp. 8–9. According to Baumann, *Vom Recht auf den eigenen Tod*, p. 19, in the late eighteenth century ignominious burials for suicides were forbidden by the state in many parts of Germany; in France, the National Assembly abolished on January 21, 1790 confiscation of property and dishonorable burials for suicides. While for England "the law of suicide remained unchanged throughout the eighteenth century," in fact, it "was not altered until the nineteenth century," only in 1870, MacDonald and Murray, *Sleepless Souls*, pp. 197, 109, 346; both Catholic and Protestant Churches follow, although hesitantly, by allowing the suicide a silent but Christian burial, although the Codex Iuris Canonici (CIC) of 1983 of the Catholic Church still upholds in CIC c. 1240 Paragraph 3 the prohibition of suicide: see Holzhauer, *Suizid*, p. 73.

[93] BB 51, September 22, 1685; CR 1664.

with straw and tightened to the wheel.[94] Except for having her corpse covered, there was thus no gender gap between these two posthumous executions. In Frankfurt's case one thus cannot argue that "women were the main privileged category in respect of corporal punishment for suicide."[95] Similarly in the complex, albeit vague, case of borderline insanity, Frankfurt's city council meted out the death sentence for serious thefts and robberies, although the culprit was already near death because of self-inflicted wounds. Since he died prior to the execution as a result of his own actions, his corpse was dragged through Frankfurt's best-known streets, passing by his home and the mayor's office to the gallows, where his head was severed and his corpse put on a wheel.[96] Again, similar posthumous procedures were carried out on sentenced criminals who died prior to their executions.

By contrast, the counterfeiter who had confessed but resorted to taking his life prior to being sentenced was spared public posthumous exposure. His corpse was put in a barrel and thrown from one of Frankfurt's bridges into the river clandestinely during the night.[97] Possibly his assertions that he had been driven to his crime out of poverty and without the knowledge of his wife and children led Frankfurt's authorities to his clandestine removal from town for, generally, non-suicide counterfeiters were publicly strangled and subsequently burnt.[98]

The two cases of attempted suicide do not disclose any particularly harsh posthumous punishments either. The culprit sentenced to death for various adulteries and incest—who had tried to stab himself prior to his execution but failed—was, due to his weakened position, tied to a chair and carried to the execution site, where he was decapitated sitting down.[99] Instead of an infamous postmortem punishment, he was buried in a special cemetery. Similarly, the woman accused of theft who had tried to end her life by jumping into a well was put into a cart because she was too weak to walk and pulled to the execution site, where she was decapitated while sitting in a chair.[100] Her corpse was not exposed, but buried underneath the gallows.

Similar posthumous penal distinctions are evident in almost all those cases where the suspects did not confess. Five of the eight had their corpses put

94 BB 81, September 16, 1690; ST September 17, 1690 and CR 1858.

95 As was advanced by Murray, *Suicide Middle Ages*, vol. 2, p. 34 for France.

96 ST December 12, 1690.

97 ST April 15, 1598.

98 ST April 15, 1598.

99 ST October 10, 1602 and CR 440.

100 ST March 15, 1637.

into barrels and dumped clandestinely into the local river during the night.[101] True, putting the corpse in a barrel and throwing it into the river was still a severe postmortem punishment. However, one could rightfully argue that a clandestine disposal of the corpse was considerably milder than having it mutilated posthumously and/or indefinitely exposed by hanging on the gallows or lying on the wheel. Such barrel punishments were not unique to Frankfurt. They are documented for various southern German and French areas as well.[102] However, in contrast to these regional barrel procedures, Frankfurt's city councilors did not mete them out randomly but reserved them predominantly for those suicides whom they suspected of committing a crime without, however, having confessed to it. And Frankfurt applied similar legal/penal steps for regular criminal suspects. In cases where the suspects had not confessed, yet Frankfurt's authorities continued to harbor doubts as to their innocence, the previously mentioned Verdachtstrafe, literally a penalty for being suspicious, was meted out. It was a milder punishment consisting in almost all instances of a banishment sentence. The conceptual and thematic connection between the two penal procedures is obvious: the removal of the might-be-guilty from the community, dead or alive, was the core objective.

True, both penalties might be interpreted as a sign of legal embarrassment for those in power for having been unable to either extract a confession or, in the case of judicial suicide, prevent the "Selbstmord" in the first place. But the penal distinction between those who confessed and those who did not, nevertheless, points to a judicious and circumspect city council, a judgment borne out by the treatment of the remaining three of the eight suicides who did not confess: they were buried—one even in the regular cemetery.[103] Thus, unlike courts in England and France, Frankfurt's city council was not "merciless toward sentenced or accused criminals who killed themselves."[104]

In fact, compared to many other regions, Frankfurt's judicial suicide posthumous punishments had generally been milder throughout. In England, even suicides unrelated to any crimes were much more severely punished.[105]

---

101 Rau, *Beiträge*, p. 66 no. 232; ST January 10, 1567; ST August 15, 1572; ST June 2, 1588; ST August 10, 1611; ST February 12, 1616.

102 See Murray, *Suicide Middle Ages*, vol. 2, pp. 37–41 for south Germany and Joblin, *Le Suicide*, p. 108 for France.

103 ST July 22, 1571; Rau, *Beiträge*, p. 106; ST June 21, 1587; ST April 14, 1651 and CR 1125. Kriegk, *Deutsches Bürgertum*, erroneously cites the year 1732 for the first such burial, p. 221.

104 Minois, *History of Suicide*, p. 285; see also MacDonald and Murphy, *Sleepless Souls*, pp. 129–30, 135, 137.

105 MacDonald and Murphy, *Sleepless Souls*, p. 75.

There, "rites of desecration" consisted of burying the corpse in a "highway or crossroad and driving a stake through the body" or they were "occasionally buried in an open field."[106] In Zurich, as late as 1692, the corpse of a suicide was burnt, while in Frankfurt the last documented burning of a suicide took place in 1522.[107] For France, especially during the reign of Louis XIV, suicide was considered one of, if not *the* worst of all crimes, entailing arguably correspondingly harsh punishments.[108] Also, unlike many other areas, Frankfurt's records do not disclose that judicial suicides who had been buried were dug up later by locals who resented such "lenient" treatment. In Zurich and its immediate vicinity, as well as in France, interred suicide cadavers were later disinterred by the people.[109] In Bavaria, the population adamantly opposed suicide burials in the first place, and "no less than eight 'suicide revolts' were registered by the Court Council in the seventeenth century."[110]

Frankfurt's archival omission of such incidences cannot be attributed to careless record keeping. On the contrary, the accuracy of related entries in the Strafenbuch demonstrates this very clearly, for in three instances the population did act up as duly recorded. But all three cases relate to sentenced criminals and not suicides, when local people ignominiously took down three hanged criminals from the gallows during the night.[111] It is thus safe to argue that with regard to the treatment of judicial suicides, judicial and popular attitudes overlapped. There was no obvious cultural polarization on judicial suicides in Frankfurt.[112]

Also, most remarkably, signs of reduced penalties for judicial suicides can be observed in Frankfurt's case already by the late sixteenth century. In 1571

---

106 Ibid., pp. 44, 48; Stevenson, "The Rise of Suicide," p. 232.

107 Schär, *Seelennöte*, p. 62; Rau, *Beiträge*, p. 76, no. 263.

108 Outlined by L'Ordonnance criminelle of 1670, Joblin, *Le suicide*, p. 119; see also pp. 94–5. Minois, *History of Suicide*, on the other hand argues that this Ordonnance criminelle did not aggravate "the repression of suicide," p. 141, for "Acquittals and compromises remained just as frequent as before," p. 142.

109 Schär, *Seelennöte*, pp. 68–9; Minois, *History of Suicide*, p. 202.

110 Lederer, "Dishonorable Dead," p. 359; see also David Lederer, "Aufruhr auf dem Friedhof: Pfarrer, Gemeinde, und Selbstmord im frühneuzeitlichen Bayern," in Signori, *Trauer*, pp. 189–209.

111 In the ST June 12, 1590 incident, the corpse had been so badly mutilated five days later that the remains were consequently buried; in the ST March 15, 1637 sentence, the criminal's body was pulled down from the gallows so that only the head remained hanging; however, three days later the corpse was hung up again. In the ST March 8, 1661 incident, the body was stolen from the gallows.

112 See divergent opinion on this topic: Lederer, "Dishonorable Dead," who argues for a "distinction between elite and plebeian perceptions of suicide," p. 350, while MacDonald and Murphy, *Sleepless Souls*, doubt its existence, pp. 215, 343–6.

a criminal suspect who committed suicide was buried in a local, though not official cemetery, while another was actually buried in the regular one in 1587. In addition, the most frequently meted out punishment for non-convicted judicial suicides, the barrel penalty, was discontinued after 1616. Instead, the woman accused of having murdered her husband, apprentice and dog but who never confessed was buried underneath the gallows; and so was the thief-soldier who never confessed despite his own son's implicating testimony.[113]

By 1695, this trend was an openly acknowledged policy. The documents in the case of the Jewish servant who took her own life state this very clearly. She was to be buried under the gallows "als für Selbstmordens," set aside for suicides.[114] While these burial practices still had a stigma attached to them, they are to be considered more lenient than having one's corpse put into a barrel with no definite resting-place in sight.

Again, this decline of severe punitive measures was, at least in Frankfurt's case, not an isolated phenomenon for judicial suicides.[115] By the early seventeenth century at the latest, with the exception of Jews, Frankfurt began to reduce the application of torture and decrease the severity of criminal punishments.[116] It was thus no historical coincidence that the last drowning of a sentenced criminal occurred in 1613, that is, three years prior to the last posthumous barrel suicide punishment in 1616.[117] These parallel punitive developments serve as a testament to Frankfurt's punitive, albeit selective, mentality change by the early seventeenth century.

However, Frankfurt's early de facto reduction of the judicial suicide penal threshold runs counter to leading legal interpretations of the time. Prominent German jurists continued to argue well into the seventeenth century and beyond that suicide was a crime.[118] In fact, it was only toward the second half of the eighteenth century that a milder legal attitude made inroads.[119] German jurists were thus not at the forefront of a more lenient suicide treatment, a trend

[113] ST February 14, 1651; ST April 14, 1651.

[114] ST June 6, 1695 and CR 2036.

[115] These findings qualify Murray's statement that "There are indications that the indignities heaped on a suicide's body and memory grew more extreme in the early modern period," *Suicide Middle Ages*, vol. 1, p. 373.

[116] See Boes, "Jews in the Criminal-Justice System."

[117] ST June 18, 1613—the offender was a woman who was sentenced to death by drowning for infanticide.

[118] Such as Benedikt Carpzov, Samuel Pufendorf, Christian Thomasius, Christian Wolff and Johann Bernhard Basedow: see Wacke, "Selbstmord im römischen Recht," pp. 40 and 37 and Holzhauer, "Suizid," pp. 71–2.

[119] Thanks to K.F. Hommel and the philosopher Moses Mendelssohn: Wacke, "Selbstmord im römischen Recht," p. 37.

clearly reflected by Frankfurt's advocates in their harsh assessment of the insanity incident. A similar pattern existed in England, where speaking of "engines of change ... the lawyers rode in the brake-van."[120]

Conclusion

Compared to Frankfurt's general criminal sentencing, the quantitative representation of judicial suicides was low, and so was their numerical representation over time: there were no noticeable increases at any given time. The personal and occupational backgrounds of the judicial suicides varied. However, not surprisingly, they all belonged to the middle or lower echelon of society, reflecting Frankfurt's general sentencing pattern, where no patrician was ever convicted for any crime. Female suicides differed from their male counterparts. They were considerably fewer in number, which, again, reflected Frankfurt's general crime sentencing trend. In contrast to men, the four women who resorted to taking their lives did so in conjunction with family-related crimes, while men almost exclusively committed "Selbstmord" in conjunction with property-related transgressions. For Frankfurt, the frequently claimed violent crime–judicial suicide correlation could not be established.

On the surface, trial proceedings disclosed that the judicial stages at which suspects took their lives varied considerably. While some did so immediately after their crimes, some resorted to suicide only after a few days in prison—one even before he was questioned; many also ended their lives only after they had been subjected to torture. Hence, fear of pain in the form of torture was not in all instances the overriding suicide causative factor. Despite these variances, the majority of suicides, however, had one judicial aspect in common: most took their lives prior to pleading guilty. Thus, the fear factor of public cruel punishments, while it surely affected some, was not the overriding causative force, as suspects who had not confessed still had a chance of being released with a considerably less painful penalty. These findings point to the personal makeup of the individual as the decisive core suicidal factor.

Frankfurt's posthumous penalties, despite variations, exhibit fine gradations depending on the sentencing status of the suicide. Those who had not confessed and were not sentenced received considerably milder postmortem treatment. And, compared to other European regions, Frankfurt handed down considerably milder punishments. While, admittedly, most of the posthumous punishments retained some of their stigma, their severity declined by the early seventeenth

120 MacDonald and Murray, *Sleepless Souls*, p. 140.

century at the latest, as most cogently exemplified by the abolition of the barrel punishment. This comparatively early trend toward milder punishments ranks Frankfurt among the leaders of the "decriminalization of suicide."[121]

However, this trend is not to camouflage the fact that German lawyers, including Frankfurt's advocates, were not at the forefront of this movement. Had they led the way, it might not have taken another 300 years before those who died of self-inflicted wounds were no longer labeled, and thus no longer treated, as "Selbstmörder" in Germany.

[121] Machiel Bosman claims that "Amsterdam was actually in the vanguard in the decriminalization of suicide," "The Judicial Treatment of Suicide in Amsterdam," in Watt, *From Sin to Insanity*, pp. 9–24, p. 9.

Conclusion

Amidst the many changes that occurred in Frankfurt, especially during the sixteenth century, the city council retained its administrative and judicial power as well as its social composition throughout the period discussed here, that is the end of the seventeenth century. Divided into three benches, which together constituted the judiciary, the first two benches were occupied by local patricians and the third by members of select guilds. While all councilors had converted to Lutheranism, this religious change did not cause them to abandon prior practices in the legal and judicial realm.

The governing patricians followed the lead of their Catholic predecessors by wholeheartedly embracing the Humanist movement and its predilection for the reception of Roman Law. They formed a local Humanist circle and entertained contacts to high-profile Humanist representatives such as Melanchthon, a devoted Protestant preacher, scholar and staunch teacher of Roman Law. While Frankfurt's Catholic Humanist patrician city councilors had been at the forefront of infusing local laws with Roman Law by issuing a revised local code already in 1509, their Lutheran successors rounded off this legal integration with the promulgation of the 1578 Reformation, as it was called, replacing Germanic laws and practices with "foreign" ones. Similar measures were taken at the imperial level where the Catholic Emperor Charles V introduced the first Roman -Law-infused imperial criminal code in 1532: the *Constitutio Criminalis Carolina*, a code which continued to be observed by Catholics and Protestants alike for centuries.[1]

However, Roman Law had a decisively negative impact on many people. It served to strengthen the power of male rulers at the expense of the less fortunate such as peasants, many women, gays and even suicides. Its adverse effect on peasants' communal rights, clearly expressed during the Peasant War, even affected Martin Luther, who not only changed his mind about the revolting peasants, his supporters, by turning against them, but also by subsequently encouraging the study of the very Roman Law that he had previously portrayed

---

1 On the continuity of Catholic practices see E.W. Zeeden, *Katholische* Überlieferungen *in den lutherischen Kirchenordnungen des 16. Jahrhunderts* (Münster: Aschendorff, 1959) and R.W. Scribner's "The Incombustible Luther: the Image of the Reformer in Early Modern Germany," *Past and Present*, 110 (February 1986): 38–68, especially p. 68, where he suggests that "the Reformation was neither as radical nor as successful a break with the past as traditional Reformation historiography has led us to believe."

with disdain. Roman Law, with its Roman principle of pater familias/patria potestas, increasingly subjected women to male authority—clearly evidenced in Frankfurt's 1578 legislation—while gays and suicides appeared as new criminal categories. They had not been cited as law-breakers in previous Germanic codes.

Criminal court procedures exhibited similar drastic changes. Material witnesses, especially eyewitnesses, replaced oath helpers or character witnesses, which represented a definite improvement over the previous vague judicial approach. By contrast, the replacement of the earlier physically painful ordeals with judicial torture did not offer a pain-free and more rational approach to seeking the truth. The unfolding of the actual court procedures also changed from an open, personal and oral accusatorial process to one officiated by the government, that is *ex officio*, where witness and suspect interrogations now unfolded primarily in secluded chambers. There, their various statements were written down and subsequently evaluated in writing, thus ushering in the legal supremacy of the written legal text, frequently and not surprisingly, composed in Latin. These new procedures drove a wedge between the illiterate majority of the people and those who became their judges, resulting in an increasing cultural divide between the alleged "educated" and the "common" people. These secretive and frequently painful procedures started under Catholic auspices but intensified and remained in effect throughout the period discussed here. Protestants did not abolish torture; nor did they reform any of the judicial procedures.

This legal transition was accomplished with the help of a newly emerging, legally cognizant professional group: advocates trained in Roman Law. They became the main actors in integrating Roman Law into the pre-existing Germanic one; and, as indispensable cooperators, they eventually formed an almost symbiotic alliance with those who fostered and initiated the reception of the new law: in Frankfurt's case, its patrician city councilors. This interconnectedness originated when Frankfurt Catholic patrician councilors offered not only financial assistance to those who wanted to study Roman Law—initially entailing long sojourns at Italian universities—but also, after successful completion, lucrative city employment as municipal advocates. With more complex laws to interpret and enticing employment offers, advocates not only increased in numbers but eventually even cemented their status by forging familial-social ties with the powerful patricians.[2] Advocates had "arrived."

That this new professional group exhibited surprising staying power as well as yielding increasing legal influence is clearly documented in Frankfurt's

2 See the seminal study by Barbara Dölmeyer, *Frankfurter Juristen im 17. und 18. Jahrhundert* (Frankfurt am Main: Vittorio Klostermann, 1993), where she correlates, among others, Frankfurt advocates' social and familial ties with local patricians.

case, where city councilors increasingly resorted to seek their advice, which, in turn, led not only to job security but also to more influence on procedural, interpretative, and subsequent punitive matters. Not surprisingly, Roman Law, with its discriminatory legal features and delineations favoring the ruling male elite, became their leitmotif.

However, the input of many local people should not be underestimated. In fact, as crime and criminal reporting agents they constituted an integral part of the initial criminal proceedings. Guided by numerous dress codes and other visible signs, they exhibited the same trend that Frankfurt's advocates would disclose: selectivity. They did not report crimes and criminals indiscriminately but favored some—no patrician was ever sentenced for any wrongdoing. They even knowingly overlooked alleged shortcomings of others, such as in the case of the two gay suspects whom they refrained from reporting to the authorities for years. By contrast, some locals immediately turned on Gypsy suspects. Arguably, many—though not all—people's most flagrant criminal reports focused on turning in Jewish people, thus taking recourse to the judicial system instead of former direct physical attacks.

In addition, many of the locals also served as witnesses on whose accounts Frankfurt's advocates frequently built their cases. However, similar to many locals, the advocates used a selective approach as to whose statements to accept and whose testimonies to discredit or even discard. Testimonies given by Jewish people carried less weight, as explicitly stated by Frankfurt's advocates, than those of Christians, and women's statements were increasingly either discarded or ignored. Judicial torture patterns exhibit a similar pattern. Advocates suggested select groups of suspects more readily to be subjected to torture than others. At their explicit recommendation, the two gay suspects who were eventually apprehended were tortured repeatedly, and so were the two women accused of infanticide. Jewish suspects suffered a similar fate, while other male suspects, especially soldiers, were not tortured at all. Instead, their statements were frequently accepted at face value without even subjecting them to harsh interrogations. In addition to the selective use of witnesses and torture, the advocates' legal opinions were frequently riddled with personal, unproven insinuation as well as flagrant omissions. They even claimed psychological expertise by asserting that one suicide only pretended not to be "in his right mind."

Yet, Frankfurt's advocates cited impressive legal sources ranging from the *Constitutio Criminalis Carolina* to various military laws, the *Kriegsartikel*, as well as divine law, even including biblical sources to buttress their legal opinions. However, it was again their selective use of such sources, especially religious citations, that is startling. In the case of Jewish and Gypsy suspects, their legal opinions even exposed racial overtones. Instead of addressing the individual suspects they turned *all* Gypsies into criminals by condemning *all* of them as "gottloses Zigeunervolk," godless Gypsy people. Similarly, when dealing with Jewish suspects, *all* Jewish people were collectively turned into "godless Jewish hoodlums." Women, while individually addressed in the advocates' legal opinions, were also subjected to their religious judgment. In fact, in their case, Frankfurt's advocates resorted to citing the harshest biblical exegeses. When addressing the women suspected of collaborative infanticide, they argued that if the city councilors granted them milder punishments they would be acting against "göttlichem Befehl," God's command—a stance which they argued exceeded their jurisdictional power. With this interpretation, Frankfurt's advocates not only turned themselves into the instrument of God's wrath but also implicitly abrogated judicial power from the city council and instead, as the harbinger of God's will, vesting it in themselves. The advocates' use of religious and theological citations thus served a multitude of legal arguments and turned into easily pliable mechanisms to discriminate; and this in a secular court. Lutheran advocates thus did not shy away from religiously laced legal arguments till the end of this study, the end of the seventeenth century. Religion remained a malleable accomplice in their legal interpretations.

Most perplexingly, however, such religious exegeses are strikingly absent from their legal opinions on criminal soldiers. In their case, Frankfurt's advocates resorted to a multitude of pragmatic and, above all, local military-serving legal excusatory arguments, including the civic status of the culprits—sons of respected citizens. The soldiers' military-honor induced killings, from the beginning of the seventeenth century and snowballing throughout the rest of that period, induced Frankfurt's advocates to overlook the various implicating factors and instead to seek exculpatory devices in sharp contrast to the honor-induced alleged infanticides by women. Honor thus did not equal honor: not all honor symptoms were equal in the eyes of Frankfurt's advocates.

However, a new legal trend emerged by the mid-1630s aimed at questioning the advocates' legal deliberations. Increasingly suspects initiated private, legally sophisticated pleas to the city council, frequently including passages in Latin, obviously the work of jurists unrelated to the court. It was during the same time frame that requests for legal defenders multiplied. This development was surely not a historical coincidence, as demonstrated in one instance when the suspect wanted the writer of his pleas to also become his official defender. Suspects thus set in motion legal and judicial challenges to disrupt the advocates' monopoly, a move which, not surprisingly, was not well received by Frankfurt's advocates. They put up various legal, moral and even time-restraining hurdles, insisting on persons of "good standing" and advancing that defenders abstain from drawn-out legal procedures, but proceed in a time-honored, prompt fashion—thus fostering the continuation of extraordinary speedy criminal trials. Yet despite these legal outside inroads, Frankfurt's advocates kept a firm grip on local court procedures as well as penal recommendations.

In fact, it was their penal suggestions that underscored their judicial power, as most of their recommendations were heeded by the city council and promptly carried out. And they were of kaleidoscopic proportions. Murderers of Jewish people were handed down considerably milder punishments, a trend which noticeably increased as of the mid-seventeenth century and which was so clearly expressed by one of Frankfurt's advocates. While he admitted that blood had been spilled, he added that it was "only Jewish blood." The four Gypsies received deliberate, explicitly stated, harsher punishments symbolically portrayed by the Gypsy woman who, while being flogged in public, held her young child in her arms—the only such penal occurrence.

Gender biases flourished as well. Frankfurt advocates' penal deliberations on the two women accused of infanticide testify to that approach most clearly. Although the women's alleged crime could not be proven the advocates, nevertheless, suggested for both of them one of the most brutal capital punishments: live burial. True, they subsequently withdrew this penal recommendation but they did so *not* on "humanitarian grounds" or through Christian mercy.[3] On the contrary, they withdrew their cruel penal recommendation, as explicitly stated, out of fear that it might cause public outcry because punishments of that nature were no longer meted out. They thus reacted to a changed public mentality rather than any benevolent attitude on their part. While, obviously, the people of Frankfurt were no longer willing to accept such former penal cruelties, Frankfurt's advocates still harbored thoughts about applying them well toward the end of the seventeenth century.

By contrast, the advocates' penal views of soldiers demonstrate a decisively milder approach from the beginning of the seventeenth century and accelerating thereafter. They advanced a multitude of penal excuses as to why soldiers ought to receive milder punishments, ranging from soldier-specific excuses to their local civic status as burghers. Even in the wife-killing case, Frankfurt's advocates laid most of the blame on the wife rather than squarely sentencing the soldier-husband for his murderous attack, while the soldier's reduced sentence for having shot a female servant as "a joke" needs no further explanation. Most soldiers were meted out non-capital punishments for manslaughter they had committed in front of witnesses. Many had to either fight the Turks or later the

[3] This disproves the thesis of "humanitarian" motivations for milder punishments as suggested by John H. Langbein, *Torture and the Law of Proof: Europe and England in the Ancient Regime* (Chicago: University of Chicago Press, 2006), p. 57.

French, military "punishments" which fell into the paradigm of soldiers' general duties: hired to fight an enemy.

By suggesting milder and explicitly soldier-related punishments the advocates not only widened the gulf between civilian and military adjudication but also indicated that soldiers were increasingly viewed in a special, exalted light, holding a privileged stake in society. Advocates thus encouraged, if not initiated, the emergence and spread of a distinct military judicial culture resulting in a quasi-militarized civilian court.[4] The increasing deployment of soldiers in the service of the judiciary as law enforcers and criminal arresting officers—so clearly depicted in numerous trials—added further momentum to this quasi-militarization. However, it would exceed the scope of this study to ascertain to what extent this trend affected general societal patterns.[5]

By contrast, one can assert that the copious legal and penal deliberations of Frankfurt's advocates extending over a period of 134 years do not exhibit an objective and uniform picture of jurisprudence, but rather one that was riddled with astonishing shortcomings and biases. While frequently seemingly carefully weighing up the various reports and witness statements, arguing from various perspectives, referring to numerous legal sources and presenting their legal arguments with increasing erudition—lacing them with Latin and Greek linguistic explanations—all this learnedness did not cover their judicial imbalances. The advocates targeted those whom they perceived as "inferior" even before they became crime suspects, and shielded others whom they considered essential allies, although they had committed their deadly crimes in front of many witnesses. While some of the "preconceived" wrongdoers resisted judicial imbalances—such as members of the Jewish community who fought back physically and verbally, and women, facing potential honor and shame-related charges forming mutual clandestine collaborative unions to shield themselves—they ultimately were no match for the advocates.

---

4 See the somewhat different argument presented by Matthias Asche, "Krieg, Militär und Migration in der Frühen Neuzeit," in Matthias Asche et al., eds, *Krieg, Militär und Migration in der Frühen Neuzeit* (Berlin: LIT Verlag, 2008), pp. 11–36, p. 18.

5 The theory of social disciplining advanced by Gerhard Oestreich, "Strukturprobleme des europäischen Absolutismus," in *Geist und Gestalt des frühmodernen Staates: Gesammelte Abhandlungen* (Berlin: Duncker & Humblot, 1969) and followed by various scholars is deliberately omitted here. For further details see Ralf Pröve, "Dimension und Reichweide der Paradigment 'Sozialdiziplinierung' und 'Militarisierung' im Heiligen Römischen Reich," in Heinz Schilling, ed., *Institutionen, Instrumente und Akteure sozialer Kontrolle und Disziplinierung im frühneuzeitlichen Europa* (Frankfurt am Main: Vittorio Klostermann, 1999), pp. 65–85, especially pp. 66–7 and 85–6.

True, many locals contributed to the criminal indictments by feeding the authorities relevant incriminating information either via the rumor mill or by direct identification aided by visible and easily identification markers. They were the policing agents—only to be replaced at a later time, when the principle of "uniforms" reversed itself in that uniformed policemen oversaw "un-uniformed" people. However, Frankfurt's people were not the final judicial arbiters. It was Frankfurt's advocates' penal deliberations and recommendations, increasingly accepted by Frankfurt's city council, that set the stage, leaving behind a bewildering legal legacy with ominous implications for the future.

Index

For Product Safety Concerns and Information please contact our EU representative GPSR@taylorandfrancis.com
Taylor & Francis Verlag GmbH, Kaufingerstraße 24, 80331 München, Germany

www.ingramcontent.com/pod-product-compliance
Ingram Content Group UK Ltd.
Pitfield, Milton Keynes, MK11 3LW, UK
UKHW021301190926
475701UK00009B/375
9781138379756